DEFINING THE CURRICULUM

DEFINING THE CURRICULUM
Histories and Ethnographies

Edited by
Ivor F. Goodson
and
Stephen J. Ball

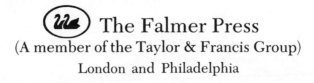 The Falmer Press
(A member of the Taylor & Francis Group)
London and Philadelphia

UK The Falmer Press, Falmer House, Barcombe, Lewes, East Sussex, BN8 5DL

USA The Falmer Press, Taylor & Francis Inc., 242 Cherry Street, Philadelphia, PA 19106-1906

First published in 1984

Library of Congress Cataloging in Publication Data

Main entry under title:

Defining the curriculum.

  Includes bibliographies and index.
  1. Curriculum planning—History—Addresses, essays, lectures. 2. Education—Curricula—Social aspects—Addresses, essays, lectures. 3. Educational anthropology —Addresses, essays, lectures. I. Goodson, Ivor F.
II. Ball, Stephen J.
LB1570.D42 1984 375 84-4024
ISBN 0-905273-94-X
ISBN 0-905273-93-1 (pbk.)

Typeset in 10/12 Caledonia by
Imago Publishing Ltd, Thame, Oxon

Jacket design by Leonard Williams

Printed in Great Britain by Taylor & Francis (Printers) Ltd, Basingstoke

Contents

Contents

Acknowledgements

The articles in this volume derive from a conference held at St Hilda's College, Oxford, in September 1982.

We would like to thank the Bursar and staff of St Hilda's for their kind hospitality over the years. We would also like to note the valuable contributions to the work of the conference made by the following: Adrian Bell, Brian Davies, Martyn Denscombe, John Evans, Andy Hargreaves, Les Tickle, Bob Moon, Harry Osser, Maurice Plascow, Andrew Pollard, Geoff Walford, Rob Walker, Sue Webb, Ian Westbury and Geoff Whitty.

Our personal thanks go to Mary Hoare and Margaret Ralph for their unfailing efforts in typing and retyping various drafts of the papers in the collection and for other support.

The Editors dedicate this volume to Lawrence
Stenhouse whose work has provided them with
a model of how scholarship can engage with
and inform practice

Introduction: Defining the Curriculum; Histories and Ethnographies

Stephen Ball and Ivor Goodson

The papers in this volume concentrate on two concerns: first, the development of historical and ethnographic studies of curriculum; secondly, their application, in particular but by no means exclusively, to school subjects.

A focal concern is to undertake, and where possible combine, historical and ethnographic work in a manner which broadens and deepens our understanding of the curriculum. The relationship between these two approaches is complex but a number of the papers (for example, Smith, Hammersley and Adelman) reflect the value of moving between ethnographic and historical studies in examining curriculum issues.

In one of his last papers Lawrence Stenhouse made two points about historical and ethnographic work, arguing that they were the two main traditions on which case study work draws. First, he argued:

> History is essentially documentary, concerned with the discussion and interpretation of evidence accessible to scholars. Ethnography, though it draws on field-notes, seldom treats them as documents to be made available for critical discussion, depending for confirmatory responses upon the reader's experience of like situations, the cogency of the theory offered, and perhaps trust in the ethnographer. (Stenhouse, 1982, p. 4)

Secondly, and more controversially, he felt that there was a sense in which

> History is the work of insiders, ethnography of outsiders. In its origins history has been how the ruling classes write about their own society, ethnography has been how they write about the societies of others. . . . The historian, assuming a shared understanding of human behaviour, deals in the foreground of action. The ethnographer, by contrast, has used a degree of naivety as a tool to call into question the commonplace. (*ibid.*)

But whilst the distinctiveness of history and ethnography can be evidenced and discussed, the concern of the conference on which these papers are based

1

was to combine the approaches in examining school subjects and the school curriculum (the St Hilda's Conference on School Subjects: Histories and Ethnographies took place in September 1982). From the beginning the complementarity of the approaches in examining common problems was stressed. Indeed, Hammersley felt that:

> Not only are history and ethnography complementary but they also share much in common. For example, they both display a primary concern with describing social events and processes in detail, and a distaste for theories which, as they see it, ride roughshod over the complexity of the social world. Often too they share a commitment to documenting 'in their own terms' the perspectives of the people involved in the events and settings they describe. (Hammersley, this volume, p. 15)

In focussing our studies on school subjects in particular the dangers should be clearly faced. Seeley (1966) has developed the distinction between the 'taking' and the 'making' of problems. If we 'take' subjects as the focus we are in substantial danger of confirming their 'taken-for-grantedness'. A historical view will confirm that the reinstatement or reaffirmation of school subjects *per se*, and certain subjects in particular, reflects a new regime of social and political control. Whilst it can be argued that research needs to follow these changes we must never forget that the focus reflects actions grounded in a new political climate — the new orthodoxy of a dominant subject-based curriculum is the opposite of 'taken-for-granted' or 'given' school worlds; it is in fact an index of intervention.

For this reason a number of papers (for example, Adelman, Burgess, Reid) deal with aspects of curriculum not organised in traditional subjects. Reid is clear on the importance of this broader focus:

> too much concentration on the idea of the 'subject' may lead resear-chers to neglect programmes like art or physical education which are essentially activity-based. The use of topic/activity avoids this problem and enables us to ask questions about how topics/activities are marshalled into various curricular patterns and called 'subjects', or shared and exchanged between subjects. (Reid, this volume, p. 69)

As yet, only limited progress has been made in these areas of study; Hammersley and Hargreaves, writing in 1983, bemoan the fact that 'our knowledge of the historical development of different communities is still rather thin.' Indeed some attempts at writing subject histories have been sociological-ly naive and historically unsound. There has been a tendency to ascribe changes in subject status or subject contents to the vague 'needs' or 'demands' at work in the society, and little serious attempt has been made to address the equally important question of why things stay the same. Writing of work done in the United States, Hazlett (1979) puts forward a trenchant critique:

> In examining the historical moment, some writers on curriculum
> curiously act as if they were reading tea leaves rather than deliberately
> and self-critically attempting to interpret a complex array of particu-
> lars. Sometimes their readings are so vague and abstract as to make it
> difficult to see a logical connection with proposed curriculum altera-
> tions, or their assertions are so categorical that they leave no room for
> alternative interpretations, or their statements imply that educational
> directives are lodged in history itself. (p. 130)

Examples of the kind of work Hazlett describes are not difficult to find, where
curriculum changes are simply related to notions like the 'demands of
technological development' or 'shifts in the economic and political climate'. The
work presented here aims to unpick and examine the variety of social and
political factors that may be at work in advancing or inhibiting changes in
subject knowledge. The papers by Cooper, Goodson and Ball make it clear that
simply reading off from the economic and political context does not provide a
coherent basis for understanding the contents of the school curriculum. These
contexts might be crucially important in setting the limits for possible contents
but even here there is substantial evidence of 'time lags' and 'contradictions'.

Hazlett is equally forceful in his criticism of the failure of historians to
come to grips with the experience of subject contents in the classroom, he
argues that the technical and methodological problems involved have been
overstated, and recent developments in the oral/biographical history tradition
(for example, Humphries, 1981 and Purvis, this volume, pp. 89–115) seem to
indicate that there are in fact considerable possibilities in this area.

> The 'lived' curriculum of the school and classroom is a level of inquiry
> that has suffered the most neglect. As a group, historians have shied
> away from the particular school because they have assumed that
> educational history is deductive and that extant records are insuf-
> ficient. (Hazlett, 1979, p. 131)

Taken together, the techniques of history and ethnography can provide us with
the tools to examine and interrogate school subjects empirically and may also
lay the groundwork for the development of theories which capture and explain
the processes of change (or absence of change) in school subjects.

A twin focussed analysis, using histories and ethnographies, allows full
account to be taken of the socially and politically constructed nature of school
subjects and tends towards a view of the structure and contents of the school
curriculum as the products of previous and ongoing struggles, within and
between subject communities. In this way the 'taken-for grantedness' of the
curriculum and its subject components is challenged. Historical work concentrating on the emergence and establishment (or decline) of school subjects
highlights the contested nature of subject knowledge, indicating the role
played by various, vested interest groups in the selection and definition of
'appropriate' contents. Ethnographic inquiry provides insights into those

factors which *mediate* between the 'espoused' and the 'enacted' curriculum as well as emphasizing the realization and experience of the different contents and forms of subject knowledge in the classroom (or laboratory, or workshop). In both cases, conflict, compromise and negotiation are key concepts. In those public arenas (subject associations, conferences, examination boards, DES and LEA committees, school staff and department meetings) where issues of content are debated and 'settled', the interests, in terms of career, status or access to resources, of particular groups may be at stake. In Archer's (1979) terms, if we are to understand the outcomes of curriculum competitions, conflicts and compromises, 'we need to know not only who won the struggle for control but also how, not merely who lost, but also how badly they lost!' (p. 23). Such disputes and settlements are also relevant in understanding the enactment of subject knowledge and the relationship between subjects in the school and in the classroom. At the institutional level access to resources and to teaching time affect and are crucially affected by subject statuses. Curriculum decisions taken in staff meetings are eminently political matters, as Hargreaves (1981) demonstrates. In the classrooms pupils may be actively discriminating between certain kinds of subjects (as Measor and Burgess and Ball indicate in this volume) or certain kinds of subject knowledge (as Spradbery's, 1976, study of the resistance of 'less-able' pupils to a curriculum innovation in mathematics teaching, which they regarded as 'not proper maths', aptly illustrates). Pupils' 'demand' and 'resistance' places them in a position of negotiating the way in which subjects are enacted and realized in the classroom.

Histories and ethnographies of school subjects can provide access to the understanding of the 'content' of education and a positive response to the exhortations of those such as Raymond Williams and M.F.D. Young to pursue the study of 'what counts as education':

> The business of organising education — creating types of institutions, deciding lengths of courses, agreeing conditions of entry and duration — is certainly important. Yet to conduct this business as if it were the distribution of a simple product is wholly misleading. It is not only that the way in which education is organised can be seen to express, consciously and unconsciously, the wider organisation of a culture and a society, so that what has been thought of as simple distribution is in fact an active shaping to particular social ends. It is also that the content of education, which is subject to great historical variation, again expresses, both consciously and unconsciously, certain basic elements in the culture, what is thought of as 'an education' being in fact a particular set of emphases and omissions. Further, when this selection of content is examined more closely, it will be seen to be one of the decisive factors affecting its distribution: the cultural choices involved in the selection of content have an organic relation to the social choices involved in the practical organisation. (Williams, 1961, p. 145)

Williams' conclusions bear a particular relevance to this volume of papers for he argues that:

> If we are to discuss education adequately we must examine, in historical and analytic terms, this organic relation, for to be conscious of a choice made is to be conscious of further and alternative choices available, and at a time when changes, under a multitude of pressures, will in any case occur, this degree of consciousness is vital. (*ibid.*, pp. 145–6)

The choices surrounding the promotion of school subjects are currently openly evidenced in the publication and reaction to the Government's White Paper on *Teaching Quality*. In the discussions which preceded its publication Sir Keith Joseph was quite clear as to his purpose in preferring PGCE subject-based training. Above all it was 'because of the need to strengthen subject expertise in the school'; he said: 'we recognise that this will mean that secondary BEd provision will in the main be restricted to certain specific subject areas in which its contribution is especially important' (O'Connor, 1982, p. 11). In fact of course it means that it will not be possible to train as a secondary teacher in geography, history, social sciences, languages, English or art through a degree level course where professional training and subject expertise are integrated partners. Maureen O'Connor has argued that it was made clear in a paper from the Inspectorate to ACSET that a powerful lobby at the DES would like to see the secondary BEd in effect restricted to subjects 'which cannot be easily taught via the postgraduate route: home economics, physical education, craft design and technology and perhaps religious education' (O'Connor, 1982, p. 11).

The ideology of subject-centredness cannot be viewed monolithically for it obscures substantial differences among subjects. Some time ago Dennis Marsden pointed to this problem:

> Hierarchies within and between subjects have hitherto been defended as the province of philosophers and educationists, but in the next few years we may be forced up against the uncomfortable fact that different subjects may entail different world-views, and, that to some extent, these have political overtones and tend to recruit and shape specialists with characteristic political stances. In other words the *political* orientations of teachers in some subjects may tend to make them more resistant to attempts to devise common curricula and examinations in their specialisms. (Marsden, 1979, p. 22)

This is reflected in the opinions about Sir Keith Joseph's preferences with regard to the subject degree in which secondary teachers qualify:

> Sir Keith would probably prefer that qualification to be in a single subject from a limited range, certainly excluding from the schools graduates in subjects such as psychology, sociology, law and others for

which there is often no exact equivalent on the school timetable. (O'Connor, 1982, p. 11)

The reinstatement of subject-centredness and of certain subjects in particular, therefore, reflects, as is often the case with curriculum change, current patterns of political control. At this time we are especially aware of how political intervention can influence what counts as education. But awareness of the new interests at work should not obscure the force of historical legacies in curriculum. It remains the case, despite the current atmosphere of crisis and change, that the school curriculum 'expresses a compromise between an inherited selection of interests and the emphasis of new interests' (Williams, 1961, p. 72).

The comments on the Government's *Teaching Quality* White Paper indicate that the reinstatement of selective subject-centredness challenges certain vested interests and cultural purposes. For Ian Morgan, Chairman of the NUT's Committee of Teacher Education, the polarised choice is clear: 'This is the classic dichotomy of English education: do we want teachers who know their subject or do we want teachers who know how to teach' (O'Connor, 1982, p. 11). His statement makes it clear that the promotion of subject-centredness and of subject preferences takes us into the heartland of cultural conflict.

Other current political initiatives, the Assisted Places Scheme and particularly the MSC industrial training schemes also underline the importance of understanding the ways in which subject knowledge is socially differentiated and distributed within and between schools. The re-emergence of Sir Keith Joseph's 'bottom 40 per cent' of 'low attainers' is in effect a reiteration of concern for the sort of curricular differentiation embodied in the elementary/ secondary school tradition, in the Norwood report, the Newsom report and the comprehensive school response to ROSLA. As Burgess (in this volume) indicates, there are certain groups of pupils for whom access to 'proper' subjects has always been problematic. The analysis of subject contents cannot be divorced from a consideration of the recipients for whom they are designed and intended. And clearly the 'status' of audiences at which particular subjects are aimed acts back decisively upon the status and long-term prospects of those subjects (Goodson's work on rural studies clearly evidences this). Status issues of this kind can also have a decisive influence on the career prospects of teachers; we only have to consider how few CDT, or art, or PE specialists eventually achieve positions as headteachers. Patterns of appointment and promotion in schools are part of the mechanism by which the hierarchy of subject statuses, and the attendant distribution of resources, are reproduced in schools despite outward changes in structure and economic climate. (In this respect *Teaching Quality* is reasserting traditional status differences.)

Histories and ethnographies of curriculum should offer perspectives on the range of choices which precede and underpin the current compromise which passes as today's school curriculum. In showing how and why choices are made, and how they are received and experienced, historical and ethnographic work should aid our understanding, for to reiterate: 'to be conscious of further and alternative choices available, and at a time when changes, under a multitude of pressures, will in any case occur, this degree of consciousness is vital.'

In the papers in this volume three general themes are to the fore, recurring and building on studies of different subjects and different settings. First, as outlined above, the conflicts, compromises and processes of negotiation involved in maintaining and changing subject contents are examined across a range of subjects (mathematics, English, rural studies and nursery schooling). Secondly, the social distribution of knowledge as maintained both in procedures for differentiating pupils within schools (by streaming, by providing separate examinations, by designing 'relevant' courses) and in the broader social structuring of educational provision which involves allocating different 'sorts' of pupils to different sorts of schools. Thirdly, a number of the papers focus on the pupils' perceptions and reception of subject contents. On the one hand, the mediation of subject knowledge in schools is considered and, on the other, the pupils' demands for and responses to different subjects and contents are presented.

Taken together these themes highlight the importance of considering and researching subjects within different arenas and at different levels of action. The rhetoric and manoeuvrings of educational politicians and subject associations may reveal a great deal about the framework of limits and possibilities within which teachers and pupils work in the classroom but neither the teacher nor the pupils are entirely passive recipients of the 'espoused' curriculum. While 'what counts as education' may be defined in political terms, what is realized as education is the outcome of the conflicts and negotiations between teachers and pupils which provide for the enactment of school subjects in the classroom.

Theory and Method

This first section contains three papers each of which attempts, in different ways, to establish a theoretical basis for the study of school subjects. In the first Hammersley argues for the need to link together historical and ethnographic analyses and he sketches out the sort of theorizing and theoretical work that needs to be done if adequate theories about school knowledge are to be established. He is critical of both historians and ethnographers for failing to take the development of theory seriously and for failing to involve themselves in the systematic testing and reformulation of those theories that they do produce. In effect Hammersley provides a programme for theoretical development. He urges the need both for more careful design of empirical investigations to make theory development possible and for a more mature approach to the use and further development of those theories that do emerge. He provides relevant examples of the sort of work that could and should be done.

Goodson's paper takes up the challenge laid down by Hammersley and presents an empirically grounded model to explain change in school subjects. Drawing on his study of the development and decline of rural studies teaching, Goodson offers a socio-historical account of the factors which would explain the evolution of a subject from the earliest stage of its establishment on the educational map to the point at which it is fully accepted (or fails to gain acceptance) in the curriculum of every school. Goodson's account draws attention in particular to the internal structure of the subject community, the material interests, status and resources of its members and the importance of changes of climates of opinion and forms of external relationship which affect the subject. Here then the potential and value of curriculum histories are powerfully illustrated. The third paper in this section takes on a task very similar to that of Goodson. Cooper again moves from a carefully conducted empirical history of the School Mathematics Project (SMP) to construct a generalizable model of subject change. In common with Goodson, Cooper stresses the internal segmentation of the subject community (drawing on the work of Bucher and Strauss) and he portrays the conflicts and alliances between rival segments as a major driving force in the processes of subject definition and change. Also, like Goodson, Cooper relates the relative power of different groups and segments to their resource base and to their position in the stratification of educational knowledge. Both draw attention to the implications for individuals' careers (positively and negatively) of proposed or enacted changes in subject knowledge. But in addition Cooper gives particular attention to the importance of subject recruitment and in this the role of the textbook as a socializing and subject-defining device. Taken together these two papers provide a set of penetrative conceptual tools for the analysis of change in school subjects. Following Hammersley's dicta we now need to take up these concepts and attempt to address them to the analysis of other so far unexamined subjects (and non-subjects); their long-term value lies in their applicability to other areas of the curriculum and in this way the frameworks offered by Cooper and Goodson may be adequately tested and reformulated.

Histories

The first paper in this section begins with some important insights derived from the work of John Meyer in the United States. Reid convincingly argues that much of the writing and research on the school curriculum is based on an assumption 'that what is taught and how it is taught results essentially from decisions and initiatives taken within educational organisations'. In questioning this view Reid argues that a crucial part of the equation is the role played by external 'publics' or 'constituencies'. These external groups act as 'gatekeepers' over legitimation, support and resources which will be required if curriculum initiatives are to be accepted, sustained and institutionalized within schools.

Reid also warns that research must focus on 'topics' and 'activities' as well as 'subjects'. This is precisely the approach adopted in Adelman's study of early childhood education where he juxtaposes some of 'the conflicts that have centred on the merits of learning through play as opposed to learning through work'. Interestingly (in the light of the aspiration of this collection to examine the complementarity of history and ethnography) he describes how initial ethnographic work led him back into history in the pursuit of meaning.

Purvis, on the other hand, reminds us that Adelman's work is exceptional, quoting Hammersley's assertion that ethnographers in the main regard history as 'someone else's territory'. Her paper examines the 'lived experience of schooling' of boys and girls in the nineteenth century. She draws on a range of personal accounts, notably autobiographies. Beyond the personal and subjective she then attempts to link these accounts to the broader social structure and culture of Victorian England. Whilst revealing both continuity and discontinuity there is an awesome familiarity to the accounts of the tedium and boredom of the pupils' experiences of schooling.

Ball's paper on the colonial curriculum in Africa also stresses that the pupil clientele is not merely a passive audience but an active transformer. Pupil demands, like external publics, feed back into the definitions emanating from the educational establishment. Advocates of greater government intervention would do well to ponder 'the enormous and enduring mismatches' which emerged between the edicts of metropolitan governments and colonial administrations and from educational provision which was offered. The forms of resistance to centrally imposed curricula are deeply analogous to the experiences documented in Stephen Humphries' excellent account of working class childhood from 1889 to 1939, *Hooligans or Rebels?*

Louis Smith's paper follows Adelman in articulating how an ethnographer in the search for meanings was driven back into the wider history of the school he was studying. The focus of the paper is, in Smith's phrase, on 'the kind of thinking that seems to be occurring as one does a blend of history and ethnography'. The fascination of the study is the evidence it provides to support the contention in Goodson's paper that history provides not just data that are complementary to ethnography but data that can actively transform the nature of the researcher's account. Above all Smith's (and Adelman's) account shows that painstaking ethnographic study often leads to the conclusion that historical work can broaden and deepen the accounts provided. Future ethnographers will ignore this conclusion at their peril, not just methodologically but experientially for Smith who has conducted a formidable range of ethnographic studies considered the introduction of history made the work he describes 'one of the most interesting research projects in which he has ever been involved'.

Ethnographies

The papers in this section illuminate aspects of the organization and experience of school subjects in contemporary comprehensive settings.

The paper by Burgess describes the attitudes and responses of pupils to

Newsom courses for the 'less able' at Bishop MacGregor comprehensive and demonstrates the low status held by the Newsom department in the eyes of both pupils and teachers. His analysis of the knowledge base, the teaching methods and the qualifications offered by the department illustrates the rigid academic criteria which are employed by teachers and pupils alike to evaluate the worth and utility of school subjects. In part, at least, the role of the Newsom department is one of containment and this, together with the absence of any examination deadlines, allows considerable licence in the negotiation and definition of what is to count as valid educational activity. Burgess shows that the pupils are fully aware of the marginal position of the department and its teachers, many of whom have other major commitments in the school. The establishment of departments like this was a standard type of response in comprehensive schools to the Raising of the School Leaving Age (ROSLA), but in the current context of high levels of unemployment among school leavers there is likely to be increased resistance from pupils to courses which are seen to have no useful outcomes either in terms of certification or vocational preparation.

In a more wide ranging review of pupils' perceptions, but again drawing on a participant observation study of a comprehensive school, Measor's paper identifies a vital link between pupils' evaluations of subject status and their actual behaviour in lessons. Her account of pupils' views and actions demonstrates how it is that lessons like needlework, art and music become valid settings for 'mucking about' and 'having a larf', even for the most academically-oriented pupils, while the high value and utility attributed to mathematics and English ensure that deviant behaviour rarely occurs. Even within their first few weeks at the comprehensive school pupils were beginning to make evaluations of their subjects based on long-term plans about employment or further education. Measor subtly portrays the behavioural interface between the formal culture of the school and the informal peer group pressures within which pupils establish themselves. Boys and girls, conformists and deviants, 'make out' in different ways, choosing the 'places and spaces' best suited to challenge or support their preferred identity and peer group status. Some tread a 'knife-edge' between the accolades of deviance and the low status label of 'dummy', others play off the benefits of doing well in maths or English against nonchalant acts of status recovery in home economics and needlework. Here the realization of a subject in the classroom is set within a dynamic cultural system of pupil responses and judgements.

Player's paper is also concerned with pupil views of and reactions to the comprehensive school curriculum. Drawing on Willis's concept of 'generalized labour' he suggests that 'unmotivated' pupils in their final years of compulsory schooling hold a 'generalized and amorphous' view of school and the school curriculum. Either as a result of previous experience or as a deliberate stance of indifference, these 'unmotivated' pupils develop an ignorance of and marginality to the basic organization of formal, day-to-day school work. In a comparative test of small groups of pupils identified as 'motivated' and 'unmotivated' Player demonstrates, through a set of simple but ingenious indicators, the vagueness and lack of engagement of the latter. These pupils know little in advance about their schoolday or their teachers and do nothing to prepare or organize themselves for school work. This paper provides a useful counterweight to those theories which overemphasize the effects of schooling upon pupils.

The paper by Woods takes the alternative perspective on school and the curriculum, that of the subject teacher. Through life-history material which concentrates on the career of one teacher, Tom, Woods isolates and examines some of the 'strategies, trade-offs, gains and losses' that produce and constrain that teacher's view of and involvement in his subject. The focus in the paper is on the teacher's self, the expression, investment and realization of the person in school and classroom work. Woods adumbrates the variety and complexity of personal and experiential influences, and values, beliefs and dispositions, which underpin Tom's views of his subject — art. The career perspective also serves to outline the limits of tolerance within which Tom is required to work and which finally lead him, somewhat disillusioned, to take early retirement. Art is clearly a marginal subject in the contemporary school curriculum; for the art teacher this both provides space for pedagogic experiment and carries the limitations inherent in having low status in the eyes of pupils and colleagues (as Burgess and Measor indicate).

Finally, in this section, the paper by Barnes and Seed takes us in another direction, to examine the ways in which the structure and content of public examination papers, in this case in English, constrain and effect pupil learning in the classroom and their conception of the subject. Through a detailed analysis of the whole range of 16+ examinations in English, two essential forms of written work — the public and private — are identified. These two forms or models also represent two 'ideal types' of English as a subject. The public relies on traditional modes of stylized and formal writing which are decontextualized and 'distant from most people's lives'. The private attempts to come close to the personal and domestic experience of the pupil, tasks are contextualized and personal responses are given emphasis. Both models, however, lay down fixed conventions for the candidate's response and 'the candidate must master the expectations implicit in the examination they are to sit'. In effect the decisions made by examiners act back dramatically and decisively upon the teaching and learning of English in the secondary classroom as pupils are prepared for ordeal by examination. The modes of expression being demanded in this examination may certainly not be readily available to all pupils and, as Barnes and Steed argue, they certainly do not reflect the cultural diversity of the pupil experiences out of school. The constraining and inhibiting affects of 'the examination' have become one of the most commonplace ways in which teachers and commentators explain the impossibility of change in the secondary classroom, but the direct impact of 'the examination' on the processes of teaching and learning 'the subject' is barely understood at all.

References

ARCHER, M.S. (1979) *Social Origins of Educational Systems*, London, Sage.

HAMMERSLEY, M. and HARGREAVES, A. (1983) *Curriculum Practice: Some Sociological Case Studies*, Lewes, Falmer Press.

HAZLETT, J.S. (1979) 'Conceptions of curriculum history', *Curriculum Inquiry*, 9, 2, pp. 129–35.

HUMPHRIES, S. (1981) *Hooligans or Rebels? An Oral History of Working-Class Childhood and Youth 1889–1939*, Oxford, Basil Blackwell.

MARSDEN, D. (1979) 'Examinations: The chains that bind comprehensive education', in RUBINSTEIN, D. (Ed.), *Education and Equality*, Harmondsworth, Penguin.

O'CONNOR, M. (1982) Education Guardian, *The Guardian*, 7 September.

SEELEY, J. (1966) 'The "making" and "taking" of problems', *Social Problems*, 14.

SPRADBERY, J. (1976) 'Conservative pupils? Pupil resistance to curriculum innovation in mathematics', in WHITTY, G. and YOUNG, M.F.D. (Eds), *Explorations in the Politics of School Knowledge*, Driffield, Nafferton.

STENHOUSE, L. (1982) *Case Study and Educational Practice*, Mimeo, CARE, University of East Anglia.

WILLIAMS, R. (1961) *The Long Revolution*, London, Chatto and Windus.

Part One
Theory and Method

Making a Vice of Our Virtues: Some Notes on Theory in Ethnography and History

Martyn Hammersley

Concern has frequently been registered, even by ethnographers themselves, about the ahistorical character of much ethnographic research. Stephen Ball, for example, has pointed out how we often neglect the temporal patterns operating in the settings we study and that this seriously threatens the validity of our accounts (Ball, 1983a). Others have pointed to the importance of biographical factors in sociological explanations (Pollard, 1982). Goodson (1983a) has noted how, over the last forty years, ethnography has come to be identified with participant observation, life history work suffering a serious decline. Fortunately though, there are now signs of a revival, Bertaux, 1981.) Lynch (1977) raises the issue in a particularly striking manner, criticizing ethnographers for a lack of interest in the 'future history' of the groups they study. He cites the case of Lofland's work on the 'Doomsday Cult' (Lofland, 1966), suggesting that we can now recognize the latter as having been one of the seed groups of 'The Moonies'. He bemoans the fact that we have no study of how this small cult was transformed into the widespread movement of today.

While these criticisms contain much truth, the days have long gone when ethnographers laboured under theoretical perspectives, notably anthropological functionalism, which specifically denied the importance of history. Indeed, recent anthropology seems to have become a major source of ideas for some historians (Walters, 1980; Stone, 1981). In this paper I want to argue not only that history and ethnography are complementary but also that they share much in common. In particular, they both display a primary concern with describing social events and processes in detail, and a distaste for theories which, as they see it, ride roughshod over the complexity of the social world. Often too they share a commitment to documenting 'in their own terms' the perspectives of the people involved in the events and settings they describe. Historians and ethnographers are often reluctant to move to general classifications of these perspectives, in which their uniqueness — and it seems much of their interest — is lost.

It is these characteristics which have sometimes led both ethnography and history to be criticized as empiricist. (For extreme examples see Sharp, 1982, and Hindess and Hirst, 1975.) They are accused of engaging in description for its own sake and of presenting their accounts of the world as if these provided theoretically neutral facts. Such criticisms have generally been rejected or ignored, and in many respects quite rightly. Often they have come from critics practising theoretical dogmatism and speculative excess. The theory demanded has simply been the critics' a priori views about how the world 'must be'; the task of the ethnographer or historian being, at most, to fill in the details.

In the face of dogmatic theoreticism, empiricism has definite virtues. In terms of method, systematic search for evidence and its careful handling must be applauded. Equally, the *products* of empiricism frequently have considerable value. The description of 'other cultures', whether of the past or contemporaneous, of other societies or of segments of our own, can often serve to challenge our routine assumptions about the nature of social life or about particular groups of people or social situations. This explains the popular appeal of historical and anthropological work like Montaillou (Le Roy Ladurie, 1978) and The Mountain People (Turnbull, 1973). But such description performs important functions for social science too. For one thing, it can challenge the preconceptions we bring to our research and which so easily get built into the accounts we produce.

Nor is the value of description limited to the 'exotic'. We often discover that there are features of even the most familiar settings of which we are unaware, recognition of which may subtly, perhaps even dramatically, change our understanding of those settings. Much recent ethnographic work in sociology has been concerned with 'making the familiar strange' in precisely this manner. Historical research can serve the same function, for instance by documenting the origins of contemporary phenomena whose existence we take for granted as 'natural' rather than as the product of history. A good example is the way in which school subjects tend to be viewed as basic forms of knowledge, forgetting the struggles which were involved in their establishment, the alternative versions which were promoted by different groups, and the changes in content undergone (Layton, 1973; Shayer, 1970; Ball, 1982 and 1983b; Goodson, 1981, 1983b and 1983c).

However, while empiricism has its virtues, it is ultimately indefensible. Description is never 'pure', a direct and unchallengeable representation of the world. All 'facts' involve theoretical assumptions. Moreover, a description or explanation is only as good as the theory by which it was produced. We neglect theory at our peril.

While defending a conception of history as idiographic, Mandelbaum (1977, p. 6) points out that historians nevertheless rely on generalizations (for which in this context we can read 'theory'):

> It is my claim that any work we take to be historical in nature purports to establish what actually occurred at a particular time and place, or is concerned with tracing and explaining some particular series of related occurrences. However, this does not entail that in fulfilling such a task

the historian may not, at certain points, have to rely on generalizations in order to offer a coherent account of some of the occurrences with which he deals. For example, in attempting to give an account of a particular revolution, a historian often has to make use of certain general assumptions concerning how individuals generally behave in particular sorts of situations, such as those that arose in the course of that revolution.

Hayek (1955, p. 72) makes the point even more strongly:

> If the dependence of the historical study of social phenomena on theory is not always recognized, this is mainly due to the very simple nature of the majority of theoretical schemes which the historian will employ and which brings it about that there will be no dispute about the conclusions reached by their help, and little awareness that he has used theoretical reasoning at all. But this does not alter the fact that in their methodological character and validity the concepts of social phenomena which the historian has to employ are essentially of the same kind as the more elaborate models produced by the systematic social sciences.

Such generalizations or theoretical claims are not difficult to find in historical and ethnographic work. In his work on the development of English as a school subject, Ball (1983, p. 65) makes the claim that 'both grammar and composition . . . served to impose and maintain the dominance of the patterns, structures and conventions of *Standard English* and received pronounciation.' Clearly here he is drawing on a generalization about what the effects of teaching of the kind to be found in grammar and composition lessons would be in the conditions prevalent in late nineteenth and early twentieth century schools. Theoretical assumptions of this kind are also routinely made in ethnographic research. For example, in his work on teachers' experiences of examining, Scarth (1983, p. 216) claims that if the practical solutions which teachers develop to cope with examining 'work', 'they become synonymous with examining itself'. Here we have reliance on a psychological theory about habitualization (Berger and Luckmann, 1966).

There has, of course, been considerable debate about the nature of the assumptions involved in historical explanations, for example about whether they are empirical generalizations or rational principles (for a discussion see Dray, 1964). In my view the most plausible account is still that of Hempel (1959 and 1963). On this account a theory is a statement which explains what will happen and why under given circumstances, and whose validity can be tested by checking whether or not its predictions are accurate. The claims which theories make are conditionally universal. In other words, they hold generally, given certain conditions, and the latter must not refer to particulars, to limits of time and space (Willer, 1967).

It seems that much of the reaction against this view of theory has been founded upon misinterpretation of its implications. Often, for example, the conditional nature of this kind of theory has been ignored. Leff (1969, p. 3), for instance, denies the applicability of universal laws to history because of 'the absence of uniformity from human affairs'. But the positivist model of universal laws, in the form outlined above, does not presuppose uniformity in the sense that identical situations undergoing identical processes of development must be readily identifiable. It is not 'historicist' in the sense popularized by Popper (1957). Nor does it involve the claim that all social events are causally determined:

> the covering law analysis of explanation presents a thesis about the logical structure of scientific explanation but not about the extent to which individual occurrences in the world can be explained: that depends on what laws hold in the world and clearly cannot be determined just by logical analysis. In particular, therefore, the covering law analysis of explanation does not presuppose or imply universal determinism. (Hempel, 1963, pp. 149–50)

Of course, Hempel (1959) also argues that many of the laws pertinent to history, and presumably to ethnography too, are likely to be probabilistic rather than universalistic in character.

Perhaps the most important misconception, though, is the idea that this model of explanation implies that conventional ethnographic and historical work must be abandoned in favour of attempts to develop and test theories. In reaction against this implication conventional modes of historical explanation have been defended on the grounds that explanation is pragmatic in character. It has been pointed out that in order to provide an adequate explanation of a phenomenon it is often not necessary to specify the underlying theory and the evidence which supports it. Often, for example, citing a particular fact about the events to be explained is enough in itself (Scriven, 1959).

Another line of defence has been the argument that historical explanation diverges from the covering law model because of the wide range of different factors which may be appealed to in explaining social events. Historical explanations draw, it is argued, not on a set of interrelated laws but on a collection of diverse assumptions about the way the world works, and in particular about why people act in the way they do. (Scriven, *ibid.*, calls these 'truisms'.)

These features of historical explanations have often been taken to reflect fundamental differences between the natural and social sciences. This, however, is a serious mistake, as Hayek (1955, pp. 66–7) points out:

> If I watch and record the process by which a plot in my garden that I leave untouched for months is gradually covered with weeds, I am describing a process which in all its detail is no less unique than any event in human history. If I want to explain any particular configuration of different plants which may appear at any stage of that process, I

can do so only by giving an account of all the relevant influences which have affected different parts of my plot at different times. I shall have to consider what I can find out about the differences of the soil in different parts of the plot, about differences in the radiation of the sun, of moisture, of the air-currents, etc., etc.; and in order to explain the effects of all these factors I shall have to use, apart from the knowledge of all these particular facts, various parts of the theory of physics, of chemistry, biology, meteorology, and so on. The result of all this will be the explanation of a particular phenomenon, but not a theoretical science of how garden plots are covered with weeds.

In an instance like this the particular sequence of events, their causes and consequences, will probably not be of sufficient general interest to make it worth while to produce a written account of them or to develop their study into a distinct discipline. But there are large fields of natural knowledge, represented by recognized disciplines, which in their methodological character are no different from this. In geography, e.g., and at least in a large part of geology and astronomy, we are mainly concerned with particular situations, either of the earth or of the universe; we aim at explaining a unique situation by showing how it has been produced by the operation of many forces subject to the general laws studied by the theoretical sciences. In the specific sense of a body of general rules in which the term 'science' is often used these disciplines are not 'sciences', i.e., they are not theoretical sciences but endeavors to apply the laws found by the theoretical sciences to the explanation of particular 'historical' situations.

The distinction between the search for generic principles and the explanation of concrete phenomena has thus no necessary connection with the distinction between the study of nature and the study of society. In both fields we need generalizations in order to explain concrete and unique events. Whenever we attempt to explain or understand a particular phenomenon we can do so only by recognizing it or its parts as members of certain classes of phenomena, and the explanation of the particular phenomenon presupposes the existence of general rules.

It is important, then, to draw a distinction between what we might call theorizing and explaining and to recognize that this distinction operates independently of the nature of the subject matter. Moreover, as Hayek makes clear, these two activities are complementary:

> Theoretical and historical work are ... logically distinct but complementary activities. If their task is rightly understood, there can be no conflict between them. And though they have distinct tasks, neither is of much use without the other. (Hayek, *ibid.*, p. 73)

Explaining a particular set or sequence of events is a pragmatic matter;

what counts as an adequate description or explanation depends on the context (Scriven, 1959; Garfinkel, 1981). In explaining any set of events one may draw on many different theories, and which ones one appeals to will depend on one's purposes, varying, for example, according to whether one is concerned with the ascription of blame or with identifying available remedies. Moreover, in producing explanations we tend to treat the truth of the theories we rely on as given. Our primary interest is in whether they fit the facts of the case with which we are concerned. We are interested in their applicability not their general validity.

Theorizing involves a rather different orientation. The aim is not to explain a particular event but to develop and test a theory, an interrelated set of propositions making claims of a conditionally universal or probabilistic nature about general classes of events. Here propositions relating to particular factors are not included or excluded on the basis of extrinsic purposes, but according to whether or not they seem likely to form part of a coherent theory. Our primary interest is not in the events themselves. Indeed their only significance is the opportunities they provide for developing and testing the theory. Moreover, theorizing demands investigation of a range of cases, both those where the conditions specified in the theory hold, despite other differences among them, and some where the conditions do not hold but where one might expect the relationships specified by the theory to occur on the grounds of competing theories. Central to theorizing, in the sense intended here, is the comparative method.

The character of such comparative analysis is usefully summarized in Sewell's (1967) commentary on the work of the historian Marc Bloch:

> If an historian attributes the appearance of phenomenon A in one society to the existence of condition B, he can check this hypothesis by trying to find other societies where A occurs without B or vice versa. If he finds no case which contradicts the hypothesis, his confidence in its validity will increase, the level of his confidence depending on the number and variety of the comparisons made. If he finds contradictory cases, he will either reject the hypothesis outright or reformulate it and refine it so as to take into account the contradictory evidence and then subject it again to comparative testing. (Sewell 1967, pp. 208–9)

This process of testing, reformulating and retesting through comparative analysis is also to be found in the ethnographic tradition in the form of 'grounded theorizing' (Glaser and Strauss, 1967; Glaser, 1978) and analytic induction (Lindesmith, 1947; Cressey, 1950; Denzin, 1978).

Unfortunately, however, within neither history nor ethnography have these attempts to apply the comparative method in the development and testing of theory proved very influential. In large part this probably stems from paradigmatic conflict between positivists and anti-positivists and a consequent ambivalence towards theory on the part of historians and ethnographers (Hammersley, Scarth and Webb, 1984).

Of course, there is no shortage of promising theoretical ideas in ethnographic and historical work. Take, for example, Measor's (1983) work on girls and science. She argues that girls have been socialized into a set of attitudes about what kinds of knowledge and activity are appropriate and inappropriate to their sexual identity. Science, particularly physics and chemistry, is very definitely regarded as masculine. Moreover she suggests that in school some girls actively use this feature of science to establish identity and status, and in the process put pressure on their peers to do likewise. While further work is necessary to develop and test this idea, I think it is clear that we have a promising theory here. We could formulate it as follows: if children are socialized into a perspective in which different types of knowledge are thought of as appropriate to men and women, then they will not only tend to react more favourably to that knowledge which is 'appropriate' to their own sex, but they will also tend to use displays of ignorance and incompetence in relation to 'inappropriate' skills and knowledge in order to underline their sexual identity. Also this tendency will be greater to the extent that the children are insecure about their own sexual identity, or where there is strong competition for inter-sex relationships.

Within the history of school subjects, too, we have a plethora of theoretical ideas. Goodson (1983b and 1983c), for example, drawing on an idea of Layton's (1973), proposes a three-stage model of the process through which new school subjects become established. Initially, the subject is composed of useful knowledge which satisfies both the interests and the needs of pupils. In the interim stage, while the usefulness of the knowledge remains important, much effort comes to be given to the systematic and rigorous development of the subject's content and rationale. As a result it acquires some academic status and this starts to become an important motivation for pupils taking it. In the final stage of development, the most influential people within the subject are not schoolteachers at all but specialist scholars working in the universities, and it is they who determine what is and what is not to count as part of the subject. Teachers are charged simply with the task of transmitting the knowledge, and pupils with passively learning it.

Goodson explains why the development of subjects tends to follow this path by claiming that it is 'not so much [the result of] domination by dominant groups as solicitous surrender by subordinate groups' (Goodson, 1983b, p. 198). He argues that the rules currently defining what counts as high status knowledge were established by dominant interest groups in the early twentieth century, but that it has been the pursuit of high status and the material rewards associated with that by teachers since then which has sustained and reinforced this hierarchy of knowledge. Because of 'the legacy of curricular, financial and resource structures inherited from the early twentieth century ... able pupils and academic examinations are linked and consequently resources, graded posts and career prospects are maximized for those who can claim academic status for their subject' (*ibid.*).

We can reformulate the central core of Goodson's account as a theory in the following way: given an examination system controlled by the universities, resources and rewards within schools will tend to be distributed in such a way as to maximize, or at least achieve a 'satisfactory' level of, examination results; and to gain a place, or to expand its role, in the school curriculum a subject will have to take on an academic cast. Clearly further specification of terms is needed — what indicators should we use for the academicization of subjects, for example — and of the conditions under which the theory holds. And, of course, further testing of the theory is required. But here too we clearly have a plausible set of theoretical ideas.

Measor and Goodson go further than most ethnographers and historians in the work of developing and testing their theoretical ideas. Measor compares girls' reactions to science with boys' responses to domestic science. Goodson compares the histories of geography, biology and rural/environmental studies. Even so in both cases there is a considerable way to go before we have well-developed and well-established theories.

My fear is, of course, that these theories, and others like them, will be left in this early stage of development and not taken any further. This is what previous experience would lead us to expect. While there is no shortage of theories within ethnography and history, few have been developed and tested to any degree. Virtually all of our effort goes into descriptive and explanatory work, little into what I have called 'theorizing'. In the case of research on school subjects such a charge may seem unfair. After all, work in this field is relatively new. Nevertheless, the fact that there has been an upsurge of research in this area reflects in part, I suggest, the fact that ethnographers have moved out of other fields, notably the study of classroom interaction and pupil perspectives. Moreover, they have done this, I suggest, because these areas have become saturated with descriptive/explanatory studies. In other words, a point had been reached where, without theoretical work, little more news seemed to be available. If the same is not going to happen to the study of school subjects, it seems that theorizing must be given some priority. The logic of progress in ethnography and history is, in my view, from descriptive/explanatory accounts through theory development and testing to better descriptions and explanations. If this is correct, I suggest that we are rapidly reaching the stage in the study of curricular knowledge when theorizing, of the kind I have recommended here, becomes an essential prerequisite for further progress.

References

BALL, S.J. (1982) 'Competition and conflict in the teaching of English: A socio-historical analysis', *Journal of Curriculum Studies*, 15, 1, pp. 1–28.

BALL, S.J. (1983a) 'Case study research in education: Some notes and problems', in HAMMERSLEY, M. (Ed.) *The Ethnography of Schooling*, Driffield, Nafferton.

BALL, S.J. (1983b) 'A subject of privilege: English and the school curriculum 1906–35', in HAMMERSLEY, M. and HARGREAVES, A. (Eds) *Curriculum Practice: Some*

Sociological Case-Studies Lewes, Falmer Press.

BERGER, P. and LUCKMANN, T. (1966) *The Social Construction of Reality*, London, Allen Lane.

BERTAUX, D. (Ed.) (1981) *Biography and Society: The Life History Approach in the Social Sciences*, Beverley Hills, Calif., Sage.

CRESSEY, D.R. (1950) 'The criminal violation of financial trust', *American Sociological Review*, 15, December, pp. 738–43.

DENZIN, N.K. (1978) *The Research Act*, 2nd ed., New York, McGraw Hill.

DRAY, W. (1964) *Philosophy of History*, Englewood Cliffs, N.J., Prentice Hall.

GARFINKEL, A. (1981) *Forms of Explanation*, Yale University Press.

GLASER, B.G. (1978) *Theoretical Sensitivity*, San Francisco, Calif., The Sociology Press.

GLASER, B.G. and STRAUSS, A. (1967) *The Discovery of Grounded Theory*, Chicago, Ill., Aldine.

GOODSON, I. (1981) 'Becoming an academic subject', *British Journal of Sociology of Education*, 2, 2, pp. 163–80.

GOODSON, I. (1983a) 'The use of life histories in the study of teaching', in HAMMERSLEY, M. (Ed.) *The Ethnography of Schooling* Driffield, Nafferton Press.

GOODSON, I. (1983b) *School Subjects and Curriculum Change*, London, Croom Helm.

GOODSON, I. (1983c) 'Defending the subject: Geography and environmental studies', in HAMMERSLEY, M. and HARGREAVES, A. (Eds) *Curriculum Practice: Sociological Case-Studies*, Lewes, Falmer Press.

HAMMERSLEY, M., SCARTH, J. and WEBB, S. (1984) 'Developing and testing theory. The case of research on student learning and examinations, in BURGESS, R. (Ed) *Issues in Educational Research: Qualitative Methods*, Lewes. Falmer Press.

HAYEK, F.A. (1955) *The Counter-Revolution of Science: Studies in the Abuse of Reason*, Free Press.

HEMPEL, C.G. (1959) The function of general laws in history', in GARDINER, P. (Ed.) *Theories of History*, New York, Free Press.

HEMPEL, C.G. (1963) 'Reasons and covering laws in historical explanations', in HOOK, S. (Ed.) *Philosophy and History*, New York, New York University Press.

HINDESS, B. and HIRST, P.Q. (1975) *Pre-Capitalist Modes of Production*, London, Routledge and Kegan Paul.

LAYTON, D. (1973) *Science for the People*, London, Allen and Unwin.

LEFF, G. (1969) *History and Social Theory*, London, Merlin Press.

LE ROY LADURIE, E. (1978) *Montaillou*, Scolar Press.

LINDESMITH, A. (1947) *Opiate Addiction*, Principia Press.

LOFLAND, J. (1966) *Doomsday Cult: A Study of Conversion, Proselytization and Maintenance of Faith*, Englewood Cliffs, N.J., Prentice Hall.

LYNCH, F.R. (1977) 'Field research and future history: Problems posed for ethnographic sociologists by the "Domesday Cult" making good', *American Sociologist* 12, April, pp. 80–8.

MANDELBAUM, M. (1977) *The Anatomy of Historical Knowledge*, Johns Hopkins University Press.

MEASOR, L. (1983) 'Gender and the sciences', in HAMMERSLEY, M. and HARGREAVES, A. (Eds) *Curriculum Practice: Some Sociological Case-Studies*, Lewes, Falmer Press.

POLLARD, A. (1982) 'A model of classroom coping strategies', *British Journal of Sociology of Education*, 3, 1.

POPPER, K. (1957) *The Poverty of Historicism*, London, Routledge and Kegan Paul.

SCARTH, J. (1983) 'Teachers' school-based experiences of examining', in HAMMERSLEY, M. and HARGREAVES, A. (Eds) *Curriculum Practice: Some Sociological Case-Studies*, Lewes, Falmer Press.

SCRIVEN, M. (1959) 'Truisms as the grounds for historical explanations', in GARDINER, P. (Ed.) *Theories of History*, New York, Free Press.

SEWELL, W.H. (1967) 'Marc Bloch and the logic of comparative history', *History and Theory: Studies in the Philosophy of History*, VI, 2.

SHARP, R. (1982) 'Self-contained ethnography or a science of phenomenal forms and inner relations', *Boston University Journal of Education*, 164, 1.

SHAYER, D. (1970) *The Teaching of English in Schools*, London, Routledge and Kegan Paul.

STONE, L. (1981) *The Past and the Present*, Routledge and Kegan Paul.

TURNBULL, C. (1973) *The Mountain People*, Jonathan Cape.

WALTERS, R.G. (1980) 'Signs of the times: Clifford Geertz and the historian', *Social Research*, 47, 3.

WILLER, D. (1967) *Scientific Sociology: Theory and Method*, Englewood Cliffs, N.J., Prentice Hall.

Subjects for Study: Towards a Social History of Curriculum

Ivor Goodson

This article scrutinizes the part which social histories can play in studying the curriculum.[1] The introduction briefly examines the use (misuse or non-use) of historical evidence in some theoretical work. Then by drawing on parts of historical studies, seeks to show, albeit in a limited way, how such work allows hypotheses to be examined and reformulated. By this view, a 'sequence to theory' emerges from historical work which not only extends the range of our studies but which, by posing questions about our current theories, can aid in generating new theories and agendas.

Partly because *Knowledge and Control* was an influential starting point for my own historical studies I want to examine briefly the use that has been made of history by some of the sociologists who contributed to this volume. I am aware that this is to generalize dangerously from the particular; I am also aware of the excellent past and recent sociological work that has employed historical perspectives, for instance, that of Margaret Archer.

Nonetheless, I think the example will establish some general points, especially as Young and Bernstein have, since *Knowledge and Control*, come to argue for historical work. Young has said that 'one crucial way of reformulating and transcending the limits within which we work, is to see . . . how such limits are not given or fixed, but produced through the conflicting actions and interests of man in history' (Young, 1977, pp. 248–9). Likewise Bernstein has argued that 'if we are to take shifts in the content of education seriously, then we require histories of these contents, and their relationships to institutions and symbolic arrangements external to the school' (Bernstein, in Rex, 1974, p. 156).

In practice, however, much of the work of these sociologists to date can be characterized in two ways: either (1) history is not used; or, alternatively, (2) history is misused, or to use Silver's elegant phrase 'raided' (Silver, 1977, p. 17). Much of the work actually ignores historical background; no evolutionary historical process is provided. Studies develop, so to speak, horizontally, working out from theories of social structure and the social order. When historical evidence is presented it is provided as a snapshot from the past to prove a contemporary point.

The use of Layton's work by Young (1977) is a good example of how history is used in this manner. Layton was describing a particular movement led by Richard Dawes towards 'The Science of Common Things' and its fate in a particular period during the nineteenth century. Layton was clear that there were striking similarities among many of the issues which engaged science educators in the mid-nineteenth century and those which occupy their latter-day counterparts, but in the first paragraph of his conclusion he warned:

> Within the last century and a quarter the social environment of science education has been radically transformed. At the time when Davies and Moseley fought their cause science was a national enterprise of limited scale, operating at the level which Derek Price has termed 'little science'. State and science had not begun to interact in any significant way and the limits of the principles of voluntaryism and *laissez-faire* applied to the growth of scientific activity, were only just be coming clear. Today, in contrast 'big science' is not only heavily dependent on state patronage, but has become inextricably interwoven into the economic, political and ethical problems of the age. Concomitantly, there has arisen a national system of secular education in which the importance of scientific studies is recognised at all levels. (Layton, 1973, p. 166)

Young, however, uses Layton's work to question Professor Jevons' *contemporary* view that in science 'we are up against something in the cognitive structure of science itself'. A historical snapshot is used to question a view about science today; moreover the implication is that our conceptions of contemporary school science can be understood from evidence of this particular period of conflict. Young is aware that 'it is not possible to draw any direct parallels with science education today' but nonetheless implies if not parallels, direct continuities — 'what is emphasized is the historical emergence and political character of the most basic assumptions of what is *now* taken to be school science' (Young, 1977, p. 245). In fact, without direct parallels and with no evidence produced of continuities it is difficult to move to *any* understanding of the basic assumptions of contemporary school science from the specific historical evidence presented from Layton's work.

Clearly the danger of 'raiding' history is that such moves can span centuries of change at all levels of content and context. A more systematic evolutionary understanding of how the curriculum is negotiated is therefore needed. The concern is to ensure that histories make evolutionary connections partly to secure against 'raiding' but more constructively to facilitate the use of such histories in developing theoretical frameworks. A continuity thesis cannot be assumed (as in Young) but has to be established over time. It is surely at the centre of the sociological as well as historical enterprise to examine curriculum transformation and reproduction at work over time: such complex undertakings simply cannot be elucidated by 'snapshots' of unique events which may be entirely aberrant and without general significance. The *recurrence* of events, however, can help in discerning explanatory frameworks in which structure and interaction interrelate. One is reminded of the humility of Lowe's comment in his seminal article on the divided curriculum:

> While it is well known that the major educational enquiries of the mid-nineteenth century culminated in an analysis of the educational needs of society by the Taunton Commissioners which in some ways prefigured [this] twentieth century tripartism, it is not widely realised that the evolution of ideas on a structured and hierarchical system of secondary education was both gradual and continuous from that time. (Lowe, 1976, pp. 139–40)

Historical studies should seek to establish the 'gradual and continuous' nature of curriculum change and do so in ways which examine negotiation and action. By this view, to seek to provide from the macro level theories of curriculum without related empirical studies of how the curriculum has been negotiated at micro level over time is a dangerous sequence through which to proceed. This article will argue that to pursue an understanding of the complexity of curriculum action and negotiation over time is a meaningful sequence through which to test, and formulate, theory.

Subjects for Study

Having made a polemical plea for the potential of curriculum history in furthering our understanding of schooling, I want to provide some instances of historical work which begins to explore that potential. By citing some of the work which is brought together in *School Subjects and Curriculum Change* I hope to (1) characterize the kinds of insights and hypotheses which are generated through undertaking curriculum histories, and (2) illustrate the capacity of such histories to aid the examination of sociological theories.[2]

My original interest in undertaking curriculum history grew out of my teaching experience. Certainly after Countesthorpe (recently described as an 'unemulated educational maverick') I was susceptible to the arguments presented by Nisbet in *Social Change and History*. Nisbet argues that we are often deluded into thinking fundamental social change is taking place because we do not take account of a vital distinction:

> between readjustment or individual deviance within a social structure (whose effects, although possibly cumulative are never sufficient to alter the structure or the basic postulates of a society or institution) and the more fundamental, though enigmatic, change of structure, type, pattern or paradigm. (Nisbet, in Webster, 1971, pp. 204–5)

To pursue Nisbet's crucial distinction into the field of curriculum demands, I think that we undertake historical work. This is true whether we seek to understand how change is contained as 'readjustment or individual deviance' as at Countesthorpe or to analyze more fundamental changes of structure over time.

In the curriculum histories undertaken, I focussed on subject groups and sub-groups in action. The particular historical context was the emergence of the environment as an influential idea and area of concern and of environmental education as a viable curriculum possibility. The location of the environmental climate of opinion within a broader structural milieu has been dealt with in a number of studies but here my particular concern was to understand how subject groups and sub-groups responded to the change in 'climate' (one subject advocate spoke of the 'changing climate' and argued that his subject group would have to 'adapt or perish'); beyond this was the need to investigate the manner in which the subject groups and sub-groups scrutinized the new climate for opportunities of promoting their interests; and why it was that one sub-group decided to promote a new subject at A-level in 'environmental studies' while other sub-groups and subject groups responded so strongly against this initiative as to threaten its viability.

Eventually a strategy for this historical investigation was designed and divided into three sections which aimed to focus on the conflict over environmental studies in the 1960s and 1970s. Beyond this paramount concern, where possible, the sections were designed so as to test hypotheses and to examine theories which related to the content studied. The first and second sections focussed on the origins and evolution of the three subjects involved in the emergence of environmental studies: geography, biology and rural studies. Here the concern was to understand the process of becoming a school subject and patterns of internal change. The third section dealt with 'external relations' between subjects and with the conflict over environmental studies, in particular the moves to promote an A-level syllabus for the subject. Hence the sections evolve chronologically: the subjects are scrutinized under construction and as they pursue status and resources; the groups, traditions and alliances within subjects are analyzed; these subjects and groups are then analyzed in the culminating conflict over environmental studies. For the purposes of this paper I do not want to provide a summary account of *School Subjects and Curriculum Change* but rather to concentrate on the way in which in constructing that account hypotheses were tested and reformulated and theories examined.

Testing Hypotheses

In the three sections of the book noted above three main hypotheses are examined within the context of the history of three subjects involved in the conflict over environmental studies:

1   'That subjects are not monolithic entities but shifting amalgamations of sub-groups and traditions. These groups within the subject influence

and change boundaries and priorities' (see Bucher and Strauss, 1971; Musgrove, 1968; Young, 1971, Kuhn, 1970 and 1972);

2 'That in the process of establishing a school subject (and associated university discipline) base subject groups tend to move from promoting pedagogic and utilitarian traditions towards the academic tradition' (see Layton, 1972; Ben-David and Collins, 1966);

3 'That in the conflict over environmental studies much of the curriculum debate can be interpreted in terms of conflict between subjects over status, resources and territory' (see Ben-David and Collins, 1966; Musgrove, 1968; Young, 1971).

1.   Obviously this pattern would appear most strongly in subjects representing 'fields' rather than 'forms' of knowledge. The history of geography, for instance, shows that in the early stages the subject was made up of a variety of idiosyncratic local versions devised or taught by specialists from other disciplines. During the period in curriculum history that is the concern of the book, the battle over environmental education in the late sixties and early seventies, the sub-groups within geography can be seen 'pursuing different objectives in differeent manners' (Bucher and Strauss, in Hammersley and Woods, 1976, p. 19). So much so that in 1970 Professor Fisher wrote, 'The light-hearted prophecy I made in 1959 that we might soon expect to see the full 57 varieties of geography that have seriously been put forward in professional literature now stands at well over half that number' (Fisher, 1970, pp. 373–4). At about the same time, the President of the Geographical Association was warning that 'new' geography created a problem because 'it leads towards subject fragmentation', so that ultimately 'the question must arise as to how much longer the subject can effectively be held together' (Garnett, 1969, pp. 368–9). The potential danger of new versions of geography was touched on by Walford who argued that 'unity within the subject' was 'a basic requirement for its continued existence' (Walford, 1973, p. 97).

The tendency to fragmentation in geography through the proliferation of sub-groups and sub-versions is a recurrent feature of the subject's history, and was echoed by the Norwood Report's (1943) fear about the 'expansiveness of geography'. At this earlier stage, they saw geography as 'the study of man and his environment from selected points of view' — a definition at that time leading to fears that through its expansiveness geography was becoming 'a "world citizenship" subject, with the citizens detached from their physical environment' (pp. 101–2). As a result 'by then, geography had become grievously out of balance; the geographical synthesis had been abandoned.' The problem was fairly rapidly addressed and a decade later Garnett claimed that most departments were headed by specialists so that 'the initial marked differences and contrasts in subject personality had been blurred or obliterated' (Garnett, 1969, p. 368).

The means by which the fragmentary sub-groups were monitored, controlled and periodically unified will be dealt with later. However, in the period of the battle over 'environmental education', two, or more accurately three, major sub-groups within the subject were actively concerned: the regional geographers, the field geographers and, the fastest-growing sub-group, the 'new' geographers. The first two groups, representing strong traditions within the subject had large support among school geography teachers. The latter group was largely derived from new developments in the subject within the universities. The first two sub-groups were considerably more sympathetic to environmental initiatives than the new geographers. This was because the environmental lobby offered aid and sustenance to the field and regional geographers. Hence, we find eminent regional geographers like Professor Bryan promoting conferences in environmental studies because this expressed more clearly than new geography 'his own life's work and ambitions as a geographer' (Millward, 1969, p. 93). Thomas explained the affection for environmental approaches entirely in terms of the struggle for survival of the regional sub-group (Thomas, 1970, pp. 274–5), and a college lecturer in geography judged that the new crisis among geography sub-groups 'caused traditional [regional and field] geographers to flee into environmental studies for a time' (interview, Scraptoft, 14 December 1976). This flirtation proved a short-run phenomenon because of the overwhelming desire for fully-fledged academic status among all geographers; because new geography carried within it the seeds of this final acceptance; and because the activities of the Geographical Association and the university schools of geography together helped direct and manage the change towards a new 'geographical synthesis' where once again the sub-groups were 'delicately held together'.

The pattern discerned among geography sub-groups in the period of environmental education's emergence is partly echoed when considering biology. Again the subject began with a variety of idiosyncratic versions and groupings devised and taught by specialists from other disciplines, in botany and zoology. By the 1960s biology had also developed a major sub-group whose concern with ecology and field biology bordered on the new environmental approaches. For a time this sub-group gained considerable momentum from initiatives like the Keele Conference which saw this version of biology as promoting environmental awareness.

Alongside field biology a sub-group promoting biology as a 'hard science' based in laboratories gained increasing adherents. The rise of molecular biology, symbolized by the Nobel prizewinning work of Crick and Watson in the late 1950s gave renewed impetus to the work of this group. In the new universities opening in the 1960s and in many schools following the Nuffield project, this group managed to dominate the versions of biology that were accepted. Hence the 'hard science' version was embodied in the new laboratories that were being built and in the departments that were set up.

So dominant did the 'hard science' group become in biology that for a time the ecology and field biology sub-group developed defensive connections with environmental studies. As with geography a number of professors associated with the sub-group appeared at events or in publications sponsored by the

National Association for Environmental Education. However, although only a sub-group on the defensive within biology, the field biologists were actively pursuing opportunities elsewhere and secured a dominant position (along with the field geographers) in the field studies movement which grew rapidly as the 'environmental lobby' gained momentum. The field biology sub-group was thereby able to develop important new 'territory' inside the growth area of field studies which partially compensated for losing the battle for mainstream biology to the hard science sub-group. By securing this leading role in field studies any permanent alliance with the rural studies groups promoting environmental studies was rendered both unnecessary and undesirable.

In both geography and biology the sub-groups allied to distinctive versions of the subject often gathered very different degrees of support according to whether school or university groups were being considered. Sometimes this reflected a time-lag effect as the new versions of the subject only slowly worked their way into the schools with new graduates taking up teaching posts in them. This was, for instance, the case in the battle between the regional geography and new geography groups: a long time after new geography was well-established in universities, regional geography retained the allegiance of the vast majority of schoolteachers.

In rural studies the varying support, according to whether one concentrates attention on school or university groups, was never an issue as the subject was not taught in universities and beyond certain individuals there was no academic reference group. The sub-groups within rural studies therefore concentrated on particular versions of the subject within schools. In the period when environmental studies was launched, the two main groups were those who wanted to quickly attach rural studies to a new examination subject with some connections in the tertiary sector and those who wanted to retain traditional rural studies as a subject of outstanding appeal to the more 'practical' pupil. The battle which ensued over the name of the subject association and the new subject was essentially between these two sub-groups and ended in resounding victory for the first group led by Sean Carson, when the name of the subject and its association was changed from rural studies to environmental studies.

2.   The second hypothesis examined within the book relates to three major 'traditions' discerned in school subjects: the academic, the utilitarian and the pedagogic. As this has been dealt with in considerable detail in *Becoming a School Subject* I will provide only the briefest of commentaries. It was thought that an evolutionary profile of the school subjects under study would show a progressive movement away from stressing utilitarian and pedagogic versions of the subjects towards increasing promotion of more academic versions. We have already seen when discussing the nature of school subjects that sub-groups representing new geography, 'hard science' biology and examinable environmental studies had come to be leading promoters of their subjects by the early 1970s. The process and rationale behind this outcome require fairly detailed understanding, representing as they do the culmination of a contest between a

range of well-supported alternative definitions within each of the subjects.

The model of subject establishment towards a culminating 'academic' discipline was found to be closely applicable to both geography and biology. Once successfully promoted as an academic discipline the selection of the subject content is clearly considerably influenced 'by the judgement and practices of the specialist scholars in the field'. Subjects defined in this way, require a base of 'specialist scholars' working in universities to continue the definition and legitimation of disciplinary content.

The strategy for achieving this final stage received early recognition in geography. MacKinder's 1903 four-point plan provides an explicit statement of a subject aspiring to academic acceptance:

> Firstly, we should encourage University schools of geography, where geographers can be made....
> Secondly, we must persuade at any rate some secondary schools to place the geographical teaching of the whole school in the hands of one geographically trained master....
> Thirdly, we must thrash out by discussion and experiment what is the best progressive method for common acceptation and upon that method we must base our scheme of examination.
> Lastly, the examination papers must be set by practical geography teachers. (MacKinder, 1903)

The key to the strategy was the first point, the establishment of 'University schools of geography, where geographers can be made'. To complete the control of the subject's identity, geography teaching and examination construction were to be placed in the hands only of teachers 'made in the universities'. The mediation between university and school was in geography placed in the hands of the Geographical Association. The Association, founded in 1893, played a central role in the promotion of geography, since in its early days the subject was confined to idiosyncratic school-based versions and had obtained a tentative place in only a few universities.

The close linkage between the growth in schools and the establishment of the subject elicited regular comment in the pages of the Association's journal, *Geography*. The President of the Geographical Association paid homage to 'fruits of inspired teaching' which have led to the 'intense and remarkable upsurge in the demand to read our subject in the universities.' The result has been 'the recognition of our subject's status among university disciplines ... together with the costly provision made available for its study' (Garnett, 1969, p. 368). The latter point shows the direct link between academic status and resources in our educational system: the triumph of the 'academic' tradition over the utilitarian and pedagogic traditions which played such a prominent part in geography's early days can be partly understood in these terms.

The establishment of 'discipline' status inside the universities which had been so systematically pursued since MacKinder's 1903 proclamation provided for a range of material improvements in the subject's place within schools. In

1954 Honeybone could claim that 'at long last, geography is forcing its complete acceptance as a major discipline in universities, and that geographers are welcomed in to commerce, industry and the professions, because they are well educated men and women' (Honeybone, 1954, p. 186). From now on geography could claim its place in educating the most able children, and thereby become established as a well-funded department inside schools staffed with trained specialists on graded posts. By 1967 Marchant noted that geography was 'at last attaining to intellectual respectability in the academic streams of our secondary schools' (Marchant, 1968, p. 133). The battle was not quite over and he gave two instances where the subject was still undesirably taught as a 'less able' option. With the launching of new geography the subject finally attained total acceptance as an academic discipline in universities and as a fully-fledged A-level subject in all schools, with the resources and 'costly provisions' which such status attracts.

In biology the evolution of the subject is distinguishable from geography because from the beginning there was an associated and well-established university base in the form of botany and zoology. For this reason and also because from the outset the subject benefited from the side-effects of the influential science lobby, the task of subject promotion never totally resembled geography's 'beginning from scratch'. Biology's task was more to present a case for inclusion within the, by then well-established (and consequently well-resourced), science area of the curriculum. This task was often pursued within the overall arena of the Science Masters Association, which from the 1930s onwards played an active role in promoting biology. In 1936 an influential biology sub-committee was formed to promote biology syllabuses, and many articles in the Association's *School Science Review* argued the case for biology's recognition as an examination subject for the able student. The problem was best voiced by the Ministry of Education in 1960: 'The place which is occupied by advanced biological studies in schools . . . is unfortunately that of vocational training rather than of an instrument of education.' The need to be seen as an instrument of education meant that the promoters of the subject had to move away from the utilitarian towards more academic versions — only then could an A-level subject command sufficient pupil numbers to warrant 'departmental' status and resources in schools. Hence we find the common theme being advocated: biology must be treated 'as a comprehensive discipline in its own right'.

In the final stages in the promotion of biology as an 'academic discipline' in the 1960s, the two main initiatives stressed the subject as a 'hard science' needing 'laboratories and equipment'. In the rapidly expanding universities it was this version of the subject which was widely introduced, thereby establishing the academic discipline base; likewise part of the Nuffield Biology Project for Schools centred on 'a crusade in terms of equipment and laboratory staff'. With the new generation of biology graduates trained in this hard science at universities, the establishment of the subject as a fully fledged academic O and A-level subject was finally assured.

Unlike biology and geography, rural studies remained for generations a low status enclave, stressing highly utilitarian or pedagogic values. This provides confirmation for Ben-David and Collins' contention; the move to a change in intellectual and occupational identity came at the time when the subject was faced with survival problems in a reorganizing educational system stressing academic examinations. The pervasive influence of this tradition can clearly be seen in the following:

> The lack of a clear definition of an area of study as a discipline has often been a difficulty for local authorities in deciding what facilities to provide. . . . It has been one of the reasons for the fact that no 'A' level course in rural studies exists at present. (Carson, 1967, p. 19)

The Schools Council Working Party in 1968 confirmed this with the broad hint that there was the 'need for a scholarly discipline' (Schools Council, 1969, p. 19).

With no tertiary base and hence no specialist scholars involved, except random specialists from other disciplines, the Hertfordshire strategy was to develop an A-level syllabus from groups working in the secondary schools, This offered the promise of tailoring 'a course to the needs of the kids' and not to 'have to meet the requirements of other people's courses'. But the crucial reason in terms of the subject teachers' material self-interest was often frankly admitted:

> I think we had got to prove that environmental studies was something that the most able of students could achieve and do something with . . . if you started off there all the expertise and finance that you put into it will benefit the rest — your teaching ratio goes up etc. and everyone else benefits. (interview, Topham)

The survival rationale was always a strong factor:

> I just thought if you're outside this you've had it in schools: it was already happening in some schools where a [rural studies] teacher was leaving, they didn't fill the place, because they gave it to someone in the examination set up. And beyond survival the reasons for an academic 'A' level were simply 'because if you didn't you wouldn't get any money, any status, any intelligent kids.' (interview, Carson)

The Hertfordshire A-level in environmental studies which was ultimately devised is a recognition of the aspiration and efforts of these rural studies teachers. What has subsequently been denied is not that environmental studies represents a valid area of curriculum but that it can thereby claim to be an academic discipline. Such claims it would appear are best validated through university scholarship and without a university base status passage to acceptance as an academic discipline has been denied.

MacKinder's strategy of using the school subject base to help bring about the creation of university departments was correctly conceived. As Carson noted at the Offley conference, new contenders for academic status are often placed in an impossible situation since they are asked, 'What evidence have you that universities would accept this sort of A-level?' On making enquiries to universities, the reply was "show us the successful candidates and we will tell you." A chicken and egg situation' (Carson, 1971, p. 6).

3.   A third hypothesis follows as one moves from consideration of the patterns of internal evolution in school subjects to investigation of the role that the pursuit of academic status plays in the relationship between subjects. In continuity with the second hypothesis we would expect established subjects to defend their own academic status at the same time as denying such status to any new subject contenders, particularly in the battle over new A-level examinations.

In the struggle, to launch environmental studies as an A-level subject, the geographers reacted strongly, and the biologists much more mildly, following the lines of the hypothesis. MacKinder, the founding father of geography's road to academic establishment, would have understood this. In explaining the geologists' opposition to geography, he saw their fear of the new subject making 'inroads in their classes' as the reason for their response and noted that 'even scientific folk are human, and such ideas must be taken into account' (MacKinder, 1913, in Williams, 1976, p. 5). In continuity with this, the geographers strongly opposed social studies, an integrated package that pre-dated environmental studies by several decades. The geographers, it was claimed, 'saw the new proposals as a threat to the integrity and status of their own subject' (Channon, 1964, in Williams, 1976, p. 112).

The growth of environmental studies was treated in similar manner by the geographers. The discussions of the Executive Committee of the Geographical Association show precious little concern with the intellectual or epistemological arguments for environmental studies. They focussed on 'the threat to geography involved in the growth of environmental studies'. Indeed, when the possibility of a dialogue with environmental studies teachers was suggested 'some members felt that to do so would be tantamount to admitting the validity of environmental studies' (Geographical Association, minutes, 1970). A plea for defence rather than dialogue came in the presidential address to the Geographical Association in 1973. Mr A.D. Nicholls laid great emphasis on the 'practical realities' for 'practising teachers'. 'With constant pressure on teaching time, headmasters are ever searching for new space into which additional prestige subjects can be fitted, and the total loss of teaching time to environmental subject may be considerable.' Beyond these practical fears about the material interests of geography teachers, environmental studies evoked a particularly emotional response among geographers because of its proximity to geography's continuing identity crisis. Nicholls provides an unusually frank admission of the need for territorial defence being placed above any intellectual imperatives:

> Ten years ago almost to the day and from this platform, Professor Kirk said 'modern geography was created by scholars, trained in other disciplines, asking themselves geographical questions and moving inwards in a community of problems; it could die by a reversal of the process whereby trained geographers moved outwards in a fragmentation of interests seeking solutions to non-geographical problems'. Might not this be prophetic for us today? Could it not all too soon prove disastrous if the trained teachers of geography moved outwards as teachers of environmental studies seeking solutions to non-geographical problems? (Nicholls, 1973, p. 201)

The fears which geographers expressed so strongly and emotionally about the emergence of environmental studies were not shared to the same degree by biologists. As we have seen, only the field biology sub-group was threatened and they managed to expand into the growing territory of field studies. However, in the negotiations at Schools Council the science sub-committee, which included a number of biologists, joined forces with the geographers in their opposition to the environmental studies A-level. In both sub-committees 'concern was expressed at the heavy overlap between this syllabus and syllabuses in both geography and biology.' The pursuance of this allegation involved a clever strategy. First, the committees argued that the A-level must delete 'irrelevant topics' not related to geography or biology. Then the committees stated that 'if irrelevant topics were envisaged as removed, the effect would be to reveal how close the resulting syllabus would be to existing syllabuses in geography and to a less extent biology' (Herts File SS/L/G/191).

A judgement from Sean Carson that the Schools Council sub-committees 'jealously guarded the preserves of their subject' was confirmed by the comments from the geography sub-committee when the decision on the A-level was finally announced. They were plainly fairly satisfied with their territorial defense and 'noted with approval that candidates could not take this examination together with geography'. A final point was added that there was 'as yet no indication that universities would be prepared to accept a pass in this subject as an entry qualification for degree courses' (*ibid*). The restriction on environmental studies being offered with geography, together with an initial restriction to a five-year 'experimental' period and to a limited number of schools, placed enormous practical obstacles in the way of any widespread adoption of the subject. By ensuring these obstacles faced the new subject in the early years, when the momentum for change was strong, the opponents of the new subject effectively extinguished its chances of establishment in the secondary school curriculum.

Examining Theory: An Example

Since we began by instancing the non-use or misuse of history by sociologists who contributed to *Knowledge and Control* it would be instructive to examine their theories with respect to school subjects. This way we can examine an earlier contention that 'to seek to provide from the macro-level theories of curriculum without empirical investigation or understanding of how the curriculum has been negotiated at micro-level over time is a poor sequence through which to proceed to theory' (Goodson, 1976).

The first point to recognize in Young *et al.* is the assumption in a number of the papers that subjects are monolithic. This would not seem a promising starting point from which to develop the theme that the curriculum is subject to patterns of control by dominant interest groups. The papers in the book reflect Bernstein's contention that 'how a society selects, classifies, distributes, transmits and evaluates the educational knowledge it considers to be public, reflects both the distribution of power and the principles of social control' (Bernstein, in Young, 1971, p. 47). Young likewise suggests that 'consideration of the assumptions underlying the selection and organisation of knowledge by those in positions of power may be fruitful perspective for raising sociological questions about curricula' (*ibid.*, p. 3). The emphasis leads to general statements of the following kind:

> Academic curricula in this country involve assumptions that some kinds and areas of knowledge are much more 'worthwhile' than others: that as soon as possible all knowledge should become specialised and with minimum explicit emphasis on the relations between the subjects specialised in and between specialist teachers involved. It may be useful, therefore, to view curricular changes as involving changing definitions of knowledge along one or more of the dimensions towards a less or more stratified, specialised and open organisation of knowledge.

> Further, that as we assume some patterns of social relations associated with any curriculum, these changes will be resisted in so far as they are perceived to undermine the values, relative power and privileges of the dominant groups involved. (*ibid.*, p. 34)

The process whereby the unspecified 'dominant groups' exercise control over other presumably subordinate groups is not scrutinized although certain hints are offered. We learn that a school's autonomy in curriculum matters 'is in practice extremely limited by the control of the sixth form (and therefore lower form) curricula by the universities, both through their entrance requirements and their domination of all but one of the school examination boards' (*ibid.*, p. 22). Later Young assures us that 'no direct control is implied here, but rather a process by which teachers legitimate their curricula through shared assumptions about "what we all know the universities want"' (*ibid.*). This concentration on the teachers' socialization as the major agency of control is picked up elsewhere. We learn that:

> The contemporary British educational system is dominated by academic curricula with a rigid stratification of knowledge. It follows

> that if teachers and children are socialised within an institutionalised structure which legitimates such assumptions, then for teachers high status (and rewards) will be associated with areas of the curriculum that are (1) formally assessed (2) taught to the 'ablest' children (3) taught to homogeneous ability groups of children who show themselves most successful with such curricula. (*ibid.*, p. 36)

Young's explanation of patterns of curriculum control therefore hinges on his belief that universities 'control sixth form curricula' through 'their entrance requirements and their domination of all but one of the school examination boards'. Direct control is not apparently meant; rather indirect control through the shared assumptions into which teachers are socialized.

Curriculum histories present evidence of a more complex process at work. The role of dominant groups shows perhaps most clearly in the victory of the academic tradition in the early years of the twentieth century. This victory was embodied in the influential 1904 Regulations and, most significantly, the 1917 School Certificate. *Once established*, however, these curricula patterns (and their associated financial and resource implications) were retained and defended in a much more complex way and by a wider range of agencies. It is therefore correct to assume that initially the rules for high status knowledge reflected the values of dominant interest groups at that time. But it is quite another issue to assume that this is *inevitably* still the case or that it is dominant interest groups themselves who *actively* defend high status curricula. It is perhaps useful to distinguish between domination and structure and mechanism and mediation.

By focussing on subjects in evolution and the conflict over A-level examinable knowledge the studies in the book clearly indicate the central role played by school subject groups and sub-groups. The most powerful of these agencies are those groups promoting the academic tradition — successfully in geography and biology but unsuccessfully in environmental studies. These groups *demanded* the creation of an academic discipline based in the universities. The 'academic tradition' subject groups act in this way because of the legacy of curricula, financial and resource structures inherited from the early twentieth century (when dominant interests *were* actively defended). Because of this legacy able pupils and academic examinations are linked and consequently resources, graded posts and career prospects are maximized for those who can claim academic status for their subject.

The evidence indicates not so much domination by dominant forces as solicitous surrender by subordinate groups. Far from teacher socialization in dominant institutions being the major factor creating the patterns discerned it was much more considerations of teachers' material self-interest in their working lives. Since the misconception is purveyed by sociologists who exhort us 'to understand the teacher's real world' they should really know better. High status knowledge gains its school subject adherents and aspirants less through the control of the curricula which socialize than through well-established connection with patterns of resource allocation and the associated work and career prospects these ensure. The study of curriculum histories argues that we must replace crude notions of domination with patterns of control in which subordinate groups can be seen actively at work. A tentative explanatory framework at this level is provided in the next section.

School Subjects and Curriculum Change: An Explanatory Framework

The Structure of Material Interests: Status, Resources and Careers

The historical investigation of the curriculum conflict over 'environmental studies' suggests the pursuit of material interests as a major explanatory factor in understanding curriculum change. This is not to provide an overarching theory but to suggest that this aspect has been substantially neglected in previous accounts.

The similar aspirational patterns discerned in the subject histories provided direct our attention to the structuring of material interests — how resources and career chances are distributed and status attributed.

Essentially the structure emerged in the period 1904–17. The 1904 Regulations defined the subjects suitable for the secondary grammar schools. These were largely academic subjects and they were subsequently enshrined in the School Certificate examinations launched in 1917. From then on these examination subjects inherited the priority treatment on finance and resources directed at the grammar schools (Smith, 1980, pp. 153–6).

The structure has effectively survived the ensuing changes in the educational system (although it is now becoming subject to major challenges). Byrne, for instance, states 'that more resources are given to able students and hence to academic subjects' (the two are still synonymous) since 'it has been assumed that they necessarily need more staff, more highly paid staff and more money for equipment and books' (Byrne, 1974, p. 29).

The material interests of teachers — their pay, promotion and conditions — are broadly interlinked with the fate of their specialist subject communities. The 'academic' subject is placed at the top of the hierarchy of subjects because resource allocation takes place on the basis of assumptions that such subjects are best suited for the able students who, it is further assumed, should receive favourable treatment.

Hence in secondary schools the self-interest of subject teachers is closely connected with the status of the subject in terms of its examinable knowledge. Academic subjects provide the teacher with a career structure characterized by better promotion prospects and pay than less academic subjects. From this viewpoint the conflict over the status of examinable knowledge is therefore essentially a battle over the material resources and career prospects available to each subject community.

Subjects as 'Coalitions'

The process model developed by Bucher and Strauss for the study of professions provides valuable guidelines for those studying school subjects. Within a profession, they argue, are varied identities, values and interests. Hence professions are to be seen as 'loose amalgamations of segments pursuing different objectives in different manners and more or less delicately held together under a common name at particular periods in history' Bucher and Strauss, 1976). The most frequent conflicts arise over the gaining of institutional footholds, over recruitment and over external relations with clients and other institutions. At times when conflicts such as these become intense, professional associations may be created or, if already in existence, become more strongly institutionalized.

The Bucher and Strauss model of professions suggests that perhaps the 'subject community' should not be viewed as a homogeneous group whose members share similar values and definitions of role, common interests and identity. Rather the subject community should be seen as comprising a range of conflicting groups, segments or factions (referred to as subject sub-groups). The importance of these groups might vary considerably over time. As with professions, school subject associations (for example, the Geographical Association) often develop at a particular time when there is an intensification of conflict over school curriculum and resources and over recruitment and training.

Subject Coalitions in Evolution: Internal Curriculum Change

In the subjects studied (further work is of course needed), a pattern of evolution can be discerned in the process of becoming a subject. Initially a subject is a very loose amalgamation of sub-groups and even idiosyncratic versions, often focussed on pedagogic and utilitarian concerns. A sub-group emerges arguing for the subject to become an academic discipline so as to be able to claim resources and status. At the point of conflict between earlier sub-groups and the proselytizing 'academic' sub-group, a subject association is often formed. The association increasingly acts to unify sub-groups into a *dominant coalition* promoting academic status. The dominant coalition calls for discipline status and for university departments to be set up to train its disciplinary specialists (see MacKinder's manifesto). Some subjects (for example, rural/environmental studies) are blocked at this point (university admissions policies play a role here).

For the successful subjects a final stage is the creation of a university discipline base. The subject is now defined increasingly by university scholars and it is to the structure of their material interests and resulting aspirational patterns that we must look to explain curriculum change (for example, new geography, molecular biology) and any resultant tensions for the school subject.

Changing Climates and External Relations: Defining a New Subject

The emergence of the environmental climate of opinion offered new opportunities for subject groups and sub-groups in the promotion of their interests. (I have not dealt with the structural origins of this new climate as other work has attempted this. For example, 'the climate of opinion which made environmental studies a credible label for curriculum innovation in the '60s and '70s is best understood in terms of the historical circumstances of post-war capitalism', Gomm, 1977.)

In this respect Ben-David and Collins' hypotheses were substantially proven. They argued that for a new subject or discipline:

1 the ideas necessary for creation are usually available over a relatively prolonged period of time and in several places;
2 only a few of these potential beginnings lead to further growth;
3 such growth occurs where and when persons become interested in the new idea, not only as intellectual content but also as a potential means of establishing a new intellectual identity and particularly a new occupational role. They conclude: 'the conditions under which such interest arises can be identified and used as a basis for eventually building a predictive theory' (Ben-David and Collins, 1966, p. 452).

Applying this to subject groups and sub-groups a number of factors would be relevant:

1 subject group/sub-group position in hierarchies of subjects (current power and status);
2 their current position regarding resource allocation in schools (current resources);
3 patterns of career and age position of practitioners (current career patterns).

Subjects with low status and resources and poor career patterns, like rural studies, therefore embraced the opportunity to establish a new intellectual identity and occupational role. Established high status subjects conversely ignored the opportunity but contested the new contenders' right to claim similar academic status (and thereby establish parity of status and resources and a share therein). Carson has provided the rationale for the rural studies sub-groups' move to promote an environmental studies A-level: 'because if you didn't you wouldn't get any money, any status, any intelligent kids.'

Conclusion

I have been concerned to show that curriculum histories can be a valuable complement, indeed at times an active agency, in the development of explanatory frameworks. The essential value of such histories is that they are immersed in the complexity of the social process. They develop from the desire to understand particular events not from a desire to prove particular theories. The curriculum historian will often travel with ideological and theoretical baggage packed away. This implicitness, whilst avoiding the primacy of theoretical verification, should not limit theoretical aspiration. The curriculum historian *should* be concerned to aid the generation of theories about actions and events in specific historical conditions. In this way the historian can play an important role in the theoretical enterprise and in the making of agendas for further studies.

Of course, the specificity of curriculum histories often acts against their capacity for generalization. The model of subject change developed herein clearly has many limitations. What about pastoral systems, falling rolls, whole curriculum planning, pupil demands? Does this apply to subjects like classics, economics or, dare we mention it, sociology? What about subjects where industrial and external forces are more clearly involved? What are the factors behind 'the changing climates for action' that have been discerned? What about current changing climates where the autonomy of the educational system and the rules of the game defined therein are challenged?

But beyond the problem of the specificity of curriculum histories lies the problem of the *nature* of curriculum histories. Clearly (following hypothesis 1), history is no monolithic subject or method. In history there are schisms which resemble those in other subjects — notably the disagreement between the 'general law' school of historians and what we might call the 'uniqueness' school (for example, 'the special interest of the historian is not in classes of events but in the uniqueness of each event').

At one level the argument for curriculum histories merely reiterates the need to study how the curriculum has evolved, to understand historical background and origins so as to provide a context for contemporary inquiry. By this view historical studies can *extend* the range of our accounts. I would want to go further than this and argue that histories are important because of their potential to *transform* our accounts: to pose fundamental questions and to point towards new agendas for study, for instance, reformulating notions of 'domination', changing the priority given to prior socialization in accounts of subject change or stressing the importance of professional subject groups in the evolution of the curriculum.

The specificity and nature of history leave us with a dual challenge in conducting future curriculum histories. First, where possible, they must pursue the gradual and continuous nature of curriculum change (certainly in systems as decentralized as ours) so as to illuminate *contemporary situations*; this argues against too rigidly 'periodized' histories. Secondly, they must aspire not only to *extend* our range of data but to contribute to the examination and reformulation of hypotheses and theories, thereby offering the potential for *transforming* our accounts.

These aspirations have to be set against the limitations of the studies reported here. I hope, however, that some progress has been indicated as well.

Curriculum histories point to the evolutionary nature of subjects as coalitions 'more or less delicately held together under a common name at particular periods'. The nature of these coalitions responds to both the structuring of material interests and the 'changing climates' for action. Because of the manner in which resources (and associated career prospects) are distributed, and status attributed, 'academic' subject groups normally develop as 'dominant coalitions'. The conflict over the status of examinable knowledge therefore becomes the crucial conflict arena where the subject coalitions (and their representative associations) contest the right to material resources and career prospects.

This article suggests that it is a dangerous enterprise to develop theories of curriculum whilst underusing or misusing historical studies. Disturbingly significant is the constant harking back to the early nineteenth century for analogies with which to support contemporary theory. Structural and interactional features are not continuous and to assume continuity is at best to oversimplify and at worst wilfully to mislead.

A particular problem in those studies which generalize from the early nineteenth century to the contemporary situation has been identified in the work reported here. Namely, that by raiding history in this way sociologists have been returning to a *pre-professional era* with respect to curriculum groups. The evidence presented here points to the power and importance of professional subject groups; they cannot be dismissed as powerless agencies in the face of structural change.

The use of socialization as a kind of black box theory of causation seems a common but inappropriate device; postulating causation without presenting evidence is poor theorizing, particularly when professionalization has been substantially ignored. The evidence presented here suggests that is not so much prior socialization as the structuring of material interest which provides the mediating mechanism between structural and interactional levels.

The dominance of 'academicism' can be shown over the last century or more. But historical studies pose questions about in whose interests this dominance prevails: professional groups, culturally dominant groups or industrial or financial capital. Academicism may be the past cultural consequence of previous domination rather than a guarantee of future domination.

Notes

1. This paper was presented at the Conference on School Subjects: Histories and Ethnographies, St Hilda's College, Oxford, September 1982 and in modified version appeared in the *Journal of Curriculum Studies*, December 1983.
2. *School Subjects and Curriculum Change* was issued by Croom Helm in hardback in 1982, reissued in paperback 1983.

References

BEN-DAVID, J. and COLLINS, R. (1966) 'Social factors in the origins of a new science: The case of psychology', *American Sociological Review*, 31, 4 August.
BERNSTEIN, B. (1971) 'On the classification and framing of educational knowledge', in YOUNG, M. (Ed.) *Knowledge and Control*, London, Collier Macmillan.
BERNSTEIN, B. (1974) 'Sociology and the sociology of education: A brief account', in REX, J. (Ed.) *Approaches to Sociology*, London, Routledge and Kegan Paul.
BUCHER, R. and STRAUSS, A. (1976) 'Professions in process', in HAMMERSLEY, M. and WOODS, P. (Eds) *The Process of Schooling*, London, Routledge and Kegan Paul.
BYRNE, E.M. (1974) *Planning and Educational Inequality*, Slough, NFER.
CARSON, S. (1967) 'The Use of Content and Effective Objectives in Rural Studies', unpublished MEd thesis University of Manchester.
CARSON, S. (Ed.) (1971) *Environmental Studies, the Construction of an 'A' Level Syllabus*, Slough, NFER.
CHANNON, C. (1964) 'Social studies in secondary school', *Educational Review*,
FISHER, C.A. (1970) 'Whither regional geography', *Geography*, 55, 4, November.
GARNETT, A. (1969) 'Teaching geography: Some reflections', *Geography*, 54, November.
GEOGRAPHICAL ASSOCIATION (1970) notes of meeting of Chairman of Section/Standing Committee, 28 September.
GOMM, R. (1977) *Environment and Environmental Studies*, monograph.
GOODSON, I. (1976) *Towards a Social History of Subjects*, mimeo.
HONEYBONE, R.C. (1954) 'Balance in geography and education', *Geography*, 34, 186.
LAYTON, D. (1973) *Science for the People*, George Allen and Unwin.
Letter, Schools Council, Herts File, 21 February 1973, SS/L/G/191.
LOWE, R. (1976) 'The divided curriculum: Sadler, Morant and the English secondary school', *Journal of Curriculum Studies*, 8.
MACKINDER, H.J. (1903) *Report of the Discussion on Geographical Education*.
MACKINDER, H.J. (1913) 'The teaching of geography and history as a combined subject', *The Geographical Teacher*, 7.
MARCHANT, E.C. (1968) 'Some responsibilities of the teacher of geography', *Geography*, 3.
MILLWARD, R. (1969) 'Obituary: Patrick Walter Bryan', *Geography*, 54, 1, January.
MINISTRY OF EDUCATION (1960) *Science in Secondary Schools*, Pamphlet No. 38, London, HMSO.
NICHOLLS, A.D. (1973) 'Environmental studies in schools', *Geography*, 58, 3, July.
Norwood Report (1943) London, HMSO.
SCHOOLS COUNCIL (1969) *Working Paper No. 24*, London, Evans/Methuen Education.
SILVER, H. (1977) 'Nothing but the past, or nothing but the present?', *The Times Higher Educational Supplement*, 1 July.
SMITH, M. (1980) 'The evaluation of curriculum priorities in "Secondary Schools 1903–4"', *British Journal of Sociology of Education*, 1, 2, June.
THOMAS, P.R. (1970) 'Education and new geography', *Geography*, 55, 3.
WALFORD, R. (1973) 'Models, simulations and games', in WALFORD, R. (Ed.) *New Directions in Geography Teaching*, Longmans.
WEBSTER, J.R. (1971) 'Curriculum change and crisis', *British Journal of Educational Studies*, 3, October.
WILLIAMS, M. (1976) *Geography and the Integrated Curriculum*, London, Heinemann.
YOUNG, F.D. (1971) 'An approach to the study of curricula as socially organised knowledge', in YOUNG, M. (Ed.) *Knowledge and Control*, London, Collier Macmillan.
YOUNG, F.D. (1977) 'Curriculum change: Limits and possibilities', in YOUNG, M. and WHITTY, G. (Eds) *Society State and Schooling*, Lewes, Falmer Press.

On Explaining Change in School Subjects

Barry Cooper

During the late fifties and early sixties a major reform of the content of selective secondary school mathematics was carried out throughout Europe and the USA. In a climate in which a 'crisis' was believed to exist within the subject, elements of 'modern mathematics' were introduced into new textbooks and syllabuses and much previously valued content seemed destined to disappear. Recently, nearly twenty years after these events, various individuals and groups have again successfully argued that a 'crisis' exists in mathematics and another phase of redefinition is currently in progress (Keitel, 1982; Cockcroft, 1982). It is therefore clearly important that sociologists interested in the curriculum continue to develop conceptual tools for understanding such apparently cyclical processes of redefinition. In a recently completed study (Cooper, 1982) I have attempted to contribute to this development by constructing a sociological account of the social process of subject redefinition in English secondary school mathematics in the late fifties and sixties, concentrating on the origins of the School Mathematics Project (SMP) and the Midlands Mathematical Experiment (MME). Here, drawing on this work, I wish to stimulate further discussion of sociological approaches to the study of subject redefinition by examining several theoretical issues which had to be resolved in constructing my account. In particular, I shall be presenting a model for the explanatory analysis of those social processes which determine the reproduction and/or transformation of the legitimacy of established definitions of school mathematics and science at the level of the textbook and syllabus. I shall argue that, in order to understand change in these subjects, we have to understand the nature and effects of interaction across a series of boundaries between subject sub-cultures practising (that is, teaching, developing, applying) mathematics and science in different social locations, and between these sub-cultures and other non-disciplinary arenas. To the extent that, over time, within these relatively insulated social settings, different versions of mathematics or science and their practice are constructed we are therefore concerned with understanding the responses of actors to various 'discontinuities' which may be perceived to threaten their occupational interests.

Defining the Curriculum

I began my work with the outlines of a programme available. Musgrove (1968) had argued that sociologists should (following the sociologists of science) regard subjects as social systems, usefully directing us to Ben-David's important work on intellectual innovation in the sciences (Ben-David, 1960; Ben-David and Collins, 1966). Various contributors to *Knowledge and Control*, although in many instances implicitly concerned with change over longer periods than I was, had offered useful insights into processes of curriculum change (Young, 1971). Like Musgrove, they had recommended the sociology of science but also symbolic interactionist approaches to the study of the professions. There was also some relevant historical work (Layton, 1973).

In developing my own preferred approach, drawing on a range of literature and my own empirical work, I have been especially concerned to make possible the articulation of structural and interactional levels of analysis. As Bernstein argued, in his review of the sociology of education:

> It is a matter of some importance that we develop forms of analysis that can provide a dynamic relationship between 'situational activities of negotiated meaning' and the 'structural' relationships which the former presuppose. Indeed it is precisely what is taken as given in social action approaches which allows the analysis to proceed in the first place. Neither can the relationships between structural and interactional aspects be created by metasociological arguments as in the case of Berger.... The levels, if they are to be usefully linked, must be linked at the *substantive* level by an explanation whose conceptual structure directs empirical exploration of the relationships between the levels. (Bernstein, 1974, p. 155)

Here, partly for presentational reasons, I shall develop my argument from an examination of Kuhn's early analysis of scientific education which, while suffering from a number of inadequacies, is a useful preliminary insight into the nature of both scientific and mathematical education.

Kuhn on the Textbook

Kuhn's original analysis of theory change in the sciences is now well-known (Kuhn, 1962). Simplifying, in *The Structure of Scientific Revolutions*, he argues (in a somewhat functionalist tone) that the history of established sciences is characterizable in terms of periods of 'normal science' during which a community of scholars sharing a 'paradigm' engages in puzzle-solving, punctuated by periods of crisis and revolution during which the previously dominant paradigm, having succumbed to 'anomalies' generated by the practice of normal science, is displaced by a new contender from amongst those developed by scientists increasingly insecure in their paradigmatic understanding of the world. The strengths and weakness of his account, and his modification of it in

46

the face of criticism, have been usefully reviewed by a number of authors, most recently Barnes (1982).

At the same time, however, both in *The Structure* and elsewhere, Kuhn presented an account, less well-known, of scientific educational practices (which, incidentally, he saw as generally 'immensely effective') (Kuhn, 1970, p. 165). Education in the natural sciences was seen as 'a dogmatic initiation in a pre-established tradition that the student was not equipped to evaluate' (Kuhn, 1963, p. 346), an initiation relying primarily on the pedagogic device of the textbook:

> The single most striking feature of this [scientific] education is that, to an extent totally unknown in other creative fields, it is conducted entirely through textbooks. Typically the undergraduate and graduate student of chemistry, physics ... acquires the substance of his field from books especially written for students. Until he is ready, or very nearly ready, to commence work on his own dissertation, he is neither asked to attempt trial research projects nor exposed to the immediate products of research done by others, i.e. to the professional communications that scientists write for each other. There are no collections of 'Readings' in the natural sciences. Nor is the science student encouraged to read the historical classics of his field — works in which he might discover other ways of regarding the problems discussed in his textbook, but in which he would also meet problems, concepts and standards of solution that his future profession has long since discarded and replaced. (*ibid.*, pp. 345–6)

He notes that, in periods of normal science, that is, whilst scientists share a paradigmatic consensus, textbooks, while they may differ in level of difficulty and pedagogic emphasis, '[do] not in substance or conceptual structure' (*ibid.*, p. 346). Neither do they describe the sorts of problem that a professional scientist may be expected to solve and proffer a variety of techniques available for this work. Rather:

> these books exhibit concrete problem solutions that the professional has come to accept as paradigms, and they then ask the student, either with a pencil and paper or in the laboratory, to solve for himself problems very closely related in both method and substance to those through which the textbook or the accompanying lecture has led him. Nothing could be better calculated to produce 'mental sets'. (*ibid.*)

Textbooks, however, do change. Since he sees normal science as subject to periodic redefinition and since textbooks are the major device for initiating students into paradigms, it follows that 'one characteristic of scientific revolutions is that they call for the rewriting of science textbooks' (*ibid.*, p. 347).

Clearly, we have here an important insight into the nature of the education received by future scientists (and, I would argue, mathematicians). I shall argue that it provides a key element for an adequate model of redefinition in these subjects by suggesting an analysis of one of the key boundary relationships within them. There are, however, a number of weaknesses in Kuhn's account. His apparent (functionalist) assumption that the necessary rewriting does eventually occur is perhaps questionable. Furthermore, it is clearly necessary to pay more specific attention to the nature of the educational system itself if we are adequately to conceptualize *processes* of change. Therefore, I shall, before outlining my preferred approach, discuss ways in which we might need to modify or expand Kuhn's account. In doing so I shall illustrate important points by reference to my own work on mathematics but I shall not be presenting any overall account of the evolution of such projects as SMP and MME. My concern here is with theoretical issues.

The Discipline

Kuhn's account of scientific education seems to have been intended to be primarily relevant to the community of scientists involved in both teaching and research, that is, institutionally speaking, to university science. This gives us good grounds for expecting that his analysis will need modification before it can be applied to school subjects. I shall, therefore, in this section, advance two lines of argument. The first criticizes Kuhn's analysis within his own frame of reference. The second introduces the complications arising from a concern with school rather than college textbooks (or curricula).

Kuhn's original account of the nature of the discipline remains ambiguous in a crucial respect. As he recognized later, it is unclear in the original edition of *The Structure* whether he wished to differentiate disciplines by reference to ideas or social organization. In a postscript to the second edition he argued:

> The term 'paradigm' enters the preceding pages early, and its manner of entry is intrinsically circular. A paradigm is what the members of a scientific community share, and, conversely, a scientific community consists of men who share a paradigm. Not all circularities are vicious..., but this one is a source of real difficulties. Scientific communities can and should be isolated without prior recourse to paradigms; the latter can then be discovered by scrutinizing the behaviour of a given community's members. If this book were being rewritten, it would therefore open with a discussion of the community structure of science, a topic that has recently become a significant subject of sociological research and that historians of science are also beginning to take seriously. (Kuhn, 1970, p. 176)

The work of Hagstrom, Price, Crane and Mullins to which Kuhn refers in this postscript has been usefully summarized by Mulkay (1972) whose work I will therefore quote at some length:

> The basic research community is divided into a great variety of social

groupings. At the most general level it is made up of broad academic disciplines, such as physics, chemistry and mathematics. These disciplines are largely responsible for passing on the body of established knowledge to each new generation of researchers.... As these new entrants become actively engaged in research, their intellectual concerns become increasingly specialised. Consequently, they find that they are members of a speciality within the parent discipline, for example high-energy physics, solid-state physics, ..., and so on. Often these scientific specialities have various formal organs, such as conferences, journals, funding committees and possibly specialised training courses and university departments. By means of these organs the members of any speciality are able to exercise some control over the work of their colleagues and to attempt to maintain acceptable levels of conformity to cognitive and technical norms widespread within the speciality. However, all specialities are further divided into various problem networks. Most scientists are members of several such networks, but they seldom belong to more than a few of those extant in their speciality. Furthermore, the problems of different networks vary sufficiently to limit the scientific competence and interest of most researchers to the few networks directly bordering their own. As a result, it is within the problem network that intellectual control is largely exercised and new ideas either approved or rejected. (Mulkay, 1972, p. 55)

In spite of his awareness of such findings Kuhn still clung to what I shall argue (at least for the case of mathematics and, I suspect, for many sciences) to be an over-integrated view of the discipline:

There are schools in the sciences, communities, that is, which approach the same subject from incompatible standpoints. But they are far rarer there than in other fields; they are always in competition; and their competition is usually quickly ended. As a result, the members of a scientific community see themselves and are seen by others as the men uniquely responsible for the pursuit of a set of shared goals, including the training of their successors. Within such groups communication is relatively full and professional judgement relatively unanimous. (Kuhn, 1970, p. 177)

Ironically, given this partial move away from his original position, it was Kuhn's earlier view which seems to have influenced the early programmes for a sociology of the curriculum, certainly those of Young (1971), Bernstein (1971) and Esland (1971). But the segmentation into networks reported by the sociologists and historians of science clearly raises the possibility of there being, to varying degrees, a lack of consensus on purposes and norms within the scientific disciplines. Given sociologists' own experience of working within a cognitively fragmented discipline it is, perhaps, especially surprising that most sociologists of education writing on the subject have tended to stress consensus.

In the particular case of university mathematics, such fragmentation certainly has characterized the subject in recent decades (Cooper, 1982). Since the nineteenth century, the nature of the mathematics practised in universities had undergone many changes. There had not been any simple paradigm shift. Rather mathematics, by 1955, consisted of various sub-groupings working, to some extent, within different sets of cognitive and technical norms on different kinds of problem and with different goals and purposes. What, with some exceptions, had changed was the relative numerical strength and status of these sub-groups within the overall discipline. Alongside these changes, there had also been developments within sub-groups.

A broad line of division existed between pure and applied mathematicians. Applied mathematicians were much more likely than pure mathematicians to be concerned primarily with modelling and solving a problem (often from another discipline) than with the elegance and generality of the method of solution itself. Within each of these broad groupings there were further subdivisions. Practitioners might favour 'classical' or 'modern' approaches to their subject. With the increasing availability of computer technology, applied mathematicians were working to develop the fields of numerical analysis and linear programming. Within pure mathematics, adherents of 'modern' approaches (broadly, post-1800 structural algebraic approaches) were gradually gaining ground within the discipline. As a result, within pure mathematics, a debate on the degree of philosophical rigour necessary to the practice of mathematics at various levels and on the merits of a very general approach to algebra and geometry paralleled that within applied mathematics on the role of the computer in the development of mathematics.

If, for the sake of argument, we were to make the unreal assumption of *a* textbook being rewritten to introduce undergraduates to mathematics, we could easily see that conflict would be likely to arise over its contents. (In practice, students are introduced through a variety of speciality-specific textbooks at university level. Conflict is over the range of specialities to be studied.) More realistically, discipline members could be expected to react differently to any particular proposal for the reform of the selective schools' mathematics curriculum which, in Kuhn's terms, served to initiate their students and potential successors. This can be illustrated by quoting two comments on SMP's earliest proposals for a new A-level mathematics course, proposals which embodied elements of 'modern' trends from both pure and applied mathematics. The comments are, respectively, from professors of pure and applied mathematics:

> The syllabus looks like the work of someone interested in applied mathematics; there are a number of interesting novelties on that side, but on the pure side it appears to be away behind what are likely to be the views of the examining board. (Thwaites, 1972, p. 57)

And:

> it is absolutely essential for anyone who is going to apply his
> mathematics in such divergent fields as nuclear physics, aeronautics,
> meteorology, crystallography, astronomy or geophysics, to acquire a
> geometrical sense. This cannot be acquired by pretending that
> geometry is a part of algebra, as your syllabus appears to do. It can be
> acquired only by some form of exercise in which people are forced to
> think in geometric terms. (*ibid.*, p. 59)

Furthermore, I found that debates at various conferences concerned with the
redefinition of selective school mathematics in the late 1950s and early 1960s
could be broadly characterized in terms of pure versus applied, and 'classical'
versus 'modern', perspectives. Indeed, Hammersley, an applied statistician
who, in 1957, as organizer of the important Oxford conference of university
mathematicians, schoolteachers and industrial representatives, had initiated
the sequence of events leading to such projects as SMP, was later to attack
SMP, which in part embodied modern algebraic approaches, under the title,
'On the enfeeblement of mathematical skills by "modern mathematics" and by
similar soft intellectual trash in schools and universities' (Hammersley, 1968).
One obvious consequence, therefore, of the intra-subject differentiation described above is that, given the endlessly changing balance of forces within the
discipline, the legitimacy apparently granted to any definition of 'feeder'
curricula by representatives of the subject is likely to be temporary and always
subject to attacks.

A second problem with Kuhn's analysis arises from his focus on *university*
science. One can see that a research and teaching community might reorganize
its own curricular emphases in ways that his analysis could, retrospectively,
loosely describe (if not explain). But university scientists and mathematicians
had no simple direct control over English selective school curricula. Furthermore, the teachers of these feeder schools, in age-dependent ways, had been
socialized into a variety of versions of mathematics in a variety of institutions.
They had career-related interests in these versions (see below). For the
university practitioners, therefore, a problem of resocialization — across
institutional boundaries — appeared. Teachers, furthermore, as members of
various professional sub-cultures, held, as well as different versions of
'appropriate' mathematics, perspectives on pedagogy which conflicted in a
variety of ways with the perspectives of university practitioners. 'Rigour', for
example, was often pedagogically frowned upon. This directly conditioned
responses to modern algebraists' claims. Similarly, teachers responded negatively to some applied mathematicians' demands for the introduction of 'more
realistic' (and hence less predictable) examination problems (Cooper, 1982, p.
162).

I have said enough to indicate that we must include in our model an
explicit concern with the vertical and horizontal differentiation of academic
subjects. This has been increasingly recognized for the arts and social sciences

(Gouldner, 1971; Goodson, 1983; Ball and Lacey, 1980; Ball, 1982) but less clearly for natural sciences and mathematics.

A related problem remains. While a concern with differentiation will help us understand interaction across the school/higher education boundary we must also attend to relationships across the boundary of the educational system, something to which Kuhn pays little attention.

Extra-Disciplinary Relationships

The problems these relationships lead to for Kuhn's analysis can be seen by merely noting that it is not only discipline members who have an interest in the socializing device of the textbook (or the curriculum in general). Members of other disciplines and industrial and commercial enterprises also receive the socializees. This is especially important to understand in the case of 'applicable' subjects like mathematics and science (notwithstanding the obvious interest of all employers in the effects of the curriculum in its broadest sense). It is also important to take account of the differing perspectives of discipline members practising within industrial and commercial settings, especially so as they may undertake, on behalf of their employers, the task of communicating the 'needs' of the economy to teachers and researchers in the educational system.

In the case of the process of redefinition of selective school mathematics, representatives of industrial, commercial and governmental enterprises were centrally involved — not only in the initial sequence of conferences, but also through funding, and, eventually, in the reactions to such materials as those of SMP. To note this involvement and its effects is not, however, as far as we might wish to go in our attempt to explain change. We also need to consider what changes in industrial and commercial organization ground changing levels of involvement of industrial and commercial personnel in educational debate. While the imperatives of capital accumulation may be taken to account, at a general level, for the interest of the employing classes in educational processes, we need to search for more specific causes of changing levels of concern. In doing so, we shall be providing accounts of changes in the conditions for action of subject members. This can be illustrated for the case of mathematics (Cooper, 1982).

After the war, as the computer (in the context of increasing industrial and commercial concentration) became more widely employed within industry, more and more graduate mathematicians were employed in non-educational settings. Mathematical techniques were increasingly used in planning and research departments. This occurred alongside a growth in sixth form numbers, especially of those studying mathematics, and, furthermore, in the context of a governmental and media concern with the production of scientific and technological manpower. The rate of production of mathematics graduates was, however, fairly static. As a result, a 'shortage' of mathematics teachers could be identified by subject members, with a range of occupational interests, by making reference to previously accepted criteria of adequate staffing (such as percentage of new entrants with 'firsts', and so on). Similarly, a shortage of mathematicians for industry could be predicted by various interested actors.

These changes in employment patterns and in the permeability of the disciplinary boundary offer an explanation of the increased involvement of industrial and commercial employers with the discipline of mathematics in the late fifties, although it must be emphasized that subject members, perceiving opportunities for forging alliances and generating resources for the subject (or their segment of it), partially activated this involvement (by playing roles analogous to those of Becker's moral entrepreneurs in the field of deviance, Becker, 1963).

I have now indicated the range of groups that might be involved in the 'rewriting of the textbook' pointed to by Kuhn. I now wish to consider ways of analyzing their interaction and its redefining outcomes.

Interaction, Power and Resources

From what I have already argued of the segmented nature of disciplines and of the relationships between educational and other arenas, it is clear that any model of subject redefinition must be capable of capturing differentiation of perspective and interest. Kuhn, unsurprisingly given his historical method, provides no general account of such an approach. Neither do all of the writers in *Knowledge and Control* seem to have realized the importance of this. Young discusses *the* criteria of high status knowledge, without adequately describing who shares in this implied consensus (Young, 1971, p. 38). Classicists and engineers? Pure and applied mathematicians? Bernstein (1971) assumes monolithic subjects. Esland (1971), although recognizing conflicting perspectives between subjects, tends to equate subjects with a paradigm. Only Keddie (1971), at the level of classroom realization, seems to allow within-subject differentiation a central place in her analysis.

Esland does, however, point us to work, that of Bucher and Strauss, which, if suitably developed, can provide the concepts we need. Bucher and Strauss (1961) recommend the analysis of professions in terms of a process model and differentiation:

> the assumption of relative homogeneity within the professions is not entirely useful: there are many identities, many values, and many interests. These amount not merely to differentiation or simple variation. They tend to become patterned and shared; coalitions develop and flourish — and in opposition to some others. We shall call these groupings which emerge within a profession 'segments'. . . . We shall develop the idea of professions as loose amalgamations of segments pursuing different objectives in different manners and more or less delicately held together under a common name at a particular period in history. (Bucher and Strauss, 1961, pp. 325–6)

This clearly captures the major features of the mathematics and science disciplines described earlier. A number of researchers have recently followed Esland's suggestion, making use of Bucher and Strauss' ideas in analyzing processes of subject redefinition (for example, Goodson, 1983).

The analysis offers important insights into process. Segments, with different missions, are seen as social movements employing a range of strategies to achieve these. These include control over recruitment, alliance with other professional and non-professional groups and the creation of favourable public images in various arenas. I found that similar strategies characterized the campaign of those striving to achieve change in selective school mathematics. Bucher and Strauss also stress, as Griffiths and Mullins (1972) do in their account of innovation in science, the importance of adequate organizational and intellectual leadership. The key roles played by certain 'entrepreneurs' within the mathematics community clearly demonstrated the importance of the latter. The success of Thwaites, the founder of SMP, in using *The Times*, the Commons and the Lords to carry his argument that a 'crisis' existed within mathematics into non-subject arenas was a particularly significant example (Cooper, 1982, pp. 227–43).

In using their analysis, however, I became increasingly dissatisfied with one aspect of it. While the centrally important concept of 'power' is employed implicitly in their work, it is not adequately explicated. In particular, I wished to be able to understand why it was that some segments appeared more 'powerful' (in relation to achieving their mission against actual and potential opposition) than others. One way of putting this might be to argue that Bucher and Strauss, while adequately describing the dynamics of professional process, do not pay adequate attention to the statics. In their concern to understand action, they neglect structure. Their one-sided approach can usefully be compared to that recently developed by Archer (1979) to bring this out more clearly.

In her *Social Origins of Educational Systems*, Archer has elaborated a simple but useful analytic model of the relationships between structure and action in social life. Social interaction is seen as structurally conditioned but as leading, simultaneously, through what she terms structural elaboration, to a new structural conditioning of action. Simple reproduction is not, therefore, determined in advance. As a general scheme, this clearly has much in common with Bhaskar's (1979) 'transformational model of social activity' as well as Gidden's recent work (Giddens, 1979). But, especially important here is her reminder that power must be conceptualized in terms of the resources available to actors. Following Archer, and Bhaskar, I wish to argue that, if we are to *explain* change sociologically, these resources must be seen as differentially (and non-randomly) distributed to actors by virtue of their location in various sets of structured social relationships. As Bhaskar argues, such a 'relational conception' of sociology:

> allows one to focus on a range of questions, having to do with the
> *distribution* of the structural conditions of action, and in particular with

differential allocations of (i) productive resources (of all kinds, including for example cognitive ones) to persons (and groups) and (ii) persons
(and groups) to functions and roles (for example in the division of
labour). In doing so, it allows one to situate the possibility of different
(and antagonistic) interests, of conflicts *within* society, and hence of
interest-motivated transformations in social structure. (Bhaskar, 1979,
pp. 52–3)

And, I would add, of interest-motivated changes in the legitimacy of various
definitions of subjects.

While, therefore, actors can clearly use their available resources to
generate more (through alliance, proselytizing, and so on), it is clearly crucial
on this view that any attempt to explain the outcomes of processes of
intra-subject conflict explicitly concern itself with the delineation of the
resources available, at key points in time, to subject members and others.

It might be claimed that such a semi-positional view is too simple, that it
fails to capture the interactional and negotiated character of social life. But this,
I would argue, would be to confuse the social world with its analysis. As Archer
notes of her work:

We open up with the results of *prior* interaction. Here, for the
purpose of analysis, such phenomena have been treated as elemental
— that is, no attempt is made to account for how the structure we take
as our starting point had developed from previous interaction between
groups and individuals in the context of antecedent structures even
further back in history. The decision to do this was governed by the
need to avoid ultimate regress to historically distant and sociologically
complex interrelationships. Quite simply, one has to break into the
historical sequence at some point, and that point was chosen with
reference to the problem in hand. Some things always have to be taken
as given. (Archer, 1979, pp. 44–5)

Without such a working agreement with ourselves no empirical study could be
completed.

For such reasons, I took the differentiated nature of school and university
mathematics in the 1950s largely as given in my own study, setting out to
describe relevant features in some detail (Cooper, 1982, pp. 40–77). To
understand the process of redefinition, that is, it was necessary to map out the
distribution of resources across the segments of the mathematics community
and interested extra-subject groups. I worked with a broad definition of
resource. I included academic and general status (reflected in degree of
self-confidence and, for example, ease of access to the media and political
arenas), access to time for proselytization, access to financial resources, access
to particular social networks and organizations, control over entry to institutions and positions, previous access to 'valued' definitions of mathematics, and
the degree of fit potentially available between a segment's mission and those of
other 'powerful' groups.

This approach allowed me to attempt to move beyond description to explanation of outcomes. It allowed, for example, the consequences of university applied mathematicians' alliance with representatives of major industrial concerns to be understood. While the boards of large manufacturing companies, by granting financial resources to some groups of potential 'reformers' within the subject and denying them to others, could exercise some control over redefinition, the fact that other important resources (such as entry to higher education) were controlled partially by pure mathematicians favouring modern algebraic approaches ensured that industry-sponsored projects like SMP would reflect both paradigms in their materials. (It is obviously also relevant here that supporters of modern algebra strove to present their 'mission' in ways that were consonant with the technology-orientated climate of opinion. Similarly, many mathematicians, while resources were at stake, denied the relevance of a pure/applied distinction, Cooper, 1982.) The approach also allowed an explanation to be offered of why it was that SMP, rather than competitors offering similar products such as MME, succeeded in both gaining major financial support and widely diffusing their materials, an explanation in terms of its members' well-resourced occupational locations (the universities and public schools) and in terms of the relations of deference which operate (as a resource for some) within subject communities (*ibid.*, pp. 254–72).

Hopefully the discussion so far provides analytic tools adequate to the task of accounting for many aspects of redefining processes. We are still left, however, with the task of explaining why some schoolteachers appear more ready to be 'resocialized' (whether it be Lacey's, 1977, internalized adjustment or strategic compliance) than others by university and industrial personnel. It is in this regard that work in the sociology of science on the relationships between individuals' career interests and intellectual innovation is particularly useful.

Careers and Subject Redefinition

Kuhn paid little attention to this area but, in a seminal paper, Ben-David and Collins (1966) have used the notions of career blockage and consequent intellectual migration to account successfully for the emergence of experimental psychology in nineteenth century Germany. Holt (1970), who has followed this approach in his study of the growth of the British chemical profession, summarizes its key ideas thus:

> What happened in a particular time and place that caused the communication of ideas in a particular discipline to become significantly effective? It is assumed that (i) ideas necessary for the emergence of a new discipline are usually available over a comparatively long period of time and in various places; (ii) only some of these embryos continue in further growth; (iii) such growth occurs in time and place because individuals become interested in the new idea, not only for its

intellectual content but also as a means to the end of a new intellectual identity and, even more importantly, a new occupational role; (iv) the conditions under which such interest emerges can be identified and form the basis for building a predictive theory. (Holt, 1970, p. 181)

Of course, in the case of redefinition of school subjects we are considering not the emergence of a new discipline (see Goodson, 1981) but a new definition of an existing discipline.

It is not difficult to see that teachers' career interests will be intimately related to their responses to powerful segments' missions. Generally speaking, all other things being equal, we might expect older teachers, who owe their positions to achievements under established definitions, to resist redefinition more strongly than younger teachers who are not only likely to be more sympathetic to the new definitions (having possibly been partially socialized in their terms) but who also might be seen as having an interest in undermining the ideational basis of their seniors' positions. Furthermore, generally speaking again, we might expect well-resourced institutions, especially those which in a period of teacher 'shortage' could still attract well-qualified graduates, to be more ready to respond to university-led demands than less well-resourced competitors. Certainly, the major independent schools were one grouping at the forefront of redefining processes in mathematics and science (Waring, 1979; Cooper, 1982). Their relatively high degree of contact and interchange with university personnel is another important factor here, as is their concern to do well in the competition for Oxbridge entrance.

It is also important that we relate the issue of career to that of professional sub-culture, as Bucher and Strauss (1961, p. 334) argue. Within the non-selective sector in the 1950s teachers were increasingly promoting their careers through becoming examination-orientated subject specialists. This was leading to some redefinition of the arithmetic-based 'mathematics'curriculum for some pupils in these schools (Cooper, 1982). Furthermore, in so far as it involved a remodelling, for some pupils, of the mathematics curriculum in terms of the existing selective school definition it was also to lead eventually, within the context of comprehensivization, to elements of 'modern maths' being incorporated into CSE syllabuses. This diffusion of 'modern maths' into the syllabuses (if not always into the classrooms) of the 'less able' would produce a number of responses from various sources in the 1970s.

Within the schools, it had the twin effects of partially deskilling older non-graduate teachers and of introducing material and approaches which their educational perspectives could not easily accommodate. Furthermore, since younger graduate teachers promoting 'modern maths' represented a threat to their sense of seniority during reorganization their reactions tended to be motivated by both perspectival differences and material interests (Riseborough, 1981). This can be seen clearly in the comments of older non-graduate teachers in a boys' comprehensive school in which I carried out a case study as part of my research, a school in which the secondary modern head of department had lost his post to a young graduate on reorganization (Cooper, 1982). The displaced man, an emergency-trained teacher, argued:

> Half a person's life is spent calculating. It's an everyday activity. This is surely the main reason for maths for most children — not those in the grammar stream though. But even of those only a few will go on to do maths. Most will just need calculating. Most kids now can't use maths after school, especially with the modern syllabuses. Modern maths is not very relevant, except perhaps for the top grammar school pupils. Sets we used to call factors. It's all just name-changing except for matrices and graphs. The kids usually ask me what's the point of it? For them there is no point.... I've no time for the S.M.P. books at all. A crowd of people got on the bandwagon. A fiddle ... S.M.P. doesn't have enough examples for ordinary kids.... Practical work, like dice, is really science.... The average kid isn't interested in mathematical principles.

Another, 57 years of age, an ex-general subjects secondary modern teacher who had specialized in mathematics for twelve years, similarly claimed:

> It all depends on ability levels. With the average pupil and downwards, maths is all about getting a job.... I avoid the modern sort of rubbish. I prefer the traditional maths as it has been in syllabuses up till now. C.S.E. is far too wide. Most of the modern topics should go. There aren't a lot of applications for reflections or whatever they call them now.... Modern maths is an attempt to teach maths to kids who shouldn't be doing maths anyway. It's too time-consuming.... Arithmetic is enough for those with I.Qs. less than a hundred, and the more formal the better.

A third, about 60 years of age, also emergency trained, thought similarly:

> I'm not favourably impressed by the S.M.P. books. They're too wordy. There's too much reading, and not enough exercises.... It's all unrelated to real life. We should talk about things like car cylinders. S.M.P. is only suitable for brighter children. Women tend to go for it ... as it's soft.

In fact, in this school, the curriculum was differentiated along the lines favoured by these teachers. As the graduate head of department explained in some detail in describing his 'aims':

> Well, for the top thirty per cent, the same philosophy as the old grammar schools. Appreciation of the subject for its own sake, elegance. We don't do totally modern but we can do as much as we want with the top groups. They're the sort of kid receptive to the

philosophy behind the modern maths.... The middle forty per cent, the C.S.E. candidates, the good to moderate: maths is a subject like any other for them.... They must be able to do the basics and know something of the rest. I develop a few things in depth, that's all they can take. We're preparing them for apprenticeships. I carefully select topics from modern maths. I wouldn't do matrix algebra with them. Nor topology — not for the average school-leaver and technical apprentice.... Mostly we do pragmatic maths.... Bottom thirty per cent: my concern here is to give them a lot of optimism and enjoyment.... We must give them success, stuff they can get right.... They have a limited span of concentration.... Number work, money, metric units, some appreciation of what you can do with fractions and decimals.... Any modern topics are strictly for entertainment value only.... Optimism and confidence-boosting are critical, and accepting that their level of performance will be limited, even in arithmetic.

As he explicitly recognized during the interview, this differentiation actually allowed staff to teach their preferred definition of mathematics and, hence, helped to 'keep the peace'.

We can now see, retrospectively, that while 'modern maths' may have entered the comprehensives via the grammar schools of the sixties through processes of imitation motivated partly by something akin to deference and partly by career interest (as well as sometimes by a concern to see a more common curriculum), this very success has ironically produced much of the negative reaction to the redefinition of the sixties, a reaction grounded in the resulting involvement of groups not involved in the original negotiation of that compromise. (This was as true of some employers' reactions as of the non-graduate teachers quoted above.)

Here, I have only indicated some of the ways in which attention to career can help us provide adequate accounts of change. In my study, I was also able to offer an explanation of divisions within the Association for Teaching Aids in Mathematics (a more broadly-based rival to the long-established Mathematical Association) in terms of members' varied occupational locations (Cooper, 1982, pp. 78–102). A concern with how the influences on actors' perspectives varied according to their location also enabled some understanding of the different emphases that characterized actors' missions to be developed. Actors, for example, in colleges of education were much more likely than those from university mathematics departments to invoke Piagetian psychology in support of redefinition. It was also noteworthy that a number of key actors in the process of redefinition (including Thwaites, the founder of SMP) had straddled occupational boundaries in their professional lives and, furthermore, that many of those associated with SMP were subsequently occupationally mobile, (Thwaites, 1972, pp. 225–8). As they moved across locations, the sets of influences they were subject to changed. It is important that we appreciate this complexity in our attempts to account for changes in actors' perspectives over time.

I shall now present the main features of a model for the analysis of changes in the legitimacy of particular versions of school science and mathematics.

The Model

1   By analogy with Bucher and Strauss' account of a profession in conflict terms, and following the suggestions of Esland and Musgrove, a 'subject' should be seen as a set of segments, or social movements, with distinctive missions, or perspectives, and material interests.

2   The relations of conflict and cooperation between these segments, and their alliances with groups inside and outside the subject, should be seen as major explanatory factors in accounts of changes in what counts as school mathematics and science.

3   The relative power of these segments, and of individuals, should be analyzed in terms of the resources available to them. This availability will partly be a reflection of the segment's position in a set of structured relationships and associated sub-cultures constituting a stratified educational (and social) system but also, again partly, a reflection of the segment's success in forging alliances with other powerful (resource-controlling) groups.

4   Particular attention should be paid to understanding changes in the conditions for action for subject members, especially changes in the distribution of resources over time. This will require, in many cases, analysis of changes in extra-subject arenas (such as the industrial, commercial and the political) which may motivate changing degrees of involvement of extra-subject personnel in processes of subject redefinition.

5   Accepting the central thrust of Kuhn's analysis of the function of the textbook as being to initiate students into a paradigm, but placing it in the context of Bucher and Strauss' analysis of intra-professional conflict over recruitment and the accounts of the sociologists of science of the differentiated nature of subjects, we should expect segments within university subject communities (and industry/commerce) to compete for influence over the redefinition of relevant subjects in feeder secondary schools, and, in textbook-based subjects, especially over the nature of the textbooks utilized.

6   Missions should be seen as partially negotiable in the interests of the careers of individuals and segments. Furthermore, following Ben-David's analysis of scientific change, we should consider the perceived career consequences of various proposals for redefinition to be important factors in accounting for the responses of interested actors to these proposals.

7   Similarly, the relative diffusion rates of textbooks, materials and proposed changes in practice might be understood, in terms of this approach, by examining whose missions and interests are represented therein, and the relation of these missions and interests to those of potential adopters. Reactions to the materials and proposals, and their situated curricular realization, might be similarly accounted for as consequences of sub-cultural conflict of perspective and interest.

8   Finally, since any redefinition of a school subject is characteristically a compromise between the demands of various 'powerful' groups, we should expect its legitimacy to be continuously subject to attack as changes occur in the distributions of resources and climates of opinion in various arenas.

Conclusion

I have argued for a model of school subject redefinition which allows articulation of structural and interactional approaches. While I have only, thus far, claimed its relevance to the areas of mathematics and the sciences, subjects in which the textbook is a major initiating device, I see no major reason why it should not be applied to other school subjects. Here, instead of focussing on the textbook we would focus on curricular materials and practices in a more general way. Presumably, different individuals and segments would be found important according to whether 'curriculum', 'pedagogy' or 'evaluation' (Bernstein, 1971, p. 47) became the focus of study. I have no doubt that interesting conclusions would emerge from such a comparative analysis, in these terms, of change processes in subjects with and without university bases, 'applicable' and 'non-applicable', and so on. We now have a number of useful studies with which to proceed (Layton, 1973; Waring, 1979; Ball and Lacey, 1980; Ball, 1982; Goodson, 1983 and 1984; Burgess, 1984).

Finally, I must stress that this paper has been written with the formal curriculum in mind and, no doubt, a different form of analysis (and a concern with change over longer periods of time) might be more appropriate for a study of the 'hidden curriculum'. In this respect, it is noteworthy, for example, that SMP's ideas offered little challenge to dominant assumptions about 'ability'. This may well have been a necessary if not sufficient condition for its eventual 'success'.

Acknowledgements

This paper is based on a thesis prepared in the Education Area of the University of Sussex. I should particularly like to thank my supervisor, Colin Lacey, for his help and encouragement over several years. Discussions with my Sussex colleagues, Trevor Pateman, Stephen Ball and Ivor Goodson, have also affected the final form of this paper, an earlier version of which was presented to the St Hilda's Conference on Histories and Ethnographies of School Subjects in September 1982.

* This paper appeared previously in the *British Journal of Sociology of Education* (1983) 4, 3, pp. 207–222 and is reproduced here by kind permission of the Publisher.

References

ARCHER, M.S. (1979) *Social Origins of Educational Systems*, London, Sage.

BALL, S.J. (1982) 'Competition and conflict in the teaching of English: A socio-historical analysis', *Journal of Curriculum Studies*, 14, pp. 1–28.

BALL, S.J. and LACEY, C. (1980) 'Subject disciplines as the opportunity for group action: A measured critique of subject subcultures', in WOODS, P. (Ed.) *Teacher Strategies*, London, Croom Helm, pp. 149–77.

BARNES, S.B. (1982) *T.S. Kuhn and Social Science*, London, Macmillan.

BECKER, H.S. (1963) 'Moral entrepreneurs', in BECKER, H.S. (Ed.) *Outsiders*, New York, Free Press, pp. 147–63.

BEN-DAVID, J. (1960). 'Roles and innovation in medicine', *American Journal of Sociology*, 65, pp. 557–68.

BEN-DAVID, J. and COLLINS, R. (1966) 'Social factors in the origin of a new science, the case of psychology', *American Sociological Review*, 31, pp. 451–65.

BERNSTEIN, B. (1971) 'On the classification and framing of educational knowledge', in YOUNG, M.F.D. (Ed.) *Knowledge and Control*, London, Collier-Macmillan, pp. 47–69.

BERNSTEIN, B. (1974) 'Sociology and the sociology of education: A brief account', in REX, J. (Ed.) *Approaches to Sociology*, London, Routledge and Kegan Paul, pp. 145–59.

BHASKAR, R. (1979) *The Possibility of Naturalism*, Brighton, Harvester Press.

BUCHER, R. and STRAUSS, A. (1961) 'Professions in process', *American Journal of Sociology*, 66, pp. 325–34.

BURGESS, R.G. (1984) 'It's not a proper subject: It's just Newsom', this volume, pp. 181–200.

COCKCROFT, W.H. (1982) *Mathematics Counts*, London, HMSO.

COOPER, B. (1982) *Innovation in English Secondary School Mathematics: A Sociological Account with Special Reference to S.M.P. and M.M.E.*, DPhil thesis, University of Sussex.

ESLAND, G.M. (1971) 'Teaching and learning as the organization of knowledge', in YOUNG, M.F.D. (Ed.) *Knowledge and Control*, London, Collier-Macmillan, pp. 70–115.

GIDDENS, A. (1979) *Central Problems in Social Theory*, London, Macmillan.

GOODSON, I.F. (1981) 'Becoming an academic subject: Patterns of explanation and evolution', *British Journal of Sociology of Education*, 2, pp. 163–80.

GOODSON, I.F. (1983) *School Subjects and Curriculum Change*, London, Croom Helm.

GOODSON, I.F. (1984) 'Subjects for study: Towards a social history of curriculum', this volume, pp. 25–44.

GOULDNER, A.W. (1971) *The Coming Crisis of Western Sociology*, London, Heinemann.

GRIFFITHS, B.C. and MULLINS, N.C. (1972) 'Coherent social groups in scientific change', *Science*, 177, pp. 959–64.

HAMMERSLEY, J.M. (1968) 'On the enfeeblement of mathematical skills by "modern mathematics" and by similar soft intellectual trash in schools and universities',

Bulletin of the Institute of Mathematics and Its Applications, 4, pp. 66–85.

HOLT, B.W.G. (1970) 'Social aspects in the emergence of chemistry as an exact science: The British chemical profession', *British Journal of Sociology*, 21, pp. 181–99.

KEDDIE, N. (1971) 'Classroom knowledge', in YOUNG, M.F.D (Ed.) *Knowledge and Control*, London, Collier-Macmillan, pp. 133–60.

KEITEL, C. (1982) 'Mathematics education and educational research in the U.S.A. and U.S.S.R.: Two comparisons compared', *Journal of Curriculum Studies*, 14, pp. 109–26.

KUHN, T.S. (1962 and 1970) *The Structure of Scientific Revolutions*, 1st and 2nd ed., University of Chicago.

KUHN, T.S. (1963) 'The essential tension: Tradition and innovation in scientific research', reprinted in part in HUDSON, L. (Ed.) *The Ecology of Human Intelligence*, Harmondsworth, Penguin, pp. 342–56.

LACEY, C. (1977) *The Socialisation of Teachers*, London, Methuen.

LAYTON, D. (1973) *Science for the People*, London, Allen and Unwin.

MULKAY, M.J. (1972) *The Social Process of Innovation*, London, Macmillan.

MUSGROVE, F. (1968) 'The contribution of sociology to the study of the curriculum', in KERR, J.F. (Ed.) *Changing the Curriculum*, University of London pp. 96–109.

RISEBOROUGH, G.F. (1981) 'Teachers' careers and comprehensive schooling: An empirical study', *Sociology*, 15, pp. 352–80.

THWAITES, B. (1972) *SMP: The First Ten Years*, Cambridge University Press.

WARING, M. (1979) *Social Pressures and Curriculum Innovation*, London, Methuen.

YOUNG, M.F.D. (1971) 'An approach to the study of curricula as socially organized knowledge', in YOUNG, M.F.D. (Ed.) *Knowledge and Control*, London, Collier-Macmillan, pp. 19–46.

YOUNG, M.F.D. (Ed.) (1971), *Knowledge and Control*, London, Collier-Macmillan.

Part Two
Histories

Curricular Topics As Institutional Categories: Implications for Theory and Research in the History and Sociology of School Subjects

William A. Reid

In this paper I make the assumption that the object of studying the history of school subjects, or of examining them from sociological perspectives, is to increase our understanding of how and why topics and activities acquire (or lose) educational significance. This view I contrast with one which would hold that work of this kind should be directed towards responding to historical or sociological rather than educational questions.

If it is an educational agenda that holds our attention — the aim to understand better the purposes and events of schooling, or the aspiration to manage and control schooling processes and outcomes — then the success of the endeavour depends on working with a conception of what education *is*. In other words, as a preliminary to asking the question, what do subjects do?, we need to have some answer to the question, what do schools do?

What Do Schools Do?

All educational research proceeds on some assumption, which may or may not be made explicit, about what it is that schools, and more particularly school systems, do. Sometimes the assumption is that they are self-organizing systems which transmit specific skills and knowledge. Other researchers see them as instruments of society at large which reproduce its social and economic structures.

In this paper, I want to explore a plausible alternative view which avoids simplistic assumptions about the self-directive nature of educational systems but, at the same time, allows that what actors within them do is the result of rational decision rather than of social forces over which they have little or no control. I find this alternative conception, which is expounded by Meyer (1978,

1980) plausible both in the sense that its predictions about the behaviour of actors fit with my own experience as student and teacher and in the sense that it is consonant with many of the findings of recent research into the history and sociology of school subjects.

Meyer's ideas are a reaction against the commonly held assumption underlying much writing and research on the school curriculum that what is taught and how it is taught results essentially from decisions and initiatives taken within educational organizations. In his writings, external forces and structures emerge not merely as sources of ideas, promptings, inducements and constraints but as definers and carriers of the categories of content, role and activity to which the practice of schools must approximate in order to attract support and legitimation. The world external to the schools is conceived not so much in terms of formal bodies and conventional groupings (trades unions, universities, parents, employers) as in terms of more loosely conceived 'publics' or 'constituencies' for whom the elements of the curriculum have importance; for example, the public for whom history as a school subject is significant because its members provide resources to support it or because they value it as something which enhances the social or intellectual standing of those who take courses in it. These interested publics which pay for and support education hand over its work to the professionals in only a limited and unexpected sense. For while it may appear that the professionals have power to determine what is taught (at school, district or national level, depending on the country in question), their scope is limited by the fact that only those forms and activities which have significance for external publics can, in the long run, survive.

Such forms and activities Meyer terms 'institutional categories', where the word 'institutional' connotes a 'cultural ideology' and is contrasted with 'organizational', meaning enshrined within unique and tangible structures such as schools and classrooms. Institutional categories comprise schooling levels (such as primary), school types (such as comprehensive), educational roles (such as college principal) and, importantly for our purpose, curricular topics (such as reading, the Reformation or O-level mathematics). In each of these instances, the organizational form as created and maintained by teachers and others is paralleled by an institutional category which is significant for some wider public or publics. When curricular practice strays too far and too visibly from the category as understood by interested publics the result is loss of support, student alienation and failure and the collapse of efforts to sustain the legitimacy of the activity. The demise of William Tyndale School (ILEA, 1976) provides a particular local example; the retreat from innovatory mathematics programmes in primary schools a more general one. Innovation is not impossible — it may even be demanded; but innovation which is generated internally to the organization without much regard for wider publics is problematic. As Meyer puts it: 'innovations sacrifice the categorical meaning of topics' (Meyer, 1980, p. 54).

The unexpected power that teachers retain is not to introduce on their own initiative new topical categories, but to represent the topics that are taught as properly belonging within existing categories. Categorical meaning is either accorded or withheld; the professional art of the teacher lies in activating and maintaining the categorical status of what he teaches. He is most importantly not a manipulator of realities, but a purveyor of rhetorics, and professional ideologies are a means to the successful accomplishment of this role.

Thus far, the impression created is one of cynicism. In fact, once the initial step is taken of seeing the schooling system as being essentially concerned with offering membership in significant categories, that is, with status, rather than with the implanting of cognitive or affective skills and knowledge, then the way is open to allow that eduational actors behave with a good deal of genuine rationality in the resolution of real choices about what to teach and what to study. Students, in Meyer's view, are centrally concerned with constructing educational careers connected to desired social and occupational statuses, while teachers (whom he considers 'not much less sensible than young persons' (Meyer, 1980, p. 47) devote their efforts to ensuring that the categorical memberships on offer are, in the public eye, fully accredited and capable of conferring 'properly schooled' labels.

Topics and Activities As Institutional Categories

Thinking of school systems as organizations which are shaped from without (Meyer uses the metaphor of the exoskeleton to convey the essence of his idea) cautions us against analyzing them according to definitions and variables proposed by insiders. For this reason it is appropriate to suspend, temporarily, our use of the word 'subject' in order to work instead with 'topics' and 'activities'. If the successful teaching of X, in the sense of its survival in school programmes is related to the rhetorical skills of those who teach and organize it, then the actual content of X in topical terms may be more problematic than we might at first suppose. Provided that no clues are given by changes in labelling, English literature may turn out to be topically quite close to sociology, or geography to statistics. However, we also need to import the idea of 'activity'. School programmes may become categorically legitimate as much through the promotion of certain kinds of activity as through the inclusion of appropriate topics. Science in the secondary school legitimates itself through laboratory work which is only loosely related to the demands of specific content (secondary modern schools in the 1950s and 60s were frequently barred from claims to be teaching science because they had no labs). It is also the case that too much concentration on the idea of 'subject' may lead researchers to neglect programmes like art or physical education which are essentially activity-based. The use of topic/activity avoids this problem and enables us to ask questions about how topics/activities are marshalled into various curricular patterns and called 'subjects', or shared and exchanged between subjects. (From this point on, 'topic' will be understood to subsume 'activity'.) It also directs attention to the critical role that certain topics may play in the organization of school subjects.

Calculus as a topic within mathematics or classical texts in the teaching of languages would be examples.

A further point to be made is that the translation of a *topic* into 'schooled status' may be a different matter from the translation of a *subject*. The constellations or sequencings of topics in school programmes do not necessarily reflect those found in other contexts where subjects are taught or practised. One of the problematic features of modern mathematics was its attempt to distort conventionally understood topic sequences so that undergraduate topics began to figure in primary school programmes (this disjunction between subjects and topics as content in schools, and as content in other places, is generally ignored by philosophers of education seeking an epistemological base for the school curriculum).

Of all the topics which might serve as the content of schooling, only a limited sub-set actually supplies the subject matter of the curriculum, and the sub-set of topics which achieves categorical status is even smaller. Over time its composition changes. Old topics drop out of favour and new ones are adopted within subject curricula as teachers and administrators seek status for those claimed to be within their jurisdiction, disassociate themselves from those which are losing esteem and make bids for those which they think will enhance the prestige of their disciplines.

Four key and related characteristics of topics determine their attractiveness: centrality, universality, sequential significance, and status-relatedness. A *central* topic is one that is essential to categorical membership. For example, in English schools enrolment in an A-level programme has traditionally been a condition of membership in the categorical role of sixth former. Students have understood this and have committed resources to mastering the A-level programme at a sufficient level to maintain themselves in good standing. On the other hand, in spite of the entreaties of educators, they have consistently failed to show commitment to general studies programmes which are not central to the claim of *bona fide* status as a sixth former. When publics recognize topics as critically related to membership in significant role categories these have centrality and will be accorded economic resources and the attention of politicians and planners.

Some topics which are central are also *universal* (such as mathematics). That is, there is agreement that enrolment in them is essential for all, or nearly all, students whatever the academic career they are embarked upon. However, universality does not necessarily imply centrality. Physical education programmes are practically universal, but hardly anywhere central. In countries such as England where education systems direct resources to 'abler' students, subjects tend to stress topics which permit them to be central without being universal since this offers greater prestige. Modern languages, even if universally taught at the outset of the secondary school, rapidly becomes a curricular option; mathematics is compelled to be universal but continues to stress high status content (hence the problems discussed in the Cockcroft Report, DES, 1982, p. 133); high status subjects in decline which try to rescue themselves by seeking universality may fail dismally — Latin is an example (Reid and Filby, 1982; Goodson, 1983).

Sequential significance characterizes topics which are prerequisites for future student progress. Reading is a simple case. Students who cannot read at a minimal level are debarred from higher status programmes. Topics in science are sequential in a more complex way. Elaborate chains of topics can be created which mesh with choice points in student educational careers and enable science content to become a significant marker of progress. Some innovatory science programmes have failed because they interfered with this process. The Schools Council Integrated Science Project, for example, rendered problematic the connections, previously well understood by students, teachers and publics, between O- and A-level programmes.

Subjects which chain topics in sequences with career significance are frequently, though not always, strong on *status-relatedness*. Enrolment in the A-level mathematics programme becomes the mark of the outstanding student and is linked to entry to high status university courses. On the other hand, progress through metalwork activities, where the curriculum moves from lower to higher skill levels, does not confer status. In fact, metalwork teachers are often keen to exchange technical skill sequencing for the less clear progression of a curriculum based on 'design', with the idea that the importance of design in the modern world can enable them to teach topics with claims to universalism and centrality. This illustrates the point that status-relatedness (which may or may not be linked to sequencing) works both ways; while some programmes are associated with high status futures, others lead to low status or stigmatized careers and occupations.

Centrality, universality, sequential significance and status-relatedness are socio-historical or ideological rather than educational or epistemological facts. Much as teachers might like to believe that the categorical significance of a subject relates to its intrinsic character, curriculum history demonstrates that this is not the case. For many years, classics enjoyed all these marks of the successful school subject and teachers maintained its supportive rhetorics with ease, even when there was evidence to show that actual levels of student achievement were quite low. Eventually, however, a shift in public appreciation of the categorical status of Latin and Greek created an opposite situation. Now the work of rhetorically defending classics in the secondary curriculum is impossible in the face of scepticism on the part of students, parents and employers.

But in the absence of such shifts in institutional categories, the work of establishing new topics is difficult. Where publics have been exposed to pervasive rhetorics of persuasion (computer studies), professional activity within the school system can result in innovation. Where this is not the case (integrated humanities programmes), modifications in the topical content of curricula may prove to be of a temporary nature.

Since the attribution or non-attribution of topical status by publics is a social fact (though not necessarily in the sense that all publics are in agreement), school programmes tend towards topical uniformity within politically united or culturally homogeneous territories. This is true even where control over the content of the curriculum rests with local jurisdictions (the United States). It is still more the case where there is *de iure* central control (Sweden), or where national systems of assessment or accreditation result in *de facto* limitations on acceptable practice (England and Wales). In Meyer's view, such administrative features of educational systems have the effect of reinforcing an already strong tendency towards isomorphism between organizational practice and institutional categories.

Teachers As Managers of Topical Content

Most teachers (and educational administrators) understand instinctively that the work of teaching consists importantly in promoting and exhibiting the isomorphism between practice and category. This helps to explain the resistance of educational forms in the face of arguments for their reform on the part of educational theorists and teacher educators. Pedagogical forms (the recitation) persist because they are identified in the public mind with 'teaching' while other activities (class discussion, meditation) are not, unless they take place under special labels which limit their scope (debating society, yoga club). Even where proponents of pedagogical reform can convince professional colleagues of the value of their ideas, they still face the more essential and highly difficult task of converting outside publics.

There is also an understanding on the part of teachers that the categorical status of topics creates a special kind of logic that has to be observed in handling the rhetorics that surround them. An act of teaching, or the inclusion or exclusion of a topic, can never be judged on a scale of correctness. Event X is either a clear case of a categorically acceptable occurrence or it is not. There is no question of something being 'probably' a remedial reading class, or 'possibly' an instance of the teaching of calculus (though there is more scope for variation in practice in the former). This explains a special difficulty that new subjects have in becoming accepted as a legitimate part of high status curricula. Since they have not been previously taught, no one knows what a proper example of topic or teaching would look like. Yet the subject has to be *totally* acceptable or not accepted at all (there are few genuine examples of 'trials' or 'feasibility studies' relating to high status content, even where this has been the declared strategy of curriculum projects).

Where subjects already have full acceptance, nothing must be allowed to jeopardize it since the least departure from total affirmation of categorical legitimacy can result in a collapse of credibility. This is so even in the case of high status schools. A nineteenth century head of Eton College was quick to reject the suggestion of the Clarendon Commissioners that his pupils' knowledge should be tested by an examination with the comment that such 'interference with the authority and responsibility of the Head Master is calculated to produce serious evil' (Reid and Filby, 1982, p. 217). Where the evidence cannot be withheld, Meyer notes, the damage may be contained by the adoption of 'a permanent posture of reform'.

Since few subjects can claim all the possible marks of status, the judgement that teachers have to make is about when it is prudent to abandon one kind of legitimation for what they teach and offer another (the case of metalwork versus design has already been noted). Perhaps the hardest judgement to make in recent years has been that between claims for universality and claims for status-relatedness, since these are to a high degree mutually exclusive. The advent of the organizational change to comprehensive secondary education in English schools beginning in the 1960s gave the impression that participation was to become a major system goal and that subjects should embrace topics which enabled them to enrol the widest possible clientele. In the event, it seems that, though politically sanctioned, the changes which took place were more properly organizational than institutional. The norms imposed by university entrance requirements and by GCE examining continue to set the parameters for educational categories which have proved remarkably resistant to attempts to 'democratize' them (notably, the removal of the pass/fail boundary from GCE O-level has met with no response in terms of public categories; students, parents and most teachers still talk of 'passing O-level'). Subjects such as science, which a few years ago were trying to develop topics accessible to a wide range of students, are now once again stressing high status content and de-emphasizing innovative teaching styles.

Students As Consumers of Topical Content

Students, as rational consumers, are less concerned with knowing than with the status that comes from categorical membership and the future promise that this implies. They are essentially engaged in building educational careers which have implications for future social and occupational careers. Like teachers, they judge the appropriateness of committing themselves to curricular topics in the light of estimations of centrality, universality, sequential significance and status-relatedness. Topics which rank high on these criteria will be accorded substantial levels of commitment; those which do not will attract lower levels of personal investment. In this way students maximize the possibility that, for a given expenditure of effort, they can maintain their good standing as categorical members and secure their chances of moving to other desired categorical positions. The goal is success in the system as opposed to success in learning (though the two are inevitably related). Hence the kind of innovation which 'sacrifices the categorical meaning of topics' will meet with low student commitment and will survive with difficulty or not at all. This was the fate of many 'ROSLA' programmes which emphasized 'relevance' and 'life skills' instead of academic, 'properly schooled' content. Students identify such curricula as connected with low status futures and find them meaningless in terms of their understanding of educationally significant categories.

Given that student commitment is closely related to the perceived significance of topics to an educational career, and that, as Meyer (1980) puts it, 'programmatic membership is more certainly vital than knowledge', (p. 26) it follows that students are likely to be only marginally concerned with attempted innovations in teaching and method which are ostensibly to their benefit. Subjects which reform their pedagogy cannot count on student support. Many studies show that 'one way', authoritarian teaching continues to predominate in schools. Yet it is also the case that students seldom experience it that way. This, Meyer suggests, is because 'they are attending to the larger reality of "teacher" as an institutional category' and are 'surprisingly inattentive to the particular characteristics of their individual teachers' (Meyer, 1980, p.54).

Implications for Theory and Research

If we regard the notion of 'institutional categories' as providing a plausible key to the understanding of what schools do, what consequences follow for how we should study the evolution of those constellations of educational topics we call 'school subjects'? Most broadly, we should be cautioned against attempting to interpret the history or sociology of subjects solely in terms of the accounts given by actors directly concerned — teachers and students. Especially, we should be on our guard against drawing our evidence about how subjects behave mainly from the activities and statements of teachers. What teachers can achieve may be importantly limited by what the understandings of outside publics impose in the way of parameters within which choices must be made. At least students provide us with a bridge between the school as organization and the external institutional categories. But preferably we should look for evidence also from the carriers of categorical ideologies, parents, employers, scholars, politicians, administrators and others.

Further, we should be encouraged to consider that the fate of school subjects may be, to a large extent, in the hands of students as rational consumers rather than be led to construe subjects as the means by which school systems and teachers produce effects in students. Understanding the evolution of the topics of the curriculum depends on a sophisticated knowledge of the behaviour of students as clients of academic disciplinary professionals. Subjects and subject topics are the elements out of which students build careers, so that one central question to be asked about school subjects is, how are the topics they offer significant for student careers? And what effect do changes of topic have on this significance? That is, the histories of subjects need to contain also the histories of those for whom they have provided access to categorical membership.

Next, though the press to isomorphism between practice and category is strong, change does take place and has to be accounted for. In the construction of such accounts, we need to focus upon those features of the external, institutional world which cause categories to evolve so that spaces for innovation are created. It is not to be denied that some of the initiative for this comes from educators and actors in school systems, but the primary changes that need to be described are those in the external category system, not those within organizational structures: Latin did not collapse because of failure on the part of teachers.

Finally, we have to take seriously the logic of categories and accept that, within the terms of such a logic, successful rhetorics *are* realities. Though teachers and administrators have to be careful that disjunctions between practice and belief do not escalate to the point where credibility collapses, nonetheless it remains true that what is most important for the success of school subjects is not the delivery of 'goods' which can be publicly evaluated, but the development and maintenance of legitimating rhetorics which provide automatic support for correctly labelled activity. The choice of appropriate labels and the association of these in the public mind with plausible rhetorics of justification can be seen as the core mission of those who work to advance or defend the subjects of the curriculum. The study of how they take such action will provide an essential key to the writing of subject histories. Here too, a condition of the conduct of research is that we focus not only on the professional actors themselves, but also on the evolution of institutional categories among external publics.

References

DES (1982) *Mathematics Counts*, London, HMSO, p. 133.

GOODSON, I.F. (1983) *School Subjects and Curriculum Change*, London, Croom Helm.

ILEA (1976) *William Tyndale Junior and Infants Schools Public Inquiry*, London, Inner London Education Authority.

MEYER, J.W. (1978) 'The structure of educational organizations', in MEYER, J.W., MARSHALL, W., *et al.* (Eds) *Environments and Organizations*, San Fransisco, Jossey-Bass.

MEYER, J.W. (1980) 'Levels of the educational system and schooling effects', in BIDWELL, C.E. and WINDHAM, D.M. (Eds) *The Analysis of Educational Productivity*, 2 vols, Cambridge, Mass., Ballinger.

REID, W. and FILBY, J. (1982) *The Sixth: An Essay in Education and Democracy*, Lewes, Falmer Press.

The Play House and the Sand Tray

Clem Adelman

... For education is but the drama of culture set upon a small stage.
(Lawrence Stenhouse)

The title of this article refers to artifacts that have become associated with early childhood education. Drawing on my more extensive research, I suggest relationships between the different theories of the child mind and moral being upon which curricula, pedagogies and the institutions of early childhood education have been founded. Through historical and ethnographic research I have endeavoured to trace some of the conflicts that have centred on the merits of learning through play as opposed to learning through work. The presence of particular artifacts does not signify that either learning through play or learning through work is dominant or in contradiction. More significant are the educational purposes to which the objects have been designed to contribute. I have found that a long prevalent tension amongst early childhood educators is that of whether to place priority on fostering children's independence of thought and reflective action or to press towards inducting the children into conformity with adult social conduct and literacy. Historically, around versions of this tension have formed alliances, institutions and curriculum.

In 1974 I received the first of three small grants from the Social Science Research Council to engage in a study entitled 'The Use of Objects in the Education of Three to Five Year Old Children'. The grants terminated after fifteen months. I had collected a considerable volume of fieldwork notes, interviews, classroom transcripts and audio-visual recordings. The analyses I made of those data were in terms of the matrices of objects, spaces, participants and of rules which appeared to regulate interaction within those matrices. Although I considered that my aspiration to conduct a naive ethnographic study of 3–5-year-olds in school classrooms had been fulfilled, I was neither satisfied with the analysis nor with my understanding of how the 'traditions' of nursery and infant schooling had been formed historically.

Given the labour intensive demands of ethnographic observation, I envisaged that I could only conduct fieldwork in a maximum of three classrooms. I wanted to look at children between the ages of 3 and 5 years and found that children within the LEA in which the study was conducted usually began nursery at the age of 4, although allowances were made for children of $3\frac{1}{2}$ years or so to enter.

I decided to take as the third class a reception class of 5-year-olds, along with the nursery class in a primary school and a nursery class in a self-contained nursery school. I hoped that by making this choice I would gain comparative data about the influence on the classrooms of school schedules, school curricula and even what might count as legitimate pedagogy within the different schools.

I wanted to pursue what Walker and I had called 'negotiation towards mutual realities', particularly as this pertained to what was called the resource-task complex (Adelman and Walker, 1972). One of the difficulties in pursuing these concepts in primary and secondary classes was that much of the process of 'negotiation towards mutual realities' was linked to literate activities — reading texts, instructions, reference books. Furthermore, neither the teacher nor the pupils provided fully referenced accounts during their conversations. Referents were signified by pronouns, phatics, often based on assumptions about shared knowledge that pupils had gained from reading. Only 'completely new' topics and objects would be fully referenced and it was on these occasions that the process of negotiation towards mutual realities was most explicit.

I reasoned that preliterate classrooms would give me access to a more consistent 'negotiation towards mutual realities' and furthermore that the referents — toys, games, art work, puzzles — would be visible and probably large and well-differentiated in shape and colour. Instead of inferring relationships among cognition, learning and utterance, I thought I might be able to collect, directly, complete segments in which the relationships between the resource and task and, in Cicourel's terms,[1] those between the topic and the resource would be manifest rather than occluded by literate pursuits. For these reasons I decided to study the relationships of resource to task and the 'negotiation of mutual realities' in nursery classrooms. Here I envisaged that the relationships among objects, place, thought, learning and utterance would be sufficiently manifest to gain rich audio-visual and fieldnote records.

I sought recent detailed descriptions of nurseries to orientate my enquiries; to help me to form an agenda of putative issues that might be worth giving priority for initial observation and recording. At that time the most recent British study was that of Parry and Archer (1974). This did not provide the rich descriptions that I sought. Indeed, this research took for granted precepts, rhetoric and values which the authors exemplified as 'good' or 'bad' practice. Little context was provided, analysis was superficial, and the methodology of investigation inadequate. I was similarly disappointed in the few other descriptive studies of nurseries and began to seek earlier work, guided initially by Whitbread (1972). This lead me to the work of Susan Isaacs (1933). The observations and practice of Isaacs and her colleagues remain remarkable as detailed and sustained studies of children. However, what Isaacs selects as worthy of reporting tends to be those instances that pertain to social and emotional development of children, particularly those that may be cited as manifestations of the work of the psyche according to Freud. I was seeking less theory-laden observations — those of an ethnographic type. Knowing that such descriptions had been part of the work of the Chicago sociologists in the 1920s and 1930s, I was pleased to locate a reference to Koshuk's study of a kindergarten, through reading Faris' (1970) book on the history of Chicago sociology.

In 1974 I read the microfiche of Koshuk's 1931 PhD dissertation, referred to in Faris. I was impressed by the ingenuity of the methodology and the instrumentation and was encouraged by the similarity of Koshuk's lines of enquiry to my researches in the nursery. Subsequently, I looked to American studies of the kindergarten as a source of ethnographic description.

My report to the SSRC (1976) attempted, within severe constraints of time, to provide ethnographic descriptions from which analytic categories were derived. The extraction of analytic categories was my attempt to represent at a more general level the social structure and the process of acculturation of the children into the institution of the nursery. Methodologically I drew on the 'constant comparative method' (Glaser, 1969) in drawing on participant observation in my derivation of these categories. As rules were explicitly stated by teacher and children, especially during the early phases in the process of acculturation, I used these explicit statements along with the 'invisible' rules derived from my constant comparative analysis of the ethnographic data. By those means I was able to suggest sets of rules upon which children's legitimate behaviour in the nurseries was intended to be based. These rules differed somewhat in type and number in the three classrooms; some rules were common to all three.

Two questions became prominent in my thoughts. To what extent were those rules common to nursery classrooms in general, and to what extent were they idiosyncratic to each of the three teachers I had studied? How did the objects of these nurseries come to be formed historically and, as a corollary, why were these objects so ubiquitous in the USA and Great Britain? To begin to answer these two questions, I turned to historical accounts of the kindergarten. I began to read the works about Froebel, his being a name that I knew was important in the history of early childhood education. These tended to provide descriptions of Froebel's recommendations for pedagogic method and his ideas about curriculum material.

David Hamilton at the University of Glasgow and I had begun work independently on the education of young children. Hamilton used a case study approach to study a reception class teacher in a newly opened Scottish primary school. In conversation during a conference in Autumn 1974, we found we had both become interested in what we had come to see as the material culture of the classrooms we were studying. This reflected our mutual interest in cultural anthropology. We had both seen as significant the distribution of milk in the classrooms we were studying. We had noticed that the distribution of milk was an activity dependent for its continuity on the existence of the material culture.

We jointly developed our ideas about the relationship between material and the symbolic culture and the economy of the classroom in a paper entitled 'The milk ceremony', the ethnographic descriptions of which were taken from my study. David Hamilton at this time (Autumn 1974) was already engaged in historical enquiry and in subsequent exchanges of letters he recommended G. Compayré's (1877) book, *The History of Pedagogy*, as containing a more detailed historical account of the work of Froebel than I had come across thus far.

Compayré's work provided me with the first instances of disputes about the ideas and practice of Froebel; of misunderstandings as well as successes. The accounts I had read up to that time were descriptions of his ideals and precepts embedded in a chronological history. Reading the chapter on Pestalozzi in Compayré made me realize that Pestalozzi's work was a source, if not *the* source, of progressive teachers' practices and ideals as I had come to understand them. On reflection I can see that I was dividing pedagogy into two broad categories, that of the nursery/kindergarten along with the few progressive primary and even fewer secondary schools and, by contrast, that of the elementary school which I saw as employing an instructional, even rote, pedagogy.

My 'simple' questions, arising from consideration of my ethnographic data had, so it emerged, complex historical roots. I began to seek descriptions of the early kindergartens. I wanted to ascertain the extent of continuity or change in the kindergarten objects and in pedagogic practices, particularly those relating to the resource-task negotiation. Initially I came across brief descriptions, those cited in Compayré (1877), Gutek (1978) and Owen (1971). From these I could not distinguish the rhetoric and precepts, which were well documented, from descriptions of practices. Ideally, I wanted to compare and contrast recent ethnographic descriptions with similarly detailed descriptions of the early kindergartens.

Such sources are hard to find, occurring in letters or as recollections, often about what someone else said about what they had seen. In his autobiography Robert Owen says this about his visit to Pestalozzi's school in 1817:

> Our next visit was to Yverdun, to see the advance made by Pestalozzi
> — another good and benevolent man, acting for the benefit of his poor
> children to the extent of his knowledge and means. He was doing, he
> said, all he could to cultivate the heart, the head, and the hands of his
> pupils. His theory was good, but his means and experience were very
> limited, and his principles were those of the old system. His language
> was a confused 'patois', which Prof. Pictet could but imperfectly
> understand. His goodness of heart and benevolence of intention were
> evident in what he had done under the disadvantages which he had to
> encounter. His school, however, was one step in advance of ordinary

schools, or the old routine schools for the poor in common society, and we were pleased with it as being this one step in advance, for the rudiments of common school education for the poor, without attention to their dispositions and habits, and without teaching them useful occupation, by which to earn a living, are of little real utility. We left him, being much pleased with the honest homely simplicity of the old man. His one step beyond the usual routine had attracted and was attracting the attention of many who had previously known only the common routine. (Owen, 1971, p. 177)

I have pieced together from various contemporary sources an image of Pestalozzi's practices. Briefly, Pestalozzi believed in the worth of mental arithmetic and the rhythmic repetition of rules of number. He developed ways of questioning individual children within the class about their apperception of objects. Above all, he respected each child as a developing individual, or at least he did in precept. The children sat at desks facing the teacher and worked from 6 to 8 a.m. and from 4 to 6 p.m. The last hour of the day the children could work for themselves — they could choose a task. Pestalozzi did not use the term 'play'. He considered that these destitute orphans would have no opportunity to indulge in the leisure of the better off. There are no records of dolls or any toys in Pestalozzi's classrooms. The study of natural objects and phenomena and the induction of qualities of objects as apperceived by children using their own words were the activities he fostered through his pedagogy. Pestalozzi considered that sophisticated adult terminology should always be the final stage in any exploration of an object or phenomenon, rather than the reverse, which was conventional at the time. Pestalozzi stated that boys and girls should receive equal attention from their teacher but according to his teacher/tutee, Neff, Pestalozzi only addressed the boys in his lessons (Gutek, 1978).

The destitute children in Pestalozzi's classes had become orphaned as a consequence of the Napoleonic wars which ravaged Europe, including Switzerland, between 1790 and 1812. Prussia's confidence as a military state had been deeply shaken by its defeat at the battle of Jena in 1806 and by subsequent capitulation to the arrangements of the Treaty of Tilsit (1807). Fichte, the ethical idealist philosopher, was a member of the faculty of the University of Jena during that time. He appealed for Prussian/German unification and 'moral rearmament'. In his *Addresses to the German People* (1808) he tried to awaken unification. One of his recommendations was that Pestalozzi's educational methods should be institutionalized nationally as part of the programme of 'moral rearmament'. He considered that Pestalozzi's method would restore a moral health to the German leadership families, particularly to the parent/child relationship, which Fichte considered to be one which spoiled the child by giving in too readily to the child's will. This in turn had led to self-indulgence and a lack of self-regulation in adulthood and as a consequence had contributed to the inadequate resistance of the Prussian army to the Napoleonic forces.

Fichte sent his student, Frederick Froebel, to Pestalozzi's school at Yverdun. Froebel remained at the school observing the methods of Pestalozzi between 1808 and 1810. In a letter to the Princess Regent of Schwarzburg-Rudolstadt, Froebel expressed his admiration for Pestalozzi's humanitarian efforts, but considered that he was misplacing his energies in trying to educate the children of the poor. Like Fichte, Froebel was concerned to re-educate the children of the ruling classes. Pestalozzi was criticized by Fichte and Froebel for his lack of stated 'educational theory'. For Froebel, theory meant a preordained system of purpose and values upon which the educational practice was to be designed and practised. As a German ethical idealist philosopher, Fichte believed in a superior, all encompassing unity which the individual was to be educated to appreciate. For Froebel, this unifying force was the deity. Pestalozzi placed his faith in man's capacity for brotherly love, creative acts, responsibility for self, leading to respect for others, yet was accused of being atheistic. In these humanistic ways Pestalozzi resembled Kant, although he had never formally studied Kant. (Pestalozzi had read widely and was aware of the contemporary and philosophical views including those of the German idealists. He wrote critically about these views and also objected to Rousseau's ideas about individualism expressed in *Emile* for their lack of recognition of the individual's mutual responsibilities to a community.)

Theory worked out before practice was widely acceptable amongst philosophers and educationalists at this time. Froebel's major contribution, following a suggestion by Fichte, was to devise a material curriculum that corresponded to the theory of the unity of the 'inner and the outer'. To this Froebel added a refinement of the notional phases of development of the child which Pestalozzi had noted. Froebel devised the Gifts and the accompanying occupations.[2] These were manifestations of the sense of order, of resolution between the inner and the outer, with a penchant for three-dimensional form that reflects Froebel's university studies in crystallography.

The child in Froebel's kindergarten was to be under the guidance of the teacher; the teacher under the prescription of Froebel's *Pedagogics of the Kindergarten* (Froebel, 1907). The child's contemplations of the contrasts and similarities within a Gift and across Gifts with the complementary occupations would, in Froebel's scheme, lead to the gradual realization by the child of the unity of the inner and the outer. Froebel believed that this structured scheme and specific teacher instructions for use with the Gifts and occupations, would release in the child's mind insights into the intellectual relationships between and across Gifts and these insights would be extended into moral precepts. This model of learning based on innate ideas contrasts with that of Pestalozzi. For Pestalozzi all children have an innate propensity for reflection on the world of objects and phenomena, animate and inanimate. To Pestalozzi it mattered little what the object of contemplation was. Far more important was the ability of the teacher to draw out of a child and reflect back to the child the child's apperceptions of the object or phenomenon. Pestalozzi's pedagogic approach was in this respect similar to the dialectic between the noumena and phenomena of Kant. Pestalozzi's cognitive approach to learning is the precursor of the work of Vygotsky and Bruner.

Froebel's curriculum was metaphysical in its long-term aims, yet was more acceptable, probably because it was a material manifestation of an instructional system. Teachers could be trained in the system and their work could be visibly evaluated. Pestalozzi's curriculum centred on children's developing minds, did not prespecify outcomes in the sense of uniform, standardized results and relied on the ability and insight of the teacher to sustain understanding and a holistic view of the long-term development of the child.

Pestalozzi had thirty or so apprenticed teachers during his lifetime. Although he envisaged the establishment of a teacher training school on a larger scale, he never had the resources to realize this. However, his educational ideas and pedagogic approach were taken to the USA (1806) and schools were established in his name, particularly in German speaking areas such as the St Louis region. In Europe, for all Fichte's recommendations and the interest of the enlightened thinkers in France, Pestalozzi's influence and practice were not extensive. However, the Home and Colonial Society was founded in 1836 partly to promote Pestalozzi's practices in Great Britain. The Rev. Charles Mayo, one of the founders, had taught at Yverdun in the early 1820s (McCann and Young 1982). Mayo adapted and systematized the idea of Pestalozzi's innovation of the object lesson into a set of structured exercises which ignored the essential quality of the child's apperception of the object.

Compayré suggests that Pestalozzi's democratic educational ideals were not attractive to a Europe that was dominated by military states. Compayré recounts the story of Pestalozzi's visit to Paris during which he was, as a representative of Switzerland, to meet Napoleon. On being informed of Pestalozzi's imminent visit, Napoleon is reported to have said, 'I have more important things to do than talk about the ABC.'

Froebel's ideas were systematic and materially realized and as such were what we would now recognize as a behavioural basis for a training programme for teachers. Froebel's considerable ability at organization and his financial backing by members of the aristocracy led to rapid establishment of teacher training in his system. The graduates of the colleges were appointed to Froebel's schools that were being established, particularly in Hanover and Saxony. This rapid and successful adoption of the Frobelian curriculum was halted between 1848 and 1878. Julius Froebel, a nephew of Frederick Froebel, was a leading member of the 1848 Prussian revolution (Hamerow, 1969). After the suppression of the revolution, the state closed all schools bearing the name of Froebel. (Frederick Froebel had not been involved in revolutionary activity.) Frederick Froebel's acolytes, who were mainly minor aristocrats and intellectuals, fled Prussia. Some were invited to England, particularly to London and Manchester. Initially, German-speaking communities in these areas adopted some of them as governesses and teachers. The first Froebelian kindergarten was established by the Ronges in London in 1851, initially for German-speaking children. Amongst the influx was Countess von Boulow who, through lecture tours, was influential in spreading Froebel's ideas; von Boulow raised funds from wealthy liberal families to found Froebelian kindergartens.

Froebel's ideas and practice spread far more extensively and rapidly than Pestalozzi's. By the 1890s in the USA numerous kindergartens based on Froebel's principles had been established. Substantial financial and moral support of the anthro-theosophists, notably Elizabeth Peabody, Sarah Quincey-Adams and Mrs Nathaniel Hawthorn in the Boston area, assisted in the spread of the kindergarten. The child study movement initiated by another anthro-theosophist, Stanley Hall, with non-anthro-theosophist associates, Edward Thorndike and John Dewey, engaged in observational and questionnaire research whose findings were critical of the practice, yet supportive of the principles of the kindergarten. Froebel's systematics were now being inculcated in trainee teachers without attending to the details of educational principles and purpose (Weber, 1969). The technical use of the Gifts and the occupations became emphasized to the detriment of attention to the child's apperceptions. The Froebelian curriculum had become technicist and object-rather than person-orientated. At the meetings of the International Kindergarten Union of 1895, 1900 and 1905, this neo-Froebelian orthodoxy was criticized.

During these meetings, evidence of children's lack of interest in this teacher-dominated neo-Froebelian curriculum was presented. The children did not exercise their large muscles sufficiently. They developed hunched postures and poor eyesight trying, for instance, to thread needles and perform intricate patterns of some of the Froebelian occupations.

Much of the evidence for this and the lack of adequate illumination and ventilation in the kindergartens was provided by the enquiries initiated by the Child Study movement founded by G.S. Hall, John Dewey and Edward Thorndike. At the National Kindergarten Union meeting of 1895, Stanley Hall's censure of the orthodoxy was responded to — thirty-three of the thirty-five delegates walked out in protest (Lazerson, 1971). The reformers, notably Anna Bryan, Patty Hill and other members of the Child Study movement, wanted not only improved illumination and ventilation but also the introduction of toys and apparatus used in the home and children's games. In his curriculum plan, Froebel had divided off play in the home and play in the street from his idea of the plays of the kindergarten. Play in the kindergarten had its own teleology, leading the child to insights about the unity of man, nature and God, although Froebel did not reject play with dolls and other toys (indeed, he mentions children's play with dolls as an extension of play with the second Gift). The neo-Froebelian had followed the 'letter' rather than trying to understand the principles and philosophy which the *Pedagogics of the Kindergarten* represented.

The reformers, whilst respecting and acknowledging children's individuality and creativity, were not sanctimonious. They advocated interest and pleasure as criteria for judging the worth of play and play objects. The reformers also wanted more of the kindergarten day devoted to children being able to follow their own inclinations to choose their tasks without direct teacher supervision or intervention. This selection of activities by children was called 'free play' and had been introduced into a kindergarten in Santa Barbara in 1896 (Weber, 1969). Child study observations of children engaged in free play indicated that children could not only sustain their interest but were able to cooperate (rather than fight) in the course of their play.

Learning through work represented by the ethics of the elementary school encroached upon the kindergarten and learning through play in the USA and Great Britain. In the national infant schools under the revised code (1862) the kindergarten was designated a functional subject drawing on adaptations of Froebelian occupations, weaving, threading, sewing and in the 1880s particularly on wood carving technique known as 'sloyd'.

In the Boston region, in exchange for state support, the kindergartens had to teach the rudiments of literacy and numeracy. Here we have to note that the kindergarten in the USA was, by about 1910, mainly for children aged 5 to 6, whereas the kindergarten or nursery in Great Britain was for children of 3 to 5 years. In the nursery in the USA it became usual for children of 4 to 5 years to be encumbents and in these USA nurseries the demands of the elementary school were not felt, although in the context of compensatory education there has been an increasing emphasis on cognitive development.

By 1910 the neo-Froebelians and their curriculum had given way, but not without resistance. Sometimes this took the form of compromise, for example, when the Froebelian Gifts were enlarged in order to provide weight and dimensions sufficient for the exercise of the large muscles! By 1920 the material curriculum of the kindergarten was similar to today. The children no longer sat at set tables dominated by the teacher's guidance in their contemplation of the Gifts and specified occupations. Dolls, rocking horses, the play house and the sand tray had appeared. The large blocks and other child study equipment replaced Froebel's Gifts. (Water play was an innovation introduced by Margaret McMillan — see Bradburn, 1976). The array of artifacts became similar to that of any well-equipped middle-class home of the time. The emphasis on moral development of the child engendered through the mystical qualities apperceived from the Gifts was successively supplanted by emphasis on child mental health, child development and cognitive development.

Pestalozzi, Wilderspin and Froebel in related but different terminologies espoused learning through play, particularly for children under the age of 6. But unlike Robert Owen who integrated play by making it continuous with schooling and schooling with an industrial economy that sustained the community, Pestalozzi, Wilderspin and Froebel depended for the continuation of their schools on the monies from benefactors and pupil fees. If the benefactor or the parents withdrew support from the school, as in the case of Pestalozzi and Wilderspin, then the schools foundered. Whilst Robert Owen could enforce his belief that reading should not be taught to children under the age of 7 without losing financial support, the apparent deviation from the teaching of reading by Samuel Wilderspin led to the withdrawal of two-thirds of the children.

The presence of apparatus such as the sand tray and the play house does not necessarily indicate that children will engage in play. Indeed, tasks defined by adults using these apparatus are regarded by children as work. For children this work involves trying to give the right answer or perform a skill appropriately, efficiently and effectively; whereas learning through play engages the child's actuality, learning through work requires the child to find a solution that fits with the reality and the adult that has set the task. Learning through play requires the nurturing or the presence of an adult or teacher who has developed or redeveloped their sense of actuality. Learning through play, the children become the agents of their own intellectual and moral development, their individuality being formed in collaboration with others, often mediated by artifacts. Learning through work leads to techniques of adult definitions of proper social conduct, 'right solutions' and progress and achievement. The manifestations and products of learning through work are more visible (Bernstein, 1975) than the cognitive, connative and self-development of learning through play.

Learning through work is premised on children's minds being like *tabula rasa*, the adult being the fount of knowledge, of definition and convention. Learning through play is premised on children's minds having an inherent capability to structure sense impressions and a preferment for morally good acts rather than bad.

My research into the history of kindergarten curricula, drawing on ethnographic studies of kindergartens and nursery classes, reveals the continuity of tension between pedagogies that demand that children conform to pre-specified norms of 'proper behaviour' learning what is deemed as useful knowledge, in contrast to pedagogies that endeavour to foster individuality within a developing sense of responsibilities to community. This tension reflects two quite contrary ideologies concerning the moral being and mind of the child and, with these, a different range of teacher intervention and criteria for judging the value of schooling.

Notes

1. The relationship between topic and resource, although usually credited to Cicourel, is given a full exposition in a relatively early paper: ZIMMERMAN, D.H. and POLLNER, M. (1971) 'The everyday world as a phenomenon', in DOUGLAS, J.D. (Ed.) *Understanding Everyday Life*, London, Routledge and Kegan Paul.
2. The Gifts were as follows:
   Solids:
   First Gift: six coloured worsted balls about one inch and a half in diameter.
   Second Gift: wooden ball, cylinder, cube, one inch and a half in diameter.
   Third Gift: eight one-inch cubes — forming a two-inch cube.
   Fourth Gift: eight brick shaped blocks $2 \times 1 \times \frac{1}{2}$.

Fifth Gift: twenty-seven one-inch cubes, three bisected, three quadrisected diagonally forming a three-inch cube.

Sixth Gift: twenty-seven brick-shaped blocks, three bisected longitudinally, six bisected transversely.

Surfaces:

Seventh Gift: squares — entire and bisected; equilateral triangles — entire, half, thirds.

Lines:

Eighth Gift: straight — splints of various lengths; circular — metal or paper rings.

Points:

Ninth Gift: beans, lentils, seeds, pebbles.

Reconstruction:

Tenth Gift: softened peas or wax pellets and sharpened sticks or straw. To reconstruct the surface and solid synthetically from the point.

References

ADELMAN, C. (1976) *The Use of Objects in the Education of Children of 3–5 Years*, Final Report HR/3234/1 and HR/3661/1 to Social Science Research Council.

ADELMAN, C. and WALKER, R. (1972) *A Grounded Theory of Classrooms*, mimeo, Centre for Applied Research in Education, University of East Anglia.

BERNSTEIN, B. (1975) 'Class and pedagogies: Visible and invisible', in *Class, Codes and Control*, Vol. 3, London, Routledge and Kegan Paul.

BRADBURN, E. (1976) *Margaret McMillan: Framework and Expansion of Nursery Education*, Redhill, Surrey, Denholm House Press.

COMPAYRÉ, G. (1877) *The History of Pedagogy*, London, Swan Sonnestein.

FARIS, R. (1970) *Chicago Sociology 1920–1932*, Chicago University Press.

FROEBEL, C. (1809) 'On H. Pestalozzi: Letter to Princess Regent of Schwartzburg-Rudolstadt, Yverdun', in LANGE, W. *Friedrich Frobel's gesammelte padagogische Schriften*, Vol. I, Berlin, Enslin.

FROEBEL, F. (1907) *Pedagogics of the Kindergarten*, trans by JARVIS, J., London, Sidney Appleton.

GLASER, B. (1969) 'The constant comparative method of qualitative analysis', in McCALL, G. and SIMMONS, J. (Eds) *Issues in Participant Observation*, Reading, Mass., Addison-Wesley.

GUTEK, G.L. (1978) *Joseph Neff: The Americanization of Pestalozzianism*, University of Alabama Press.

HAMEROW, T.S. (1969) *The social Foundations of German Unification 1858–1871: Ideas and Institutions*, Princetown University Press.

HAMILTON, D. (1977) *In Search of Structure*, London, Hodder and Stoughton.

ISAACS, S. (1933) *Social Development in Young Children*, London, Routledge and Kegan Paul.

KOSHUK, R. (1931) *A Comparative Study of Child Contacts with Play Materials in Four Pre-School Settings*, PhD dissertation, University of Chicago, Department of Sociology.

LAZERSON, M. (1971) *Origins of the Urban School*, Cambridge, Mass., Harvard University Press.

McCANN, P. and YOUNG, F. (1982) Samuel Wilderspin and the Infant School Movement, Beckenham, Croom Helm.

OWEN, R. (1971) *The Life of Robert Owen by Himself 1771–1859*, Introduced by John Butt, Charles Knight and Co.

Parry, M. and Archer, H. (1974) *Pre-School Education*, Schools Council Project on Pre-school Education 1969–1971, London, Macmillan.

Weber, E. (1969) *The Kindergarten: Its Encounter with Educational Thought in America*, New York, Teachers College Press, Columbia University.

Whitbread, N. (1972) *The Evolution of the Nursery/Infant Schools: A History of Infant and Nursery Education in Britain, 1800–1970.* London, Routledge and Kegan Paul.

The Experience of Schooling for Working-Class Boys and Girls in Nineteenth-Century England

June Purvis

It is fitting in a collection of papers concerned with histories and ethnographies of school subjects that we give some consideration to the nineteenth-century classroom. After all, some of our present-day ideas about, and practices within, education reflect the past. Yet curiously enough, most books within the sociology of education, especially those on ethnography, are ahistorical. Ethnographers, as Hammersley (1982) notes, largely regard history as 'someone else's territory'.

If we look to historians for accounts of the nineteenth century classroom, we find a neglect of the subject too. The history of education has been traditionally concerned with the documentation of educational provision and administration. In 1973, for example, Simon pointed out that there had been little attempt within the history of education to assess education from the point of view of those experiencing it (p. 123). Some four years later, Silver (1977) made a similar point, though this time specifically in relation to education in the nineteenth century:

> 'There are no published studies of possible varieties of educational experience in monitorial schools, workhouse schools, factory schools, dame schools — indeed *all* schools'. (p. 60)

Silver failed to consider, however, Horn's scholarly book, *The Victorian Country Child*, first published in 1974. In this, and in a subsequent book on education in nineteenth-century rural England, Horn includes some material offering vivid accounts of the experience of schooling for working-class children in rural areas. Her approach to the education of the working-class child was, however, the exception rather than the rule.

The early 1980s have witnessed the publication of some major historical studies that focus more specifically on the point of view of those who experience schooling. For example, Dyhouse (1981) offers a stimulating account, drawn from documentary sources, of the 'experiences' of growing up, and of school and family size, for girls in late Victorian and Edwardian England. Humphries (1981), using a rich array of oral information, details the experience of childhood and of youth for some working-class boys and girls over the period 1889–1939. As yet, however, there is no one account that attempts to document the variety of educational experiences that may have been the lot of working-class boys and girls in nineteenth-century England. This paper, despite the methodological issues involved,[1] is a first attempt to do that.

An immediate problem arises. Unless we have access to oral history, how can we find out about the experiences of schooling for working-class boys and girls in the nineteenth century classroom? I will consult a range of sources, but draw particularly upon personal accounts that might be found in a variety of texts, especially autobiographies.[2] I will attempt to relate these individual, subjective accounts to various aspects of the social structure and culture of Victorian society. The use of biographical material in historical research can be an invaluable tool for the sociologist. As C. Wright Mills (1959, 1967 ed.) said some years ago:

> The sociological imagination enables us to grasp history and biography and the relations between the two within society. . . .
>
> No social study that does not come back to the problems of biography, of history and of their intersections within a society has completed its intellectual journey. (p. 4)

Class and Gender in the Organization of Schooling

Nineteenth-century England was a clearly stratified class society as well as a patriarchal society.[3] Social class divisions were evident in the forms and content of educational provision. Thus elementary education, which usually involved the teaching of reading, writing and arithmetic, was associated with the working class and was clearly segregated from the forms of secondary schooling offered to middle-class boys and girls. The basic education for working-class children might be provided by the working classes themselves, by middle-class philanthropic organizations or individuals, or by state-aided voluntary bodies. But irrespective of who provided elementary schooling, it was seen as inferior in quality and status to that provided for middle-class children. Working-class boys and girls, as members of the working class, learnt through a range of experiences, including the experience of schooling, that they were of the 'lower' social orders.

The social construction of masculinity and femininity varied within the working class, and over time, but both working-class girls and boys learnt that an essential part of their gender would involve paid employment of some kind. Paid employment in childhood was likely to be particularly persistent for the poor and poorest strata of the working class who were engaged in a constant struggle to earn sufficient income to support the basic necessities of life. For such families, the extra income that a child's paid employment might bring, however small, was often vital for the family's existence. In addition, though some schools were free, others charged a fee of one penny to fourpence per week, and such fees were not abolished until 1891. Within the context of working-class childhood, therefore, schooling often had to compete with a child's economic potential or usefulness to family life in a range of free domestic servicing such as baby-minding, cooking, cleaning and going on errands. Nevertheless, for most working-class boys and girls, some form of schooling was likely to be a part of childhood, even if that amount of schooling was minimal. At Tysoe, in Warwickshire, for example, there were 'only one or two families' whose children did not go to school at all (Ashby, 1974, p. 20), and that was some twenty years or so before elementary schooling was made compulsory by the Education Acts of 1876 and 1880. But attendance could be irregular and intermittent — even towards the end of the century.

In addition to this handicap of their social class, working-class girls also learnt about the patriarchal nature of nineteenth century society. In particular, they learnt that masculinity was the dominant gender form, and this was evident in a wide range of social and cultural phenomena. Legally, for example, for much of the century a wife was regarded as the property of her husband. Inequalities between men and women in other spheres of life, such as paid employment, politics and education, gave men many advantages too. The general conclusion that Gavron (1966, p. 3) draws is that legally, politically, economically and socially, women of the nineteenth century were 'second-class' citizens. Though the patriarchal nature of nineteenth century society was never total or secure for all working-class girls and women at any one time, working-class girls within the home, within paid employment, within the community and within the school, learnt that they were inferior to boys and men and less important than their brothers who might one day be the main financial providers of families themselves.

Working-class parents were likely to give more priority to the schooling of their sons than their daughters. In particular, a working-class daughter would learn that domestic duties such as child-care, cleaning, washing clothes and cooking were a 'natural' part of femininity, and that she might be kept at home to help out in this way rather than sent regularly to school. In some cases, such domestic work might release a mother or neighbour for paid work and a daughter might be given a penny or two, but in most cases it would appear that domestic duties were just 'expected' from a daughter — to the detriment of her schooling. As late as 1897 a report from one London school stated:

> It seems to the mothers only natural that a girl should help to clean, or baby-mind; and if there is no need of her services at home, then she can 'oblige' a neighbour. In the latter case she may get 6d., instead of 1d. or 2d. from her mother; but even if only 2d. or 3d. were offered, she would do the work all the same. (cited in Hogg, 1897, p. 239)

Before 1870 a working-class boy or girl might attend a range of educational institutions such as Sunday schools, ragged schools, dame schools, charity schools, factory schools, schools of industry, and various day schools organised by the National Society for Promoting the Education of the Poor in the Principles of the Established Church (the Church of England) or the much smaller British and Foreign School Society (largely supported by religious dissenters). The working-class family itself might also have been another important educational resource, but as Johnson (1979, p. 75) comments, we lack an adequate study of this. After the 1870 Education Act, the variety of schools that working-class boys and girls might attend began to dwindle but provision by the two main religious bodies was still widespread. It was not until well into the twentieth century that a unified state system of education was built. As Lawson and Silver (1973, p. 314) noted, the 1870 Education Act did not introduce free or compulsory education, though it made both possible: it did not supersede the voluntary schools, but supplemented them and, though it created school boards, the most democratic organs of local administration of the century, it also left the boards' opponents in positions of strength.

The experience of schooling for working-class boys and girls within such a wide range of institutions would obviously be varied. In this paper, I shall concentrate upon the main forms of schooling that working-class children might attend — dame schools, Sunday schools, the day schools of the two influential religious bodies — the National Society and the British and Foreign Society — and the day schools of the school boards.

Dame Schools

Although the term 'dame school' has been applied to a range of infant schools that might be attended by children in all social classes, it usually refers to those small private schools that were common to working-class culture. Dame schools 'grew out of' the working-class community and were not institutions 'imposed' by those outside it. In times of financial hardship, a woman or a man might open a 'dame' or a 'gaffer' school in part of her or his own house. It would appear that there were more dame than gaffer schools.

Dames were untrained teachers, and the quality of their schools varied greatly. The vast majority appear to have been child-minders (Sutherland 1971, p. 12), but others might teach a child the alphabet and perhaps to read, do a few simple sums and knit or sew. Of course, the more children a woman took into her dame school, the more she could earn; and the daily or weekly fee varied considerably. Even in the 1830s, a dame school could charge 4d. a week. The fact that working-class parents would pay this amount illustrates, as McCann (1976, p. 29) has noted, the 'class consciousness' of the poor: they would rather pay high prices for their children to be taught to read in a school that they chose than send them to the free schools teaching the 3Rs, free schools that were maintained by middle-class philanthropy.

Attendance at a dame school was an expected part of childhood for large numbers of working-class boys and girls. Many began attending at the age of 3 or 4 as Charles Shaw, born in 1832, did. His father was a painter and gilder, and Charles had 'a poor little bit of education' at 'old Betty W's school' which was the only room on the ground floor of her little cottage. The room, about four yards square, was sparsely furnished. Two or three little forms, about eight inches high, were in the room, for the pupils to sit on. On the wall were a few pictures, 'blazing with colour'. Charles Shaw's (1903, 1977 repr.) experience of his dame school is best told in his own words:

> The course of education given by the old lady was very simple, and graded with almost scientific precision. There was an alphabet, with rude pictures, for beginners ... though she never taught writing, her scholars were generally noted for their ability to read while very young. I know I could read my Bible with remarkable ease when I left her school, when seven years old.
>
> Betty's next grade, after the alphabet, was the reading-made-easy book, with black letters, making words in two, three and four letters.
>
> The next stage was spelling, and reading of the Bible. For those successful in these higher stages old Betty had peculiar honours. They were allowed to take the ashes from under the fire-grate to the ash-heap outside the house. This ash-heap was a common meeting-place, as everybody used it, and on its elevation many doughty battles were fought....
>
> Another honour of old Betty's was to allow a successful scholar to sit on the highest visible stair in the winding staircase leading to her bedroom. It was a rare joy to see and be seen by your fellow scholars from this vantage-point of honour. There was yet another distinction the old lady had to bestow. She taught both boys and girls who were successful in reading how to knit stockings. She was a remarkable knitter herself, and could carry on this occupation with the regularity almost of a machine, while her eyes were everywhere in her school. I knew boys who knitted stockings for their families. They thus learnt reading and knitting, instead of reading and writing. (pp. 2–3)

We see in Shaw's account that at this dame school boys and girls appeared to follow a common curriculum that was based not on the sex and gender of the child but on the ability to master each task that was set. Old Betty, like many teachers, used various 'incentives' to motivate her pupils. For Charles Shaw, however, such a form of schooling within the private home of the teacher abruptly came to an end when, at 7 years old, he became a full-time waged worker as a mould runner in a pottery works. The work was hard and demanding, and left little time for his passion for reading — something that he bitterly resented.

Other examples may be found of dame schools which, like Old Betty's, offered a common curriculum to working-class boys and girls. For example, Mary Paley, born in 1850, the daughter of a country vicar, recollects that in their parish there was one dame school which was supposed to teach reading, writing, summing and knitting to both boys and girls. The dame who ran the school was a Mrs Sopps, who was 'a washerwoman by profession and also a monthly nurse' (Paley, 1947, p. 2). Mrs Sopps exercised stern discipline over her charges and kept a birch rod tied with blue ribbon. When a child told a lie, a tongue of red cloth was fastened to its chin. Though Mary Paley did not herself attend this dame school, she remembers quite clearly that the pupils there were taught to bow and curtsey 'to their betters'. Such forms of deference were probably more prevalent in rural areas where the dame school might be more subject to patronage and control by the church and local gentry than in the cosmopolitan urban areas.

It is difficult to establish to what extent a common curriculum was the norm in dame schools in the nineteenth century. However, some autobiographical accounts do record the existence of curricula differences for boys and girls. Thomas Cooper, for example, born in 1805, attended a dame school where both boys and girls were taught to read and to spell but knitting was taught only to girls. This dame school which Thomas (whose father was a dyer by trade) attended at the age of 5, was kept by:

> aged Gertrude Aram: 'Old Gatty', as she was usually called. Her school-room — that is to say, the larger lower-room of her two-storied cottage — was always full; and she was an expert and laborious teacher of the art of reading and spelling. Her knitting, too — for she taught girls as well as boys — was the wonder of the town. I soon became her favourite scholar, and could read the tenth chapter of Nehemiab, with all its hard names ... and could spell wondrously. (Cooper, 1872, 1971 repr., p. 7)

The dame school that Thomas Cooper attended was a mixed sex school. But some dame schools were for girls only. Mary Smith, whose father was a small tradesman, a boot and shoe maker, attended a series of dame schools, from the age of 4, but then, when 7 years old, was sent to another dame school, just for a few months, for the sole purpose of learning to knit and sew. This dame school was in Cropedy, Oxfordshire, where Mary was born in 1822, and the dame who ran the school was so diseased that she was unable to move from her chair or lift her hand to her mouth. Nevertheless, the dame kept control of her female pupils by means of a long white stick which could reach to any part of the cottage floor where the school was held. Mary recollects that the knowledge of the dame was: 'very small. The girls had a lesson once a day in the New Testament, and the little ones read out of the "Reading Made Easy". But knitting and sewing occupied nearly the whole time of the girls, who perhaps might average from nine to ten' (Smith, 1892, pp. 24–5). Sewing was a practical skill considered particularly suitable for the female sex. It could be utilized as unpaid domestic work within a girl's family and also be vocational preparation for low paid women's work as a sewing woman, a milliner or a dressmaker.

The experience of schooling in the more conventional dame schools might involve the quicker and brighter children who could read teaching those who could not. When Thomas Cooper attended his first dame school, at the age of 3, he could already read, and so he taught an older boy, Master Bodley, his letters. Similarly, John Wilson, born in 1833 at Greatham, near Hartlepool, whose father was a labourer at that time, recollects that before he was 6 years old, he was teaching older boys to read the New Testament in the gaffer school he attended (Wilson, 1910, 1980 repr., p. 52). Acting as a dame's or gaffer's helper did not necessarily mean that a child became a 'good' pupil. John Wilson, for example, who spent much of his childhood travelling around with his father, attended yet another gaffer school (when he was 11 years old) where the strictness of the old man irritated him considerably. One day the gaffer had some business in the town and, recollects Wilson (1980 repr.), the old man:

> locked the girls in a room to keep us separate. This was too much, and the boys resolved to have them out. We had just achieved our purpose when suddenly the master appeared on the scene, and without inquiry he marked me as the ring-leader (on the principle that if I had not been in mischief I would be), and gave me as much of the cane as his strength would allow. This was more than I could bear, and, seizing an ink-stand, I hurled it straight at his head. It did not miss the mark, but caught him in the face. As soon as he recovered he took my slate and books and put them, with me, outside; and so ended my school days. (p. 57)

Acts of defiance such as this illustrate only too well some of the problems that a dame or gaffer might encounter when trying to impose discipline, and autobiographers record many instances of discipline problems. At the first dame school that Mary Smith (1892, pp. 16–17) attended, for example, when she was just 4 years old, the stern old dame used to pin the small children to her knee as a form of punishment. John Wilson (1980 repr., p. 49) remembers that at one dame school the old dame used 'to fasten me to her apron with a darning needle' attached to the pinafore he wore, simply to 'keep me under her eye'. Other dames adopted different methods that induced greater fear in their pupils. Frederick Hobley, born in 1833 in Thame, Oxfordshire, was sent to one dame school kept by Ma'am Lund who used to supplement her living by selling bull's eyes and brandy-balls, sweets that were commonly bought by children at that time. When a boy was naughty, however, he was shut in her 'dark pantry' as a form of punishment. Frederick Hobley (1905) retained little affection for this dame school: 'Occasionally at this time, I was taken out for a walk on a Sunday, and if we went near this school, I remember, I used to run by as fast as possible lest I should be taken into it' (p. 178)

For many working-class boys and girls, then, attendance at a dame or gaffer school would have been a part of childhood. For some children, a dame may have been a substitute parent, offering the care, warmth and affection that is possible in a child-minder, while for other children a dame may have been a stern person who attempted to discipline and channel their behaviour. Some children learnt to read, do sums, knit and write while others learnt little.

The popularity of dame schools with working-class parents, in comparison with the cheaper and more efficient day schools offered by the National and British Societies, was pronounced up to the 1850s. The latter schools were attracting increasing amounts of state grant and were seen by the working class as essentially 'public' education that was controlled by others and carried the stigma of 'charity' (Laqueur, 1976a, p. 201).

By the 1870s, however, the state aided day schools of the religious bodies had gained a hold on educational provision for the working class. Dame schools now attracted only a minority of working-class children, though some of these institutions did survive into the twentieth century. For the first half of the century in particular, the dame school had been an important form of schooling for working-class children. This form of schooling was often combined with attendance at a Sunday school — about which I will say something now.

Sunday Schools

Robert Raikes, who in the 1780s established some Sunday schools for poor children in Gloucester, is generally regarded as the founder of the Sunday school movement. Though the motives of those who established Sunday schools varied considerably, the Sunday school movement in its early years is generally seen as an attempt to rescue and save the souls of children in the poorest strata of society.

In a study of Sunday schools from 1780 to 1850, Laqueur (1976b) makes the controversial suggestion that by the early nineteenth century Sunday schools were not an imposition by the middle class upon the working class, but a part of the working-class community. Many of those people active in the founding of Sunday schools were, he claims, from the working class, and after 1810 some 60 per cent of all Sunday school teachers had once been students themselves (p. 189). Elsewhere, Laqueur (1976a, p. 201) suggests that the Sunday schools were 'strange halfway houses' between the dame schools which were fully integrated into the working-class community and the externally imposed public school of the National and British societies.

Particularly in the first half of the nineteenth century, Sunday schools were an important form of part-time education for working-class children, offering both religious instruction and some secular education. In a Sunday school a boy or girl might learn to read and, if lucky, to write. The teaching of writing was, however, controversial and often limited to a weekday rather than a Sunday class. At other Sunday schools writing was considered a privilege.

By 1850, 2 million working-class children were enrolled as Sunday school scholars. During the second half of the nineteenth century the curriculum of the Sunday schools changed: secular instruction began to disappear while religious instruction became more systematic (Laqueur, 1976b, p. 250). The decline in the teaching of reading and writing was directly linked to the decline in the number of children employed in full-time waged labour, the increase in the number of children in day schools and the advent of legislation in the 1870s and 1880s to enforce compulsory school attendance.

So how did working-class boys and girls experience the schooling and other activities that were offered in the nineteenth-century Sunday school? Some Sunday schools taught boys and girls separately, in single sex groups, while others organized mixed sex groups. Obviously much would depend on the size of the Sunday schools and the availability of teachers. But even if boys and girls were educated together, this does not mean that they would experience what was taught in the same manner. In particular, curricular content undoubtedly contained messages, explicit or implicit, about the appropriate place of boys and girls, men and women in society. The Bible, biblical texts and other religious material were frequently used as teaching aids. Mary Anne Hearne, for example, born in 1834 in Eynsford, Kent, vividly recollects in her autobiography that reading material published by the Sunday School Union omitted any reference to poor girls who had risen to be rich and great:

> My father gave us two monthly magazines published by the Sunday School Union, the 'Teacher's Offering', and the 'Child's Companion'. In one of these was a series of descriptive articles on men who had been poor boys, and risen to be rich and great. Every month I hoped to find the story of some poor ignorant *girl*, who, beginning life as handicapped as I, had yet been able to live a life of usefulness, if not of greatness. But I believe there was not a woman in the whole series. (Farningham, 1907, p. 44)

The content of Sunday school literature could contain, therefore, a sexist bias, a hidden gender message that while poor boys might have ambition and rise in the world, this was not so for poor girls. To what extent poor girls were socialized into, and accepted, such a subtle form of social control, we do not know. But Mary Anne Hearne was at least one poor girl who questioned the content of religious literature and the implied hierarchy of men over women.

Mary's father was a small tradesman and also a village postmaster, so we may see her as belonging to the artisan stratum of the working class. When her mother died, it was expected that Mary, as the eldest girl in the family, would leave the Eynsford British school and look after the four younger children:

> Of course I had to leave school and do the 'housekeeping' and the work of the house, and I am sure that it was done very badly. But I was only twelve years and a few months old, and the others were younger.... I was very bitter and naughty at that time. I did not pray, and was not anxious to be good. (*ibid* p. 44)

Here we can see quite clearly the way that a working-class daughter, especially an eldest daughter, was expected to serve the needs of her father and of her younger brothers and sisters. Patriarchy was not an abstract notion — it could extend into the daily life and lived experience of a working-class girl. Mary claims that it was the love of her Sunday school teacher that saved her at this difficult time in her life. Later, in 1853, when she was 17 years old, Mary became a Sunday school teacher and it was not until the late 1890s that she gave up such teaching. One of her old pupils remembers the help that Mary gave to the girls in her Bible class: 'If we were in any difficulty or trouble, and needed advice or comfort, our teacher was at home on Saturday afternoons always, and if our difficulties and troubles were not all removed, the love which was given us without stint made us strong to meet them' (quoted in *ibid.*, p. 128).

Mary Anne Hearne earned her own independent living, first as a teacher and then as a writer. In 1884 she became the editor of *The Sunday School Times*. Throughout her life the influence of her religion and of the Sunday school remained strong. She was a working-class girl for whom the Sunday school was a means of support and comfort, as well as a means of social mobility.

Other working-class girls and boys, especially those who were very poor, may have attended no other school than the part-time Sunday school. George Edwards, for example, born in a Norfolk village in 1850, experienced a childhood of extreme poverty. When he was born his father was a bullock feeder, earning just 7s. for a seven-day working-week. It was necessary for all seven children to contribute in some way to the family income, and in 1856, when he was 6 years old, George secured his first job — scaring crows. He was paid 1s. for a seven-day week. He recollects that Sunday school was the 'only schooling' he ever had: any literacy skills he might have learnt were lost during his teens since he claims that at the age of 22 'I could not read, I merely knew my letters' (Edwards, 1922, pp. 21 and 32). However, when his name was included as an 'Exhorter' on the preachers' plan for Aylsham Primitive Methodist Circuit, this provided a strong incentive to become literate. Despite the economic hardships of his social class position, and despite the fact that George Edwards did not become literate until his early 20s, he was eventually elected to parliament in 1920 as a Labour MP. Throughout his life, the Sunday school and the Primitive Methodist religion remained powerful influences.

Countless other working-class children, who have left no record of their lives, were undoubtedly less fortunate than Mary Anne Hearne or George Edwards. Nevertheless, the Sunday school may have been appreciated by such children — especially those whose childhood was experienced before the expansion of elementary schooling that was possible after the 1870 Education Act. Working-class children in the first half of the nineteenth century were likely to be engaged in paid employment at an early age, and the Sunday schools could offer not only emotional support and comfort but also the chance to acquire literacy skills. Such a form of schooling could involve not only formal instruction but also the reading of books that were borrowed from the Sunday school library. Charles Shaw of Tunstall, whose experiences of the dame school we have already considered, was one such child who benefited in this way when he was employed as mould runner in a pottery works:

the Sunday school was the most powerful factor in giving any education to poor children.... We had a few books in our small Sunday school library which attracted my attention. I read 'Robinson Crusoe' and a few other favourite boys' books, but there were not many there. After these the most readable book I could find was Rollin's 'Ancient History'.... I regarded it as remote from Tunstall and England as those other worlds I read of in Dick's 'Christian Philosopher' which book I found in the library too....

Then I read Milton's 'Paradise Lost', Klopstock's 'Messiah', and, later on, Pollock's 'Course of Time', and Gilfillan's 'Bards of the Bible'. (Shaw, 1977 repr., pp. 218–19)

Charles Shaw, through his strong association with the Sunday school and chapel, became a local preacher — as did George Edwards and John Wilson. Similarly, Ellen Wilkinson (1938, pp. 400–1), born in 1891, recollects that her father, who had been a half-time worker in a cotton mill when he was 8 years old, had all his formal education at the local Sunday school where he learnt to read and write: he was lent books, his 'only contact' with education, and at the age of 15 he became a local preacher. For Ellen herself the Wesleyan Sunday school offered a training in public speaking that was to aid her entry into politics. She made speeches, dressed as a Chinese or Indian girl, at various missionary meetings, and recited poetry at the Band of Hope, a temperance organization (*ibid.*, p. 411).

Sunday school could play an important part in the life of a working-class child. But just because some working-class people remembered their Sunday schooling with affection does not mean that all did so. In particular, the experience of Sunday school may not have been a happy one for those boys and girls who found reading, and any writing that was taught, difficult. Others may have been bored since the curricular content was similar to the religious instruction taught in the day schools of the two main religious societies; in addition, the teachers were amateurs with only their 'personal sincerity and integrity' to recommend them (Horn, 1974, p. 141). For some children, such as William Edwards, born in 1870 to working-class parents in the Lotting Fen area of Huntingdonshire, the Sunday school was a place of fear:

I used to be frit to death at the old men who run the chapel when I were a child . . . the leaders in chapel were associated in my mind with the tales they used to tell us littl'uns at Sunday school about hell-fire and the bottomless pit, and the Angel of Death coming to fetch good children to heaven and the Devil coming to fetch bad children to hell, and so on. I used to sweat all over wondering which one on 'em 'ould come to fetch me, for I used to come out o' Sunday school convinced I coul'n't live till the next Sunday. (Marshall ed., 1980, p. 94)

Even if some children were, like William Edwards, frightened by the tales of heaven and hell that might be taught, some compensation might be found in the various recreations that the Sunday school might offer. Joseph Ashby, born in rural Tysoe in 1859, left the day school just before his eleventh birthday to work on the land. The Sunday school 'treats', when the Vicar was 'at his best', were something to look forward to. Such treats could involve tea at the vicarage where there would be cake instead of the bread and lard common to working-class diets. Games on the hill behind the vicarage might end the day for the children (Ashby, 1974, pp. 43–4). John Purser (1966), born in 1878 in the village of Ilmington in the county of Warwick, recollects that when the day arrived for the annual summertime treat at the rectory, some of the boys 'would have no dinner, so that they could have a good "tuck in". It was good fare, such as they were not used to: fresh bread and butter, tea brought round in big jugs to fill their tin mugs, and two sorts of cake. The Rector, with his wife and four daughters, enjoyed the fun of serving, and seeing them eat' (p. 19).

The importance of the Sunday school as a centre for recreational life is recalled too by Kate Edwards. In the 1880s and 1890s, in the Lotting Fen district of Huntingdonshire, the Methodist Sunday School Anniversary was an annual event for everyone, however poor, to look and do their best:

> The last high day of the year, except for Ramsey Fair, were the Sunday School Anniversary. This were the child'en's very own day.... The Sunday school teachers had been teaching 'em special hymns for weeks, and between the hymns such children as dared and could learn their 'piece' said recitation or sung little hymns in pairs or even an occasional solo. It were a terrible ordeal to stand up facing all the people and "say your piece". We used to practice it for days and nights at a time just before "the anni", but when you stood up there wer'n't a single word of it left in your head.... Every mother, however poor she was, had to get her child'en looking smart for the anniversary, and if they couldn't buy new clothes for their families every child had to have one thing new. Among the girls, the secret o' what they were going to wear were kept as if their lives depended on it, and many a mother has dragged out to work for weeks in the field to be able to buy the new things for the anni. This were the part we loved best, because although we were as poor as anybody there, we knowed we could trust our mam to get us the prettiest frocks as well as better quality ones than anybody else's there. (Marshall ed., 1980, p. 206)

Similarly, Louisa Hamer (1967), born in 1873, remembers that in Rawtenstall, Lancashire, in the 1880s the Sunday school was a focal point for village life: 'We had no theatre no picture house, no dance hall no public library, no trams, no taxis.... For entertainment well the Sunday Schools were "Tops"—bazaars, sales of work, bring and buy's, American Teas, At homes and amateur operatic societies' (p. 10). Just how effective Sunday schools were as educational institutions during the nineteenth century is debatable. But overall they did teach thousands of working-class girls and boys how to read. As Laqueur (1976b, p. 123) argues, though Sunday schools did not provide an adequate substitute for extended day education, nevertheless, within the context of working-class childhood, the three to five hours of instruction offered each week for an average of four years, in small classes graded according to scholastic ability, had a significant impact on the creation of mass literacy in nineteenth century England.

Day Schools

The two main providers of day schools in the nineteenth century were the National Society and the British and Foreign Society. By 1870 these two societies were providing over 90 per cent of voluntary school places (Hurt, 1979, p. 4). The Church of England National Society was particularly influential, and this influence extended to the end of the century. It has been estimated that by 1895 61.6 per cent of all elementary schools in England and Wales were Church of England schools, 6.2 per cent were British and Foreign schools and 24.2 per cent schools connected with the school boards created by the 1870 Education Act (Horn, 1974, p. 133). While dame schools and Sunday schools were largely seen as a part of working-class life and of the working-class neighbourhood, the day schools of the religious societies and of the school boards were seen as extraneous to the working-class community, a form of education that was 'provided' by middle-class personnel.

The two religious societies attracted government grants from as early as 1833, and the education they offered was often seen as a form of charity. In addition, the aims of the two societies were not just to impart some rudimentary knowledge, especially religious knowledge, but also to instill certain habits considered suitable for children in this social class location. The aims of the National Society, for example, were stated in 1812 as being to communicate to the poor 'such knowledge and habits, as are sufficient to guide them through life, in their proper stations', and especially to teach the doctrine of the Established Church and to offer training for the performance of religious duties (First Annual Report, 1812, p. 18). The experience of schooling in these day schools was likely to be sharply different from that in either dame or Sunday schools. In particular, I would like to highlight the following factors that helped to structure the learning experience.

First, in these day schools the sexual divisions between boy and girl pupils were developed in a much more pronounced way than in dame schools or Sunday schools. Though there were wide regional variations in the way these schools were formally organized, many of them — especially those large day schools in urban areas — built sexual divisions into their formal structure. For example, the day schools of the National Society included both single sex and mixed sex schooling. Yet even in mixed sex schooling there could be separate rooms for boys and girls and separate departments. At the Central School of the National Society, in Baldwin's Gardens, we find in 1814 a boys' room to hold 600 pupils and a girls' room to hold 400 (Second Annual Report, 1814, p. 194).

Whatever pattern of single sex or mixed sex schooling was offered, fewer places were provided for girls than for boys; within a patriarchal society, the education of working-class boys was considered more important than that of their sisters. But perhaps the area where sexual divisions in the day schools were most evident was in the curriculum. At the Central School in Baldwin Gardens, both boys and girls were taught prayers, ciphering, religious exercises, writing and reading in the morning, but in the afternoon the curriculum was gender-specific. While boys continued with ciphering, writing, reading and arithmetic, the girls were taught knitting and needlework till half past four and then arithmetic till five o'clock (*ibid.*, p. 195). Similarly, the British schools offered a basic curriculum of the 3Rs and religious knowledge with needlework for girls only. Though other subjects such as history and geography were gradually added to the curriculum, not all day schools were teaching these by 1870. Irrespective of whether the new subjects were taught or not, the sewing afternoon for girls was still retained. This meant that girls had less time to study the other subjects. The frequent result was a lower educational standard in the 3Rs, especially in arithmetic, than that attained by their brothers. The total effect of these sexual divisions within the day schools of the two societies was to disadvantage girls in comparison with boys. As girls, fewer places were provided for them, and as female pupils, they were taught a gender-specific curriculum that devoted a large amount of time to the low status, manual skill of sewing (Purvis, 1981, pp. 105–12).

A second feature of the day schools which was particularly influential in structuring the experience of schooling for working-class boys and girls was the fact that a monitorial method of teaching was used, especially up to the first half of the nineteenth century. This method relied upon older pupils or 'monitors' teaching younger pupils in a mechanistic way. Compared with the teacher/pupil ratio of dame and Sunday schools, these day schools had a high teacher/pupil ratio. Under this system one teacher only was usually attached to a school and it was his task to run the school in an orderly, efficient manner and train the monitors. Joseph Lancaster of the British Society, usually credited along with Andrew Bell of the National Society as the 'inventors' of the monitorial system, organized his school at Borough Road in this way. He was the sole teacher at his school, which had about 1000 pupils. He organized the school and trained and employed sixty-seven monitors.

As Sturt (1967, p. 31) has observed, under the monitorial method of teaching everything was reduced to its basic elements. Reading, for example, began with making letters in sand while the monitor watched carefully; then the spelling and writing of two-letter syllables would begin. Chanting of dates, verses from the Bible and other set replies were common too. The great advantage of this method of teaching was that it was cheap. There was only the salary of the teacher (usually a man) to be paid, plus a small fee to the monitors. Slates and sand, which could be used again and again, were the only writing tools that had to be bought for the pupils.

The mechanistic reply that the monitorial method evoked in children held a number of implications for the way schooling was experienced by the pupils. Endless repetition of certain lessons may have occurred until each class provided, or appeared to provide, the correct answer. It is highly probable that many children copied each other, aped words that were similar to the expected reply and did not necessarily understand what they had said.

Unfortunately, as Burnett (1982, p. 148) has noted, few autobiographies by monitors or by those they taught have survived. The few that have come to light include those of Thomas Dunning, James Bunwick and Frederick Hobley. Thomas Dunning, for example, was sent in 1820, when he was 7 years old, to the National School at Newport Pagnall. He claims that he learnt 'but very little'. As he could read moderately well, he was appointed a monitor. As a monitor, he had 'very little time allowed' for either writing or arithmetic, and none whatsoever for grammar and geography (Vincent ed., 1977, p. 120). Frederick Hobley (1905, p. 180), born in 1833, recollects that at a National School in Oxfordshire he was 'promoted to be a monitor' and paid a halfpenny a day. He regarded this income from his monitorial duties as pocketmoney.

Other accounts condemn the monitorial system more forcefully. James Robinson, for example, aged 15 years old in 1836, who had attended one of the central schools of the National Society in Baldwin Gardens, did not stay at the school long. He played truant one day, and was beaten for it so severely that he would not return any more. Anyway, he claimed that he learnt little 'because boys taught you' (Central Society of Education, 1837, p. 24). Monitors would often play with the pupils and then the boys would get a hiding for being naughty. Thomas Shepherd, aged 14 in 1836, claimed too that monitors could be bribed with favours of various kinds: 'if you gave the monitor anything, he would let you off your lessons, and if you did not, he would have you up to the master and get you a good hiding' (*ibid.*, p. 25).

The monitorial method of teaching was particularly popular up to the 1840s. In 1848 a pupil-teacher training system was adopted, and the state became much more actively involved in the recruitment and training of teachers. A five-year, state-aided, pupil-teacher apprenticeship could be offered to pupils of either sex who had completed elementary schooling up to the age of 13. The number of female pupil-teachers rose rapidly during the second half of the nineteenth century. In 1849 about 32 per cent of pupil-teachers were female, but by the 1890s this had risen to about 78 per cent (Tropp, 1957, p. 22; Horn, 1978, p. 66).

The training schemes for teachers during the second half of the century should have meant that the quality of the educational process within the classroom of day schools was vastly improved. To what extent this is so is difficult to judge. In particular, one external constraint upon the educational system during the second half of the century undoubtedly brought a less than beneficial effect upon the experience of schooling — that was the constraint exercised by the Revised Code of 1862. This Code initiated a system of payment by results whereby a grant of twelve shillings for each child could only be earned under certain conditions. Thus four shillings could be earned if a child attended regularly (under a qualified headteacher), while the rest of money would only be awarded if a child attained a satisfactory standard in the 3Rs in the annual examination to be conducted by an HMI. If a pupil failed in any one of the 3Rs, two shillings and eightpence was to be deducted from that pupil's grant (Horn, 1974, p. 41). Each child was expected, under the Code, to pass the annual examination and proceed to the next stage. The Revised Code encouraged certain aspects of monitorial teaching — such as chanting, recitation and drilling. The experience of schooling for working-class girls and boys continued as a daily grind in the 3Rs and religious knowledge, with sewing only for the girls. It is little wonder that many pupils experienced extreme boredom.

One such pupil was Joseph Ashby, born in 1859, who attended the local National School in rural Tysoe. For Joseph, and doubtless countless other children, schooling was something to be endured, not enjoyed:

> Right up the school, through all the six standards (there was a special class of a few boys and one or two girls above this) you did almost nothing except reading, writing and arithmetic. What a noise there used to be! Several children would be reading aloud, teachers scolding, infants reciting, all waxing louder and louder until the master rang the bell on his desk and the noise slid down to a lower note and less volume.
>
> Reading was worst; sums you did at least write on your slate, whereas you might wait the whole half-hour of a reading lesson while boys and girls who could not read stuck at every word. If you took your finger from the word that was being read you were punished by staying in when others went home. A specially hard time was the two 'sewing afternoons'. While the girls were collected together for sewing, the boys merely did more sums or an extra dictation, just the sort of thing they had been doing all morning. As they craned their necks to see what sort of garments, what colours, were coming out the vicarage basket of mending, they were unusually tiresome to the poor pupil-teacher, losing their places over and over again or misspelling words they knew perfectly well — forgetting everything. He rapped with a stick; he shouted; he called out, 'Jack, Tom, stay in half an hour!' — a rather effective threat. To remain in school was the thing above all others the children did not want to do. (Ashby, 1974, pp. 17–18)

The 1870 Education Act, which enabled a state system of elementary schooling to develop out of the previously fragmented provision, may have done little to alleviate the sense of boredom experienced by many working-class boys and girls. Flora Thompson (1954), for example, born in 1877 at Juniper Hill on the Oxfordshire-Northampton border, remembers in her semi-autobiographical book that the interest of the pupils was not in books, but in life, and especially the life that lay immediately about them. At school they worked unwillingly, upon compulsion, and the life of the schoolmistress was a hard one (pp. 194–5). The main subjects were still reading, writing and arithmetic with a scripture lesson each morning. The scripture lesson for the older children was taken by the Rector and it embodied many aspects of curriculum content and pedagogy that had been common earlier in the century:

> His lesson consisted of Bible reading, turn and turn about round the class, of reciting from memory the names of the kings of Israel and repeating the Church Catechism. After that, he would deliver a little lecture on morals and behaviour. The children must not lie or steal or be discontented or envious. God had placed them just where they were in the social order and given them their own especial work to do; to envy others or to try to change their own lot in life was a sin of which he hoped they would never be guilty. (*ibid.*, p. 191)

The writing lesson consisted of the copying of copperplate maxims such as 'A fool and his money are soon parted', 'Waste not, want not' or 'Count ten before you speak'. The reading lesson was extremely tedious since it involved each child reading out loud, in turn. Such tedium was particularly onerous for the more able children such as Laura (assumed to be Flora Thompson):

> Many of the children read so slowly and haltingly that Laura, who was impatient by nature, longed to take hold of their words and drag them out of their mouths, and it often seemed to her that her own turn to read would never come. As often as she could do so without being detected, she would turn over and peep between the pages of their own 'Royal Reader', and studiously holding the book to her nose, pretend to be following the lesson while she was pages ahead. (*ibid.*, p. 193)

For an able child like Laura the tedium of school was lightened by some pleasures. It was one of her greatest joys, for example, to recite her school books since she knew 'every piece in the books by heart'. Similarly, many descriptions of faraway places fascinated her, such as this description of the Himalayas: 'Northward of the great plain of India, and along its whole extent, towers the sublime mountain region of the Himalayas, ascending gradually until it terminates in a long range of summits wrapped in perpetual snow' (*ibid.*, p. 193).

Other working-class girls and boys may, of course, have found little tedium in their lessons. Annie Barnes (1980), for example, born in 1887, whose father ran a high class fruiterer's and confectioner's shop in Stepney, London, remembers that she 'loved' every minute of her education in a local board school:

> I went to Ben Jonson School and I loved every minute. I liked all my teachers and the discipline was such that we never wanted to be naughty. But we had one girl in our class who was a demon. Her name was Harriet Vincent. She had ginger hair and she used to throw things

at the teachers. That sort of thing was never known in my school. She used to tell the teacher to shut up. (p. 7)

However, Annie's ambition to become a pupil-teacher had to be abandoned when her mother became ill. As with many other working-class girls through-out the century, it was 'expected' that a daughter (especially an eldest daughter) rather than a son should leave school and take over the household responsibilities when some kind of family emergency or crisis arose:

> Unfortunately I had to leave school in 1902, which was my sixteenth year, because my mother was taken ill. She wouldn't have anyone else to look after her. It was a great blow to me. I was very interested in teaching and was really keen to stay on, but there was a lot for me to do at home. There were all the children and the meals to see to and, of course, I had to help in the shop. (*ibid.*, p. 8)

Not all working-class children were as fortunate as Laura and Annie in liking their teachers and finding some pleasure in schoolwork. Henry Teague, born in Bristol in 1885, whose father was a labourer, remembers that he did not try hard at his school lessons and was unable to concentrate because he was afraid of the teachers who were 'brutes in them days' (quoted in Humphries, 1981, p. 77). Mabel Bennett, born in Bristol in 1886, whose father was a carpenter and joiner, remembers how she was always punished for being late: 'I had to take the children to school, and then I had to go nearly a mile to my school, so I was late. I always came in for the cane ... they'd lay it on so that it would nearly cut your hand in half' (quoted *ibid.*, p. 55). Kate Edwards recollects that in the Lotting Fen area in the 1880s all the pupils hated 'Old Daddy Rigby', the schoolmaster, and his family who helped to run the school (Marshall ed., 1980, p. 191). Other working-class pupils, such as James Brown, born in the Tyne Valley in 1872, regularly played truant. He attended a local school which, after the 1870 Education Act, came under the jurisdiction of the Newcastle School Board and the rural dean of Corbridge. His grandson recollects:

> My grandfather used to say that if he did not feel like school he just stayed away 'playin' the wag' and keeping well away from 'the school board man'. It is clear from the log books that given the choice of a run with the Heddon Hunt, a farm sale, a pig killing or a funeral, certainly casual work of any kind, and school, the children would 'play the wag'. The abolition of school pence in 1891 helped matters a little but the chronic problem of erratic attendance remained. (Williamson, 1982, p. 27)

The Education Acts of 1876 and 1880 made elementary schooling compulsory, but the 'truancy' amongst boys may have been viewed more seriously by teachers, school board officials and parents than 'absence' amongst girls (Davin, 1974). Girls were expected to be involved in domestic activities such as child care, cooking and cleaning, and a blind eye was probably turned to school absences for such reasons. One headmistress stated that girls could not be prevented from 'helping' their parents but a boy 'ought never to miss' an attendance unless there was not an older girl in the family (quoted in Adams, 1982, p. 54). School log books at this time bear endless witness to the way that the demands of housework for girls made their attendance at school more irregular than that of their brothers — 'several girls absent, it being wash day at home', 'cleaning time and the militia being in the town the girls required for extra work where they are lodging', 'Wakes cleaning', 'Spring cleaning', 'Autumn cleaning' (quoted in Johnson, 1970, p. 193). Working-class girls could experience not only the inferior educational provision that was common to their social class location but also the burden of their gender. It was regarded as a 'natural' part of their femininity that they should be involved in domestic duties and, as a consequence, their schooling was more irregular and intermittent than that of their brothers. Indeed, some girls did not even attend school on an irregular and intermittent basis but were kept at home as domestic drudges. Hannah Mitchell, for example, born in 1871, to poor farming parents, was the fourth of six children and anxiously awaited her turn to attend school. Her two elder brothers were sent first, and then two of her sisters. But Hannah's turn at school never came: all she experienced was 'a fortnight's schoolin' (Mitchell ed., 1968, p. 46). Hard manual domestic work in the daytime was followed by lighter domestic work in the evenings. Unlike the boys in the family, the girls were allowed little free time:

> On winter evenings there was sewing by hand, making and mending shirts and underwear. At eight years old my weekly task was to darn all the stockings for the household, and I think my first reactions to feminism began at this time when I was forced to darn my brothers' stockings while they read or played cards or dominoes.
>
> Sometimes the boys helped with rugmaking, or in cutting up wool or picking feathers for beds and pillows, but for them this was voluntary work; for the girls it was compulsory, and the fact that the boys could read if they wished filled my cup of bitterness to the brim. (*ibid.*, p. 43)

As the state became increasingly involved in elementary education, attempts were made not only to enforce compulsory attendance but also to control the curriculum. In 1872, for example, singing became grant earning. In 1878 domestic economy was made a compulsory specific subject for girls, and in 1882 and 1890 respectively grants were available for teaching cookery and laundry work. In 1891 drawing was made compulsory for older boys, and in 1895 'Object Lessons' (on subjects such as animals and plants) were made compulsory for younger children (Hurt, 1979, pp. 179–81; David, 1980, pp. 123–4). Some of these subjects had been taught in elementary schools for many years. But as the state exercised increasing control over what was taught in the elementary school, some changes were occurring too, especially in some of the more enlightened infant schools, in how children were taught. A Derbyshire woman, for example, who was in the 'babies' class' in Church Gresley National School in 1884 recalls that there was 'much play and singing'. Another Derbyshire school, Matlock Church of England Infant School, introduced a toy train and rails 'for use in object and conversation lessons' in 1899, and other schools in the county included a range of activities for young children — such as colour drawing, bead threading, tablet paying, guessing games, ball making and picture lessons (Johnson, 1970, pp. 208–9). But for older working-class boys and girls in the elementary schools, where class numbers were large, attendance intermittent, equipment scarce and teachers hard-pressed to keep order, the drilling and recitation so common in earlier decades probably continued. Charles Cooper (1964), born in a Yorkshire mining village in 1872, remembers the way that reading, writing and spelling were taught:

> For reading, the same books were used year after year until they were ready to fall to pieces. Usually then they were sent up to the Hall to be patched up and made usable again. . . .
>
> For writing, Copy Books were used and the correct holding of the pen was insisted upon — 'Thumb on the left side of pen, first finger on top, second finger on right side, little finger resting on the paper, wrist flat and end of pen pointing towards the right ear.' Blots and finger marks were punishable by cane; and the correct size, shape, height and length of each letter had to be as shown in the copy.
>
> Pens in those days had steel split nibs; the nibs often got crossed and they dripped ink readily. There were no fountain pens or ballpoint pens. All these disadvantages tended to make us very careful and nervous, with the fear of the cane ever before us. . . .
>
> And now we come to the case of spelling. . . . Each mistake had to be written out correctly a given number of times. Simple rules were taught, and correct spelling was insisted upon and was regarded as being very important. (p. 194)

Another pupil remembers that when she was at school in the 1880s the class stood and recited the trial scene from *The Merchant of Venice*, which they had learnt by heart, since only the teacher had a copy of the words (Johnson, 1980, pp. 210–11).

The sexual divisions in elementary schooling became more pronounced after 1870 as girls spent more time on the various domestic subjects that were made compulsory or offered as 'choices'.[4] This, of course, meant less time for non-domestic subjects such as history and geography. Even when new subjects were introduced into the higher forms of the board schools, the range of subjects for girls was restricted to botany and domestic economy while boys could take animal physiology, physical geography, mechanics, algebra, chemistry and physics (Adams, 1982, p. 47). The listing of a subject for both boys and girls did not mean the sharing of a common curriculum — especially when there were separate schools or separate departments for the sexes. At the

London School Board, for example, 'Experimental Science' was gradually introduced in the boys' and girls' departments around the turn of the century. But gender differences between the sexes were upheld in the content of their science lessons:

> The girls . . . study the difference between conduction, convection and radiation of heat. From a simple experiment, which they themselves perform, they can tell you why a cotton fabric is to be preferred to a woollen one in the summer; why the water in the boiler behind the kitchener rises to the cistern in the bath room; or whether water boils more quickly in a kettle covered with soot than in one new and polished. The boy can explain why ice is packed in flannel or felt in summer, and why it is necessary, when descending into mines, that the safety-lamp should be surrounded by a gauze of close mesh. (Spalding, 1900, p. 212)

The emphasis upon domesticity for girls in elementary schools may be seen as an attempt, by the middle classes, to make working-class girls into good wives and mothers and competent domestic servants (Dyhouse, 1981, pp. 89–104). But the experience of such a schooling may have been interpreted rather differently by the pupils themselves. Some of the female respondents in Elizabeth Roberts' (1975) oral research remembered that when they were schoolgirls in the closing decades of the nineteenth century the practical domestic lessons were of little value in real life:

> Respondents remember as schoolgirls learning to wash socks, iron handkerchiefs, lay fires, make bread and scones, but they are unanimous in the belief that it was their mothers' training which was of real value and that they learned little or nothing at school. 'It was never any help. . . . They never taught me anything.' (This respondent took home some dirty looking scones which the family refused to eat, and also had to wash a collar which her mother then washed again.) (p. 16)

Grace Foakes, who spent her childhood in East London around the turn of the century, remembers that the housewifery course, held in a house set aside for the purpose, was the highlight of the week. While the busy teacher was inspecting a task in one part of the house, the girls in another part would play about, doing exactly the opposite to what they had been taught: 'We jumped on the beds, threw pillows, drowned the doll and swept dirt under the mats' (quoted in Adams, 1982, p. 46).

The increased emphasis upon sexual divisions between boys and girls after 1870 was not evident only in the curriculum. Some of the more academic elementary schools prepared some pupils for scholarships in the fee-paying, secondary school sector. It was usually boys, rather than girls, who were promoted and sponsored in this way. At Kennington National School in London, for example, boys began to win scholarships from 1881. On at least one occasion a girl 'was also successful' (Silver and Silver, 1974, p. 127). The Technical Instruction Act of 1889 enabled counties and county boroughs to make grants to secondary schools to provide scholarships for able boys and girls in the elementary sector. Though the total number of scholarships was severely limited and really only for exceptionally able children, the number available to girls was well below that available to boys. In addition to this barrier, able working-class girls might also find that both their parents and teachers discriminated against them when they had scholastic ambitions for secondary education. The parents of Nora Lumb would have paid 'for a boy, but not for a girl' to attend a grammar school. So Nora, born in 1912, had to gain one of the ten scholarships that Sunderland offered in order to enter the grammar school (quoted in Burnett ed. 1982, p. 163). The parents of Reginald Farndon, born in Ealing in 1904, allowed him to attend the grammar school though his three elder sisters had had to leave school when they were 13 years old. As Burnett (1982) observes, here, as in many cases, the boy took educational precedence over any girls (p. 163). The teachers too may have encouraged the able working-class boy rather than the able working-class girl. Ellen Wilkinson, for example, born in 1891 to working-class parents, won a series of scholarships that eventually enabled her to attend Manchester University — despite the fact that she had been a pupil at a 'filthly elementary school ... with five classes in one room'. She bitterly recollects that in this school: 'The masters would often give extra time, lend book and so on to a bright lad. I never remember such encouragement. I was only a girl anyway' (Wilkinson, 1938, p. 404).

Even if a working-class boy or girl did pass the scholarship to a secondary school it was no guarantee of attendance. Money was usually needed for the school uniform, for books and for sports equipment. Such expenditure had to compete with other things that a working-class family needed, such as money for rent, for food and for clothes. Thus some working-class children who passed a scholarship failed to take up a place in a secondary school or left early. Lavinia Swainbank, for example, born in Newcastle-upon-Tyne in 1906, whose father was a blacksmith-striker, recollects that even though she passed the eleven plus exam, she could not attend the secondary school since there was no money to spare for books or the uniform (Burnett ed., 1974, p. 221). Cyril Willis, born in Bristol in 1901, was a scholarship boy at Hanley grammar school, but felt obliged to leave since his father was slowly dying and his mother was forced to work long hours to earn enough to support the family:

> my mother was having to work like a slave to keep the family. And I think subconsciously it was getting me down. . . . Nobody said anything to put pressure on me to leave but I desperately wanted to earn some money to make it easier for her. I was aware I was sacrificing my education when I left, and I valued education. . . . But I wanted to leave to hand my wage packet over to her so it wouldn't be such a struggle all the time. And I wasn't the only one. My friend Freddie Potts, he left, and several others did as well that term, because they

felt their families couldn't support them any longer. (quoted in Humphries, 1981, p. 59)

The fact that the economic conditions of a working-class family could determine the fate of the scholarship girl or boy must not blind us to points mentioned earlier — that more scholarships were provided for boys than girls and that more boys were encouraged to compete for such awards. Working-class girls could experience, in relation to the scholarship system, not only the handicap of their social class position but also the handicap of their gender. In a patriarchal society their education was considered less important than that of their brothers. That minority of working-class girls who managed to break through the barriers of inequality in educational provision between the social classes and inequalities in educational opportunity between boys and girls, and enter a secondary school might feel, only too keenly, the social differences in life style, speech and dress between themselves and the daughters of fee-paying parents. Doris Frances, for example, whose father was an illiterate bus-cleaner, won a scholarship to a grammar school in 1919. She experienced many embarrassing moments as on one occasion when the headmistress asked her to wash her hair with soft green soap and to comb it with a fine-tooth comb. She recollects: 'The insinuation behind the message was all too clear. It is doubtful whether such an offensive message would have been sent to the parent of a fee-paying girl, especially without positive justification' (quoted in Burnett ed., 1982, p. 164). Of course working-class boys might experience social inferiority within a secondary school too. But secondary schools for girls were likely to be more socially exclusive than those for boys and to give greater emphasis to the learning of middle-class social skills.

The proportion of children from elementary schools entering secondary education at the turn of the century was small.[5] By 1900 the vast majority of working-class girls and boys were being educated in the elementary sector, and their experience of schooling was still likely to be that of a daily grind in the 3Rs with some history, geography and elementary science, together with domestic subjects for girls. In 1893 the school leaving age was raised to 11, and so the daily grind was endured by pupils for some six years. It was to be many years before so-called 'progressive' methods of teaching and changes in curriculum content were to open up wider possibilities for individual fulfilment and expression amongst pupils educated in the state-maintained sector.

Conclusion

In conclusion I would like to make the following points. First, I have tried to provide an account of the experience of schooling for working-class boys and girls in nineteenth century England by drawing upon a range of texts, especially autobiographies. Secondly, I have tried to relate this account of the experience of schooling to both the social structure of the nineteenth century and to the biographical details of the individuals concerned. Thirdly, I have tried to demonstrate that the experience of schooling for working-class boys and girls was shaped by their social class position and by their gender, and that the differences in educational experience between girls and boys were probably most pronounced in the day schools of the National and British Societies and in the board schools that were established after the 1870 Education Act. In particular, the growth in the latter decades of the century in domestic subjects for girls meant that female pupils devoted less time to other non-practical subjects such as history and geography. Domestic subjects were linked with the gender of femininity and working-class girls were thus handicapped in their educational progress in a way that working-class boys were not. The differences between the sexes in educational attainment within elementary day schools were further aggravated by the fact that when scholarships to secondary schools were provided, more scholarships were offered to boys than to girls.

Finally, I would like to emphasize that the study of the experience of schooling for working-class children within the nineteenth century classroom reveals both continuity and discontinuity with today. Perhaps the main threads of continuity relate to the variation by gender and class of pupil experiences, even within one education form, and the feelings of boredom about the 'daily grind' of schooling that many pupils express.

Notes

1 The main methodological problems relate to the sources. If one consults documents written by middle-class people about the experience of schooling for working-class children then all kinds of bias may be built into the way the information is collected and recorded. If one consults documents written by working-class men and women, describing their own experiences of schooling, bias is not eliminated either. For example, such accounts may report events inaccurately and select information in order to present the writer in a favourable light. In addition, documents written by the working class overrepresent the literate and men and underrepresent the illiterate and women. It is difficult to know, therefore, just how 'typical' the experience of schooling that is recorded in such documents may have been for working-class children. For further discussion of some of these issues see PURVIS (1984). The collection of oral accounts of the experience of nineteenth century schooling presents its own particular problems. For a discussion of some of these issues see, for example, THOMPSON (1978) and PLUMMER (1983).
2 Useful sources for autobiographical extracts are BURNETT (1974), VINCENT (1977) and BURNETT (1982).
3 A number of definitions of patriarchy have been offered. BEECHEY (1979) suggests that at the most general level patriarchy refers to male domination and to the power relationships by which men dominate women (p. 66).
4 The Code of 1875 had noted that, in addition to the 3Rs (and needlework for girls only), there should be 'class' and 'specific' subjects. Class subjects were for groups of children, while specific subjects were for individuals. By the mid-1890s schools could offer not more than two specific subjects and present their pupils in one or two class subjects. Needlework could be included as a class subject and many girls were, therefore, presented only in this subject rather than in the other class subjects. In

1878 domestic economy had been made a compulsory specific subject, and by the mid-1980s girls could choose cookery, laundry work or dairy work as their second specific subject while boys could choose gardening (see HURT, 1979, p. 183).

5 LOWNDES, G. (1937, p. 101) suggests that the odds against a child in an English elementary school gaining a scholarship to a secondary school in 1894 were 270 to 1. Even in 1930 the percentage of public elementary school pupils aged 10 and under 11 entering grammar schools in England and Wales was only 12.9 — see BOARD OF EDUCATION (1939, p. 320).

References

ADAMS, C. (1982) *Ordinary Lives a Hundred Years Ago*, London, Virago.

ASHBY, M.K. (1974) *Joseph Ashby of Tysoe 1859–1919*, London, Merlin Press, first pub. 1961.

BARNES, A. in conversation with HARDING, KATE and GIBBS, CAROLINE (1980) *Tough Annie: From Suffragette to Stepney Councillor*, London, Stepney Books.

BEECHEY, V. (1979) 'On patriarchy', *Feminist Review*, 3.

BOARD OF EDUCATION (1939) *Secondary Education with Special Reference to Grammar Schools and Technical High Schools*, London, HMSO.

BURNETT, J. (Ed.) (1974) *Useful Toil: Autobiographies of Working People from the 1820s to the 1920s*, London, Allen Lane.

BURNETT, J. (Ed. with an Introduction) (1982) *Destiny Obscure: Autobiographies of Childhood and Family from the 1820s to the 1920s*, London, Allen Lane.

CENTRAL SOCIETY OF EDUCATION (1837) *Schools for the Industrious Classes; or, The Present State of Education among the Working People of England*, London, Taylor and Walton.

COOPER, C. (1964) autobiographical extract, pub. in BURNETT (1982).

COOPER, T. (1971) *The Life of Thomas Cooper, Written by Himself* (with an introduction by John Saville), New York, Leicester University Press, first pub. 1872.

DAVID, M.E. (1980) *The State, the Family and Education* London, Routledge and Kegan Paul.

DAVIN, A. (1974) 'Board school girls' (a paper read to the Feminist History Group in London, June 1974), quoted in DYHOUSE. C. (1981).

DYHOUSE, C. (1981) *Girls Growing Up in Late Victorian and Edwardian England*, London, Routledge and Kegan Paul.

EDWARDS, G. (1922) *From Crow-Scaring to Westminster*, London, Labour Publishing Company.

FARNINGHAM, M. (1907) *A Working Woman's Life*, London, James Clarke.

GAVRON, H. (1966) *The Captive Wife*, London, Routledge and Kegan Paul.

HAMER, L. (1967) *Reminiscences of Rawtenstall*, Rawtenstall, Libraries and Museum Committee.

HAMMERSLEY, M. (1982) 'Making a vice of our virtues: Some notes on theory in ethnography and history', this volume, pp. 15–24.

HOBLEY, F. (1905) autobiography written at the special request of his children, October 1905, pub. in BURNETT (1982).

HOGG, E. (1897) 'School children as wage earners', *The Nineteenth Century*, August.

HORN, P. (1974) *The Victorian Country Child*, Warwick, Roundwood Press.

HORN, P. (1978) *Education in Rural England 1800–1914*, New York, St Martin's Press.

HUMPHRIES, S. (1981) *Hooligans or Rebels? An Oral History of Working-Class Childhood and Youth 1889–1939*, Oxford, Basil Blackwell.

HURT, J.S. (1979) *Elementary Schooling and the Working Classes 1860–1918*, London, Routledge and Kegan Paul.

JOHNSON, M. (1980) *Derbyshire Village Schools in the Nineteenth Century*, Devon, Newton Abbot, David and Charles.

JOHNSON, R. (1979) ' "Really useful knowledge": Radical education and working-class culture, 1790–1848', in CLARKE, J., *et al.* (Eds) *Working Class Culture*, London, Hutchinson in association with CCCS.

LAQUEUR, T.W. (1976a) 'Working-class demand and the growth of English elementary education, 1750–1850', in STONE, L. (Ed.) (1976) *Schooling and Society*, Baltimore, Md., The Johns Hopkins University Press.

LAQUEUR, T.W. (1976b) *Religion and Respectability: Sunday Schools and Working Class Culture 1780–1850*, New Haven, Conn., Yale University Press, p. 189.

LAWSON, J. and SILVER, H. (1973) *A Social History of Education in England*, London, Methuen.

LOWNDES, G.A.N. (1937) *The Silent Social Revolution: An Account of the Expansion of Public Education in England and Wales 1895–1935*, London, Oxford University Press.

MCCANN, P. (1977) 'Popular education, socialization and social control: Spitalfields', in MCCANN, P. (Ed.) *Popular Education and Socialization in the Nineteenth Century*, London, Methuen.

MARSHALL, S. (Ed.) (1980 paperback ed.) *Fenland Chronicle: Recollections of William Henry and Kate Mary Edwards Collected and Edited by Their Daughter*, Cambridge, Cambridge University Press, first pub. 1967.

MITCHELL, G. (Ed.) (1968) *The Hard Way Up: The Autobiography of Hannah Mitchell, Suffragette and Rebel*, London, Faber and Faber.

NATIONAL SOCIETY FOR PROMOTING THE EDUCATION OF THE POOR IN THE PRINCIPLES OF THE ESTABLISHED CHURCH (1812) *First Annual Report*, London.

NATIONAL SOCIETY FOR PROMOTING THE EDUCATION OF THE POOR IN THE PRINCIPLES OF THE ESTABLISHED CHURCH (1814) *Second Annual Report*, London.

PALEY MARSHALL, M. (1947) *What I Remember*, Cambridge, Cambridge University Press.

PLUMMER, K. (1983) *Documents of Life: An Introduction to the Problems and Literature of Humanistic Methods*, London, George Allen and Unwin.

PURSER, J. (1966) *Our Ilmington* (printed privately).

PURVIS, J. (1981) 'The double burden of class and gender in the schooling of working-class girls in nineteenth-century England, 1800–1870', in BARTON, L. and WALKER, S. (Eds) *Schools, Teachers and Teaching*, Lewes, Falmer Press.

PURVIS, J. (1984) Understanding Texts, Unit 15 of E205, *Conflict and Change in Education: A Sociological Introduction*, Bletchley, Open University Press.

ROBERTS, E. (1975) 'Learning and living — socialisation outside school', *Oral History*, 3, 2, Family History Issue.

SHAW, C. (1977) *When I Was a Child*, Sussex, Caliban Books repub. facsimile of first ed of 1903.

SILVER, H. (1977) 'Aspects of neglect: The strange case of Victorian popular education', *Oxford Review of Education*, 3, 1.

SILVER, P. and SILVER, H. (1974) *The Education of the Poor: The History of a National School 1824–1974*, London, Routledge and Kegan Paul.

SIMON, B. (1973) 'Research in the history of education', in TAYLOR, W. (Ed.) *Research Perspectives in Education*, London, Routledge and Kegan Paul.

SMITH, M. (1892) *The Autobiography of Mary Smith, Schoolmistress and Nonconformist*, Carlisle, The Wordsworth Press.

SPALDING, T.A. (1900) *The Work of the London School Board*, London, P.S. King and Son.

STURT, M. (1967) *The Education of the People*, London, Routledge and Kegan Paul.

SUTHERLAND, G. (1971) *Elementary Education in the Nineteenth Century*, London, Historical Association.

SWAINBANK, L. (1974) autobiographical extract in BURNETT (1974).

THOMPSON, F. (1954) *Lark Rise to Candleford*, London, Oxford University Press, first pub. 1939.

THOMPSON, P. (1978) *The Voice of the Past*, Oxford, Oxford University Press.

TROPP, A. (1957) *The School Teachers*, London, Heinemann.

VINCENT, D. (Ed. with an Introduction (1977) *Testaments of Radicalism: Memoirs of Working-Class Politicians 1790–1885*, London, Europa Publications.

WILKINSON, E. (1938) in OXFORD, M. (The Countess of Oxford and Asquith) (Ed.), *Myself When Young*, London, Frederick Muller.

WILLIAMSON, B. (1982) *Class, Culture and Community: A Biographical Study of Social Change in Mining*, London, Routledge and Kegan Paul.

WILSON, J. (1980) *Memories of a Labour Leader*, Sussex, Caliban Books repub. facsimile of first ed. of 1910.

WRIGHT MILLS, C. (1967) *The Sociological Imagination*, New York, Oxford University Press paperback, first pub. 1959.

Imperialism, Social Control and the Colonial Curriculum in Africa*

Stephen J. Ball

One of the commonest assertions to be found in accounts of schooling in less developed countries in Africa is that the present day education systems of these countries are trapped, and inhibited in their development, by the legacies of the colonial past. Furthermore, it is normally taken for granted, both by indigenous writers and Western commentators, that these legacies stem directly from the imposition of forms of Western, academic schooling by the colonial power. While accepting the former assertion as undoubtedly true, I intend in this paper to challenge fundamentally the latter assumption of colonial imposition. I have four main arguments to put forward.

First, I would argue that one of the major features of the process of dissemination of Western educational institutions, especially with respect to the definition of school curriculum, 'what counts as valid knowledge', is the role played by the *demand* for education by indigenous peoples. This is important in a number of respects. For example, any crudely formulated notion of enforced incorporation of 'the natives', through compulsory schooling, can be discounted immediately. The examination of colonial policy for education quickly demonstrates the enormous and enduring mismatches which emerged between the wishes of the metropolitan governments and colonial administrations and the form of education provision which actually took shape.

Secondly, the analysis of these mismatches must take into account the role played by *forms of resistance*, by the indigenous peoples, to attempts by the colonial and metropolitan authorities to control and determine the school curriculum. The indigenous peoples in Africa were not simply passive recipients but played an active role in attempting to shape the education being offered to them.

Thirdly, the whole history of colonial schooling is denoted by the contestation between rival social and political groups with separate and conflicting vested interests, which Anderson (1970) calls 'the struggle for the

* A previous version of this paper appeared in *Journal of Curriculum Studies*, Vol. 15 No. 3 July–September 1983 pp. 237–264.

school'. This struggle, for the most part, is between the colonial authorities, the missionaries (of various persuasions) and particular groups within the indigenous peoples, though, in some cases, it is necessary to take into account the interests and influence of other economic groups like the immigrant Indians in East Africa and the white settlers in South and East Africa. And, from the 1920s on, the intervention of the forerunners of the modern day international aid agencies must also be taken into account.

Fourthly, much of the sociologically informed analysis of colonial schooling (in particular I am thinking of the work of Carnoy (1974)) sets itself within an essentially economistic frame of analysis, drawing primarily from Lenin's (1970) work. I shall argue that this perspective both overestimates the economic and concomitantly underestimates the political functions of the colonial school: indeed it contains a profound misreading of the objectives of British colonial education policy.

As far as the curriculum of the colonial school is concerned three competing types of curricula, based upon radically different assumptions about the nature and purpose of schooling, will be identified. These three versions of 'what is to count as school knowledge' may be termed: the evangelical curriculum; the 'adapted' curriculum; and the academic curriculum. As outlined below these curricula may be linked to particular sponsors and identified, to some extent, with particular phases in colonial history.

The Missionaries and the Evangelical Curriculum

Throughout the nineteenth century the bulk of the provision of Western schooling in colonial Africa was initiated by and remained in the hands of a wide variety of American and European missionary organizations which had entered Africa to proselytize the natives; 'they envisioned themselves as bringing a high view of life to benighted savages' (Beidelman, 1981, p. 83). The provision of schools, at least before 1900, was essentially a means to an end. The early missionaries did not hope to educate the Africans, but rather to convert them. The school played a dual role in this main aim. First of all, schooling provided the most effective means of achieving religious instruction — this was also the case in Britain itself where, in the first half of the nineteenth century, 'the Sunday school offered virtually the only formal educational experience for most of the population' (Dick, 1980, p. 28). Native colonial and British working-class children alike were taught to read the Bible, the catechism and religious texts. In the mission schools religion pervaded the whole curriculum. Bacus (1974), drawing from the reports of the Inspector of Schools in Barbados, notes that:

> In 1872 about 68% of the 3709 examinations conducted in reading were based on the old and new testaments while about 60% of the dictation examination passes were drawn from the same source. In the 'higher subjects' which included grammar, geography, etc., this influence was

even more dominant. Of the 7913 examinations conducted in this area about 88% (7022) were in 'Catechistical Religious Knowledge' (6625) and Bible History (397).

The parallels between the British working-class and native pupils are not there merely to be drawn through the distance of historical analysis. In the case of one of the largest missionary organizations, the Church Missionary Society, 'prospective overseas missionaries were encouraged to practice by evangelizing the working class and poor of East London' (Beidelman, 1981, p. 79).

So the missions hoped to use the schools to turn the Africans into 'Good Christians', which involved both 'civilizing' and converting. For many societies the success of their enterprise was often reduced to producing the largest possible number of recruits to the faith. In many areas of Africa it was soon the case that missions of different denominations were in direct competition for converts. This was to have a far-reaching significance for the development of educational provision, as we shall see later.

The second role played by the school was as an attraction and incentive for the Africans to allow their children to be subjected to the missionary influence. Nonetheless, in the earliest phases of missionary schooling the missionaries were not above offering additional material incentives to attract the reluctant Africans. Both Foster (1965) and Anderson (1970), describing educational penetration in Ghana (West Africa) and Kenya (East Africa) respectively, make the point that the 'attractions' of the mission school were firmly related to the availability of (1) models of advantage in the form of a 'normative reference group', educated Europeans and Africans, and (2) prospects of social advantage in terms of employment in the newly arrived cash economy. Foster (1965, p. 38) argues that:

> If . . . there had been an attempt to offer Western education *in vacuo* and if it had not been associated with significant change in the economy of the system of political control, it is likely that educational demand would have remained minimal.

Thus, in East and Central Africa the early missionaries who penetrated the interior far beyond the influence of the European military and economic establishment found little enthusiasm for their schools. Similarly in Ghana, where the Basel Mission ventured inland away from the coastal zone, the missionaries found that it was only possible to establish themselves by making fundamental changes to the sort of schooling they were offering, for example, by concentrating efforts into boarding schools ('a policy of detachment of individuals from the traditional milieu', Foster, 1965, p. 51) and teaching in vernacular languages. In some cases, for instance in Bechuanaland, the missionaries were actually invited to establish schools by the native rulers. But this had little to do with an interest in Christianity. Rather the 'missionaries were known to procure and repair guns, weapons which had assumed an important role in hunting and warfare' (Mutero-Chirenje, 1976).

These two interrelated aspects of missionary schooling, the prime concern with proselytization and conversion and the need therefore to attract children into the schools, are of fundamental importance in understanding the development of schooling and the nature of its impact on the natives and should not be lost sight of. If these primary concerns of the missionaries are neglected then it is all too easy to overestimate the extent of common interest between 'Bible and Flag'.

Carnoy suggests that the missionaries 'attempted to transport to Africa the ideal of the individualistic, capital accumulating small-farmer who raised goods demanded in European markets' (Carnoy, 1974, p. 118) and sees them as important agencies of the dissemination and inculcation of Western capitalist values. However, in a number of respects this argument is difficult to sustain. It appears to misconceive both the single-mindedness of the missionaries and the main concerns of the colonial and metropolitan governments and unrealistically glosses over the important differences in ideology between the different missionary societies. It also fails to take account of the important supply and demand relationship which underlay the 'success' of missionary activity.

The missionaries of the Church Missionary Society, for example, were clear in their rejection of the materialism of the capitalist industrial society which they left behind in Britain. They associated the industrial advancement witnessed in Europe with the corruption and denegation of basic Christian values. Thus:

> The missionaries were reluctant to teach secular skills to Africans because some feared to teach such skills would be to teach the wrong aspects of the world ... Even during the 1920's, the CMS still taught no skilled trades in most of its East African schools, but instead only simple tasks. (Beidelman, 1981, p. 88)

In Nigeria the hardline evangelical position of the CMS was clear in the teaching methods and curricula of their schools in the Niger Mission region. They played down the role of English, preferring to teach in the vernacular,[1] and maintained a firmly catechistic curriculum. This situation was only changed as the CMS began to lose ground to the rival Catholic Holy Ghost Fathers. Would-be pupils and converts began to see the disadvantages of the narrow catechistic education offered by the CMS schools. They turned in increasing numbers to the nearby Catholic schools where the teaching was in English. A second factor that was not insignificant in encouraging the CMS to rethink its educational philosophy at this time, just after the turn of the century, was the failure of their existing provision to qualify for government 'grants-in-aid' under the system of 'payment-by-results'. The running of the mission schools was placing an ever increasing burden on the finances of the Society. Nonetheless, the changes embarked upon could hardly be described as hurried; nor were they authorized without considerable anxiety and heartsearching by the Niger Mission representatives and the home committees of the society (Nduka, 1976).

But in February 1910 the Executive Committee authorized the introduction of several English language books into their schools:

Readers: (1) Indian Readers (to be adapted for use in Africa)
        (2) Tropical Readers
English Grammar and Composition: (1) Davidson and Alcock's Grammar
                                 (2) McDougall's 'Line upon Line'
Geography: Lawson's Geographical Series
English History: Ransom's Elementary English History
Hygiene: Dr Strachan's Hygiene.

In June 1914 the Educational Committee of the Parent Committee approved a full elementary curriculum for their schools. However, the major feature of the CMS attempt to wrest the initiative from the Catholics was even longer in its gestation. That was the introduction of a secondary school at Onitsha, the Dennis Memorial Grammar School, which opened finally in 1925.

The Society's committee proceedings throughout this period and letters written home by the missionaries leave no doubt that these innovations were directly associated with the Catholic threat to the CMS rate of conversion, and this is an indication of the role of native demand producing changes in the nature of the education being offered to them. However, not all the missionary societies were imbued with the hardline evangelical ideology of the CMS. The Church of Scotland Mission, for example, which had established schools in Kikuyu in Kenya, advocated from the time of Livingstone a strategy of 'commercialization'. They saw the incorporation of the African into wage labour as an effective means of inculcating the disciplines of their faith. One CSM missionary (quoted by Rigby, 1981), D.C.R. Scottl, argued for 'industrial work as a means of preparing Africans for conversion to the faith'. But this orientation cannot be taken outside the relationship between the missionaries and the white settler population in East Africa. It is to be remembered that there was no such population of any size in West Africa. Settlers were represented on the Kenya Board of Education from its inception in 1910 and were a powerful influence in the shaping of Kenyan education right up to the time of independence. The work so earnestly advocated by the missionaries turned out to be working for the settlers on their plantations and taking over the clerical and technical positions which were being filled in ever increasing numbers by Indian immigrants, much to the dismay of the colonial authorities. Indeed, at one point the pressure from the settlers resulted in a government circular advocating a scheme of forced labour, which was supported by many of the missionary societies. The missionaries also supported the settlers in their alienation of the native lands and, according to Rigby, they 'became the moral apologists for the expansion of capitalist settler interest' (p. 127). The result, in terms of education, was that Kenya acquired what was probably the most highly developed system of 'industrial education' in Africa. Between 1911 and 1934 both the Mission and the government schools were primarily vocational and from 1935 post-primary 'trade schools' were established. In the former period

Pupils were indentured as they entered primary school (that is after their four years of what was then called elementary school); most of their school day was organized around productive labour in the particular vocation to which they had been legally bound, and there was an opportunity to pick up the academic subjects at night school. Most pupils were indentured to follow the basic trades of masonry and carpentry, although in some missions it was possible to follow a course for hospital dressers, teachers and catechists. As the government grants-in-aid were primarily allocated for the artisans' apprenticeships, no school could attract substantial grants unless it technicalised itself. (King, 1977, p. 22)

Here then we have a point of colonial history and a set of specific structural conditions where the interests of the colonial government, the settlers and the missions appeared to coincide and give rise to a relatively well coordinated schooling system. The only group in this instance which did not find its needs and interests being served was the Africans themselves. However, this coordination of colonial interests is not typical of all the colonies. In Ghana the Basel Missions were the only ones to establish successfully a trade and agricultural training curriculum in their schools. In Nigeria attempts to introduce 'adapted' curricula had virtually no impact in the schools.

It is in the Kenyan case that we find probably the clearest support for Carnoy's contention that the missionaries may be considered as disseminators of capitalist ideology. But in general terms Carnoy's emphasis remains too crudely economistic. As social groups, the missionaries carried their own particular ideologies 'within the overall context of the intrusion of peripheral capitalism in its colonial form' (Rigby, 1981, p. 98). However, the materialistic superiority of the missionaries over the Africans certainly provided an image of wealth and power that the Africans sought to imitate and emulate.In this respect it may be argued that the missionaries 'stood for' the advantages and superiority of the culture and the economy of the colonizers. Even when the missionaries sought to reduce their own standards of living to the simplest level, they were materially far better off than the Africans to whom they preached. Despite the spiritual message of the missionaries, especially the rejection by the more evangelical societies of the teaching of secular skills, the Africans came to identify and value education as a source of individual material betterment. Sorrenson notes that 'no matter how genuine their motives, the missionaries could not avoid the African suspicion that a missionary was no better than a settler' (Sorrenson, 1968, p. 270). It is in this respect that the missionaries may be seen as 'carriers' of a capitalist ideological message.

Nonetheless, as suggested previously, the missionaries were not in every circumstance welcome partners in the colonial enterprise. I shall offer one brief illustration of conflict between missionary and commercial interests and then go on to examine the attempts by the colonial and metropolitan governments to influence and change the curriculum of the African colonial school.

The role of the missions in the West Indies provides a clear instance of a conflict of interests. Before the official ending of slavery in 1833 the missions were prohibited from establishing schools on the slave estates and were forcibly discouraged from establishing them elsewhere on the islands. As noted already, proselytization and conversion was normally achieved via a catechetical, functional literacy. To the slave owners literacy represented a threat to stability and to the maintenance of a compliant labour force. After abolition, the demand for schooling increased enormously as literacy came to be seen by the ex-slaves as a source of power and prestige previously monopolized by the whites. While the missionaries were not seeking in any way to undermine the established social order (indeed, they used their religious teaching to extol the virtues of obedience, thrift, etc.), the slaves and their children were 'not merely passive recipients of white middle class values, they reacted and modified such values in a sociological dynamic which in many ways helped create their own history' (Rooke, 1980, p. 74). Rooke notes that eventually even the missionaries came to see the educated catechists as rivals for their own jobs.

Colonial Policy and the 'Adapted Curriculum'

This distrust of the effects of literacy was not limited only to the settlers, estate owners and traders in the colonial territories. From the earliest point of intervention by the metropolitan government in the field of education of 'the natives', two themes are evident in their policies, recommendations and comments. One is the criticism of the 'bookish' nature of the curriculum offered in the native schools; the other is the criticism of the attributes and attitudes of the graduates of these academically oriented schools. The first systematic expression of British government views on education came in 1847 in the report by the Education Committee of the Privy Council to the Colonial Office.

> A short and simple account of the mode which the Committee of the Council on Education considers that industrial schools for the coloured races may be conducted in the colonies and to render the labour of the children available towards meeting some part of the expenses of their education.

There is also an indication here of the notion which was to become one of the major tenets of colonial policy. That is, that the provision of education should be self-financing. This was to have a considerable inhibiting effect, especially during periods of economic depression in the colonies. The other striking feature of this report is its anticipation of issues and policies that are currently being aired in the context of the so-called 'world education crisis'. According to the committee, the principal objectives of the education of the natives in the colonies should be:

1   to inculcate the principles and promote the influences of Christianity by such instruction as can be given in elementary schools;

2   to accustom the children of these races to habits of self-control and moral discipline;

3   to diffuse a grammatical knowledge of the English language as the most important agent of civilization;

4   to make the school the means of improving the condition of the peasantry by teaching them how health may be preserved by a proper diet, cleanliness, ventilation and clothing, and by the structure of their dwellings;

5   to give practical training in household economy and in the cultivation of the cottage garden as well as in those common handicrafts by which a labourer may improve his domestic comfort;

6   to communicate such a knowledge of writing and arithmetic and of their application to his wants and duties as may enable a peasant to economize his means, and give the small farmer the power to enter into calculations and agreements;

7   improved agriculture is required to replace the system of exhausting the virgin soils and then leaving to natural influences alone the work of reparation. The education of the coloured races would, therefore, not be complete for the children of small farmers, unless it included this object;

8   lesson books should teach the mutual interests of the mother country, and her dependencies, the natural basis of this connection and the domestic and social duties of the coloured races;

9   lesson books should also set forth simply the relation of wages, capital and labour, and the influence of local and general government on personal security, independence and order.

As Foster notes, 'The general aim was the development of "habits of steady industry" leading to a "settled and thriving peasantry" ' (p. 58). In the first aspect at least there is a direct comparison to be drawn with the contemporary attitudes towards the education of the working classes in Britain. As in the British context, these attitudes represented the dismissal and the stigmatization of a whole way of life. In the second aspect there is an illustration of the desire on the part of the metropolitan government, which as we shall see is constantly reiterated, *not to attract the African away from the land into the modern sector of the colonial economy.* Nor is it clear that this is an exhortation to teach the native African the skills of cash crop production. For those pupils who were to stay on into the period of secondary education two sorts of institutions were envisaged: 'Day Schools for Industry' with their own model farms, intended to be partly self-supporting, and 'Normal Schools' for the training of teachers. The latter were to have a curriculum including: Bible instruction; chemistry and its application to agriculture; land surveying and practical mensuration; the theory and practice of agriculture and gardening; and the management of farm stock. Not only does this report mark the first in a continuing series of attempts to 'adapt' the school curriculum in the colonies, but it also represents the first in a long line of failures to have such adaptation accepted by the Africans. As Foster points out, the view of the school embodied in the report's recommendations rests on two assumptions, both of which were to prove to be unfounded: first, that 'the creation of schools and curriculums' based on the economic development of agriculture 'would generate demand for such education among the "coloured races"' (Foster, 1965, p. 58); and secondly, that 'African expectations regarding the potential functions of educational institutions were congruent with those of Europeans, or could be made so' (p. 58).

The primary weakness of these recommendations lay in the failure of the Privy Council Committee to take into account the basis of 'attraction' for the existing colonial schools and the concomitant distribution of the schools. The vast majority of the existing schools were in the expanding urban areas and were attracting those Africans who saw opportunities of employment within the expanding commercial and government sectors of the colonial economy. The schools were not seen as a means to improve agricultural skills, but a route of escape from agricultural work altogether. Indeed, the number of low-level white-collar jobs available to the literate African was to keep expanding for sometime to come, alongside the increased penetration and exploitation by metropolitan economic interests. Thus, in several respects the scheme put forward in the report was unrealistic in its appraisal of the situation in the African colonies.

It must also be registered that there was a second agenda of concerns which underpinned the orientation of the report. These concerns were very much related to the initial impetus for the production of the report, and again constitute what may be seen to be another major factor of continuity in government policy towards colonial education. That is the perceived problem of unemployed school graduates whose knowledge and attitudes make them unsuitable for and unprepared for agricultural work or a trade. I shall return to this issue shortly.

The expansion of educational provision in the second half of the nineteenth century was marked by continuing African support for the traditional literacy-based schooling being offered by the missions. Indeed, there was increased pressure for a wider 'academic' curriculum and teaching in English, as we have seen in the case of the Niger missions. Here again there is the basis of the emergence of a conflict of interests between the missions and the metropolitan and colonial governments. However, paradoxically, the opportunity to 'bring the missions in line' which occurred towards the end of the nineteenth century, by means of 'grants-in-aid' payments, backed by government inspection of schools, reinforced aspects of the academic curriculum as well as providing a vehicle for the introduction of 'technical' subjects. Foster reports that in Ghana (The Gold Coast):

> the minimal curricular requirements, upon which grants were to be
> based included the provision of instruction in reading, writing, English

language, and arithmetic, with needlework for girls; grants could be
obtained for optional subjects such as English grammar, History and
Geography. (p. 82)

In 1898 drawing, industrial instruction and physical exercises were added to
the basic curriculum and singing, elementary science, book keeping, shorthand
and mensuration added to the list of options. In Barbados in 1900 the Inspector
of Schools reported on the initiation of a special grant-in-aid scheme for those
schools which gave two hours of 'technical instruction' each day. In 1907 in
Barbados agriculture for boys and needlework for girls were included in the list
of basic subjects for examination. In Kenya experimental grants for mission
schools offering 'technical instruction' were first offered in 1909 and, with the
establishment of the Education Department in 1911, a scheme of 'payment by
results' for industrial instruction was initiated. Anderson (1970) reports that 'by
1912 industrial training in basic skills such as smithing, carpentry, agriculture
and even typing was successfully under way' (p. 37). In Nigeria, however, in
relation to the employment needs of the colonial administration, the 'payment
by results' scheme was used almost exclusively to establish an 'academic'
curriculum based on the British elementary school of the time. In all these
areas the introduction of 'grants-in-aid' coincided with growing economic
difficulties among the missionary societies in maintaining their educational
provision. Few of the societies were able to resist for very long the attraction of
the 'grants-in-aid'. But, at very much the same time, another imported policy
innovation from Britain strengthened the hold of the missionaries over education at the local level: the attempt to introduce a system of local School Boards
along the lines of the 1870 Education Act. In most cases, especially outside the
towns, the missionaries were virtually the only people recognized as capable of
serving on such Boards.

One additional factor, applying in the West African colonies (Nigeria, The
Gold Coast, Sierra Leone and The Gambia), in the Educational Ordinance of
1882, was the making of religion optional in 'assisted schools' and its total
prohibition in government schools. This clause, again deriving from educational legislation in Britain, served to exacerbate the conflict between the state and
the missionaries over the purpose and the content of schooling.

From 1900 onwards three distinct themes are marked out in the conflict
over educational provision in the colonies: (1) the increasing level of reaction
within the colonial authorities to the 'dysfunctions' of the academic/literary
school curriculum; (2) the increasing emphasis given by colonial education
authorities to the need for a 'relevant' agricultural/technical curriculum; (3) the
increasing level of overt African resistance to such an 'adapted' curriculum in
their schools. These themes are obviously strongly interrelated. One interrela-
tion is that of *social control*. I want to argue that there is more than one
dimension to such an analysis of educational provision in the colonies. The
major strategy of social control with regard to education is not the emphasis on
socializing the African and producing an obedient and industrious worker,

although that is strongly represented in educational policy. The main feature of social control is the denial of schooling to the vast majority of the African population. Both of these aspects of social control, limited access and limited provision on the one hand, and attempts to impose an 'adapted' curriculum on the other, can be seen to be related to previous colonial experience and to the increasing manifestation of social problems of various kinds among educated school leavers in the African colonies.

To some extent educational policy in the colonies in the early years of this century is representative of the dilemma faced by the colonial administration: on one side the demands for educated personnel in the rapidly expanding areas of government bureaucracy, trade and industry, together with the demands of the Africans themselves for formal education; and on the other side the political and social disturbance created by the unemployed or dissatisfied among the educated Africans. The writings of educationalists and government officials of this period are littered with references to the negative consequences of education for the 'coloured races'. In Nigeria Governor-General J.D. Lugard was particularly critical of the education provided by the missionaries, describing their products as 'lacking in integrity, self-control and discipline ... [and showing] ... no respect for authority.' Elaborating on this theme he also records that:

> Education has brought to such men only discontent, suspicion of others, and bitterness, which masquerades as racial patriotism.... As citizens they are unfitted to hold posts of trust and responsibility where integrity and loyalty are essential. (Lugard, 1929, p. 429)

Somewhat later Miller, in his pamphlet *Have We Failed in Nigeria* (1947), argues that the educated Nigerian was usually a 'spoiled, degenerate creature, vicious, unreliable and immoral'. In common with Lugard he sees 'the great failure in our system of education ... to be in the production of character' (p. 92). Thus in 1916 Lugard sponsored an Educational Ordinance in Nigeria aimed at rectifying the shortcomings of mission education and re-emphasizing the role of character training.

In a similar vein Gordon (1963, p. 135) quotes the West Indies newspaper, *The Echo* (18 July 1898), as critical of the schools for turning out 'lads and lasses whose memories were well stocked with fundamental knowledge but who found it difficult to find a job because of the lack of skills', adding that they were, as a result, becoming 'pests of the society'. Referring to The Gold Coast, Foster (1965) notes that the unemployed products of schools were characterized as 'dishonest, unwilling to undertake employment, and willing to live by their wits at the expense of their illiterate brethren' (p. 68). Batten, a long serving colonial administrator, wrote in his *Lectures on Education in Colonial Society* that:

> the present picture is one of ferment and conflict in which the individual, much more than in the past, sees himself and his private

interests ever more clearly, and society and his duties to it as something outside himself, demanding and frustrating. The ranks of criminals, delinquents and other social misfits appear to be most largely recruited, not from the illiterate peasants, or from the best educated, but from the products of the schools.

Even where technical schooling had taken root, as in Kenya, the outcomes in terms of the aspirations and orientations of the graduates were not always those anticipated by the providers. Thus King, discussing the graduates of the Kenyan trade schools, suggests that:

> It is quite understandable that boys and girls are in a sense the aristocracy of the school population should think of themselves as 'big people', and that even boys in technical and vocational schools should see themselves being prepared for careers of directing and supervising others rather than having a direct practical orientation to their work. (King, 1977, p. 20)

This is one indication of a typical pattern of the functional use by individuals of any kind of schooling experience and certification as a means of access to sought-after non-manual employment. This casts the school, whatever its intended training objectives, into the role of what Kinsey (1970) calls a 'conduit institution' (p. 80). He gives the example of the use made by students of the Tunisian Khalduniya college, set up with the intention of training teachers of Arabic for government schools, as a 'conduit' which 'led to non-educational jobs in the modern sector'. This kind of 'misuse' of educational provision by pupils reinforced the opinion held by some colonialists that any kind of schooling for 'the natives' would have undesirable consequences.

In the *Report of the Commission on Native Education in Southern Rhodesia* it is noted that:

> ... a clear majority of Rhodesian women, a large number of whom are fair and indulgent mistresses, have the opinion that mission-trained Natives are self-assertive and impudent. It is also said that mission natives are not as honest as 'raw' Natives.

What appears to lie behind this kind of statement is the notion that education can 'spoil' 'the native'. But the deleterious effects of education were not solely linked with the development of 'unhealthy' social characteristics on an individual level. Large-scale threats to social order were perceived by some. Anderson (1970) reports the underlying conflict of perspectives between the District Commissioners in Kenya, who held the responsibility for the maintenance of law and order at a local level, and missionaries and others interested in the expansion and development of African education. 'Too much Education for many of them [DC's] spelt too fast a pace of change and therefore disturbances which might alter the whole frame of control which they had built up in their areas' (p. 40). The fears and concerns of the anti-education Europeans and those who urged gradualist strategies of change were directly related to what they saw as the destabilizing effects of the *detribalization* of the African — the creation, that is, of a rootless class of urban 'malcontents' lacking in respect for traditional tribal authority and poorly socialized with regard to the behavioural standards of the white society. This was one of several factors which gave credence to Lugard's concept of *indirect rule*, which was to have a particular impact on British colonial education policy throughout the period up to the end of the Second World War. Access to schooling was to continue to be extremely limited especially at post-elementary level. Renewed efforts were made to orient the school curriculum to the village, to aspects of traditional culture and to bolster the traditional forms of tribal authority.

Another strand in the policy, and one which directly linked the attempt to revitalize traditional tribal authority with selection and sponsorship in education, was the attempt in several of the colonies to establish schools specifically for the sons of tribal chiefs and government appointed headmen. In The Gold Coast, as Foster reports, the traditional elites had not availed themselves of the opportunities of Western education and the emergence of an African intelligentsia with no base in the traditional authority system had led to antagonism and political instability, despite British attempts to bolster the authority of the chiefs. Support for tribal authority was fundamental to *indirect rule* and Lugard argued that the

> Identification of the ruling class with the Government accentuates the corresponding obligation to check mal-practice on their part. The task of educating them in the duties of a ruler becomes more than ever insistent; of inculcating a sense of responsibility; of convincing their intelligence of the advantages which accrue from the material prosperity of the peasantry, from free labour and initiative; of the necessity of delegating powers to trusted subordinates; of the evils of favouritism and bribery; of the importance of education, especially for the ruling class, and for the filling of lucrative posts under government ...
> (Lugard, 1929, pp. 210–11)

The Phelps-Stokes report criticized missionary schools for their failure to make any differentiation between 'the education of the masses' and 'the development and training of Native leaders' (Jones, 1922, p. 57). The report urged the need for education to be planned in relation to such a differentiation. The political service hoped that, by limiting access to post-primary education and the literary/academic curriculum, they would be able to reproduce and control a neo-traditional native elite and avoid the creation of an unemployable educated group. There are many examples in Africa and elsewhere of attempts by the colonial authorities, and in some cases also the missions, to establish schools for the sons of chiefs with varying degrees of success. In Uganda the development of the 'high school' system of schools, modelled on the British public school tradition, was based almost entirely upon the provision of boarding education for the sons and other relatives of chiefs.

> Mento High School was opened in 1905 with the aim of training the sons of chiefs. All of its first forty students were sons of chiefs ... Iganga Girls' School was built to cater for the daughters of chiefs.... Moreover, the fees paid in these High Schools were so high at that time that only sons of the rich — who were chiefs at the time — could afford to pay. (Kasozi, 1977, p. 80)

The structure of the modern Ugandan education system, and many of its problems, are directly related to the high school system which developed between 1905 and 1950 almost exclusively for the education of the traditional elite.

In contrast to the 'success' of the Ugandan schools, similar attempts to establish schools for the sons of chiefs in the Dagomba region of the Ghanaian Northern Territories made little headway against the reluctance of the local aristocracy. Staniland (1975) reports that:

> One or two divisional chiefs' sons were enrolled, but other chiefs sent the children of slaves or commoners, fearing that the European schools would turn their sons into labourers or stewards. (p. 54)

Duncan-Johnstone, a Provincial Commissioner in the Northern Territories, and a staunch supporter of the policy of indirect rule, proposed in 1930 the establishment in the government school in Tamale of a special division for the training of 'the future governing class' in the responsibilities of native administration. A curriculum including administrative studies, local history, English, animal health and road maintenance was envisaged. This straightforwardly reflects the concerns and interests of the political service. However, despite the attempts of District Commissioners to persuade chiefs to allow their sons to be enrolled, the scheme was never implemented. As far as the children of commoners were concerned, the administration used its influence to restrict the numbers of children moving beyond standard III schooling: the administration was haunted by the fear of a repetition of events in the south, where, it was thought, the authorities had 'allowed education to outstrip native administration in the race of progress' (Staniland, 1975, p. 99).

It is only in the case of the education of traditional elites that an orthodox 'education as social control' thesis can be pursued with any confidence, for it is only at this level that colonial education policies were aimed at the Europeanization of 'the native', inasmuch as 'both the missionaries and the government wanted to have an influence on society through powerful individuals sympathetic to their views' (Kasozi, 1977), p. 83). As far as the education of the masses is concerned, the strategies employed by the colonial administrations cast education in the role of disrupter of political stability rather than as a means of achieving political hegemony. The schooling of the masses must be seen in terms of policies of exclusion from schooling altogether or at least exclusion from the literary/academic curriculum.

Over and above the immediate political problems which had emerged from the colonial experience in Africa there is one other factor which supported the particular direction given to education policy: the 'lessons that were learned' from the free rein given to the development of academic education in India. The links between India and the policy in Africa and between education and social disorder are clearly made in the following comments from Arthur Mayhew, the longstanding Secretary of the Colonial Office Advisory Committee on Education. Defending the expense of attempts to develop a limited access system of technical and vocational education in Africa, he wrote:

> The high cost per head is a necessary result of our African policy, born of bitter experience in India; a policy of caution and firm foundations, advancing gradually from a few selected and well-equipped centres in slowly widening circles, secondary education being restricted with reference to local demand and the more urgent claims of primary education. (Mayhew, 1938, pp. 195–6)

And on the consequences of unchecked expansion of education:

> There is a tendency which, although natural, is capable of perversion, to guard against a surplus production of graduates which may stimulate unrest and discontent. (p. 179)

Lord Lugard, also for some time a member of the CAC, made a similar connection:

> The system which had proved so disastrous in India had its counterpart in the Crown Colonies and dependencies, and its results were similar. The lessons of India were ignored. I have already quoted the opinion of a French writer that a literary education on European lines had mischievous results, and only produces hostility and ingratitude. The results achieved by Holland, and to a lesser degree by Germany, in their Eastern Colonies are contrasted to our disadvantage. In South Africa General Smuts has recently described the existing system as 'wholly unsuited to native needs, and positively pernicious, leading the native to a dead wall over which he is unable to rise, and he becomes ready prey to the agitator'. (Lugard, 1929, p. 429)

Specifically, secondary education, in the minds of colonial administrators in Britain and Africa, became associated with political unrest. Thus the school came to be seen neither as an instrument of mass political socialization nor as a means of inculcating Western values. Rather, as more recent manpower planning theorists have urged, access to education and the rate of expansion of provision were to be directly linked to the needs of the economy (for example, in Kenya to train Africans to replace the Indian immigrant workers and provide labour for the settler-owned coffee plantations) with the majority of school attenders experiencing a village oriented, skills-based curriculum.

Support and impetus were given to these policies by the influential reports of the Phelps-Stokes Commission, an American funded investigation into

African education which visited West and South Africa in 1921 and East and Central Africa in 1924. The reports, *Education in Africa: A Study of West, South and Equitorial Africa by the African Education Commission* (1922) and *Education in East Africa* (1925), were both written by Jesse Jones. The Commission was appointed by the British government, which warmly received their reports. The original conception of the commission was very much an outcome of the concern felt by some of the protestant missions, the American Baptist Foreign Missionary Society in particular, about the state of education in Africa.

The reports of the Commission were very much influenced by the work of black American educators at the Hampton and Tuskegee Colleges, and parallels were drawn between the educational problems of the American negro and the African. As a result of this transfer of concepts, the emphasis of the reports was on the role of *rural education*. The 'wholesale transfer of the educational conventions of Europe' (p. 16) to Africa was strongly criticized as 'educational slavery' (p. 36). The commission advised in their stead 'the adaption of education to the needs of the people ... and ... to African conditions' (p. 11), to include agricultural education and 'the simpler elements of trades required in Native villages and to prepare for the less skilled occupations in industrial concerns' (p. 71).

There is an interesting parallel here with educational policies in Great Britain in the same period. There the development and spread of rural education and rural studies teaching in rural schools was encouraged in Parliament and the Board of Education as a means of discouraging the movement of young people into the cities (Goodson, 1983). A Board of Education circular published in 1925 (quoted in Goodson) concluded that '... it appears desirable at the present time to emphasise afresh the principle that the education given in rural schools should be ultimately related to rural conditions of life.' Goodson notes that 'the argument leads plainly to the need for studies particularly designed for rural children' (p. 92), and he quotes a rural studies teacher as saying that 'there is no doubt that working people resented this attempt to keep them in their place.'

Returning to the Phelps-Stokes reports, the need for a small sector of academic education to feed into the professions was also recognized. The use of vernacular languages was recommended for the lower elementary forms, with English reserved for those who reached the upper standards. It was urged that subjects like history and geography should be more related to 'the record of our own institutions and activities than that of strangers' (p. 67). These educational recommendations were then set within a wider framework of social change advocating the adaption of 'primitive' and 'civilized' culture so that 'the people shall be urged and developed according to the best experience of both ...' (p. 86).

But Anderson (1970) makes the point that no account was taken in the reports of African participation in politics and decision-making, 'it badly neglected his aspirations for individual and political advancement'. (p. 20). The reports of the Commission were closely followed by the publication by the Colonial Office Advisory Committee on Education (formed in 1923) of a *Memorandum on Educational Policy in British Tropical Africa* (1925), the main emphases of which Foster (1965) notes as being 'generally similar to those of the Phelps-Stokes Commissions but amplifications were made concerning the precise application of principles within British colonial areas' (p. 160). Significantly, increased government supervision of education was stressed. Foster summarizes the main points of this and the subsequent *Memorandum on the Education of African Communities* (1935) as follows.

1 The structure of education was to be based on the continued activities of voluntary agencies but with general direction of policy in the hands of the respective colonial governments.
2 The schools were to be adapted to native life.
3 Grants-in-aid were to be made on the basis of efficiency.
4 The use of local vernaculars in education, particularly in the lower forms, was to be stressed.
5 There was a growing need for more active supervision of schools by the colonial governments.
6 Great stress was laid on the need for technical, vocational and agricultural training at the expense of more 'traditional' subjects within the curriculum.
7 There was an increasing awareness of the need to expand educational facilities for women and girls (pp. 159–60).

Again, remarkable similarities are apparent between these policies and the literature on non-formal education which emerged in the 1970s from the analysis of the world-wide educational malaise which seemed to undercut the reliance that had been placed by developing nations on the 'take-off' effects of formal educational expansion. But in the 1920s and 1930s, while the social problems associated with formal academic/literary education were already long established, the rationale behind the attempts to limit growth in this area was motivated in a somewhat different way, as we have seen. The ramifications of Phelps-Stokes are apparent throughout the British colonies but we must not fall into the trap of assuming that there was a straightforward and unproblematic transfer of policy into practice. In particular, the role of African *resistance* to 'adapted' education must not be ignored, and this is discussed below. Nonetheless, it is possible to trace the impact of these policies in a number of ways, for example, in the holding down of educational expansion. Figures from The Gold Coast Annual Education report of 1934 analyzed by Mumford and Jackson (1938) show the total numbers of children attending school year by year for the previous twenty-five years (1911–34). The trend of increase so shown reveals that it would have taken 600 years before the number attending school would have been as great as the child population figures of the 1931 census. However, when these figures were amended to take account of the increase in population, the trend suggested it would take 3500 years before primary education would have been made available to 100 per cent of the child school-age population. In Kenya, as King (1977) notes:

> the colonial government had a very effective examination hurdle low down the primary cycle, which meant that 65 to 75 per cent of all standard four children never went on to the last four years of primary education. (p. 16)

Furthermore, as recommended in the Colonial Office memorandum, English was only taught in the upper standards. The introduction of trade schools and vocational training in Kenya has already been recorded. In The Gold Coast, Kenya and elsewhere all pressures from the Africans to establish government secondary schools were resisted by the colonial authorities and most government expenditure went in grants-in-aid to the mission schools. As a result,' in 1939 there was still no secondary education for Africans anywhere in Central Africa' (Gray, 1960 p. 142). This position was carefully sustained in Central and East Africa by a rigid racial segregation of schooling for the European settlers, the Indians and the Africans. Koinage (quoted in Anderson, 1970, p. 141) reports the Kenya government as spending £59 on each European child, £4 16s 0d on each Asian child, and £1 10s 0d on each African child per annum. In some cases it is possible to establish a direct link between political policy and the holding down or reversal of educational expansion. In 1930 Morris, Director of Education in Uganda, closed four of the eight junior secondary schools in the Protectorate because of what he saw as the consequences of the overproduction of school graduates who would be 'the political emissaries of agitation and discontent' and have no outlet for their energies 'but political intrigue and the flouting of authority' (Uganda, 1930, p. 7). In 1924 in the Northern Territories of Ghana a Superintendent of Schools was appointed, the Reverend A.H. Chandler, 'and made answerable directly to the Colonial Secretary in Accra, instead of the Education Department' (Staniland, 1975, p. 55). During Chandler's period of administration all schooling above standard IV was ended outside Tamale, the administrative centre of the Territories, and access to the Tamale schools was heavily restricted. In every case alongside these restrictions on educational provision

> officials sought to revitalize tribal authority and to restrict the ambitions of the emergent few. Black and white teachers were encouraged to regard African children as members of a traditional rural society, which slowly and cautiously would adopt the modern blessings of hygiene, morals and manure. (Gray, 1960, p. 134)

Taking Kenya again, recognizing the particular influence of the existence of a permanent and economically dominant white settler group, we can also note the particular orientation given to the rural education offered in the school agricultural programmes. The growing of plantation crops by the Africans was forbidden. It was clearly intended that they should not be allowed to emerge in competition with the white plantation owners. The Africans were interested in *ngirigaca* (a Kikuyu corruption of the English word for agriculture), learning, that is, the European skills involved in the cultivation of cash crops. They were not interested in *urime* (farming of a traditional kind) or *gicumba* (digging), although it was these last two that were represented in the rural education curricula of the bush schools. The effects of adaptation were not limited to the East African schools. In West Africa also there were attempts to change the direction of development of African education. In Nigeria, in the absence of a permanent white settler community, a limited system of secondary education had developed (twenty secondary grammar schools were established by 1930, ten of them government schools). Attempts at adaptation here included changes being made by the British overseas examining bodies in the contents of their School Certificate and Matriculation Examinations. At the instigation of the Colonial Office Advisory Committee, the English universities involved in overseas examining expressed a willingness, in the best traditions of Phelps-Stokes, to modify their syllabuses 'in order that the external examination system might be adapted to local needs' and to ensure that colonial subjects were 'not being forced into an educational mould that might deform their particular attitudes and unfit them for a life in their own country' (University of London, Minutes, 1935–36). In 1935 a Sub-Committee was set up to coordinate the activities of the examining bodies. The Sub-Committee finally recommended that three examination subjects seemed appropriate for adaptation: botany, by the substitution of local plants; geography, by giving greater emphasis to local geography; and English language, where both topic material more relevant to African interests (the forest, native markets, popular superstitions, native salutations and greetings, polygamy, the choice of career for an educated African, the good and bad characteristics of native religions) and options in vernacular languages could be introduced. The University of London subsequently accepted Hausa and Yoruba as suitable as academic subjects, as special language options. Both Efik and Igbo were rejected because, among other things, they lacked sufficient native literature for 'an adequate test of proficiency' to be conducted. Even so, a success in any of the Certificates continued to require the candidate to pass the English language paper.

In 1935 the Advisory Committee also considered a recommendation, from one of its members who had recently made a tour of Africa, for the sponsorship of textbooks on African history, but this appeared to come to nothing.

It is important to put the scale and the impact of these examination changes into perspective. The remaining subjects in the examinations were left intact (apart from some changes in art) and continued to be examined in English (see Table 1). Even the Africanized essay topics were to be written in English. The other paraphernalia, rituals and experiences of an English secondary education continued to be a part of the school careers of those Nigerian pupils who gained access to the secondary grammar schools — 'The use of uniforms, college blazers and caps, cutlery and the English language continued undisturbed' (Omolewa, 1976, p. 114).

Table 1.   School Examination Subjects in Nigeria, 1916–36

	Subjects offered to Nigerians before adaptation	Subjects offered to Nigerians after adaptation
Group I:	English	English
Group II:	History	History
	Religious Knowledge	Religious Knowledge
	Latin	Latin
		Yoruba
Group III:	Arithmetic	Arithmetic
	Geometry	Geometry
	Algebra	Algebra
	Geography	Geography
	Physics-with-Chemistry	Chemistry
		Botany
		Biology
Group IV:	Drawing	Drawing
		Book-keeping
		Shorthand
		Art

Note: Candidates were expected to pass in a minimum of five subjects taken from at least three groups including Group I.

Source: Annual Reports and Examiners' Reports of the Oxford Delegacy for Local Examinations, Cambridge University Local Examinations Syndicate, and the University of London Matriculation and Schools Examinations Council, 1916–36.

Nor was the African's motivation to obtain School Certificates abated by the adaptations, nor did the renaming of the School Certificate examination as the Overseas School Certificate

> bring any noticeable changes in the performance of Nigerian students. Many of them, who came from good, well-equipped schools, continued over the years to do very well in the examinations, whilst those from the schools where there were few competent teachers and ill-equipped library and laboratory facilities, continued to do poorly at examinations. (Omolewa, 1976, p. 114)

Again this was not in small part due to the resistance of the Nigerians to the philosophy of adaptation. There was, Omolewa reports, 'a very strong suspicion among Nigerians that they were considered unworthy of English education' (p. 109). The policy of adaptation was also heartily condemned by many established members of the educated African elite.

While it is the case that the Phelps-Stokes Commissions provided the colonial authorites with a powerful ideology of legitimation for the policy of adaptation throughout Africa and the other colonies,[2] there was also a second, but publically less acceptable, legitimating ideology at work, an ideology of *racism.* This was based on the idea of the intellectual inferiority of the African.

Thus Anderson (1970) notes that 'a recurring basic assumption made by Europeans was that the African was innately less intelligent than the European and therefore needed a long period of practical education, before any further plans for his development could be considered' (p. 61). Such an assumption is certainly evident in the views and writings of many missionary educators. It was frequently considered that a minimal ability to read the scriptures was the most that could be expected in the way of intellectual achievement from the vast majority of the mission schoolpupils. Even the achievements of the successful African pupils could be dismissed; J.W.C. Dougall (1926) writes that:

> It is noteworthy that the efforts of pupils is given to the feat of memorization and those who know the African will agree in expressing astonishment at his remarkable power of verbal memory *as against* his power of understanding meaning. (p. 497, my emphasis)

Exactly the same arguments were levelled against the examination performances of those pupils who passed junior, higher and matriculation examinations. W.H. Maclean (1932) put the exceptional performances of colonial students in these examinations down to 'their highly developed faculty for passing our usual type of examination by feat of memory without any understanding' (quoted in Omolewa, 1976, p. 122). Sir Michael Sadler, a member of the Colonial Office Advisory Committee on Education, expressed a similar view at a committee meeting in 1932. He argued that 'the natives had such a power of memorising that they gave on paper a misleading impression of skill and ability' (quoted in Omolewa, 1976, p. 112). But, as Omolewa notes, 'when the African candidates failed the examinations, they were considered by those who believed in their ineducability as true images of their backward society' (p. 112). Heads I win, tails you lose. Thus 'for long stretches of the colonial era, ... Africans as a group were thought sufficiently different from Europeans not to merit the same access to knowledge' (King, 1977, p. 15). In addition to the arguments stressing the political and social undesirability of African access to European education, and those which emphasized the need to adapt the education being offered to the 'needs' and 'conditions' of the African, it was being suggested in the 1920s and 1930s that the Africans lacked the intellectual ability to benefit in any real way from European subject matter.

African Resistance and the Academic Curriculum

As indicated already, the realities of African education cannot simply be read off from the colonial policies formulated in London. In particular, it is necessary to take account of the role of African *resistance* to colonial policy on education. This resistance takes several forms: there was the pressure exerted on the missions and the colonial governments to increase the provision of schools; in addition, there was specific pressure to provide secondary and further education opportunities for the African pupil; and finally, there was opposition to attempts to 'adapt' the curriculum of the African school. These forms of resistance are related, naturally enough, to the Africans' perception of the role of education, collectively and individually, in their future. In particular, as noted already, education was seen to be one source of the material superiority of the white colonialists, and a route for individual social mobility. For example, Anderson (1970) quotes two extracts from essays written in 1930 by Alliance High School pupils under the title 'Why I Go to School' (p. 10):

> If I go to school and get much knowledge I would not always work for others but I may have much money, I will look for many workmen.

> I myself want to go to school. But every boy who does not want to go to school is stupid. You can't be a great man without going to school. If you want to be a great man then go to school.

Where secondary education was established the emphasis on preparation for the Overseas Examinations provided the successful pupil with the opportunity to proceed to higher education in Britain or elsewhere.

Thus we find, as early as 1885 in the Cape, opposition from African school graduates to the plans to drop Latin and Greek from the curriculum of Lovedale School. Anderson (1970) records a strike of boys at Maseno School in 1908 who refused to take part in manual labour and made demands for more reading and writing. The early African enthusiasm for technical education soon wore off as they came to realize that the sort of skills being offered were directed at preparation for routine subordinate positions. Increasingly the missions and the colonial authorities came under pressure to provide an academic/literary curriculum that would prepare the successful pupil for a lucrative government or commercial post as clerk. As we have seen previously, the Africans also resisted the limitations of the narrow catechistic curricula, taught in the vernacular, by many of the evangelical missionary schools. Ndabaninga Sithole, himself a Wesleyan missionary school pupil, captures the perceptions and aspirations of the African pupil in these comments on his schooldays:

> ... to us education meant reading books, writing and talking English, and doing arithmetic.... At our homes we have done a lot of ploughing, planting, weeding and harvesting.... We knew how to do these things. What we knew was not education; education was what we did not know. We wanted as we said to Ndebele, 'to learn the book until it remained in our heads, to speak English until we could speak it through our noses.' (Sithole, 1950)

In Bernsteinian terms what Sithole is describing and demanding in this passage is the strong framing of a literary/academic education. That is to say, a strong 'boundary relationship between what may be taught and what may not be taught', between 'non-school everyday community knowledge' and 'educational knowledge' (Bernstein, 1971, p. 50). In terms of individual social mobility, the literary/academic curriculum was regarded by the African pupils as 'vocational' inasmuch as it provided the possibility of employment in the wage sector of the economy. There is perhaps a second reading of Sithole's comments, in which we can see the commitment to an academic/literary school-based education reflecting back as a rejection of, and to some extent alienation from, the traditional tribal culture 'as a whole way of life'. This may be seen more clearly in the following contrasts drawn by a 'school Xhosa' (a Christian mission educated Xhosa) between himself and the traditional, tribal 'red Xhosa'.

> The difference between a Red man and myself is that I wear clothes like white people's, as expensive as I can afford, while he is satisfied with old clothes and lets his wife go about in a Red dress. After washing I smear vaseline on my face: he uses red ocre to look nice. He is illiterate whereas I can read and write. I want to educate my children, but he just wants to circumcise his boys so that he should have a daughter-in-law. A Red man attends sacrifices but I attend church. I pray for my sins when I am sick. He knows nothing about sins, and approaches a diviner for his illnesses. I was baptized, he was sacrificed for. I may not use any words that are obscene, but he uses any type of words, even in the presence of his elders, without fear or rebuke. (quoted in Mayer, 1961, p. 21)

Discussing this cultural separation between the 'school Xhosa' and the 'red Xhosa', Mayer (1961) notes that 'the Xhosa think of this division as bisecting their entire population' (p. 20). Clearly, for the 'school Xhosa' the acquisition of a European education also involves the acquisition of European values and life style, and aspirations and consumption patterns taken from European 'models'.

It is important to reiterate the point that the perceived relationship between academic/literary certification and wage employment was at many points during the colonial period a realistic assessment of the job market on the African's part. Some at least of the claims made about levels of unemployment among school leavers during this period are unsubstantiated attempts to bolster the case for industrial and agricultural education. This is evident, for example, in the account by the Rev. Kemp of the state of affairs surrounding his mission in The Gold Coast in 1891.

> We have been told that our schools simply glutted the market with clerks. For our own part, we have most earnestly wished that there was even a shadow of truth in this statement. Were this really the case, we, as a Mission, should not find so much difficulty, when desiring teachers and catechists for our own work, in competing with merchants in their tempting salaries to our young men. And further, we should not have expressed the strong feeling of disgust that the merchants and the Government alike so constantly employed young men without references from us. But this nevertheless, has been our experience, so great

was their desire to employ the candidates, with or without testimonials. (Kemp, 1898, p. 148)

Here again is the contradiction between the metropolitan government policy of industrial and agricultural education and the colonial administration's need for literate educated clerks. The same contradiction at a much later time is recorded in the case of Guyana by Bacus (1974). Here, government attempts to orient the primary school curriculum to agricultural employment can be set against the differing levels of unemployment in the occupation market (see Table 2).

Table 2. Percentage of Employed and Number of Unemployed to Each Vacancy in Different Occupational Groups in Guyana in 1965

Occupational group	Percentage unemployed	Number unemployed to each vacancy
Professional	0.0	0.00
Non-professional with specialized training	0.3	0.47
Administrative, executive and supervisory	0.1	0.20
Clerical and sales workers	6.4	7.64
Other service workers	10.7	20.30
Craftsmen and technical workers	19.2	12.22
Manual workers	39.9	108.86

The *resistance* to 'adapted' education by pupils and parents not only took the form of representations or political action. In the day-to-day running of the schools the pupils were able to subvert the attempts to impose non-academic subjects by devoting their energies only to those subjects which they saw as being useful in terms of their job aspirations. Religious instruction and rural studies lessons were simply not attended to or taken seriously. Humphries (1981) describes similar processes at work in Great Britain, 'subverting the school syllabus', through the resistance of working-class pupils to religious instruction in schools in the period 1889–1939. He reports that 'both oral and documentary evidence suggests that school authorities met with widespread resistance to their effort to shape the religious character of working-class children' (p. 33). Humphries also traces the occurrence of school strikes by pupils during this period but here the motives tended to be concerned with getting less of what was offered at school rather than more, as was the case in Africa. In African schools pressure was also exerted on the teachers to confine themselves to those topics covered by the examination syllabuses. But the most dramatic, and in some respects, most successful line of resistance was the setting up by the Africans of independent schools of their own. In East Africa in 1929 the Kikuyu Karing'a Education Association was formed to coordinate the work of a number of already existing independent Kikuyu schools. These independent schools were closely linked to the establishment of independent African churches.

The attitude of the colonial government to these independent schools was initially sceptical. There was clearly a fear of the political role being played by these African controlled institutions. But as Anderson (1970, p. 127) reports, the government increasingly came to accept the existence of these schools as a part of the overall educational provision in the colony. From 1935 the annual reports of the Department of Education began to record these schools in its statistics (see Table 3).

Table 3. *British Colonial Records of Numbers of Schools and Pupils in Africa*

	Schools	Pupils
1935	34	2,510
1936	44	3,984
1937	54	7,223
1938	41	6,494

Source: Annual reports of the Department of Education

These are registered schools but there was also a small number that were unregistered. These schools were inspected by the Department and, according to the 1938 report, 'increased efficiency in these schools is evidenced by the results of the Common Entrance Examination to the primary schools. In 1936 five were successful, in 1937, fifteen were successful. During the present year, out of 199 candidates, 27 passed. One third of the total acceptance of Kagumo were pupils from independent schools' (Anderson, 1970, p. 127). These schools were normally built and supported by the local community and often run by a single teacher working without salary. In the larger schools headmasters were appointed or provided by the Department of Education. This independent school movement led in 1939 to the establishment of Githunguri College, an independent teacher training college and the first post-primary educational provision for Africans in the whole of Central and East Africa. The aim was to produce students, who, whilst able to handle so-called "European knowledge and techniques" remained firmly linked with their African heritage and committed to achieving an African form of modern independent society' (Anderson, 1970, p. 124). Among those who were teachers at Githunguri was Jomo Kenyatta. The College attempted to escape from the restrictions placed on the normal school curriculum by the government and was regarded with some hostility both by the government and the missions. Several of the teachers became involved in political activities, and lectures on politics and current affairs were offered in addition to the normal curriculum subjects. The College was eventually closed in 1952. Indeed, it is a significant reflection on the colonial government's view of the independent schools and their overall attitude to African education that at the outbreak of the 'emergency' in Kenya the whole independent school system was closed. The government clearly saw the independent schools as a base for political opposition. While less organized and coordinated, a similar pattern of self-help, in the founding of community schools, is to be found in Nigeria during the period 1939–60. Most of this development took place at the secondary level with the setting up of secondary grammar schools. In 1940 there were twenty-nine secondary schools in Nigeria, twelve of them government schools; by 1960 there were 227 secondary schools, twenty-six of them government schools. Almost all of this expansion was the outcome of local community effort. The schools established, while varying enormously in their facilities, equipment, quality of teachers, etc., were uniformly modelled on the British grammar school of the period and provided for 'the intensification of the process of acceptance of the literary tradition introduced by the Christian missions through formal classroom education' (Fajana, 1972, p. 381). Again the founding of these schools was closely linked to pupil and parental aspirations toward employment in the expanding modern sector of the economy. These aspirations were not limited only to those Africans who had come under the influence of the Christian missionaries. In the Muslim regions Ahmadiyyah separatist schools were set up on the basis of Western educational curricula and methods.

The effects of the African push for access to a Western literary/academic education are plainly marked in the current provision of education in most ex-colonial societies, not least because the majority of education officials and teachers had acquired their own education through the academic system. I have argued that the demand for such an education was often related to individual mobility aspirations and has to be set against the various attempts by the colonial and metropolitan governments to impose 'adapted' forms of education. However, the arguments put forward by the colonial authorities, supported by the Phelps-Stokes Commission reports, for example, were quickly 'penetrated' (Willis, 1977) by the Africans. But, as Willis argues, 'Penetrations are not only crucially skewed and deprived of their independence, but also bound back finally into the structure they are uncovering in complex ways by internal and external limitations' (p. 119). That is to say, there is 'a "partial" relationship of these penetrations to that which they seem to be independent of, and see into' (p. 119).

The African 'resistance' to forms of 'adapted' education may be seen to lie in the 'cultural insights' embodied in the demand for a Western style academic/literary curriculum, though we must bear in mind Willis' point that 'in their very formation these insights are distorted, turned and deposited into other forms' (p. 121). These 'insights' provide a penetration of the ideological complex surrounding the legitimation of 'adapted' education in terms of the 'needs' of African society, the long process of development towards self-government and the 'conditions' of economic production in the colonies. These were overlain, as I have already suggested, by expressions of African racial inferiority. The African came to see the social, economic and material advantages of the colonizers as founded upon their access to and control of education. For some this was a realization related to the potential for personal advance. For others, education was seen to be the key to mass political consciousness. In each case, the process of education was identified with the skills of literacy and separated from the known skills of agriculture: 'Education was what we did not know' (Sithole, 1950). The equality of the African and the drive for education are expressed in Nnamdi Azikiwe's poetic advice to African youth, which significantly is stated in the imagery of Greek mythology.

> There is no achievement which
> Is possible to human beings which
> Is not possible to Africans
> Your studies in Logic should
> Lead to the correct conclusions
> Therefore go forth, thou
> Son of Africa, and return
> home laden with the
> Golden Fleece.

W.E.B. Dubois, an African educationalist, has a similar message in his cry that 'we will fight for all time against any proposal to educate black boys and girls simply as servants and underlings, or simply for the use of other people' (quoted in Ekechi, 1972, p. 525).

African resistance to 'adapted' education was thus based on the recognition that agricultural training would not provide the skills of cash crop farming and was designed only to turn them back upon and 'improve' the traditional subsistence farming methods; and that industrial training was, for the most part, aimed at the production of subordinate workers skilled in routine manual tasks or in routine clerical work. Alakija (1930) argued 'Africans are not to be a nation of clerks without a future' (p. 94).

In some cases, as we have noted, the resistance to adaptation and the concomitant demand for expanded provision of formal schooling found its expression in the formation of social and political associations or in collective 'self-help' activities. Thus the 'creativity' of cultural penetration was translated from an individual to a *group level*. Willis (1977) suggests that 'creativity is in no individual act, no one particular head' (p. 120). In some respects these social formations are linked at the cultural level to more traditional forms of African social organization. Paradoxically, they are founded upon the sharing of traditional tribal agricultural tasks. So, for example, the Kenyan notion of self-help, 'Harambee', 'as a concept is a collective effort meaning "pull together"'.

> The concept embodies ideas of mutual assistance, joint effort, mutual social responsibility and community self-reliance. It embraces such activities as collectivist neighbourhood housebuilding, weeding, bush clearing, irrigation, harvesting, fundraising etc. Harambee practice is found among many ethnic groups in Kenya, for instance —

> The Luo call it Konyir Kende
> the Luhya call it Obwasio
> the Kikuyu call it Ngmatio
> the Masai call it Ematonyok
> the Kamba call it Mwethia. (Mwaura, 1978, p. 8)

This traditional conception of community collective self-reliance has been exploited recently in the development of African political culture. The second paradox of this collective recognition of, and effort towards, the potential of schooling is that it involves a commitment to institutional processes of individual competition and the notion, embodied in the didactic methods of teaching and the procedures of examining, of knowledge as private property.

It is in relation to this paradox that we can identify both the ways in which the 'insights', which give rise to resistance and self-help, are 'distorted, turned and deposited in other forms' and partially related to 'that which they seem to be independent of, and see into' — colonial domination. The commitment to 'progress' through Western education is also a commitment to the values, attitudes and orientations of Western culture and a rejection of the traditional forms of African culture, though in a different way to that meant by Willis (1977). 'A commitment to work and conformism in school is not the giving up of something finite: a measured block of time and attention. It is the giving up of the *use* of a set of potential activities in a way that cannot be measured and controlled and which prevents their alternative use' (p. 130).

The defeat of the colonial ideology of 'adapted' schooling is, as Willis puts it, a 'Pyrrhic' victory in that it 'passes a larger structure more unconsciously and more naturalised' (p. 146). That structure, in this case, is the cultural domination of colonialism and the social formations of capitalism that underlie it. These social and cultural forms are naturalized in the processes of and experience of schooling by the individual pupil. In particular, the traditional collectivism of African society is yielded to the individualism of competition, examination and success and failure in the school. Also, as Willis suggests, but again not in the way he suggests, the cultural penetrations of colonialism, which provide the basis for the demand for formal schooling, are 'repressed, disorganized and prevented from reaching their full potential ... by deep, basic and disorientating divisions.' In total opposition to the case of 'the lads', it is 'mental labour' that takes on 'a significance and critical expression for its owner's social position and identity' (p. 145). The educated African stands on that side of the line with individualism and mental activity, where manual labour is rejected as demeaning. Thus Chief J.A.O. Odebiyi (1967) condemns Nigerian secondary school graduates as 'mercenary, materialistic and complacent' and suggests that 'they tend to think that possession of a Cambridge or West African Examinations Council certificate entitles them to believe that the world owes them a living' (p. 43). One *division*, then, is that between mental and manual labour. Other divisions are attendant upon this. For example, the division between the modern African and the tribal African, between Western culture and traditional culture — the division, that is, that separates the 'red Xhosa' from the 'school Xhosa' — the division between the English speaker and the vernacular speaker, between the literate and the illiterate, or, fundamentally, between the schooled and the unschooled. But in other respects the role of education has also been to act back upon and break down divisions within traditional African society. Divisions between the sexes have been weakened as African women have gained access to school. To some extent also education has weakened ethnic and tribal divisions and has begun to replace them with a national consciousness. In another respect there is a fundamental difference between the analysis of schooling in Africa and Willis' analysis of working-class schooling in Britain. In the case of 'the lads', their cultural penetrations of schooling took a form which did not give them access to any possibility of political articulation. In the case of colonial Africa this is a significant and profound bi-product of African success in gaining access to school and higher education.

> It is obvious that by embarking on training the African in world history, freedom through the rule of law, constitutions, fellowship, equality of rights, toleration, respect, trust and free discussion the colonial government was faced with the herculean task of reconciling their teaching to the fact of colonialism with its display of power and intolerance. For education could hardly be restricted to making a harmless, colonial-dominated African since the African was also introduced to revolutionary ideas which were feared by colonial officials. (Omolewa, 1976, p. 117)

But it is here that the contradictions inherent in the relationship between education and colonialism bite deep. While education produced an elite political leadership to spearhead the drive towards independence, it also tied its leadership to a cultural dependence upon Western models of the conceptions of development. As Carnoy (1974) explains it:

> In the short run, particularly in the immediate post-World War II period France and Britain may have seen schooling as a curse, but in retrospect, European education created 'sensible' values of liberty and freedom, ones that were derived from European standards of conduct and were likely to produce a continuing cultural and economic dependency on the ex-colonial countries. As an alternative to the kind of resistance to colonization produced by the uneducated, schooling served Britain and France well. (p. 143)

The model of analysis presented here moves away from the one-way, deterministic and aggregate conception of colonial schooling towards a position which recognizes the functionally linked, interactive and mutually conditioning nature of colonizer-colonized relationships. Indeed, in the light of such an analysis, colonial education may be located firmly within the framework of the Chilean *dependencia* perspective in that:

Dependence in any given society is a complex set of associations in which the external dimensions are determinative in varying degrees of the internal ones and, indeed, internal variables may very well reinforce the pattern of external linkages. (Valenzuela and Valenzuela, 1979, p. 46)

Notes

1 As only the Bible and a few other religious texts were translated into Ibgo, the language of the Niger Mission region, the Africans were effectively prevented from employing their literacy skills to obtain clerical employment or to read other secular books.
2 D'Souza (1975) specifically mentions its application to the New Zealand Maoris, South African Blacks and the natives of the Philippines.

References

ALAKIJA, O.A. (1930) 'The African must have Western education', *Elders Review*, July.
ANDERSON, J. (1970) *The Struggle for the School*, Nairobi, Longman.
BACUS, K. (1974) 'The primary school curriculum in colonial society', *Journal of Curriculum Studies*, 6, 1.
BEIDELMAN, T.O. (1981) 'Contradictions between the sacred and the secular life: The Church Missionary Society in Ukagura, Tanzania, East Africa 1876–1914', *Comparative Studies in Society and History*, 23, 1, January.
BERNSTEIN, B. (1971) 'On the classification and framing of educational knowledge', in YOUNG, M.F.D. (Ed.) *Knowledge and Control*, London, Collier-Macmillan.
CARNOY, M. (1974) *Education As Cultural Imperialism*, New York, McKay.
DICK, M. (1980) 'The myth of the working-class Sunday School', *History of Education*, 9, 1.
DOUGALL, J.W.C. (1926) 'Religious education', *The International Review of Missions*, 15, 59, July.
D'SOUZA, M. (1975) 'Educational policy in British Tropical Africa', *African Studies Review*, 18, 2, September.
EKECHI, F.K. (1972) *Missionary Enterprise and Rivalry in Igboland 1857–1914*, London, Frank Cass.
FAJANA, A. (1972) 'Colonial control and education: The development of higher education in Nigeria 1900–1950', *Journal of the Historical Society of Nigeria*, 6, 3, December.
FOSTER, P.J. (1965) *Education and Social Change in Ghana*, London, Routledge.
GOODSON, I.F. (1983) *School Subjects and Curriculum Change*, London, Croom Helm.
GORDON, S. (1963) *A Century of West Indian Education: A Sourcebook*, London, Longmans.
GRAY, R. (1960) *The Two Nations*, London, Oxford University Press.
HUMPHRIES, S. (1981) *Hooligans or Rebels? An Oral History of Working Class Childhood and Youth 1889–1939*, Oxford, Blackwells.
JONES, J. (1922) *Education in Africa: A Study of West, South and Equatorial Africa by the African Education Commission*, New York, Phelps-Stokes Fund.
KASOZI, A.B.K. (1977) 'Education for the chiefs in Uganda becomes education for all', *Education in East Africa*, 7, 1.

KEMP, D. (1898) *Nine Years at the Gold Coast*, New York, Macmillan.

KING, K. (1977) *The African Artisan*, London, Heinemann.

KINSEY, D.C. (1976) 'Efforts for educational synthesis under colonial rule: Egypt and Tunisia', *Comparative Education Review*, June.

LENIN, V. (1970) *Imperialism; the Highest State of Capitalism*, Moscow, Progress Publishers.

LUGARD, J.D. (1929) *The Dual Mandate in British Tropical Africa*, Edinburgh, Blackwood.

MAYER, P. (1961) *Townsmen or Tribe*, Cape Town, Oxford University Press.

MAYHEW, A. (1938) *Education and the Colonial Empire*, London, Oxford University Press.

MILLER, W. (1947) *Have We Failed in Africa?* London, Oxford University Press.

MUMFORD, W. and JACKSON, R. (1938) 'The problems of mass education in Africa', *Africa*, 11, pp. 187–206.

MUTERO-CHIRENJE, J. (1976) 'Church, state and education in Bechuanaland', *Presence Africaine*, No. 99.

MWAURA, L. (1978) 'Kenya's Harambee Schools', unpublished MA project, University of Sussex, Education Area.

NDUKA, O. (1976) 'Background to the foundation of Dennis Memorial Grammar School, Onitsha', *Journal of the Historical Society of Nigeria*, 8, 3, December.

ODEBIYI, J.A.O. (1967) 'The aims of secondary education in Western Nigeria', *West African Journal of Education*, 1, 2, June.

OMOLEWA, M. (1976) 'The adaptation question in Nigerian education 1916–36: A study of an educational experiment in secondary school examinations in colonial Nigeria', *Journal of the Historical Society of Nigeria*, 8, 3, December.

RIGBY, P. (1981) 'Pastors and pastoralists: The differential penetration of christianity among East African cattle herders', *Comparative Studies in Society and History*, 23, 1, January.

ROOKE, P. (1980) 'Missionaries as pedagogues: A reconstruction of the significance of education for slaves and apprentices in the British West Indies, 1800–1838', *History of Education*, 9, 1, March.

SITHOLE, N. (1950) *African Nationalism*, Cape Town, Oxford University Press.

SORRENSON, M.P.K. (1968) *Origins of European Settlement in Kenya*. Nairobi, Oxford University Press.

STANILAND, M. (1975) *The Lions of Dagbon: Political Change in Northern Nigeria*, Cambridge University Press.

UGANDA (1930) *Department of Education Annual Report*.

VALENZUELA, J.S. and VALENZUELA, A. (1979) 'Modernization and dependence: Alternative perspectives in the study of Latin American underdevelopment', in VILLAMIL, J.J. (Ed.) *Transitional Capitalism and National Development*, Brighton, Harvester Press.

WILLIS, P. (1977) *Learning to Labour*, Farnborough, Saxon House.

Ethnographic and Historical Method in the Study of Schooling*

Louis M. Smith

An Introduction to the Issues

Most essays have an interesting origin, a beginning, which helps give meaning to the substance one wishes to present. Among several, one brief story comes to mind in regard to these thoughts on the relationship between historical and ethnographic research in the study of schooling; it comments on the Department of Education at Washington University where I work. Although most of us are quite individualistic we do talk, banter and play a variety of friendly one-upmanship games. Several years ago I had been trying to understand the concept of 'explanation' and began reading people like Scriven (1959), Dray (1957) and Gardiner (1959) on the nature of explanation in history. In the course of this I began to try to figure out how historians do their work. With my colleagues Arthur Wirth, Raymond Callahan and William Connor in mind, I came to the conclusion that historical method was *just*, nothing more than, 'participant observation with data fragments', a kind of less adequate ethnography. I don't recall their specific reactions, beyond benevolent, tolerant smiles, and I'm not sure that they believe I won that round. Cloaked in the jest, however, were two significant ideas. Essential similarities existed in the two approaches, that is, one is a form or instance of the other. Second, a major difference seemed to appear in the quality of the data that existed, that is, fragments. Malinowski's (1922) active ethnographic huntsman image seemed bounded. In a sense, my hope in this essay is to explore the hunches caught in that bit of attempted humor.

Such humor and by-play suggest also that a more fundamental issue is lurking about. I knew one day I wanted to do a real historical case study. At

* The research on which this essay is based was partially supported by NIE Contract #G78–0074 and by Washington University. The account represents official policy of neither NIE, Washington University, nor the Milford School District. John Prunty, David Dwyer and Paul Kleine are co-investigators in the project, Innovation and Change in American Education: Kensington Revisited.

first, I didn't realize the extent of the opportunity which would develop around our project, Kensington Revisited: A Fifteen Year Follow-up of an Innovative School and its Faculty. In a sense, a fifteen-year follow-up is a kind of recent history. We had studied the innovative Kensington Elementary School — open space, team teaching, individualized curriculum and instruction, democratic administration, pupil control of their own learning in 1964–65 — and had written a participant observer monograph, *Anatomy of Educational Innovation* (Smith and Keith, 1971) on the first year in the life of the school. Now we were supposed to return for an ethnography of the school today (1979–80) and a view of the further careers of the original faculty, a group of true believers, none of whom was still at the school.

In looking for some of the context of change it seemed reasonable to spend some time in the Central Office of the Milford School District, of which Kensington is one elementary school, to read documents such as the Milford Public School *Bulletin*, and to attend some of the School Board meetings. One day, while reading the file of *Bulletins* that the District sent to patrons, I happened upon some elements of conflict between the then Superintendent, Mr McBride, and the Board. In talking with the current Superintendent, Mr George, he indicated that the Board had tried to fire Superintendent McBride. We chatted a bit about the event, he wandered off, only to return a little later with a large black book, which turned out to be the bound *Minutes* of the Milford District Board of Education, the legal record of school proceedings. I was amazed at the bill of particulars against Superintendent McBride, the traces of significant human action and interaction. To my questions: Are there more of these? How far back do they go? and Can I look at them?, he said they had a closet full, they go back at least to the 1920s, and that I was free to look at them. For the last couple of years I've been reading them avidly. While we are still not 'historians' in a formal or professional sense, we have been busy developing a chronicle of the Milford District from 1915 to 1980, a sixty-five-year period. The activity has changed the definition of our problem, enlarged our final report to six book-length volumes, and demanded continued renegotiations with school district officials and with our project officer at the National Institute of Education (NIE) which has funded the effort. Most of my concrete illustrations and substantive remarks will come from our experience in this project.

Anomalies, Initial Observations and Reflections on Doing Ethnography and History

An interpretive aside is a simple, practical ethnographic technique of writing in the fieldnote records a short comment to oneself about some hunch, bright idea or insight that occurs along the way in fieldwork (Smith and Geoffrey, 1968). In the course of doing our history of Milford, a series of methodological observations and reflections arose and were noted in the fieldnotes and summary observations. I raise and elaborate a half dozen of them here. Mostly, the focus is on aspects of the data and the kind of thinking that seems to be occurring as one does a blend of history and ethnography.

The-World-Begins-in-1952 Phenomenon

One of the more interesting items we encountered is 'the-world-begins-in-1952' phenomenon. Among the various sources of data on the history of the district the Milford Public School *Bulletin* became one of the most important. Volume 1, no. 1 appeared in August 1952. That issue became the fulcrum around which the history of the district seemed to unfold. Each news item gave an indication of what had gone before and what was just beginning. It became a rock upon which inferences ran both backward and forward. For example, what was to become a deluge of pupils in the 1950s, changing the district from a semi-rural, semi-small-town to a large suburban district, was just beginning. The Milford High School listed only thirteen faculty members with 'one or more years of service'; nine new faculty arrived in the Fall of 1952. The Milford Village Elementary School listed twelve faculty and six new members. The Marquette School of fourteen faculty was increased by four. The Attucks School remained with a single teacher for all eight grades. In all, staff size increased by 50 per cent in that year. A two-class addition was being built at Marquette. Six classes were being rented from the Adams Street Community Church's Education Building, and the new Grant Elementary School was under construction. Overcrowding in the elementary schools was a real problem.

The substantive points are both interesting and important but my purpose here is to indicate that we found a rock on which to anchor our beginning story and analysis. The data produced an initial 'set of facts' and a beginning image of the nature and structure of the district. This record occasioned the raising of hypotheses about earlier years and the recency of the change from rural to suburban. It began to suggest linkages with the Kensington School and Milford District which we had encountered in our intensive observational study in 1964–65, *Anatomy of Educational Innovation*. To find a source which one could count on, at least initially, seemed very helpful. Because they started publishing the *Bulletin* in 1952, it seemed as though our world began in 1952.

The *Bulletins*, as data, had several other attributes which helped shape the label 'the-world-begins...' we gave to the phenomenon. First, the *Bulletins* were a large mass of data. Some years a half dozen were issued; they varied from four to eight pages in length. They have continued until the present. Second, by their very nature they were organized chronologically. They provided a kind of chronicle of the District for the latter-day reader. Third, they had a holistic quality — 'all' of the District news of interest to the patrons, at least as perceived by the administration. Fourth, the audience of patrons are the citizens who vote yearly for Board members, who legally direct the district, and the citizens whose support is needed for tax levies and bond issues — local democracy with a vengeance. As we will discuss shortly, the *Bulletin* is not the only perspective possible but is an interesting and important one for an ethnographer interested in documents as well as observations and interviews.

Discovering the Board Minutes: Cognitive and Motivational Consequences

The initial interpretive aside leading to the previous section, 'the-world-begins-in-1952', was written before we got into the Board *Minutes*. These became an even more fundamental rock — earlier in time and with a peculiarly important decision-making format. It reminded us of the old story of the earth resting on a rock, the rock resting on an elephant, and the elephant on a turtle, and after that 'it's turtles all the way down'. The Board *Minutes* seemed to be 'turtles' all the way down. But even here, we had not studied the community newspapers and we thought we might find them to be 'the real bedrock of turtles' to continue to mix our metaphors. Actually we used those records more selectively.

The point I am trying to make is the nature of the cognitive processes involved in this phase of this kind of research — at least as we are doing it. The finding of these sets of documents and the careful reading of them started several processes. *First*, as I indicated earlier, it set a boundary, '1952 and onward'. *Second*, it indicated that those boundaries are always provisional and tentative as new sets of records appear. *Third*, by their amount, detail, and particular form — news items for the patrons in the one instance and legal records in the second — they gave an aura and confidence of 'reality'. *Fourth*, as I started to make notes I found myself chronicling specific events on a time line. *Fifth*, commonsense strands — when buildings were built and the coming and going of superintendents — soon appeared. *Sixth*, some specific items related to contemporary events became themes, for example, a Black School was built in the mid-1920s and reference was made to it in one of the first volumes of Board *Minutes*. This linked with the contempoary racial changes at Kensington and with what Myrdal (1944) long ago called *The American Dilemma*. *Seventh*, a developing gestalt or image of what the totality or whole is like began to form. Something called the Milford School District existed in the records, in the legal settings of county and state and in the minds of individuals. We found ourselves in the midst of the Griffiths (1979) and Greenfield (1978) debate. *Eighth*, a continuous inference process about 'unknown areas' based on implications from known items occurred. For instance, what was the relationship between faculty and staff turnover in Mrs Briggs' early tenure as superintendent in 1928–30 and in her being fired after two years? What relation did the Board's stated reasons have to her personality? What was the significance of pupils being called in by the Board to discuss the problems of the school? *Finally*, what alterations occurred in each of these processes as new information, and particularly new large bodies or sets of information arose, for example, finding the District *Bulletin*, then the sixty-five years of Board *Minutes* and then the extended oral histories of early Board members and students?

Each of those eight or ten cognitive processes has become an issue in our longer methodological analysis in our project. They seem very important for thinking about the relationships between historical and ethnographic methods, at the level of a concrete practical activity of inquiry. Later, I found historians such as Gottschalk (1945) presenting examples of similar inferential thinking from documents.

In addition, finding and working for two years on the *Minutes* of the Board of Education has been a most dramatic and emotional research experience for me, second only to my original experience as participant observer in Geoffrey's class almost two decades ago (*The Complexities of an Urban Classroom*). The massive and relentless month in, month out, year in, year out quality, the written at the moment and not to be changed record regardless of what happened later quality, and the moved, seconded, and passed quality focusing on decision-making provided a 'reality' against which all other data could be compared, contrasted and triangulated.

Beyond those substantive intellectual processes, the personal consequences of this discovery of the *Minutes* seemed multiple. *First*, an energizing, exciting quality appeared. Motivation ran high. Day after day I returned to the new kind or genre of data for the surprises it contained both substantively and methodologically.

A related, but *second* aspect occurred. Creative thought was stimulated to a high degree. I was in a welter of new data, new formats, forms, or categories of data, new precepts and images, new items about which choices had to be made, and new construals or perspectives formulated. Continuously I asked, 'How do I cope with all this?' The materials were manifestly relevant, for little items kept appearing here and there and seemed to be connected. What were the patterns and structure of ideas which would encompass all this in some way relevant to our original problem and the way that too was evolving? The data transformed the problem from 'A Fifteen Year Follow-up of an Innovative School and Its Faculty' to what we now call 'Innovation and Change in American Education', a very different agenda. I was struck with the parallels to changes that occur in problem definitions as creative artists work (Beittel, 1973).

Along the way came the doubts about the degree of or levels of creativity — is it new to oneself versus is it new to the field? Were we just rediscovering the wheel? Tours occurred into the nature of history, the philosophy of history, the methods of history. Similar trips occurred into the substance of educational history — local, state and national. Even book titles with a ring of the history of curriculum, teaching or schooling in England, Australia and elsewhere caught my eye and dollar — or pound — in the book stores. Conversations occurred with my historically trained colleagues. They were assaulted with concrete particular items and with abstract and general items. What do you make of this? What do you think of that? What's the conventional historical wisdom on this, on that? And on and on.

When the energizing aspect collided with the creative aspect, the turmoil raced through all parts of my life. It got in the way of my teaching, although sometimes it blended in neatly, effortlessly and successfully. It made me impatient with committee meetings and organizational maintenance activities. It led to multiple new kinds of readings as I indicated in this instance, further histories, biographies and autobiographies of historians, and books on historical method and philosophy of history. It awakened me in the middle of the night, impatient to get some new idea down, yet unhappy that if sleep didn't come, I would be too tired to push on for more than a couple of hours the next day. It meant drinking too much coffee and eating too much to dispel the sourness. It meant the need for heavy doses of exercise — handball, walking, gardening — to tone down the mania and to take the tension out of my arms, legs and head. As I said, it was an incredibly important all-encompassing professional experience.

The Occasional Rare Document

A number of historians we have read have talked about the joy and excitement in finding a key document which made a point, unraveled a knotty problem, or illuminated an enigma. This happened to us on several occasions; but the prototypical incident concerned the genesis of Milford's Policy Handbook in the early 1960s. We had encountered several years of minutes between 1962 and 1965 and realized that Dr Steven Spanman, superintendent between 1962 and 1966, had initiated the changes. No one in Milford or at Washington University with whom I talked knew about the general intellectual origins of the particular system. The format seemed too complex and too systematic to have come whole cloth out of his head. It looked like too large and effort for any local district to have created. Then one day I ran into a Central Office staff member who had been around in those years and who tended to be a bit of a 'pack rat' in terms of keeping things. She disappeared into an old file drawer and brought out 'the document'. It was a mimeographed copy of the 'Southern City Public Schools Policy Procedures'. Southern City District was Spanman's prior work place. Scrawled all over it were Spanman's deletions and additions to alter it into a Milford Public Schools document. Rather than being addressed to Southern City's principals' meeting it was altered to a Milford Board agenda item. To become Milford District policy it required a Board vote for adoption.

The 'introduction' to the original report gave a little history of Southern City and the original researchers and consultants, Davies and Brickell. The first section dealt with administrative 'organization', who would do the reworking and implementation. A second section indicated 'steps and procedures'. A third contained 'materials to be supplied'. The first appendix contained the eight 'policy study committees' by title and personnel involved. The second appendix

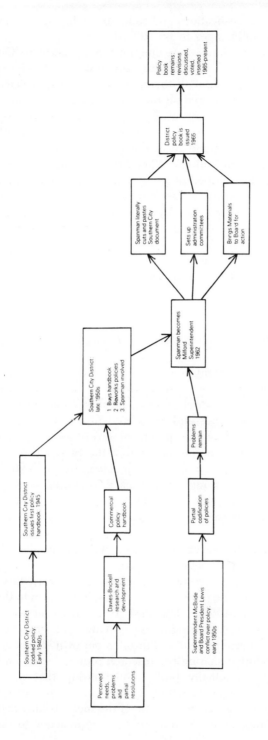

Figure 1. Origins of Milford's Policy Handbook

contained the 'policy classifications and codes' over the eight areas. Each page contained the minimal changes to fit Milford.

And there it was. My immediate emotional reactions were 'Oh, my god', 'I can't believe it' and 'ecstasy'. Methodologically, it was the lynch pin, the ribbon around, the string that pulled it all together. It had the specificity that tied all the inferences down. It answered all the questions. I got it from an individual directly involved with it twenty years before. Substantively it led us to Figure 1. Three strands of activity came together: a strand from Southern City, a research and commercial strand from the work of Dan Davies and William Brickell, and a strand from Milford. When Spanman joined the Milford School District, he brought a resolution of a long standing problem which had been a source of conflict between the Board and the prior superintendent, McBride. The nature and format of the policy handbook is such that it has remained, with revisions, in the District ever since. The meaning and implications of the vignette for a variety of problems such as policy formation, educational innovation and change, relationship of research, theory and practice, macro and micro levels of analysis seem open for analyses. This was history and ethnography at their best.

Triangulation Possibilities between History and Ethnography

It is a minor matter at one level, but critical at another. Dr George, the current Milford superintendent, gave us total access to the various sets of public records — the *Bulletin* to district patrons and the School Board *Minutes*. The latter exist in bound volumes and are stored in a locked closet just off the superintendent's office. The minor point: we never took any of these out of the Central Office building. Concretely, we kept the two or three volumes with which we were working on top of filing cabinets in the secretary's alcove. We left the volumes there over night which gave us simple access, early in the morning or late in the afternoon whenever we came up to work. When the superintendent and secretary were on vacation, we had access through one of the assistant superintendents.

The major point, however, is that by working in the Central Office building, actually in a small conference room off the main hall, we gradually came to meet most of the secretaries, clerks and Central Office professional staff. They came to know the project in two forms, 'the return to the Kensington School' and a 'history of Milford'. The most general reaction was amazement at the long involvement in reading minutes — off and on for two years. With the legitimation of the superintendent and through our own efforts to spell out our activities, which included sharing the research proposal early and preliminary documents later, we gradually built a relationship that merged helping, friendship and professional collegiality. These concrete activities and developing relationships set the occasion for some of the most striking instances I have encountered of triangulation or multi-method approaches to data and ideas

(Smith, 1979). At this point, historical method and anthropological method merged into a general open-ended set of field methods.

Figure 2 illustrates the half dozen classes of data and activities. First are the bound volumes of Board *Minutes* themselves. I don't really know much about other districts and their *Minutes* and how they are similar or different, but Milford's volumes are fascinatingly diverse. In one form or another, these Milford District records go back to 1914.

Figure 2.   Classes of Triangulated Data and Data Gathering Activities

1   Multiple items bound into the Board *Minutes*
2   Other Central Office documents: historical and contemporary
3   Creation of data files to our questions and inquiries
4   MA and PhD papers — inside and outside Milford
5   Short-term conversations and long-term vivid memories
6   Other contacts and oral histories
7   Intensive interviews

Beginning in the 1930s, each year is bound separately; before that the years are clustered. In terms of triangulation and multi-methods one of the most important aspects of these records is that they contain other kinds of documents beyond the minutes themselves. This fact seems to make them a much more powerful set of records. For instance, at different times they included:

1   notes of other meetings;
2   original copies of letters to and from the Board or superintendent to citizens, government agencies, etc.;
3   financial records: bills paid, budgets, bank loans;
4   superintendent's agendas;
5   reports on school issues by internal staff and outside consultants;
6   on several occasions stenotyped records (50–90 pages) of meetings involving severe conflict between staff and between (and within) the Board.

In short, the *Minutes* were much more than minutes, they were multiple kinds of primary documents with curious kinds of independencies and inter-dependencies, open to triangulation.

While working on the *Minutes*, a second kind of triangulation occurred. It blended document analysis with brief interviews. One of the most vivid of these is what I've called my 'Nussbaum story'. It goes like this. In reading the *Minutes* of the late 1950s a conflict arose in which the Board voted not to rehire a social studies teacher, Mr Nussbaum. Allegedly he was having discipline problems and was too familiar with some of his students. He argued that they were firing him because he had distributed some literature on the teachers' union. The *Minutes* summarized the controversy as well as contained some of the Board's allegations: Nussbaum was in his seventh year of teaching and also he was chairman of the high school social studies department. Problems in teacher student relations — discipline and familiarity — are not problems typically of experienced teachers and department chairpersons. In the vernacular, things didn't smell right. It was at this point that the triangulation occurred. One of the Central Office staff wandered by the conference room in which I was working, as he was prone to do, and stuck his head in to say 'hello'. After the greeting, in my best non-directive style, I said, 'Say Bill, did you ever know a teacher named Nussbaum?' His response was immediate, direct and vivid. 'Oh, yes, the Board and the Superintendent were really on his case for union activities.' Then he proceeded to tell me an even more devastating story:

> 'At the time, I was teaching fifth grade at Milford Village School. The Community Teachers Association (CTA) President was teaching sixth grade in the room next to mine. One afternoon, the Superintendent, the high school principal and our principal all descended on him about the upcoming CTA meeting. He was told in no uncertain terms that he was to set the agenda beforehand, to have no additional items added, and under no circumstances was Nussbaum to get on the agenda. He couldn't sleep for three days. Later Nussbaum heard about it, called him, and said he wasn't going to raise a fuss at the meeting.

The triangulating point of the story is obvious: mixed data in the documents, incongruency with my knowledge of schooling, a Central Office staff member's immediate reaction, and then the very powerful story of teachers teaching together and the trauma faced by one's friend presented a powerful view of the events.

Instances of triangulation occurred with each of the other items in Figure 2. Other dusty documents appeared off of shelves. MA and PhD papers were loaned, in some instances the District began to accumulate data files in areas where we were searching for clear records, and the network of contacts grew and grew. As we have indicated, ethnography and history merged into a series of efforts to find credible data and to build a synthesis or view of the school.

Eliminating One's Contextual Ignorance and Imagining One's Self into the Past

Being new to historical research and coming at the task from our idiosyncratic brand of ethnography left me with a continuing problem of 'eliminating one's contextual ignorance', and 'imagining one's self back into an historical period'. The phenomenon arose this way. In two separate interviews, one with a teacher who had been in the District a number of years and one with a former student of the Class of 1931, items were raised which we fumbled with because we did not know enough of the history of Milford and of Suburban County. For instance, with Mrs Irma Hall, a Kensington teacher, we didn't realize that the Milford District and the Marquette District had merged as late as 1949 and that those two schools were the elementary school program when she joined the faculty. The interview put us on to some of the issues, which we've since explored, but we did not raise key items in that early history. Similarly, in talking with and later reading through the interviews with Mr Elbrecht, from the early years of Milford High School, we did not have a view of the west end of Suburban County and Milford's relationship to the numerous other small three-director districts. Nor did we know much about Suburban County in general.

These 'fumbles' started us reading contemporary local histories and records from the turn of the century. Each source, as is true in all our academic work, tends to lead to several more, and in a few hours of searching one has three months of reading and a half dozen new problems. For example, we believe a need exists for a history of Black education in Suburban County. Similarly we believe a need exists for a biography of a Suburban County Superintendent who served for thirty-seven years in that office, an exceptionally long period in an era of incredible change. Each of these would clarify important aspects of schooling in Milford since the turn of the century.

As I have said, for an individual with minimal training in history, and with no training in historical research methods, one of the most difficult problems has been 'imagining oneself back into an historical period'. No images of Midwest State in 1870 or Suburban County in 1920 came to mind. The hurly burly of the rapid county growth in the post-war years clouds visions of an earlier more rural and small-town state of affairs in the state and county.

The two channels which seemed most helpful and fruitful in developing images were two of the main sources of data. As I indicated, open-ended, oral history type interviews with older residents of the community and professional staff filled in gaps regarding the coming of roads, electricity, volunteer fire departments and so forth. In addition, I started reading histories of all kinds. First were United States histories, particularly the splendid three-volume set by Boorstin (1978), *The Americas*. Second were books on the history of American education, such as Cremin (1980) and Butts (1978). Third, a variety of local histories appeared. A folksy history of a Suburban County school district seemed very much like the Clear Valley School before Milford became Milford. Histories of 'Big City', its neighborhoods, its schools, its politics were sought. A centennial history of Midwest State University, and especially its College of Education, provided another look at the total state educational establishment, the training of teachers and the beginnings of educational research.

Unless our label, 'eliminating one's contextual ignorance', be taken too negatively, a few positive aspects seem latent in the approach. It follows the general inductive, interactive mode of our general research style. One learns a little here and a little there and those items play into each other and into later interviews, documents, reading, analysis and writing. This is tremendously motivating, in the sense that one is always discovering something new, patterns emerge, flow and stabilize. It's very exciting intellectually, it keeps one at the task, hour after hour, day after day, month after month.

The particular configurations from established interpreters as they appear in theoretical structures and in accepted descriptive formulations do not become overly potent filters as the new information is acquired or processed. At some point, what Hexter calls 'the second record', what the historian carries about in his/her head from general reading and knowledge must come into play. As we have argued elsewhere (Smith, 1979 and 1982; Smith and Dwyer, 1980) eventually that second record has to be well filled out and articulated with the specific problem under study and with the data being developed. We're arguing that 'too much too early' may be stifling to one's imaginative construing and reconstruing of the problem and the analysis. Unless it's eventually done, one may find one's only rediscovered the wheel, and probably a lopsided one at that. Even so, in the process, one keeps eliminating one's contextual ignorance.

Several substantive outcomes of this activity seem most critical. We were struck by the recency and the magnitude of educational changes. The basic change in Suburban County from ninety school districts to about two dozen in Suburban County happened since the Second World War. This was less than a dozen and a half years before Spanman was to build a space-age open school. In the mid-1960s when we first came to the District and did *Anatomy*, that recency didn't even occur to us. Second, the 'catastrophic' current changes — race. SES, declining enrolments — seem less catastrophic when viewed from this longer perspective. Periods of high change, growth, complexity and specialization, as we have argued substantively elsewhere, have been lived through, thought about and fought about (Smith *et al.*, 1982). The current changes, modes of reaction and adaptations will become later chapters in someone else's historical account. This is not to argue for a Polyannais progress' or a 'Nihilistic doomsday'. Nor is it to argue for change, reform or innovation coming too fast (for some individuals and groups) or too slow (for other individuals and groups). Rather it is to indicate that many of the hopes, aspirations, conflicts, disagreements and action have had their counterpart in prior times and places.

Finally, and a point that first arose when William Geoffrey and I were studying his classroom at the Washington School, is the realization that his world of urban education, at the classroom level and at the school level, had its own kind of patterns and order, and that this order and pattern could be observed, analyzed, reflected upon, lived with and in some instances changed. This seemed a most important insight then. Now it seems that earlier historical times, places, events and people could similarly be ordered and patterned. This seems an important part of 'imagining oneself back into an historical period'.

On Knowing How Things Turn Out

As we began some of our historical meanderings in the multiple kinds of records and data which exist in and around Milford, another issue or two left me a bit edgy. With our 1971 book, *Anatomy*, and with the ethnography of the 1979–80 year we knew beforehand how the story and some of the sub-stories came out. In a sense, we had some of the themes defined ahead of time and our search of the records was a clarification of the origins and development of those themes. Racial issues, the neighborhood school concept, demographic changes, the role of the Federal government, the nature of the curriculum, the importance of Superintendent Spanman, the issues around buildings and physical facilities suggest some of the themes from our contemporaneous studies. Somehow we seemed to be in a game different from the positivistic prediction and control social science I had grown up with. At the time, it left me with a question of the legitimacy of the whole enterprise.

Also, for a long time, we had been in debates with various colleagues over the importance of narratives, portrayals and stories, for example, Stake's (1977) view of evaluation versus the importance of generating grounded theory — Glaser and Strauss' (1967) extreme position. We tended to follow George Homans (1950) and argued strongly for both (Smith and Pohland, 1976; Smith, 1979; Smith and Dwyer, 1980; and Smith *et al.*, 1981).

One of our recent joyful experiences has been to find that the historians split on the same kind of issues. For me, Hexter's book, *The History Primer*, broke open the narrative/analysis dilemma by offering a third alternative. He took some of the edginess out of knowing the outcome. He presents an illustration of historical writing, an American baseball game, which has received considerable notoriety among sports buffs. American baseball is one of the most documented aspects of American life. Records exist on the details of every player, every game in the season and every aspect within the game — hits, runs, errors, and so forth. Newspapers chronicle daily each game. Daily, weekly and monthly papers and magazines offer commentary. For 'important' games, as in the final game of the 1951 National League season, the commentary is unending. This is the game Hexter, the historian, chose to write about as an illustration of history with a small 'h', the mundane and unimportant. In writing his history he ignored large masses of available factual data, omitted reference to star players who were unimportant that day and selected threads and incidents that culminated in the high drama of the game, Bobby Thompson's home run in the ninth inning. This example of what he calls 'processive explanation in history', a form of explanation, is an answer to the 'why' question which has plagued historians. He comments in summary:

> It is this outcome that warrants the substance, the structure, and the tone of the introductory section of 'The Last Game'. In other words, the outcome defines the appropriate historical macrorhetoric, and the macrorhetoric in turn dictates the selection of 'facts' or more accurately data to be drawn from the record. Or to put it more bluntly, amid a mass of true facts about the past, too ample to set down, historians choose not merely on logical grounds but on the basis of appropriate rhetorical strategies. (1971, p. 190)

In effect, he is making a case for the importance of rhetorical principles as part of the historian's craft. In the course of his analyses he raises concepts such as record, focal center, event clusters, fragments, promissory notes, judicious omission, universe of discourse, pivot points and unstable active explanandum. Although he would probably disown the label, he has a 'theory' of historical method. All this we found helpful in thinking about what we were doing in our Kensington Revisited project. Processive explanation gave us a rationale for what we had been doing in a social science which knew the outcomes. It bridged history and ethnography in a way which cuts to the heart of the logic of social science, the concept of explanation.

The Merging of Methods and Theory on Ethnography and History

At this point, I want to back off a bit from the day-to-day data-based generalizations of our activities that involved ethnography and history in our Kensington Revisited project. With this detachment come several broader ideas concerning the relationships among history, ethnography and the cumulating aspects of our work. Briefly, these include (1) diversity within ethnography and history, (2) some similarities and differences, (3) a concern for process as a mode of integration, and (4) a move to broader assumptions, metatheory or paradigms.

Diversity within Ethnography and History

As I began to ground our activities further in the methodological writings of historians and anthropologists, I found myself in a quagmire of diverse opinions. I had known the anthropologists did not agree with one another. In trying to write a general essay on ethnography a year ago, I was struck by the theoretical differences among such major figures as Bronislaw Malinowski, William Foote Whyte and Clifford Geertz. The differences among functional, social interactional and interpretive anthropology suggest that the 'real' problems in resolving their diversity lay in their assumptions, their metatheory, their underlying paradigm (Smith, 1982).

Among historians similar differences exist. Morton White, an American social historian (1963) who is keen on narrative history, is a logical positivist seeking broad social laws. Jack Hexter, an American who specializes in British history, wrote, as indicated earlier, a book called *The History Primer* which is a long argument with Carl Hempel's (1942) classical paper, 'The function of general laws in history'. Lawrence Stone, an Englishman trained at Oxford and now at Princeton, has published a recent collection of methodological essays and reviews under the title, *The Past and the Present* (1981). The first, 'History and the social sciences in the twentieth century', is a cautionary note to the historians. He feels the logic of the social sciences is in real trouble and they, the historians, should be wary of their borrowings from social science. The second essay is entitled 'Prosopography' and refers to collective biography or multiple career line analysis. He raises a set of issues undergirding our study of the original Kensington faculty. The third he calls 'The revival of the narrative: Reflections on a new old history'. His new historians, after a flirtation with positivistic social science, quantification and general laws are returning to narratives 'directed by some "pregnant principle"', which sounds a good bit like Hexter's processive history. Further, he argues they are more apt to look to the interpretive anthropologists (such as Geertz and his thick description) as the more important kind of social science for stimulation.

Reading these materials by eminent anthropologists and historians suggests several tentative conclusions. (1) Intellectual ferment and turmoil are everywhere. (2) Guidance from other disciplines for educational theorists, researchers and practitioners is not going to be a simple '1 to 1' and '2 to 2' kind of borrowing. (3) Synthesis and integration, to whatever degree they occur, seem to involve a next level higher set of abstractions, a metatheory or paradigmatic level of discussion. (4) It probably should be left to philosophy, but I'm reminded of Kaplan's (1964) argument of scientific autonomy. The working scientists, the crafts people of an area, must put their own intellectual house in order on their way to solving their own particular substantive problems. This would seem a worthy goal for any academic community.

Some Similarities and Differences

Rather than tackle directly this array of anthropological and historical methodologists, I have borrowed bits and pieces to illuminate some of the procedures we used and the ideas we developed as we tried to carry out and understand aspects of our Kensington Revisited project. Some of these have been noted along the way. The fuller essay is the last volume, the methodological appendix, of that series. For the moment, I find the diversity and pluralism among historians and anthropologists helpful in suggesting ways to do the inquiry and in giving ideas toward the rationalization of what one does. But the diversity is frustrating in not providing a logical structure of criteria for judging proposals and products.

As indicated in the introduction, one of my chief guiding hypotheses of the differences between ethnography and history was the dependence of the historian on data fragments. Now, especially after reading Gottschalk's (1945) essay on 'The historian and the historical document', I believe the hypothesis remains essentially true but that it is a matter of degree. The ethnographer also deals in data fragments, but usually he has a chance at larger and more relevant chunks.

A second difference seemed to exist in the 'active huntsman' role of the ethnographer, so eloquently captured by Malinowski: 'But the Ethnographer has not only to spread his nets in the right place, and wait for what will fall into them. He must be an active huntsman, and drive his quarry into them and follow it up to its most inaccessable lairs' (1922, p. 8). It seems that it is a matter of degree; there are historians and historians. The data oriented kind chase the aforementioned 'fragments' in varied, creative and persevering ways.

A third difference, and one that now seems to be much more critical, is what lies behind the cliché of the ethnographer as the research instrument. In the historian's terms this has to do with 'primary' and 'secondary' sources. For the historian a primary source is 'the testimony of an eyewitness'. A secondary source is 'the testimony of anyone who is not an eyewitness — that is, of one who was not present at the event of which he tells' (Gottschalk, 1945, p. 11). In this framework the ethnographer who observes is producing his own primary sources. He is the witness to the event. From the historian's point of view that has to be a powerful and important difference. Although the ethnographer still deals in fragments and although the ethnographer is a more active huntsman, it is the production of an eyewitness account by the researcher which is the devastating difference. Somehow I had never quite phrased it that way. But that in turn produces complications, for the eyewitness is also the 'detached' story-teller and analyst. Does he lose more than he wins?

Within his discussion of the historian, Gottschalk is very precise on the need to examine each document in terms of the 'particulars', each item in any document. Some may be based on eyewitness testimony, other items may be secondary, information that has come to the document writer from someone else. Again, to think of ethnographic interviewees and informants from this perspective casts new meanings on them and their reports. From a psychological perspective, I'm reminded of the relationships between overall test validity and item analysis and item validity.

Note here also the contrast of the ethnographer who is an eyewitness observer and the ethnographer who uses an informant. The latter seems more like an historian. Similarly the ethnographer, or case study researcher, who relies on interviews is also more like the historian, and perhaps identical to the oral historian. Further, if one must use an interpreter or translator, one puts another item between the event and the eyewitness. The commonalities keep suggesting ways to interpret the activities of each group of researchers.

But even here the issue turns complicated, as the ethnographer is apt to say to the historian. If 'the ideas, feelings, meanings of the participants' are the 'real data', as some more interpretive ethnographers and case study researchers argue, then the words of the interviewees might be 'more primary' than the observing ethnographer's eyewitness reports. This is complicated in at least two further ways. The observer, insofar as he is a participant observer, can observe and report on his own internal states thereby producing another kind of primary document. Secondly, at least since Freud, there is theory and data to suggest that an outside observation of slips of the tongue and unintentional mistakes may have a kind of validity that self-reports do not have.

Once the limits of the data are held constant, the historian and the ethnographer seem to be carrying out the same intellectual activity when the ethnographer does his descriptive narrative and the historian does his historiography, which Gottschalk defines as 'the imaginative reconstruction of the past'.

In brief, and in spite of the pluralism and variety, reading historical methodologists has been a profitable exercise in rethinking the nature of what one does as an educational ethnographer.

Process As a Mode of Integration

One's origins seem both to help and hinder one's inquiry and thought. I came to ethnographic research from a measurement oriented kind of psychology. One of the texts I taught from was Remmers and Gage's *Educational Measurement and Evaluation* (1955). One of the parts of that book which I liked, as an educational psychologist, was the unit on measuring the environment, including teaching and the classroom. About the same time I was enthralled with Cornell, Lindvahl and Saupe's *An Exploratory Measurement of Individualities of Schools and Classrooms* (1953), as well as H.H. Anderson's dominative and integrative teacher personalities (1945) and Withall's (1948) classroom climate index. All this was pre-Ned Flanders. Bryce Hudgins and I put a lot of this into our *Educational Psychology* text (1964). To me, one of the problems with this approach was that it was static, cross-sectional, structural. It was time-free. The larger problems in teaching, it seemed, were processual, sequential, longitudinal. Ethnography, or participant observation as we tended to call it, or the micro-ethnography of the classroom as Fred Strodtbeck labeled it, seemed to put us next to the evolving and developing classroom over the semester. It permitted a view of the teacher and children as active, interacting human beings. This was one of the important lessons, for me, from my work with Geoffrey in *The Complexities of an Urban Classroom*.

We struggled mightily to produce models such as Figure 3, 'A Process Analysis of an Interactional Episode'. It was a vehicle, we thought then, useful for teachers to think about their classrooms. It enabled us to begin to think about teacher decision-making and planning, a very different kind of view of human beings from that of our non-intentional educational psychology colleagues (for example, Medley and Mitzel, 1958 and 1963) and very different from the operant/respondent theories some learning psychologists were arguing. The idea was simple. On the abscissa of the figure is a time line. The ordinate is a teacher with a personality who engages in certain behaviors and actions. There are pupils, like Sam, who have personalities also and who engage in behaviors and actions. As these actions become interactions of various sorts (such as banter, personalized interaction), a social system of roles, sentiments, beliefs and norms develops. All that seems a part of Figure 3.

Over the years and through several projects we struggled with the model. That struggle achieved a slightly larger generality in our methodological essay, *Go, Bug, Go*, as Pat Brock and I argued about units for classroom analyses and

Figure 3: A Process Analysis of an Interactional Episode between Mr Geoffrey and Sam and Its Implications

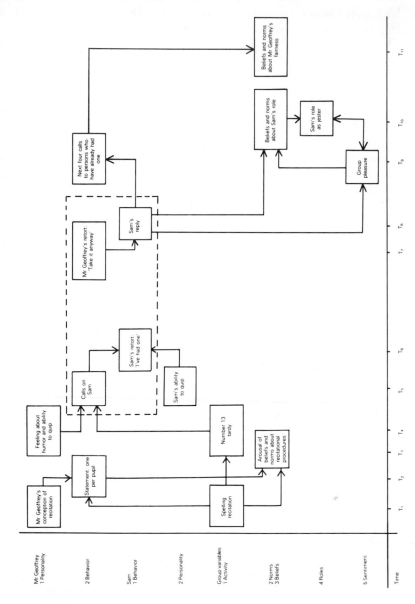

Source: Smith and Geoffrey, 1968, pp. 56–7.

classroom processes useful in thinking about her general science class (Smith and Brock, 1970; Brock and Smith, 1981).

The most significant addition to our thinking occurred as we were trying to order our data from the Kensington Revisited project. There we began talking about 'a longitudinal nested systems model of educational innovation and change'. We had gone back to the Kensington School to see the longer-term fate of an educational innovation, a specific planned change, in the Milford School District. We found the school different in a number of respects. One of the most obvious was a shift in the pupil population from 100 per cent white to 60 per cent black over the fifteen-year period. One of the obvious first answers to why this had happened was the United States Supreme Court decision in Brown versus Topeka in 1954. Before this time Midwest State law made it illegal for black children and white children to be educated in the same schools. Without that decision, or an equivalent set of changes, the school would not have been different in this regard.

The general model we present is a simple grid. The nested systems are arranged hierarchically on the ordinate; the time line was constructed on the abscissa. The generic quality of the model is suggested by the possibility of inserting any set of nested systems on the vertical axis and any time line on the horizontal. In Figure 4 we insert the systems we have seen as relevant to Kensington and Milford and add a time line from 1910 when the first records of Milford appear. Into this we place some of the items and events from the stories we have told in our narrative. Simply, we are capturing instances of innovation and change, putting them into categories that are more general and abstract, and then arranging them to demonstrate their temporal relations. We contend that each such conceptual act adds clarity and depth to the Kensington story and improves our ability to think about our original problem: What happened at Kensington? The process has not only been enlightening in this respect but has expanded the initial conceptualization of the study by suggesting further fruitful avenues of inquiry. For example, as we view the Milford District story as an important influence on Kensington events, that story becomes significant in its own right. Now one of our guiding questions is not so much 'How and why did this school change from 1964 to 1979?' but also 'Why did the Kensington School appear at all in the Milford School District?' Elsewhere we have tried to answer that substantive question (Smith *et al.*, 1981 and 1982).

When we bring the model into specific focus on the changes in the Kensington School we find a series of events, which we have drawn perhaps a bit too linearly, but which capture the flavor of international, national and state changes influencing the community which in turn influences the Milford District. Kensington's changes, 'its reversion to the old Milford type', as we predicted a decade ago, involve a complex set of demographic changes, perceived pupil changes and curriculum and instructional changes. Figure 5 specifies the items from our analysis.

This perspective has implications for both the metatheoretical and the theoretical levels of analysis. For example, it argues implicitly for a contextual-

Figure 4: Selected Events and School Personnel Arrayed on the Longitudinal Nested Systems Model

	1910	1920	1930	1940	1950	1960	1970	1980
International				Second World War (1939–45)		Sputnik (1957)	Vietnam War	
National (USA)				Post-war baby boom (1945)	Supreme Court desegregation decision (1954)	NEA intervention in district (1962)	Statewide basic achievement testing (1978)	Equal Education for Handicapped PL94–142 passed (1975)
State (Midwest)				State law for school reorganization (1948)				
County (Suburban)					Reorganization Suburban County Districts (1949–52)	County services for exceptional children (1962)	CSES involvement in Kensington (1978)	
Local Community (Several municipalities)						1 Population shifts 2 Land development 3 Extensive building of apartments	1 Community receipt of federal housing support 2 Population shifts (1975)	
School District (Milford)		Six-director Board (1925)	First superintendent appointed: Briggs (1928–30) / Grey's superintendency (1930–35)	McBride's Superintendency (1935–62) / Marquette District Annexed (1949)	Massive School Construction: Ten Buildings (1952-64)	Spanman's Superintendency (1962–66)	George's Superintendency (1966–00)	
School (Kensington)	One-room school (1910)				Shelby (1946–66)	Edwards (1966–76)	Hawkins (1976–79) Wales (1979–00)	
Classroom						Building walls (1966–00)		
Individual personality systems						Charismatic personalities (Spanman, Edwards)		

Source: Smith *et al.*, 1981.

Figure 5: *A Longitudinal Nested Systems Portrayal of the Changes in the Kensington School*

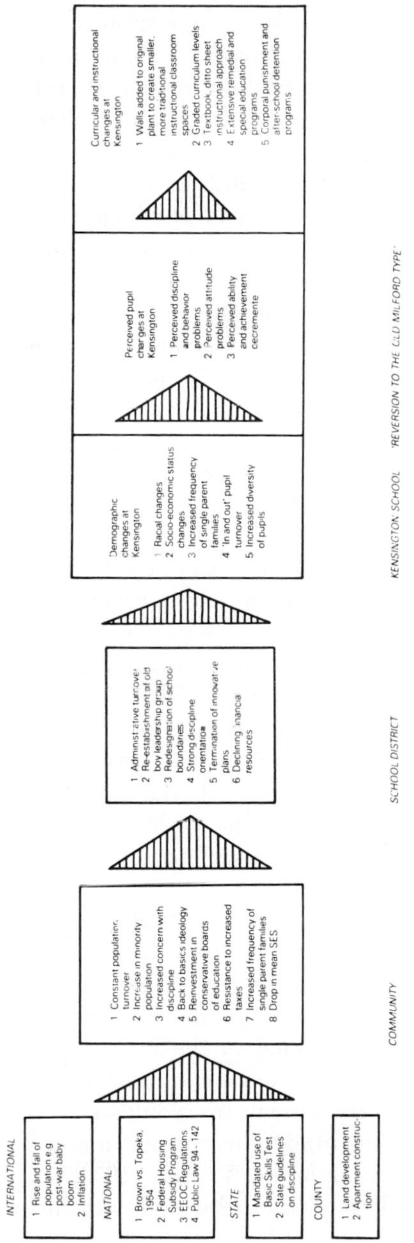

Source: Smith *et al.,* 1981.

ist root metaphor rather than a formistic, 'mechanistic or organic one (Pepper, 1942; Sarbin, 1977). Conceptually, it seems open to varied substantive theories, for example, organizational, political or cultural.

Further, the model helps locate our approach in relation to other social science studies of change and innovation in education. *First*, we find ourselves examining increasingly longer periods of time for relevant information in our inquiries. This differs from the snapshot variety of study that examines a brief, specific period. *Second*, our perspective involves a holistic view of events; we contend that one cannot understand an innovation or change in a system without considering the larger systems of which it is a part. *Third*, our model makes explicit a hierarchic arrangement among the nested systems. It high-lights the direct and indirect 'controls' one system may impose on another. *Fourth*, the longitudinal nested systems notion allows one to focus on parameters or 'givens' of the field of action set by one system upon another. *Fifth*, it assumes some autonomy both analytically and practically for each system — perhaps less than some educational theorists imply and more than some educational practitioners perceive. *Sixth*, it builds upon a psychology of individual actors, involved in events or scenes, that cumulate into meaningful structures resembling plots in drama and literature (Kelly, 1955; Sarbin, 1977). *Seventh*, it includes a respect for the chance event, the fortuitous, the serendipic, which nature forces upon us in the form of health or illness, death, and luck or natural disaster. *Finally*, and our major point here, the conception aligns closely with the perspective of some historians. We differ from some of them, too, in that our longitudinal approach carries the time line to the present, the realm of contemporary events, and sets the stage for Hexter's perspective on processive history.

In effect, what started out as an ethnographic study of a school became something very different. In part, it became an historical study of a school district. As we struggled to order this world we ended up with a process type model which has close linkages in form and purpose without earlier analyses of classroom interaction.

Partly we feel our kind of educational ethnography has had a strong process orientation. It seemed to fit some of the early interactionally oriented applied anthropologists such as Arensberg and MacGregor (1942), Arensberg and Kimball (1940), Chapple and Arensberg (1940) and Whyte (1955). However, it seems to fit less well some of the mainstream anthropologists in the functional/structural schools. When we turned to 'cultures through time' we found so far only a few individuals speaking to the issue. Radcliffe-Brown's (1958) account raised synchronic analysis and diachronic analysis but mostly argued the difficulties in the latter. Vansina (1973) and Haekel (1973) present images of the diachronic modes intertwined with historical references.

At this point in our work, I believe the diachronic or process mode is an appropriate and powerful way to join ethnographic and historical modes of inquiry. It handles well a cluster of important phenomena in the micro-world of Geoffrey's classrooms and in the macro-world of the Milford School District.

Any conceptual tool that bridges events as diverse as Sam's jester role and Kensington's transformation from an innovative school to a traditional school is a powerful addition to our ways of thinking about schooling.

In this essay, I have not taken up the process analyses of individuals and the data we have on the careers and lives of our original Kensington faculty. The interplay of life history, biography and autobiography with historical and ethnographic method is vivid, striking and informative. We will have more to say about that on another day. It seems clearly to belong in the discussion at this point.

The Move to Broader Assumptions, Metatheory or Paradigms

A second kind of serendipity also seemed to be in the offing. As our story telling and analysis was moving to a close, we found, lurking in the background, concerns that we have often labeled 'broader assumptions', 'metatheoretical issues', or 'the nature of one's basic paradigm'. Somehow we wanted a next level of consistency, which never seemed attainable, for it was too big a problem. In fieldwork, at least as we practise it, the intensive literature search often comes relatively late in the inquiry process. On those occasions we use it to help see our data and ideas in a broader, intellectual setting. We try to generalize our findings. In part, this intellectual activity is the relation of the particular instance to a larger, more general, more abstract class of events (Smith, 1979; Diesing, 1971). This becomes a practical task when one intersperses ideas and stories or when one views conclusion sections as offering the analyst and interpreter a variety of intellectual options.

As we were finishing a major piece of the Kensington Revisited project, what we called 'Milford's recent history: The school district as contemporary context of the Kensington School', and as we were doing our 'literature survey', we were brought up short. We found ourselves stunned in reading Keith Goldhammer's provocative little book, *The School Board* (1964). We remarked to ourselves that our account of Milford's recent history, heavily an account of the Board and superintendents, was quite different. In trying to isolate those differences we generated a list of a baker's dozen items. As we looked at that list, we felt that our tacit knowledge had been running well out ahead of our formalized knowledge — we knew better than we realized, a not unusual phenomenon in this kind of research, at least as we practise it. Consequently, we present Figure 6.

Obviously, our intent is not to disparage Goldhammer's work, which is provocative in its brevity and clarity, but we believe we have come out of our experience with a point of view that is quite different — not simply different in the sense of a substantive middle range theory of school boards, but that it has the potential for an integrated view of schooling across several levels of analysis. For instance, it encompasses the kinds of data one collects when one thinks about schools, the kinds of methods and procedures linked to those data, the

Figure 6:   Contrasts with Goldhammer: Toward a New Perspective

---

1   Full of people with interests, motives, and sentiments
2   who are making choices and decisions
3   which lead to actions and interactions
4   which are in a context — historical and contemporaneous
5   which gives a dynamic or processual quality
6   as a case it is interrelated and systemic
7   substantive focus is on innovation and change
8   blends/mixes/integrates the specific/concrete/particular and the general/abstract/universal
9   focuses on the 'real', the 'is' rather than an external 'ideal', on the 'ought', or the prescriptive
10 part of the real is the 'multiple ideals of the several actors and subgroups out there'
11 those ideals are often in conflict and are resolved by a variety of social/political processes
12 eventually all individuals and subgroups make up their own minds
13 ultimately integrates is/ought dichotomies in an R.M. Hare (1952) type configurated decision of principle
14 as personal experiences cumulate (and case studies are surrogates for those) one builds toward one's own syntheses of decisions of principle.

---

kinds of accounts one renders of those phenomena — both commonsense and technical — the kinds of concepts, propositions, principles and generalizations one uses in one's thinking, and finally a root metaphor, a world view, or metatheoretical perspective that is consonant with the other levels of analysis and synthesis. We believe this perspective to be the most fundamental intellectual achievement of this part of our research. Its test will be the degree to which it can subsume the substantive findings from the other parts of our study and several additional perspectives from the literature of social science and education.

For now, we have used Goldhammer as a means of articulating our perspective, essentially at the level of assumption behind the kinds of data we gathered and the kinds of substantive ideas and theory we will pose shortly. This is basically our conception of metatheory. To be more specific, the first six items on our list indicate we are making statements consonant with Pepper's (1942) contextualist world view and with Burke's (1945) dramaturgical model. Substantively we feel it puts us into the psychology of personal constructs of George Kelly (1955) and the dramaturgical sociology of Goffman (1959) as these have been brought together by Sarbin (1977) with the 'emplotment metaphor'. In education, symbolic interactionists such as Delamont (1976) and Hargreaves (1975) have a similar view.

Items 4, 5 and 6 suggest an historical framework and a systemic framework. In an early report on our findings, we used the term 'longitudinal nested systems model' to capture our meaning. For clarity, we would note that the system's idea, for us, is not the closed, convergent, mechanical model of the operations analysts but rather the open, divergent, holistic model suggested by the constructionists and the aestheticians and artists. These differences stretch into every aspect of learning, teaching and schooling.

Item 7, innovation and change, is partly our attempt to deal with the initial substantive problem at hand, but also to capture planned or intentional action on the one hand and the larger category of unplanned alterations as well. In our view, these two concepts have been separated and kept too far apart.

Item 8 attempts to dissolve one of the major dichotomies of the logical positivists (Joergensen, 1951), the split between the operational, data language, and the theoretical, conceptual language in favor of a more configurational, concatenated or patterned language and account of events. This implies a shift in the concept of explanation from a covering law model (deductive nomothetic or inductive statistical) to a pattern model (Hempel, 1965; Kaplan, 1964; Diesing, 1971).

Item 9 tries to focus on two points. The first is an attempt to be wary of judging individuals and groups, particularly from an earlier time and place, against a latter-day set of standards, ideals or ideology. The second aspect of Item 9 blends with 10–13 and attempts to take a position on the is/ought dichotomy of Hume, its extension by the positivists of the early twentieth century, and its part within the dominant ideology of American educational researchers (for example, Campbell and Stanley, 1963) if not more world wide social science.

Item 13 is fundamentally an acceptance of R.M. Hare's (1952) decision of principle. When everything has been said, which is the extended account of all the items, then one has to decide how one wants to live — and then do it. That's our understanding of his decision of principle. Finally, Item 14 individualizes and personalizes that.

As one traces out one's assumptions and the roots of the assumptions, an awesome intellectual agenda is created. While this came to focus as we read Goldhammer's book, it obviously had been brewing for some time. Equally obviously, it is a long way from being finished. For us, though, it sketches the level and kind of issues we believe are at stake at this point in our work and in our interpretation of where educational thought should be moving. More specifically, in the context of historical and ethnographic methods, the synthesis within and between groups of historians and anthropologists needs to involve items and issues of this sort.

Summary and Conclusions

These remarks began with the telling of a story or two. Beyond setting the general stage, my intention was to convey the potency of narrative accounts in explaining the origin of a set of ideas. Although they are history with a small 'h', as Hexter uses the expression, they do say some things about communities of researchers, our small niche of qualitative case study inquiry, and the sociology of educational research.

Second, my intent was to share a number of items that arose as I stumbled about in the 'Board Minutes' of what has become one of the most interesting research projects in which I have ever been involved. Mostly it's an account of attempts to raise some of the intellectual and emotional reactions to the experience. Most grew out of interpretive asides, noted along the way.

Third, as I detached myself from the details of Kensington Revisited, I was struck by the diversity among anthropological ethnographers and among historians. One might say that the within group variance was greater than the between group variance. In an earlier essay on ethnography, the reading I had done on Malinowski, Whyte and Geertz reaffirmed what Paul Pohland and I had meant when we commented that there was no such thing as 'standard participant observation methods'. My more recent tour through the historians Gottschalk, Hexter, Stone and White (not to mention such philosophers of history as Scriven, Dray and Gardiner) left me with much the same feelings.

However, it seemed to me, and I raised a number of illustrations, that the kind of thinking processes we engaged in our educational ethnographic work had a number of counterparts in the activities and thinking of historians who examine and work with documents. By starting with the hunch, the hypothesis, or the interrogative question, that history is nothing but participant observation with data fragments, I found the historians clarifying, extending and rationalizing some of the more puzzling ethnographic practices we seemed to be using at a commonsense level. In this way, we came to know better what we were doing and what we might do. We gained confidence that we could defend the practices. In addition, I believe we have both broadened the scope of our activities and moved toward a more patterned synthesis of a position. Though it's not 'the' system or 'the one right way', to borrow a phrase from one of our Kensington collegial subjects, it does represent an approach others can look at, discuss and criticize on the way to developing their own positions.

In this same, more detached mood, I raised two broad ideas which seem to further a more general rapprochement between ethnography and history. When, in the Kensington Revisited project, we begin to talk about 'a longitudinal nested systems model of educational innovation and change' we thought we were on to a way of organizing our data to give a contextual or concatenated explanatory vehicle. We believe it does link historical and contemporaneous events into a potent image or framework. The more we puzzled with it, talked about, argued with ourselves and our colleagues, the more pleased we were. Finally, when we saw the similarities to the earlier classroom models we had developed concerning the micro-processes of Geoffrey's classroom, we thought that we could subsume some of the most important events in schooling within similar frameworks. Whether that's really so, we shall see.

Mixed in with these activities is what my colleague Arthur Wirth and I have been calling a 'search for a paradigm'. For me, the most recent aspect of that search has been the perplexities which arose in reading Goldhammer's book, *The School Board*. Our Kensington Revisited account seemed so different. In detailing those differences, our thoughts skipped quickly through a number of puzzling epistemological and ethical issues, ending up with a focus on R.M. Hare's 'decision of principle'. Whether we have put as much order and pattern here as I think and hope and whether it is as important as I think and hope, I don't know. For the moment, it seems a rationale helpful to talk about, if not explain, our efforts in a kind of inquiry which seems to put us on to interesting problems, which seems to give us ways of coping with those problems, and which seems, interestingly, to blend what a number of people call historical and ethnographic methods.

References

ANDERSON, H.H. and BREWER, M. (1945) 'Studies of teachers' classroom personalities, I: Dominative and socially integrative behavior of kindergarten teachers', *Applied Psychological Monographs*, 6.

ARENSBERG, C.M. and KIMBALL, C.T. (1940) *Family and Community in Ireland*, Cambridge, Mass., Harvard University Press.

ARENSBERG, C.M. and MACGREGOR, D. (1941) 'Determination of morale in an industrial company', *Applied Anthropology*, 1, pp. 12–34.

BEITTEL, K.R. (1973) *Alternatives for Art Education Research*, Dubuque, Iowa, Wm. C. Brown.

BOORSTIN, D.J. (1973) *The Americans: The Democratic Experience*, New York, Random House.

BROCK, J.A.M. and SMITH, L.M. (1981) *Teaching Tales and Theories: A Story and Commentary on a General Science Classroom*, St. Louis, Mo., CEMREL.

BURKE, K. (1969) *A Grammar of Motives*, Berkeley, Calif., University of California Press (originally published by Prentice Hall, 1945).

BUTTS, R.F. (1978) *Public Education in the United States*, New York, Holt, Rinehart and Winston.

CAMPBELL, D.T. and STANLEY, J.C. (1963) 'Experimental and quasi-experimental designs for research in teaching', in GAGE, N. (Ed.) *Handbook of Research in Teaching*, Chicago, Ill., Rand McNally.

CHAPPLE, E. and ARENSBERG, C. (1940) 'Measuring human relations: An introduction to the study of interaction of individuals', *Genetic Psychological Monographs*, 22, pp. 1–147.

CORNELL, F.G. et al. (1953) *An Exploratory Measurement of Individualities of Schools and Classrooms*, Urbana, Ill., University of Illinois Press.

CREMIN, L.A. (1980) *American Education: The National Experiences 1783–1876*, New York, Harper and Row.

DELAMONT, S. (1976) *Interaction in the Classroom*, London, Methuen.

DIESING, P. (1971) *Patterns of Discovery in the Social Sciences*, Chicago, Ill., Aldine, Atherton.

DRAY, W. (1957) *Laws and Explanation in History*, Oxford, Oxford University Press.

GARDINER, P. (1959) (Ed.) *Theories of History*, New York, Free Press.

GEERTZ, C. (1973) *The Interpretation of Cultures*, New York, Basic Books.

GEERTZ, C. (1975) 'On the nature of anthropological understanding', *American Scientist*, 63, pp. 47–53.

GLASER, B. and STRAUSS, A. (1967) *The Discovery of Grounded Theory*, Chicago, Ill., Aldine.

GOFFMAN, E. (1959) *The Presentation of Self in Everyday Life*, New York, Anchor.

GOLDHAMMER, K. (1964) *The School Board*, New York, Center for Applied Research in Education.

GOTTSCHALK, L. (1945) 'The historian and the historical document', in GOTTSCHALK, L. *et al. The Use of Personal Documents in History, Anthropology, and Sociology*, New York, Social Science Research Council.

GREENFIELD, T.B. (1978) 'Reflections on organization theory and the truths of irreconcilable realities', *Educational Administration Quarterly*, 14, 2, pp. 43–65.

GRIFFITHS, D. (1979) 'Intellectual turmoil in educational administration', *Educational Administration Quarterly*, 15, 3, pp. 43–65.

HAEKEL, J. (1973) 'Source criticism in anthropology', in NAROLL, R. and COHEN, R. (Eds) *A Handbook of Method in Cultural Anthropology*, New York, Columbia University Press.

HARE, R.M. (1964) *The Language of Morals*, London, Oxford University Press (originally in 1952).

HARGREAVES, D.H. (1975) *Interpersonal Relations and Education*, student ed., London, Routledge and Kegan Paul.

HEMPEL, C.G. (1941) 'The function of general laws in history', *Journal of Philosophy*, 39, pp. 35–48.

HEMPEL, C.G. (1963) *Aspects of Scientific Explanation and Other Essays in Philosophy of Science*, New York, Free Press.

HEXTER, J. (1971) *The History Primer*, New York, Basic Books.

HOMANS, G.C. (1950) *The Human Group*, New York, Harcourt Brace.

JOERGENSEN, J. (1951) *The Development of Logical Empiricism*, Chicago, Ill., University of Chicago Press.

KAPLAN, A. (1964) *The Conduct of Inquiry*, San Francisco, Calif., Chandler.

KELLY, G.A. (1955) *The Psychology of Personal Constructs*, New York, Norton.

McKINNEY, W.L. and WESTBURY, I. (1974) 'Stability and change: The public schools of Gary, Indiana 1940–1970', in REID, W.A. and WALKER, D.F. (Eds) *Case Studies in Curriculum Change: Great Britain and the United States*, London, Routledge and Kegan Paul.

MALINOWSKI, B. (1922) *The Argonauts of the Western Pacific*, London, Routledge.

MEDLEY, D.M. and MITZEL, H.E. (1949) 'A technique for measuring classroom behavior', *Journal of Educational Psychology*, 49, pp. 86–92.

MEDLEY, D.M. and MITZEL, H.E. (1963) 'Measuring classroom behavior by systematic observation, in GAGE, N. (Ed.) *Handbook of Research on Teaching*, Chicago, Ill., Rand-McNally.

MYRDAL, G. (1944) *An American Dilemma: The Negro Problem and Modern Democracy*, Vols 1 and 2, New York, Harper and Row.

PEPPER, S. (1942) *World Hypotheses: A Study in Evidence*, Berkeley, Calif., University of California Press.

RADCLIFFE-BROWN, A.R. (1958) *Method in Social Anthropology*, Chicago, Ill., University of Chicago Press.

REMMERS, H.H. and GAGE, N. (1955) *Educational Measurement and Evaluation*, rev. ed., New York, Harpers.

SARBIN, T.R. (1977) 'Contextualism: A world view for modern psychology', in COLE, J. (Ed.) *Personal Construct Psychology. Nebraska Symposium on Motivation, 1976*, Lincoln, Nebraska, University of Nebraska Press.

SCRIVEN, M. (1959) 'Truisms as the grounds for historical explanations', in GARDINER, P. (Ed.) *Theories of History*, New York, Free Press.

SMITH, L.M. (1978) 'Science education in the Alte Schools: A kind of case study', in

Stake, R. and Easley, J. (Eds) *Case Studies in Science Education*, Washington, D.C., NSF.

Smith, L.M. (1979) 'An evolving logic of participant observation, educational ethnography and other case studies', in Shulman, L. (Ed.) *Review of Research in Education*, Chicago, Ill., Peacock Press.

Smith, L.M. (1982) 'Ethnography', in Mitzel, H. (Ed.) *Encyclopedia of Educational Research*, Chicago, Ill., Rand-McNally.

Smith, L.M. and Brock, J.A.M. (1970) 'Go, Bug, Go': Methodological Issues in *Classroom Observational Research*, Occasional Paper Series, no. 5, St Ann, Mo., CEMREL.

Smith, L.M. and Dwyer, D.C. (1980) *Federal Policy in Action: A Case Study of an Urban Education Project*, Washington, D.C., NIE.

Smith, L.M. and Geoffrey, W. (1968) *The Complexities of an Urban Classroom*, New York, Holt.

Smith, L.M. and Hudgins, B.B. (1964) *Educational Psychology*, New York, Knopf.

Smith, L.M. and Keith, P. (1971) *Anatomy of Educational Innovation*, New York, Wiley.

Smith, L.M. and Pohland, P. (1976) 'Grounded theory and educational ethnography: A methodological analysis and critique', in Roberts, J. and Akinsanya, S.K. (Eds) *Educational Patterns and Cultural Configurations*, New York, David McKay.

Smith, L.M. *et al.* (1981) 'Observer role and field study knowledge, an essay review of *Usable Knowledge* and *SAFARI I Educational Evaluation and Policy Analyses*', 3, pp. 83–90.

Smith, L.M. *et al.* (1982) *Kensington Revisited: A Fifteen Year Follow-up of an Innovative School and Its Faculty*, Washington, D.C., NIE.

Stake, R. (1977) 'Description versus analysis', in Hamilton, D. *et al.* (Eds) *Beyond the Numbers Game*, London, Macmillan.

Stone, L. (1981) *The Past and the Present*, Boston, Mass., Routledge and Kegan Paul.

Vansina, J. (1973) 'Cultures through time', in Naroll, R. and Cohen, R. (Eds) *A Handbook of Method in Cultural Anthropology*, New York, Columbia University Press.

White, M. (1963) 'The logic of historical narration', in Hook, S. (Ed.) *Philosophy and History*, New York, New York University Press.

White, W.T., Jr. (1982) 'The decline of the classroom and the Chicago Study of Education 1909–1929', in *American Journal of Education*, 90, pp. 144–74.

Whyte, W.E. (1955) *Street Corner Society*, rev. ed., Chicago, Ill., University of Chicago Press.

Withall, J. (1948) 'The development of a technique for the measurement of social-emotional climate in classrooms', unpublished PhD dissertation, University of Chicago.

Part Three
Ethnographies

It's Not a Proper Subject: It's Just Newsom

Robert G. Burgess

For some years sociologists of education have focussed on elements of 'success' and 'failure' in the school system, paying special attention to the relative failure of working-class pupils.[1] In turn, those sociologists of education working within the interactionist tradition have, like sociologists of deviance, taken the perspective of the 'underdog' and conducted studies among those pupils who have encountered difficulties in schooling and who have been failed by their teachers. Accordingly, the focus of several studies of classroom interaction between teachers and pupils has been on the school leaver, the anti-group, pupils who create disruption in the classroom (cf. Furlong, 1976; Gannaway, 1976; Birksted, 1976; Davies, 1979). This theme has also been picked up by researchers working within a Marxist perspective (Willis, 1977; Corrigan, 1979) who have also focussed on similar groups of pupils. Yet, despite all these studies we have little or no knowledge about the 'education' at which the pupils 'failed'. Within empirical studies of schools and classrooms we have learned much about the interactions, strategies and negotiations that have taken place but we know very little about the curriculum content of the lessons. Even when sociologists have focussed on the school curriculum they have turned their attention to conventional school subjects.[2] As a consequence they have failed to analyze the non-subject courses that are provided for pupils who are regarded as the 'less willing' and the 'less able'.

In some respects, this neglect is not unusual. Indeed, a brief glance at many secondary school timetables would indicate that subjects lie at the heart of the secondary school curriculum; they are the basic building blocks out of which the formal curriculum is constructed. In this respect, sociologists have posed questions about those aspects of the curriculum that are highly visible in schools: subject disciplines. Even in cases where some innovation is taking place, the teaching of 'humanities' is often based on history, geography and religious education, while 'life sciences' will be constructed out of chemistry and biology. In itself this is not surprising as teachers in secondary schools are predominantly recruited as subject specialists. In their initial training in universities and colleges they will have focussed on subject specialisms (cf.

Lacey, 1977; Ball and Lacey, 1980) and will have entered secondary schools in order to teach their subjects. For subject expertise gives many secondary school teachers their identity and their status (cf. Hargreaves, 1982, pp. 192–200).

Secondary schools are predominantly organized in terms of subject departments. Teachers and pupils are timetabled to teach and learn about subject disciplines which are subsequently evaluated in public examinations. Here, knowledge may be seen as an end in itself with the consequence that it becomes difficult to adapt and adopt new approaches to teaching and learning. Nevertheless, teachers have introduced some new approaches into secondary schools. When the school leaving age was raised to 16 (DES, 1971) several developments took place in terms of attempts to provide a more attractive curriculum for the 16-year-old who would not be taking many external examinations. Among those approaches that were widely canvassed were: team teaching, an integrated curriculum and interdisciplinary enquiry. Teachers who worked with 'less able' pupils planned to use these approaches as for many of their children the traditional subject curriculum was deemed inappropriate when they had already failed at conventional school subjects (cf. Hannam *et al.*, 1971). However, we might ask: How are 'new' approaches planned and used? How are they perceived by teachers and by pupils?

During the course of conducting an ethnographic study of a purpose built co-educational Roman Catholic comprehensive school that I called Bishop McGregor (Burgess, 1983)[3] I focussed on an area that lay outside the traditional subject structure by looking at courses that were provided for those pupils who were generally regarded as 'non-academic', 'non-examinees' or 'Easter-leavers'. At McGregor they were also called 'Newsom pupils' as their course and their department took its name from the Newsom Report (Newsom, 1963) that had made recommendations on the education of secondary school pupils of average and below average ability. Within the Newsom Department I found that there was considerable flexibility in terms of courses, work and discipline. The headmaster indicated that Newsom was an experimental area where teachers might expect to meet with considerable success and some failure. Many teachers made comparisons between educational activities that took place within subject departments and the activities that took place within the Newsom Department and among Newsom pupils with the result that the phrase 'It's just Newsom' became a shorthand summary not only for the noise and disruption that pupils brought into classrooms, but also a description of the courses that were provided by the Department. As a researcher who taught in the Newsom Department I learned first-hand about the Newsom course, the pupils' conception of the course and their views about it.

Just as the teachers made comparisons between the Newsom Department and subject departments so did the pupils. I found that, like their teachers, pupils were quick to comment that Newsom was 'not a proper subject' and as a result they considered that Newsom teachers did not need qualifications. This topic was pursued in conversation during lessons and during informal or unstructured interviews that I held with pupils. Several of these perspectives were summarized by pupils during the course of one of my Newsom lessons. I had set my group some work and was walking around the classroom when I noticed that Terry Nicholls was not working so I asked:

RB: Why aren't you working?
Terry: What's the use of this work?
RB: What do you think you ought to do?
Terry: I wanna do as little as possible for as long as possible. I wanna do as little as I can. Anyway this work don't give you any qualifications. It don't get you anywhere.

I said nothing and Terry continued:

Terry: What subjects do you teach besides this? What qualifications do you have?
RB: I'm qualified to teach sociology and geography.
Terry: It's not important to have these qualifications to teach Newsom.

At this remark, Peter Vincent joined in the conversation.

Peter: What's the sense of teaching Newsom with these qualifications? You don't have to be clever to teach Newsom. I don't think you're a proper teacher. What else do you do?
RB: Why do you think I'm not a proper teacher?
Peter: Newsom isn't proper teaching.[4]

This conversation summarizes several elements of the pupils' perspective of the Newsom course: the work provided no qualifications for the pupils, teachers did not require qualifications to teach the course, teachers were involved in teaching other subjects, and Newsom was not 'proper teaching'. Implicit within this conversation and in further conversations with pupils, with teachers and with the headmaster comparisons were made between Newsom courses and subject department work. In these terms, by focussing on Newsom courses it is possible to outline the characteristics of a non-academic course and by implication to consider the characteristics associated with conventional subjects. It is these issues that are explored within this paper by drawing on ethnographic material on Newsom courses. However, before focussing upon the Newsom courses at McGregor School, it is essential to locate the term 'Newsom course'.

The Newsom Report and Newsom Courses

In 1963 the Newsom committee reported on the education of average and below average children in the 13–16 age-range in secondary schools (Newsom, 1963). In commenting upon the education of these pupils the committee indicated that their education should be practical and realistic, and should be vocationally orientated. Indeed, they considered that the pupils should be involved in choosing what they should learn. As a consequence they argued: 'We believe that these four words — practical, realistic, vocational, choice — provide keys which can be used to let even the least able boys and girls enter into an educational experience which is genuinely secondary' (Newsom, 1963, p. 114). The committee stressed the importance of basic skills in reading, writing and calculation being reinforced throughout the whole curriculum. In turn, they argued that science and mathematics were important to these pupils who would be living in a scientific world and they also recommended that the pupils should have the opportunity to learn a foreign language. There was also the idea that the education provided for such pupils should be 'deliberately outgoing — an initiation into the adult world of work and leisure' (p. xvii). Accordingly, a vast list of practical subjects was discussed that included art and the studio crafts, handicrafts, rural studies, housecraft and needlework, physical education and music. Meanwhile, under the heading 'Humanities', the committee considered the teaching of English (including film and television) and drama, a foreign language and 'the proper study of mankind' which was taken to include history and geography.

Several commentators (Shipman, 1971; Lawton, 1973; Eggleston, 1977) have been critical of the curriculum recommendations in the report, for as Shipman indicated the Newsom committee had recommended separate forms of schooling which resulted in 'relevant' courses for the average and below average children compared with examination courses based on the traditional subject framework for above average pupils. Indeed, he remarks:

> The new curriculum, involving topic centred approaches, interdisciplinary enquiry, projects taking the children outside the school and experience of social service and working conditions, will probably increase the motivation of the pupils and give them an insight into the working of the world around them. They are often lacking in real academic discipline and at worst can be a pot-pourri of trivia chosen because they are believed to be of interest to the young. But regardless of their worth, they could separate the education of the Newsom child from that of the future elite as effectively as when these groups were educated in different schools or systems. (Shipman, 1971, pp. 103–4)

Further criticisms along similar lines were also made by Lawton (1973) who argued that:

> What has happened in many schools since the Newsom Report has been some effort to set up a curriculum organisation for the fourth year leavers, in preparation for the time when they will be fifth-year leavers, which will somehow keep them quiet and prevent them breaking up the furniture. Outward looking curricula have degenerated into watered-down meaningless outside visits; 'real experience'

has degenerated into watered-down life-adjustment courses. (Lawton, 1973, p. 115)

With these comments in mind, we turn to the Newsom course at Bishop McGregor School to see whether these critical comments and those of the pupils are justified.

Newsom Courses at Bishop McGregor School

The headmaster at Bishop McGregor School had previously held a headship in a secondary modern school where he had gained considerable success in devising and teaching courses for pupils that he defined as 'non-academic' school leavers. Much of the content of these courses rested upon the recommendations that were contained in the Newsom Report. It was, therefore, not unusual that this aspect of secondary schooling should be introduced into McGregor School.

On this point, Mr Goddard (the headmaster) was explicit. Before the school opened in 1969 he spoke to parents in the feeder junior schools about the aims and objectives that he had for the school. During the course of his talk he discussed his ideas for the school curriculum which he indicated would be derived from other forms of secondary education. In particular, he indicated that McGregor would organize courses that would come from the grammar school tradition with 'streaming, setting and high standards'. Technical courses would be available, and there would be Newsom courses which would be based upon successful practice in secondary modern schools. In these terms, Goddard's curriculum was based upon elements of a tripartite system of school organization which brought inequality into the curriculum arrangements of this new school (cf. Shipman, 1971 and 1980).

From the time Goddard started to make appointments to his teaching staff he had sought out teachers who had experience with non-academic pupils. Indeed, teachers who were applying for posts in houses and departments were specifically asked if they were prepared to teach a course or part of a course to Newsom pupils. Yet at this stage McGregor had no senior pupils as it was a new school. However, Goddard was already thinking about future developments, including the possibility that the school leaving age would be raised to 16 which at that time (1969) was being widely canvassed. In an interview with me he discussed his early plans:

> I knew that even if ROSLA [the raising of the school leaving age to 16] did not come I would have non-academic youngsters. I knew that it took at least twelve months to draw up programmes for these youngsters, to keep them interested and to do something for them.[5]

On the basis of his earlier experiences in designing such courses he explained: 'I knew I would need a variety of staff and a variety of talents. I wanted to spot who would be useful to me.'[6]

Plans for the Newsom course were laid within the first four terms. Staff had to be appointed during the second year in which the school operated as Newsom teaching would begin with fourth year pupils just three years after the school had opened.[7] However, Goddard indicated that he had planned this course because: 'I realised that if we did not do something for them [the non-academic pupils] they would destroy the rest of us.'[8]

In these terms, Newsom courses were not merely for those pupils for whom the courses were designed, but were also for the benefit of other pupils and their teachers who were engaged in examination classes in the fourth and fifth years. Subject teachers regularly commented on the positive aspects of not having Newsom pupils in examination group options and indeed so did the pupils in these groups. One boy (Malcolm Jackson) who had been in examination group options until the end of the autumn term in the fifth year, summed this up by saying: 'Maybe it's [Newsom's] boring but I think it's the best thing really. 'Cos if you don't do your exams it's no use staying in hindering the exam people.'[9]

In his terms, Newsom was seen as a direct alternative to examinations; a view that was shared by teachers and expressed in the headmaster's definition (the official school definition) of Newsom that was contained in reports and memoranda on the department and in further particulars on posts in the department. Goddard summed up the school's view of Newsom work by stating:

> For better or for worse we at McGregor use the word Newsom and define it as 'work on non-examination material designed for pupils for whom the maximum expectation of success in public examinations seems likely to be 3 CSE Grade 5's or less'.[10]

The main strands of Goddard's philosophy behind the Newsom Department were summarized in an interview with me. As far as he was concerned, there were three main elements to the 'Newsom programme' as he called it:

> First, it must not take a child totally away from the peer group. It is a part programme rather than a full programme. Secondly, it is an alternative to the exam programme for the more academic. Thirdly, it is designed to develop and strengthen those talents in the non-academic which will be most useful to that youngster in society; job wise, marriage wise, recreation wise.

The Newsom course was, therefore, an alternative to the traditional examination course in the fourth and fifth year. However, Newsom pupils were in classes with their peers for subjects that were part of the core curriculum in the upper school (tutorial, English, mathematics, religious education and games). In addition, Newsom pupils also had the opportunity to choose two practical subjects from a range of options that were available for other fourth and fifth year pupils. As McGregor operated on a thirty-five-period week at least twelve lessons each week were devoted to the Newsom course. Unlike examination

Table 1: *Newsom Teachers at Bishop McGregor School in the Summer Term 1973*

Newsom teachers	Qualification	Responsibility in the school	Main subjects taught	Newsom courses taught
Sylvia Robinson	Teachers' Certificate, main subjects in Physical Education and Mathematics	Head of Careers (scale 4)	Careers and General Subjects (Religious Education and some Science)	Money Matters, Project Work, First Aid
Keith Dryden	Teachers' Certificate, main subject in Art	—	Art	Woodcarving
Stanley Booth	Teachers' Certificate, main subject in Art	Head of House (scale 5)	Art	Horse Riding
David Smith	Graduate in Art	—	Art	Camping
Terry Goodwin	Teachers' Certificate, main subject in Home Economics	—	Home Economics	Food, Mothercare
Jim Parkes	Graduate in Science	Scale post for Audio-Visual Aids (scale 2)	Biology	Film Making, Wine Making
Geoff Goddard	Graduate with qualifications in Science and Religious Education	Headmaster	Variety of subjects especially Religious Education and Science	Safety, Organized course with Fire Service

Note: At the time this research was conducted teachers were awarded posts of responsibility on a scale 1 (basic) to 5 (maximum) subjects where a set syllabus was available for the teacher, no such prescribed material existed for Newsom courses as at McGregor: 'the actual content of the course depends on: (a) the abilities and talents of the members of staff taking the group; (b) type of rooms available as well as the use of materials'.[11] During the period I was in McGregor one group followed a Newsom programme in the fourth year which in addition to the subjects in the core curriculum included workshop mathematics, project-based science courses, project options on government, economics, local history, mining and the post office, leisure time pursuits and external courses organized by the Fire Service, the St John Ambulance Brigade and the local technical college. Meanwhile, in the fifth year the pupils' work included government, law and general studies, workshop mathematics, courses that could be selected from mothercare, woodcarving, jewellery making and food, a course on going to work and a leisure course.

These courses were designed and taught by teachers who were drawn from a variety of other areas in the school. In my first term in the school the teachers who were working on Newsom courses were as shown in Table 1. All these teachers except Sylvia Robinson, who had initially joined the school for a joint post in careers and Newsom work, had volunteered to take Newsom courses. They had found that they 'got on' with the pupils and for those without any scale post of responsibility it was a possible avenue for promotion.[12] Keith Dryden and Terry Goodwin considered it unlikely that they would get promotion of any kind within their subject area but as they were prepared to teach Newsom pupils some promotion seemed possible within this department. For these two teachers and for a new teacher who was appointed to the school in the academic year 1973–74, scale two posts were provided for their work with Newsom pupils. Together these teachers and other volunteers constituted the Newsom Department.

Not a Proper Department?

In a school which organizationally was subdivided into houses for pastoral work and departments for subject work, Newsom was part of the departmental structure. However, it was different from other departments. Newsom had no head of department which had political and status implications as departments were represented at heads of departments meetings that were held on alternate weeks during each term and where key decisions were taken that could affect departmental resources. The only Newsom teacher who attended these meetings was Sylvia Robinson but as far as she was concerned she was present to represent careers for which she held a scale four post of responsibility. As a consequence no individual teacher fully represented the Newsom Department. The department therefore had no direct means of contributing to school policy which was developed by the heads of departments. Furthermore, it had implications for staffing and for departmental resources.

The Newsom Department had only one room available to it; apart from that it had to use rooms that were a part of other departmental accommodation and which were vacated by department staff during free lessons. As far as staff were concerned, Newsom, unlike all other departments, had no teachers who held full-time appointments for that work alone. In these terms, even teachers with scale posts in the Newsom area were considered to be 'on loan' from subject departments to the Newsom Department. This became especially clear when departmental meetings were held at the beginning of each academic year. Subject departments could use the day before the start of term to hold their meetings. Here, it was assumed that Newsom teachers would go to subject department meetings for as Sylvia Robinson indicated in a letter to Newsom teachers outlining the arrangements for the beginning of term:

> It is quite obvious that when all the departments use 30th August for departmental meetings, all of us engaged in Newsom studies will already be involved. I hope, therefore, that we can meet as soon as possible after the beginning of term and that the scheme [of work] is clear enough for us to make a start immediately.[13]

Invariably Newsom meetings had to be carved out of the existing timetable with the result that several days elapsed at the beginning of the academic year when teachers organized the teaching and their groups in response to the final timetable arrangements to which they had not been a party and which provided limited resources in which to teach practically orientated courses.

Departments in McGregor School were given status on the basis of their physical resources, the size of their staff and the scale posts given to members of the department (cf. Burgess, 1983). In addition, success in public examinations enhanced the status of the departments who were publicly congratulated or admonished by the headmaster in the first staff meeting at the start of an academic year. In this instance, Newsom which had been defined as a 'non-academic', 'non-examination' group was involved in a competition in which it had no means of competing. On the basis of the criteria used it could never be mentioned. Overall, the criteria that were used by teachers to judge departments produced an unfavourable result for Newsom as it had few resources, no permanent members of teaching staff and no head of department. However, in terms of the points available for scale posts it did have a total allocation of three which placed it alongside religious education, geography, careers and remedial education and above music, audio-visual aids, humanities and general hospitality. However, unlike other departments where posts were given for administrative responsibilities Newsom teachers were given posts just for teaching. Yet what constituted Newsom teaching was often questioned by the Newsom teachers, by teachers in other departments and by the pupils.

Not a Proper Subject?

We have already seen that Newsom teachers held qualifications in a variety of disciplines but with a distinct orientation towards practical subjects. However, when it came to teaching classes the knowledge that was disseminated to pupils was modified and simplified. The teachers devised courses whose content and titles were thought to be suitable to capture the pupils' imagination (cf. Hargreaves, 1982, pp. 50–2). The main courses that were devised are shown in Table 2. In Newsom, not even the subject areas were recognizable. New titles had been substituted with the idea of making courses more 'practical', more 'relevant', more vocationally orientated and to include some elements of choice. However, as we shall see, the pupils were critical of what was on offer.

Table 2.   The Content of Newsom Courses

Areas of study	Course titles	Subjects
Government, Law and General Studies	Mining The Post Office The Fire Service Local Studies	History Geography Social Studies
Workshop Mathematics Project Options	Money Matters	Mathematics
	Mothercare Food	Home Economics
	Woodcarving	Woodwork
	Jewellery Making	Art and Craft
	Electricity in the Home Wine Making Safety	Science
Careers Guidance	Going to Work	Careers
Leisure	Camping Horse Riding Swimming	Physical Education

   The Newsom Report had indicated the importance of subject labels as it stated:

> A subject name is not only a signpost to the pupils of what a lesson will be about, it also provides a similar reminder to the teacher. It marks out in intelligible shorthand the kind of contribution he is to make to the educational programme. It also links this contribution with his own adult field of knowledge. He speaks with more conviction in this field. When he is on his own ground, his pupils should feel that this lesson is not just textbook stuff. (Newsom, 1963, p. 125)

As far as subjects were concerned, these were no longer visible in the course titles given to pupils. The knowledge that was transmitted included simplified versions of subject material and commonsense knowledge that the teachers considered would be relevant to 16-year-olds who would leave school without taking many examinations. For the pupils this was perceived as very low status. Indeed, many of the pupils talked about 'doing nothing' in their classes which they compared with real learning that had taken place in subject classes in earlier years. In a conversation with Sheila Brown, Jenny Nelson and Sarah Molinski, these comparisons were continually made. Sheila and Jenny summed up the situation as follows:

Jenny: My best year here [at McGregor], I thought was my first year. It was really great.

Sheila: Yes. Geography, English, Maths, tutorial, R.E., You learnt loads here you know. It would be great if it went through all the years.

Jenny and Sarah: Yes.

Sheila: Yes you could learn the whole lot, never mind what anybody else wanted to do.

Jenny: I get very fed up when I'm sitting at home and I think well why do I have to do this Newsom?

Sheila: Yes.

Jenny: I sometimes even cry because I get that depressed about it.[14]

Indeed, Jenny considered that they were no longer taking subjects like geography and history where *real* learning took place.

This view was also shared by the boys who also saw Newsom as 'doing nothing'. This view was summed up in a conversation with Terry Nicholls who compared Newsom adversely with work in examination groups.

RB: You do nothing?

Terry: No not much.

RB: Surely you do something?

Terry: No just sit around and do woodcarving. I also do Art but well Art's taking a CSE.

Malcolm: Well you done a lot in Newsom in the fourth year didn't you? Cooking and woodwork and metalwork.

Terry: I didn't do metalwork, I got chucked out. I don't reckon much to Newsom but the rest of the school is all right. If you're taking an 'O' level course it's all right. The teachers are pretty good then but when you're in Newsom it's just a mess around. It's a wasted two years.

RB: Why is it a wasted two years?

Terry: Because I'm achieving nothing am I? You come to school to achieve something like the kids trying to get their 'O' levels and their CSE's while we are just sitting around watching the world go by.[15]

In these terms, Newsom courses were criticized as not involving learning and not providing opportunities for pupils to achieve in comparison with subject courses in earlier years and examination courses in the fourth and fifth years.[16] In turn, some girls complained that the practical courses that were on offer in woodcarving, jewellery making and building were 'boys' courses' that were not of interest to them.[17] The boys also complained of boredom and about courses that the teachers considered would be relevant to them. Patrick McConnell presented this perspective:

> *Patrick:* The kids in Newsom complain how bored they are and how they want to do something interesting and the teachers say, 'right we'll do something about banking'. The things they do about it are just no good to us. They're going to do us no good when we leave anyway.
>
> *RB:* Why not?
>
> *Patrick:* Well the things they teach us, like this decorating or say that Money Matters. You do how to spend your money. Now they told you, they kinda told you, showed you, how to buy a house, decorate it and insure it and all that kinda stuff you know. But the way they taught it, the way they taught you how to do it you'd either have to be a mathematician or a multi-millionaire.[18]

In this respect, classes which were perceived by the teachers as practical, relevant and vocationally orientated were defined by the pupils as boring. For them Newsom classes and subject classes in the core curriculum (that were seen by many teachers as really further Newsom groups) had little to offer. As a consequence classes were missed, whole days were taken off school and attempts were made by pupils and teachers to modify the activities that occurred within classes.[19]

The course titles were only guides to what was occurring in each period. As far as teachers were concerned, flexibility was involved in teaching Newsom courses. In practice, in some groups only a minority of pupils would be working on the topic involved. Keith Dryden indicated that in a woodcarving group some boys would work on woodcarving while others might sit around or go to sleep. Indeed, he described a class where four pupils were woodcarving and another four sat around and played cards while one boy who was unwilling to join in any of the activities laid out across a table and went to sleep. In most Newsom classes pupils were allowed to make cups of coffee and to sit talking to each other. In some groups teachers played games with the pupils so that in a Money Matters class the activities alternated between topic work in one week and games the following week, which was justified by the teachers who argued that this helped them 'to get to know the pupils'. Indeed, Sylvia Robinson regularly reminded teachers that 'Newsom isn't teaching a subject it's teaching a whole person'. In her terms Newsom work cross-cut the traditional division of subjects and pastoral care as it involved transmitting knowledge and getting to know the pupils as people. However, on this the pupils were critical as they interpreted such conversations as attempts by teachers to get to know about 'your private life'.

These aspects of Newsom work were ridiculed by some teachers in other departments who joked about the notion of Newsom project work. A typical remark came from the Head of the Mathematics Department who said, 'I hear they are going to get Newsom pupils carrying Bibles around the school. It's to be called project work.' Similarly, comments were directed to me and to other Newsom teachers by the Head of the History Department and the Head of the Geography Department who enquired, 'Are you going off to make a few more cups of coffee?' as we made our way to lessons at the end of morning breaks.

On this basis, the Newsom teachers considered that their work was perceived by other teachers as little more than containing pupils who had been removed from examination classes so that *real* work could continue uninterrupted in examination groups. After one heads of departments meeting in which some teachers indicated that Newsom groups were too small and that resources could be used more effectively, a memorandum was circulated by Sylvia Robinson in which she outlined the size of each Newsom group in the fifth year. Lists of names were provided for each group, some of which included as many as thirty-five pupils. After the names in one group, who were taking a cookery course, was the remark, 'Get this lot to wash up dishes!!' At the end of her paper the difficulties that confronted the Newsom teachers were well summarized:

> I shall only be too pleased to challenge anyone on the difficulties of coping with the above type of pupil without a definite subject and without many exam prospects. What can we appeal to?[20]

Not Proper Teaching?

In her paper Sylvia Robinson had indicated that Newsom work involved little subject work and few examinations. Her question at the end of the paper leads us to consider what Newsom teachers did and how Newsom teachers worked. In short, what constituted Newsom teaching?

As far as the teachers and the headmaster were concerned flexibility was the keynote of Newsom teaching. Mr Goddard considered that those who got most success with Newsom classes could 'roll with the punches', they could understand why pupils went to sleep in lessons without taking offence. In short, he argued that within Newsom courses there could be an alternative form of discipline. This was never discussed in any Newsom Department meetings that I attended, although teachers indicated to me privately that they allowed pupils to smoke and to swear in classes as this allowed them to cope with 'difficult pupils'; it was a survival strategy for teachers (cf. Woods, 1979; Burgess, 1983). This strategy was substantiated by the pupils who indicated that the way they were treated by teachers helped them to accommodate to school life. Jenny Nelson and Sheila Brown discussed this aspect of Newsom teaching and the work of Newsom teachers:

> *Sheila:* It's like some teachers have a good laugh. I get on great with
>   Mr Dryden and Mr Davies.
> *RB:* Why do you get on great with them?
> *Sheila:* I don't know.

> *Jenny:* You can talk to them more.
>
> *Sheila:* It was like Mr Smith. He was youngish and fuzzy hair and all that. He was absolutely fantastic. I had him for a couple of lessons and it was great. It depends on what you want to do and the boys in Newsom used to work really hard for him. It was unusual really because he got on with everybody.
>
> *Jenny:* But he didn't get on with the teachers, that's why he left. The reason he left was because he didn't get on very good with the teachers. It was the way that he dressed and the way he mucked around with the children. In his lessons he used to let the kids go in the cupboard where they keep all the stuff and that and have a sly puff of a fag or something. He was really great.[21]

Similar accounts were given by other pupils of Newsom teachers with whom they could 'have a laugh' and who allowed them to smoke in certain circumstances. It was these characteristics, they argued, that made Newsom teachers different from other teachers who worked in subject departments and in houses.

As far as the teachers were concerned, getting to know the pupils was a major part of their work.[22] Sylvia Robinson considered that finding the pupils' talents and counselling them was the main task involved in work with Newsom pupils and

> At all times the programme must be flexible. Staff must be ready to change group or members and even content. The general interest of Newsom pupils rises and falls and so change is necessary.[23]

This emphasis upon flexibility and upon getting to know pupils was reiterated by the headmaster who had spent several lessons playing board games with the pupils to this end.[24] He explained that while this approach was used with Newsom, it was not appropriate with examination groups. He pointed out the difference in approach by commenting:

> Within the context of any Newsom class, if I am playing Scrabble with Newsom I am saying it's worthwhile. If I find someone doing this with fourth year top set Biology I'd scrabble him. If I'm drinking coffee I find it acceptable with Newsom but not in 'O'-level Religious Education.[25]

It was differences between teaching in Newsom and in subject classes for examinations that were also identified by the pupils. This was summed up by Terry Nicholls who had indicated along with several other pupils that he did not regard Newsom teaching to be 'proper teaching':

> *RB:* What do you think of Newsom?
>
> *Terry:* I don't reckon much to Newsom. It's just a way of teachers getting out of work. It's just like a free lesson. They just sit around.
>
> *RB:* What do you mean, they just sit around?

> *Terry:* When they come to us they just sit around. They don't do anything specific like standing at the front of the class. They don't use conventional methods.
>
> *RB:* What are conventional methods?
>
> *Terry:* Standing up and giving a talk, telling them [the pupils] what to do and pupils doing it.

At a later point in the interview, Terry returned to this theme:

> *Terry:* It's not the kids that need disciplining. It's the method of teaching.
>
> *RB:* What method of teaching is there?
>
> *Terry:* It's really taking any method, give them a book and let them sit around reading the book and making them read the book. In most schools they have the same method all the way through.[26]

Here, Terry indicates a desire for a traditional mode of teaching which involves reading and listening to teachers and where teachers use their authority. In contrast, he considered that Newsom involved 'a new method' as teachers were sitting around listening to them. This was also raised by other pupils who pointed out that in Newsom lessons teachers sat around talking to them and of this they were critical. Yet for the teachers, talking with pupils and listening to them was a crucial part of real Newsom teaching; it enabled them to get to know the pupils as individuals.

This method of teaching resulted in a minimal transmission of knowledge and was adversely compared with methods of teaching that were used in examination classes. As Terry Nicholls explained to me, he would have preferred to take a conventional course like geography or English or mathematics as this would have given him access to conventional lessons with traditional teaching methods. This view was supported by the girls who thought they should have been given geography and history lessons. They argued that if they had been given the same course as other pupils in the fifth year they could have taken the examinations and they might have passed them. Indeed, one girl told me that she had taken the examination and got one mark below the pass mark but she argued 'I would have got a long way on if I had've taken the course.' Certainly, examinations were important to the Newsom pupils[27] and were often discussed; it is, therefore, to examinations for Newsom pupils that we now turn.

Not a Proper Qualification?

In earlier sections we have drawn attention to the point that Newsom was officially defined as a non-examination course with the result that teachers found it difficult to provide some specific form of subject instruction. However,

195

in the fourth year, members of the St John Ambulance Brigade were invited into the school to give a course to the fourth year Newsom girls.

Here, it was found that the pupils responded to the course, were pleased with their results and the reward of a certificate. On this basis the Newsom teachers decided that this could be extended into the fifth year when the girls could take the examination of the National Association for Maternal and Child Welfare. This examination was held in March and was subdivided into an oral examination and a written paper. Eighteen girls were entered for the examination but only ten attended both the oral test and the written papers. When the results were declared Sylvia Robinson went around the staff commonroom telling everyone of the pupils' success. They had passed with results that ranged between 53 and 88 per cent. The pupils were equally delighted by their results in both First Aid and in the Child Care examination and went to great pains to tell me that not only had they passed but they had gained certificates.

At first sight, all seemed well. Both the Newsom teachers and their pupils had, it appeared, met with success in an area that was normally reserved for subject departments and for GCE and CSE pupils. However, a letter from the headmaster to the Director of Education in January put it into perspective as the key section read as follows:

> *National Association for Maternal and Child Welfare.* This Association provides course work and a final exam in 'Child Care and Human Development'. This, they say, leads to the award of Certificates of Instruction. These are not qualifications but they do have a number of quite specific advantages, not the least among which is that they enable a group of slow but hard working girls to display a certificate earned on merit in an examination situation. These are known nationally and for Newsom youngsters may well help them to use more profitably their last two years at school and to hold their heads high.

Here was the final irony. Certainly, the pupils had followed the course, they had taken an examination and they had gained a certificate but they had not gained a recognized qualification.

Conclusion

This paper started from the assumption that the bulk of research on teaching and learning in secondary schools focusses upon subject disciplines that are assessed in public examinations. Accordingly, an attempt has been made to explore the characteristics associated with an area of study that was officially defined as non-academic and non-examination. On the basis of an analysis of ethnographic data collected at Bishop McGregor School, I found that the Newsom course was regularly compared with work in academic subject departments against which the Newsom course was timetabled. Newsom had been given departmental status but lacked the resources and the staff that were given to other departments. Indeed, Newsom teachers were qualified in subjects, and taught in subject departments. There was, as the pupils indicated, no qualification to teach Newsom, apart from experience and a desire to work with non-academic pupils.[28] While this course had been designed as an alternative to the courses provided in academic, examination orientated subject departments, I found that it was nevertheless judged by teachers in departments and particularly by the Newsom pupils themselves in relation to the following criteria: subject knowledge, teaching method and qualifications; all of which were associated with other school subjects. Accordingly, the Newsom course was seen to be associated with the following characteristics:

1   it was a non-subject where little subject knowledge was transmitted;
2   teaching methods were claimed by the pupils to be unconventional; there was no book learning, it relied upon the teachers' experience;
3   teachers adopted different standards concerning the curriculum and discipline;
4   there were no opportunities to take public examinations that would provide qualifications in the courses that were offered in the Newsom Department.

In short, the Newsom Department was judged adversely in comparison with other departments and so was the course and the teachers. The major message of the school curriculum was that conventional subjects count, while non-subjects were of less value. However, within this evaluation there is the assumption that subject teaching is concerned with the transmission of knowledge, with conventional teaching methods, standards of discipline, examinations and a set of qualifications.[29]

Clearly, not all subjects would meet these criteria. In this respect, we need further studies among teachers and pupils to examine what constitutes 'subjects', what counts as 'teaching method' and what counts as 'learning'. We also need to look at the extent to which pupils as well as teachers are socialized into subject disciplines where the expectation is that public examinations will be taken. Furthermore, we need to assess the impact of subjects upon attempts to innovate in terms of reshaping and modifying curricula and teaching methods.

These data have been used to examine the provision of an alternative course within a comprehensive school that teachers and pupils have judged by the yardstick of subjects and examinations. In these terms, it was impossible for the Newsom course to match the subjects offered in other parts of the upper school curriculum. For just as there were always stark contrasts between the curriculum of the grammar school and the secondary modern school, so similar contrasts are apparent between the examination orientated subject courses and Newsom courses. In these terms, Newsom underlined the dimensions of inequality within the school system to which Shipman (1971) and other commentators have alluded.

Yet as long as we organize our schools in terms of departments with subject disciplines and subject teachers, there will be little chance for Newsom type courses and associated innovations to attain any status. The future looks bleak and there are few signs that we are shifting from the subject base. Indeed, the government white paper entitled *Teaching Quality* (1983) emphasizes subject disciplines for it assumes that secondary school teaching should be subject-based and that secondary school teachers should mainly focus on one or more subjects.[30] On this basis, we might ask what hope is there for non-academic, non-examination, non-subject areas within our schools?

Acknowledgements

I am grateful to the members of the 'Histories and Ethnographies of School Subjects' Conference that was held at St. Hilda's College, Oxford in September 1982, who provided many helpful comments on an earlier draft of this paper. In particular, Stephen Ball and Ivor Goodson provided many detailed editorial suggestions which I found very useful. Any weaknesses in this paper are, of course, my own.

Notes

1 For a review of some of this literature see, for example, Silver (1973), Mortimore and Blackstone (1982).
2 See, for example, Ball and Lacey (1980) on English, Goodson (1982) on biology, geography and rural studies and Young (1976) on science.
3 For the complete study see Burgess (1983) and for methodological commentary on this study see Burgess (1982, 1984a and 1984b).
4 Extract from fieldnotes.
5 Extract from a tape-recorded interview with the headmaster.
6 *Ibid.*
7 The school had opened with first and second year pupils, the latter being drawn from other comprehensive schools.
8 Extract from a tape-recorded interview with the headmaster.
9 Extract from a tape-recorded interview with Terry Nicholls and Malcolm Jackson.
10 Statements included in a set of further particulars for the post of Newsom teacher at Bishop McGregor School that was advertized in 1973.
11 Extract from a report on the Newsom course in 1972–73 written by the headmaster.
12 In 1973–74 assistant teachers could gain promotion by obtaining posts of responsibility on a scale two to five, as scale one was the basic position for all assistant teachers while scale five was the highest assistant teacher position.
13 Extract from a letter written by Sylvia Robinson to Newsom teachers.
14 Extract from a tape-recorded interview between Jenny Nelson, Sheila Brown and Sarah Molinski.
15 Extract from a tape-recorded interview between Terry Nicholls and Malcolm Jackson.
16 Cf. Spradbery (1976), where pupils comment on what constitutes 'proper maths' teaching. Material that had been specially prepared for pupils of 'less than average

ability' was seen by the pupils as an obstacle to progress in working for an examination.

17 For further discussions of sexism in schooling see, for example, the papers in Deem (1980) and the evidence provided by Delamont (1980 and 1983).

18 Extract from a tape-recorded interview with Patrick McConnell.

19 For a discussion of definitions, redefinitions and negotiations over curriculum content during lessons see Burgess (1983), especially part 2.

20 Memorandum entitled 'Amendment to 5th Year Withdrawals', written by Sylvia Robinson, March 1974.

21 Extract from a tape-recorded interview with Sheila Brown, Jenny Nelson and Sarah Molinski.

22 This approach can be compared with that used by the teacher in Woods's account (this volume, pp. 239–261) who saw developing close relationships with pupils as what constituted 'important teaching'. Such an approach raises the question: What is 'teaching'?

23 Extract from a document written by Sylvia Robinson for the headmaster.

24 This was three years before the attack on the teachers at William Tyndale School for using similar teaching methods. Cf. Gretton and Jackson (1976), Ellis *et al.*, (1976).

25 Extract from a tape-recorded interview with the headmaster.

26 Extract from a tape-recorded interview with Terry Nicholls and Malcolm Jackson.

27 For similar views on the instrumental value of school subjects see the reports from pupils in Measor (in this volume, pp. 201–217).

28 A similar point which is also made in the White Paper entitled *Teaching Quality* (1983).

29 For a discussion of the criteria associated with subject definition see Cooper (in this volume, pp. 45–63).

30 For similar views see DES documents (1979, 1982a and 1982b). In a DES press release (DES, 1982b) Sir Keith Joseph has justified a swing towards postgraduate teacher education because of the 'need to strengthen subject expertise within the schools'.

References

BALL, S.J. and LACEY, C. (1980) 'Subject disciplines as the opportunity for group action: A measured critique of subject subcultures', in WOODS, P. (Ed.) *Teacher Strategies: Explorations in the Sociology of the School*, London, Croom Helm.

BIRKSTED, I.K. (1976) 'School performance viewed from the boys', *Sociological Review*, 24, 1, pp. 63–77.

BURGESS, R.G. (1982) 'The practice of sociological research: Some issues in school ethnography', in BURGESS, R.G. (Ed.) *Exploring Society*, London, British Sociological Association.

BURGESS, R.G. (1983) *Experiencing Comprehensive Education: A Study of Bishop McGregor School*, London, Methuen.

BURGESS, R.G. (1984a) *In the Field: An Introduction to Field Research*, London, Allen and Unwin.

BURGESS, R.G. (1984b) 'The whole truth? Some ethical problems in the study of a comprehensive school', in BURGESS, R.G. (Ed.) *Field Methods in the Study of Education*, Lewes, Falmer Press.

CORRIGAN, P. (1979) *Schooling the Smash Street Kids*, London, Macmillan.

DAVIES, L. (1979) 'Deadlier than the male? Girls' conformity and deviance in school', in BARTON, L. and MEIGHAN, R. (Eds) *Schools, Pupils and Deviance*, Driffield, Nafferton.

DEEM, R. (Ed.) (1980) *Schooling for Women's Work*, London, Routledge and Kegan Paul.

DELAMONT, S. (1980) *Sex Roles and the School*, London, Methuen.

DELAMONT, S. (1983) 'The conservative school? Sex roles at home, at work and at school', in WALKER, S. and BARTON, L. (Eds) *Gender, Class and Education*, Lewes, Falmer Press.

DES (1971) *Raising the School Leaving Age to Sixteen*, Circular 8/71, London, HMSO.

DES (1979) *Aspects of Secondary Education in England*, London, HMSO.

DES (1982a) *The New Teacher in School*, London, HMSO.

DES (1982b) 'Initial teacher training target intakes announced for next three years', *Press Notice* (175/82), London, HMSO.

EGGLESTON, J. (1977) *The Sociology of the School Curriculum*, London, Routledge and Kegan Paul.

ELLIS, T. *et al.* (1976) *William Tyndale: The Teachers' Story*, London, Writers and Readers Cooperative.

FURLONG, V. (1976) 'Interaction sets in the classroom: Towards a study of pupil knowledge', in HAMMERSLEY, M. and WOODS, P. (Eds) *The Process of Schooling*, London, Routledge and Kegan Paul in association with the Open University Press.

GANNAWAY, H. (1976) 'Making sense of school', in STUBBS, M. and DELAMONT, S. (Eds) *Explorations in Classroom Observation*, London, Wiley.

GOODSON, I.F. (1982) *School Subjects and Curriculum Change*, London, Croom Helm.

GRETTON, J. and JACKSON, M. (1976) *William Tyndale — Collapse of a School or a System?* London, Allen and Unwin.

HANNAM, C. *et al.* (1971) *Young Teachers and Reluctant Learners*, Harmondsworth, Penguin.

HARGREAVES, D.H. (1982) *The Challenge for the Comprehensive School: Culture, Curriculum and Community*, London, Routledge and Kegan Paul.

LACEY, C. (1977) *The Socialization of Teachers*, London, Methuen.

LAWTON, D. (1973) *Social Change, Educational Theory and Curriculum Planning*, London, University of London Press.

MORTIMORE, J. and BLACKSTONE, T. (1982) *Disadvantage and Education*, London, Heinemann.

NEWSOM, J. (1963) *Half Our Future*, Report of the Central Advisory Council for Education, London, HMSO.

SHIPMAN, M. (1971) 'Curriculum for inequality', in HOOPER, R. (Ed.) *The Curriculum: Context, Design and Development*, Edinburgh, Oliver and Boyd in association with The Open University Press.

SHIPMAN, M. (1980) 'The limits of positive discrimination', in MARLAND, M. (Ed.) *Education for the Inner City*, London, Heinemann.

SILVER, H. (Ed.) (1973) *Equal Opportunity in Education*, London, Methuen.

SPRADBERY, J. (1976) 'Conservative pupils? Pupil resistance to curriculum innovation in mathematics', in WHITTY, G. and YOUNG, M. (Eds) *Explorations in the Politics of School Knowledge*, Driffield, Nafferton.

Teaching Quality (1983) London, HMSO.

WILLIS, P. (1977) *Learning to Labour*, Farnborough, Saxon House.

WOODS, P. (1979) *The Divided School*, London, Routledge and Kegan Paul.

YOUNG, M. (1976) 'The schooling of science', in WHITTY, G. and YOUNG, M. (Eds) *Explorations in the Politics of School Knowledge*, Driffield, Nafferton.

Pupil Perceptions of Subject Status

Lynda Measor

In a book on curriculum we should include the pupils' viewpoint and know something about the reaction of the 'consumers' to the package of curriculum they are given. Most of the research on curriculum has concentrated on how it is shaped and formulated at the top. The other end of that process, where curriculum is realized and practised, has been neglected. Both teachers and pupils have a role in defining the curriculum at classroom level. They have a real input. The point is the basic interactionist one: neither teachers nor pupils just receive and digest what is handed out from above. They make space, they negotiate and they affect the realization of school subjects. Peter Woods, in his paper, concentrates on the viewpoint of a teacher; this paper is focussed on the pupils.

The interest here is in the ways pupils receive school subjects, on what their reactions are to different areas of the curriculum, and on how they view school subjects. The curriculum is realized by people in social interactions, and the realization is partly a product of meaning constructions they make (Berger, 1971). The suggestion is that different areas of the curriculum have different meanings for pupils, and specifically have different kinds of status in their view. A number of factors influence pupil meaning constructions. Adolescent culture is certainly important, as are gender codes about appropriate activities. Social class and ethnic origins can equally exert an influence. Most contain a particular orientation to the world of work and adult occupations, and school subjects are viewed through these perspectives. The meanings and the status attributed by pupils to school subjects act as a very significant constraint upon teachers, and more generally limit the realization of certain areas of the curriculum.

The data upon which this paper is based were taken from a participant observation study of part of the intake year of a large urban comprehensive.[1] This included a period of research with the intake year while they were still at middle school. The research was done in 1980 in an area of the East Midlands where the recession had not then been felt. It is possible that the looming prospects of unemployment could have had a significant effect upon the perceptions of these pupils since then.

The research was done over an eighteen-month period; it involved a longitudinal perspective; and the data are presented chronologically as they occurred. This is intended as a methodological note, for it indicates the process by which they emerged. I was 'alerted' to the fact that pupils viewed different areas of the curriculum differently by comments they made at middle school. The attitudes expressed resulted in particular sorts of behaviour once the pupils were at secondary school. When pupils were interviewed about the issue, they agreed they saw different subjects in different ways.

It is clearly absurd to talk about reactions of 'pupils' as if they were a uniform whole, with shared reactions to school life. Individual variations were obvious, pupils had different preferences and different abilities. Nevertheless, some classification of their reaction is possible. Gender, unsurprisingly, seemed to affect the way pupils view school subjects. The impact of gender upon the sciences has been dealt with in detail elsewhere (Measor, 1983). The basic orientation that the pupil has to the school is another factor: whether he or she takes primarily a 'conformist' view of school, assuming that schooling is a worthwhile activity, or a 'deviant' orientation, where school is not given any primacy. Recent research has cast doubts upon any simple dichotomized view of orientation to school (Hammersley and Turner, 1980). The concept is used here with some reservations, which are discussed later.

All the same, there were some shared perspectives amongst pupils. At middle school a pattern of response became clear; certain curriculum areas had more value than others. Everyone agreed that maths and English were the most important subjects; they were referred to as 'the basics'.

Amy: Maths is one of those subjects you have really got to have.
Researcher: What are the others?
Rebecca: English and Maths.
Researcher: Which subjects do you think are the most important?
Keith: Maths and English.
Researcher: Why?
Keith: Because you need English and Maths and that when you go out to work. The other areas are not so important really.

This answer was standard, coming from boys and girls, whatever their orientation to school. It corresponds with Ball's (1981) findings in Beachside about subject status. This also fills out the picture given by Bob Burgess in his paper, where he indicates the 'Newsom courses' are held in low esteem by pupils; they fail to match the rigid academic criteria which grant a subject high status. There is a suggestion of a hierarchy of school subjects, stratified in the perspective of the pupils.

By the end of the first few weeks in secondary school, it was clear that this evaluative perspective was influencing classroom behaviour. Pupils behaved in markedly different ways in different subject areas. The first phase of school life, which Ball has termed 'Initial Encounters' (Ball, 1980), is characterized by extreme conformity on the part of the pupil to the demands of the new institutional culture. In other research (Measor and Woods, 1984) we have suggested that both pupils and probably teachers put on 'a front' during this period. The 'front' crumbles over time and 'real' identities emerge. Deviance appears, but it does not occur evenly throughout all lessons. Some subject areas attracted deviant, oppositional strategies earlier than others. A lot of research has documented the basic fact that pupil actions and behaviour vary according to the context they are in. The area is 'mapped out' quite well, but we don't understand a great deal about the reasons for these variations. A few largely *ad hoc* suggestions have been made; clearly the personality and competence of the teacher is crucial. Furlong's work (1976) would suggest that the composition of the pupil groups influences things too. The suggestion here is that because some subjects are given lower status than others they become suitable arenas for deviance.

It is important to get a detailed picture of this process to see where exactly the deviance occurred first and worst. The data which follow are taken from observation of one form of first year pupils in their first week at secondary school. English and maths, which were highly valued, were marked by hyper-conformity. In maths, for example, on the second day the pupils were fully attentive while the teacher held the centre stage, and, when asked to work, did so at first without talking. There was an absolute quiet in these lessons, a silence which was quite unnatural to anyone familiar with British secondary schools. Pupils were rigidly attentive to any information or instructions given by a teacher. When the maths teacher turned his back to write on the board, the pupils did not even use that opportunity to talk. When another teacher entered the room and distracted the attention of their own teacher the pupils just went on working. They showed a real anxiety to get absolutely everything right, and were entirely unwilling to take any initiative on their own. One girl asked if she might cover her maths book to keep it clean. Pupils asked permission to turn pages to go onto the next section of their work sheets. They wanted absolute clarification of what side of the page to write on, of which titles to underline and what spaces to leave in their books. English lessons saw a similar pattern, although because the particular teacher's style was different they were more relaxed. Nevertheless, pupils rushed to complete their work and showed a keen interest in answering questions and doing well. Pupils were conforming exactly to the formal demands of the school culture. The formal took precedence.

This picture needs to be contrasted with that in other areas of the curriculum where the situation was very different. It was the teaching of music which aroused the most overt opposition from these pupils. This same class, as in maths, had their first music lesson on the fourth day in school, and it is worth documenting this in some detail, for this lesson saw the first major challenge to the school's culture. On his way to the lesson, one boy, Pete, removed his tie and hid it beneath his jumper; this was specifically against school rules. The class was lined up outside the classroom door, the cue was familiar from middle school, it signals a demand for quiet, for ordered preparation for the lesson. Yet

Pete and Roy entered the room whispering and giggling. The teacher then called a register, and attempted to learn some names. As David had his name called out, he made a silly face at the teacher, when she looked back down at the register. Keith sat messing around with his pens and rulers, making some noise as he did so. While the register was called Pete did an imitation of a boxer, attacking Roy, imitating punches without allowing them to actually land. Mrs Skye learned a few names, Keith's, for example, since she knew his brother. A few minutes later in the lesson she addressed him directly by name. Keith denied that his name was Keith, which put the teacher in a difficult position. Her response, however, was immediate. She said loudly to him, 'Watch it . . . [pause] . . . it's quite a short journey from your chair to the other side of the door, Sunshine.' Mrs Skye then asked the class what they wanted to do in music. There was a loud and predominantly male chorus of 'Nothing.' She laughed and went on to give them some ideas of what they *would* do in music. As she talked, Pete and Roy began a murmured conversation to each other. Mrs Skye instantly responded to this challenge: 'Someone is talking while I am', which effectively silenced them. The class was then asked to work alone on some written materials. There was almost immediately quite a loud buzz of noise as the class settled to work, in marked contrast to the strained silence of the maths class. At first the conversation that caused this noise dealt with work, pupils asking each other spellings, what the title was, how long has it to be, and can I borrow your ruler? As the noise grew louder, Mrs Skye asked the whole class to be quiet. For a short while they were, but then the chatter began again. This time the conversation was far more general. Carol discussed with Pat, 'Did you see them dragonflies in the showers? (they had just finished a PE lesson). They both shared an inarticulate expression of disgust, 'Uggh!', thus cementing a growing friendship. Again, as the noise increased, Mrs Skye interrupted. This time she singled out Keith, who was being especially noisy and could be heard above the others, 'Look, Sunshine, you had better watch your step in here.' He then turned around to the researcher and grinned. The teacher's intervention created quiet for a few minutes, but then the chat began again. Rosemary asked Sally if she could see her book. Jenny then questioned Rosemary about the musical instruments she plays. Janet showed Sally her work.

It has to be emphasized that these activities occurred on only the fourth day the pupils had been in the school, for clearly they do not compare with the sophisticated strategies of Paul Willis' (1977) much older lads, for example. Nevertheless, such actions had significance in the terms of the participants. We need explanations of such differences in behaviour in different subject lessons. In terms of music it seems that several factors come together. Pupils when questioned stated that they did not rate music highly; 'It's not very important is it' was a typical response. One boy, Pete, said, 'I don't think music's necessary, it's a waste of time, you're not learning anything from that, nothing at all.' Subject status, as it is perceived by pupils, then, seems to affect their behaviour within the subject's lessons, and the extent to which they are prepared to cooperate with the formal demands of the subject's teacher.

There are other reasons for the opposition pupils offered to music; and the input of the informal values of adolescent cultures within schools has to be taken into account. Hostility derived in part from the distinction Vulliamy (1977) has elaborated between 'Our music' and 'Their music', where adolescent subcultures take musical style as a cardinal point in their definition. Such issues were at stake in this context, as Roy said, 'We should do things that we want, like punk rock or something ... we have to enjoy it.' Later in the school year pupils were observed beating out 'rock rhythms' on their drums and attempting to achieve 'heavy metal' sounds on their tambourines, in contravention of their instructions to play more 'classical' melodies.

There was another issue, again deriving from the 'informal' area. Pupils identified school music as involved with the world of childhood. It offended their new sense of adult or adolescent identity. Roy said, 'We're only doing triangles, we should be getting on to trombones and things.' Keith was in agreement.

> *Keith:* I don't like that Mrs Skye, the music teacher. We get tambourines to play with, and we were using tambourines when we were at the very first school. When we went to Hayes we were still using tambourines.
>
> *Researcher:* What do you think you should be doing in music?
>
> *Keith:* I wanted to learn to play the guitar; my mum bought me a guitar for Christmas, and I can't play it, it is sitting in my room, all dusty.
>
> *Researcher:* And you think the school should teach you?
>
> *Keith:* Yes, most schools do, I asked Mrs Skye, but she goes 'I don't think it is the kind of thing you would want to do', because she reckons I muck about too much. I only muck about because I don't approve of music, can't stand it, because the kind of music we do is for the babies.

The pupils demoted school music in accordance with certain of their own concerns, which drew from the informal culture and its values. Activities which did not meet their sense of a new age-graded status and adolescent interests were likely to be denigrated. In addition, music was perceived as having a low, devalued status anyway within the curriculum. It all ensured that school music was given no chance by the majority of pupils, and it is not surprising that it was music lessons which witnessed the first real deviance initially and later in the year some of the worst deviance.

The informal concerns are likely to constrain severely any teacher's practice of the subject. This does not mean, however, that the subject was without value for the pupils. Conversely, it is a useful resource for the playing out of pupils' informal interests. Music lessons offered an opportunity for signals to be sent about pupils' involvement in informal adolescent subcultures. In the examples given, Pete could publicly assert his serious allegiance to punk rock in school music. Keith could use the arena to make a claim for adult treatment and status. Questions of orientation to school were at stake, especially in the first few weeks at the new institution. Pupils could use music lessons to make statements about their priorities and their preferences for the informal as opposed to the formal culture of the school. Identities were established in these ways as individual pupils differentiated themselves from the anonymous cohort which had entered the school. Music was not without value for pupils, but the values attributed to it still form a serious constraint upon the teacher at classroom level.

Art and design subjects were also marked by considerable deviance by the second week of term. The patterns and concerns identified in music lessons seemed to be operating in the art area too. Pupils like Pete, Roy and Keith made exploratory forays, to find the discipline limits, consolidating their identities as deviants in the process. Pete forgot his pencil, Keith his art book. The class was set a piece of work, and asked specifically not to discuss and share ideas for it. The majority of pupils settled quietly to the task set. Pete, Roy and Keith did talk and laugh quite loudly, they obeyed instructions like 'Put your pencils down' reluctantly and so slowly that they earned a public reprimand. It was also noticeable that other pupils followed into the territory that Pete, Roy and Keith had opened up. Boys like Phillip and Stewart had shown themselves to have an eager conformist orientation in other subjects. In art they engaged in 'out of line activities'. Phillip sat for a while making faces at his drawing and grimacing, then he giggled loudly at it, and started to discuss a better way of doing the drawing with Stewart. Furthermore, as this activity went un-punished, some of the girls began to join in. Some of the girls began to talk quietly together about their work. Both the girls and Phillip cooperated and chatted in a quiet way, without the noise and laughter that characterized the other group. Differences in orientation were beginning to show through 'the front'.

The pupils began to blend their 'informal' concerns on to the formal framework. In design lessons Pete and Roy soon inscribed 'PUNK ROCK' on their protective aprons. Such subjects also offered the opportunity for 'friendship forming' activities to go on apace. Pupils discovered a pathway to unauthorized chat in these lessons. They would discuss their work; when asked to work alone this acted as a cover, in case they were challenged, but the talk rapidly progressed to other subjects, like family, pets and TV, which had 'friendship forming' implications and openings. The physical arrangement of lessons like design, art and also music, with groups of pupils around tables, presented more opportunities for 'friendship forming' activities than more formally organized classrooms (Stebbins, 1976; Denscombe, 1977). 'Making friends' was a major concern of the pupils who found themselves in a new school, quite frequently bereft of the easy network of friends they had built up at middle school — a concern documented more fully elsewhere (Measor and Woods, 1984).

Art and design, like music, seems to be selected as an area for the playing out of informal interests. Again, pupils said that they did not rate the art and design area of the curriculum highly. 'It's not very important is it', was a typical response when questioned. There were extra data available on this matter. Pupils made a distinction between 'work' and 'art' when it came to school life.

Researcher: Have you worked quite hard at middle school?

Gary: I have worked quite hard, but not as hard as ... we have missed a year you see ... well half a year. We had a teacher Mrs Smith and she wasn't very good at all because every day we done art, then of course we thought it was good, but now — we are about six months behind, and we have got to work much harder to get up to the standard of the other kids. We hardly done any work in that year.

Even at middle school age the pupils seem to have a view of what is really important, what counts as 'proper' work. Pupils' perception of 'work' is now a fairly well researched area (Woods, 1979, for example).

Data of this kind coincide with evidence from general and journalistic sources which suggest real opposition to many of the creative and liberal teaching policies of primary education on the part of the public. Evidence was available later in the school year which gives a further indication of parental attitudes. On the evening parents came to school for reports on their children, Janet reported: 'My mum only got to the basic area, you know. English, Maths, Science. I wanted her to go and see my art and things like that, because that's one of my keenest subjects, but she never got round to it.'

The other subject which attracted attention was the sciences; and here the gender issue became important. Girls reacted to the physical sciences, boys to the domestic ones. A full account of this has been given elsewhere (Measor, 1983). A number of reactions existed, ranging from deviant oppositional through half-heartedness to indifference. In the three classes under observation, however, a pattern was clear. The vast majority of the girls signalled their objections to doing physical sciences; they avoided doing work whenever possible, they bungled their experiments, loudly made clear their dislike of the noise, smells, fumes and activities of the lessons, and stated themselves quite incompetent to deal with the complex machinery in the laboratories. The few girls who failed to object to physical sciences met with a degree of hostility from their peers. These data support the general conclusions drawn by Kelly in her recent work on the sciences and sex-role differentiation (Kelly, 1981).

In the domestic sciences the boys displayed negative reactions. In needlework the boys in the study were completely passive for the first week of term. In the second week they became more adventurous, giving silly answers, driving wedges of illegitimate activity or talk into lesson turning-points, and overplaying the pupil role (Willis, 1977). One example of the latter was when a boy used a sewing machine, tried to see how fast it would go, making a great deal of noise and breaking the needle. It has to be said that none of the boys began to take this subject seriously, and the same was true to a lesser extent of home economics.

207

Researcher: What do you think of cookery?

Roy: I think that's a waste of time as well.

Andy: I don't mind cooking, it's a laugh. I cooked some soup yesterday and nearly choked on it.

Pete: When we're in cooking we really have some rolics in there.

It is also the case that none of the domestic science teachers ever felt they gained disciplined control of these mixed first year classes, and they complained repeatedly about their difficulties.

Among the bargaining counters of the teacher, perceived value of the subject is basic. Pupils saw these subject areas as having low value for them in the formal sphere. Furthermore, there were pressing concerns from the informal culture which could not be ignored. Boys in this study saw the domestic sciences as 'sissy' and as something boys did not do, not if they were proper boys that is. The girls objected to the physical sciences on gender grounds. The pattern was the same. Paradoxically, pupils valued the science subjects; they were prime resources in the process of sex role differentiation. They could be used to give signals of gender allegiance. Informal concerns predominated in the science area of the curriculum; and the informal concerns of the adolescent pupil acted as a significant constraint on teachers in classroom practice of the subject.

By the second week of term the pattern was set. English and maths escaped much of the pupil deviance that art, music and the sciences attracted and witnessed. During the school year pupil strategies of deviance grew in sophistication and confidence and the strength of their challenges grew. Nevertheless, this opposition remained uneven throughout the curriculum. Pupils remained more attentive in maths and English than they did in the devalued art, design, music and sciences. Yet there were always several factors involved and teacher style was crucial. All of the teachers observed have to be seen as being of roughly equal skill, that factor was constant, for there were no real incompetents amongst them. At the same time, subject culture could not save an incompetent teacher from problems. A supply teacher in maths was to face a real take-over bid from pupils. A temporary woman teacher came to take physical science, and boys as well as girls joined in a full frontal assault on her discipline.

Other factors became clear during the year. It seems as if pupils make a classification of oppositional strategies and attach values to them. There is a kind of hierarchy, some are viewed as being far more seriously challenging than others. 'Skiving' and truanting is the zenith, but was rarely indulged in by first year pupils. 'Mucking about' seemed to be placed in the top position on their hierarchy. Those who are described as real deviants do it; the defining word for them is that they 'muck about'. It is the characteristic of the ace deviant, for it was seen to challenge teachers and it was known to rate 'trouble'. Sheila was one such example: 'She is always messing about, and cheeking teachers and getting other people into trouble.' One pupil, Kevin, refused to accept he was ever deviant enough to rate the term. He said, 'We just have a laugh, we never really muck about.'

This 'mucking about' could be contrasted with the activities at the other end of the scale, which were not so serious — 'talking' or 'whispering' or 'having a chat'. It is interesting that when pupils discussed them, they usually put the word 'just' in front of them. It acts as a qualifying word, 'just talking', or 'just chatting'. They signify the lack of weight, the non-seriousness of the activity.

> *Emma:*   In our form, there is a lot of boys that muck about with the teacher.
>
> *Lucy:*   In our class the girls just chatter and giggle.
>
> *Janet:*   Some of the girls in our class whisper and giggle, but the boys are the ones who make remarks out loud. The girls don't make the remarks out loud it is the girls who whisper and giggle.
>
> *Christine:*   I think the boys muck about more in our form.
>
> *Keith:*   I play up a little, not a lot. Our form teacher was really getting at us, she gave us detention. She said it was all the boys' fault. So I stood up and said 'No it's not the girls natter on, more than we do', and she said 'I don't agree, you lot play up'. We play up but they chatter.

It became clear that there was a distinction made between the private verbal exchanges and public verbal challenges. The latter were regarded far more seriously, as Janet's comment indicates. It is saying things 'out loud' that pushes the act up the deviancy scale. We have termed this kind of deviance *centre stage challenges*. They occurred when a teacher claimed the centre stage of the classroom to give instructions or new information. Pupils could intrude jokes or comments into the discourse and effectively divert the whole flow of a lesson. They were serious, they rate, yet they do not rate the cane. On two occasions boys were caned for such activities and pupils objected. The negative case brings out the value again.

> *Roy:*   Keith ain't done much has he . . . he just sits there and every now and again makes a joke, that's about it. I thought he caned Scotte for nothing, he done it for nothing.

Yet many pupils were shocked by these kinds of deviant activities.

> *Sally:*   Dominic Melton's quite a big head, because in music, did you notice, he said he wouldn't play the instrument — straight to the teacher — that was being a bit cheeky, seemed to me.
>
> *Researcher:*   What did you think of that?
>
> *Sally:*   I was shocked really, because sometimes he is really brainy, and I thought he was posh and I didn't think he would ever do that.
>
> *Amy:*   I was really shocked when he did that, couldn't believe it.
>
> *Rebecca:*   I thought it was shocking as well, I wouldn't have the guts

to say that to a teacher.... I am not a little Mummy's girl ... but ... I do that to my mum and dad sometimes, I argue with them.

At the bottom end of the scale is day-dreaming, which has a low value. In Jacqui's view it did not deserve, it did not rate 'trouble' from a teacher. When Mrs Gates disagreed with this and challenged her, Jacqui was very annoyed: 'We were just day dreaming, and she picked on us, I hate that Mrs Gates.'

Other acts like eating sweets and bubble gum tended to fit into the middle ranges of the hierarchy. They were regarded as 'taking liberties' but they did not fit in at the top of the scale. The other type of activity is work avoidance. There are various ways of achieving this: pupils could be late for lessons; they could do very little work themselves, but get others to help them out; they could lose equipment and projects.

The point at issue here is that there were curriculum variations in the deviant acts. The same act has a different meaning and value according to which area of the curriculum it takes place in. Pupils were far more willing to be deviant and to engage in the strongest actions in the low priority areas of the curriculum than they were in maths and English. Mucking about in home economics might be far less serious than 'talking a bit' in maths, for example, and a pupil who went so far as to 'skive off' maths or English as opposed to music would be making a very definitive statement indeed. Pete and Roy described the 'real rolics' they had in home economics; clearly their activities there went beyond mere 'mucking around'. The girls saw the boys' activities in home economics as worth describing.

Rebecca: The boys don't like needlework.
Sally: They always muck around more with a lady teacher, they are not as strict as the men like in cooking, they can get away with a lot more. Pete and Roy they are always mucking about with Amy in there.
Amy: In cooking they got moved; we had to make cheese on toast and set the table, and we got marks for it [so it was a serious activity]. Their table was everywhere, and they had all this sauce round their mouths.
Rebecca: They did individual toast, nobody did the whole thing like they should. They all did their own toast, their own coffee.
Sally: Pete had about three pieces of toast — about five cups of coffee.

These pupils were also willing to engage in more extreme work avoidance strategies there than elsewhere. Pete, for example, boasted 'I ain't brought my fabrics money. I have paid for art, that's all.'

Researcher: Why haven't you brought your fabrics money?
Pete: Come on, it's rubbish. Look we have to bring the money in for it, don't we, and we have to buy our own material. I never use anything — I only get round to drawing it, and then go on to

something else. I ain't doing my mum out of 75p for a load of rubbish.

Pete basically removed himself from real participation in this lesson. We have suggested that the girls objected to science; they defined themselves as involved in more serious actions there than elsewhere.

Sheila: We misbehave, we take liberties in Mrs Lines' science lesson.
Pamela: Yes, we eat Polos.
Researcher: Would you do that in anybody else's lesson?
Sheila: No!

The form's other teacher for science was the headmaster himself, and the girls still employed more opposition and half-hearted participation there than in other subjects. This is instructive for it shows the strength of the girls' objection to science, that they were prepared to take on their headmaster in their first term at secondary school.

So far in this paper we have adopted the terms 'deviant' and 'conformist' without question. Research such as that by Hammersley and Turner (1980) has, however, raised serious problems about these concepts. In the wider research, we have suggested that while pupils do seem to have a basic orientation to school life, which can be defined along the deviant-conformist line, yet members of both groups engage in what we have called *'knife edge' strategies*; to maintain a balance between the formal and the informal pleasures and pressures of school. Similar data are discussed in Fuller (1979) and Lambart (1976).

What this means is that both groups engage in actions which keep them out of a range of different kinds of trouble. The conformists can be faced with accusations that they are 'goody-goodies' or 'snobs', they can find themselves friendless and isolated. Many pupils seek out places and spaces where they can engage safely in deviant acts, and where they *can be seen* to engage in deviant acts. They therefore select these low priority areas of the curriculum and use them for what is usually limited to fairly minor deviances. Needlework and home economics, for the boys, physical sciences for the girls, art and music are the obvious subjects. This would help explain the data given in the paper about the early art and design lessons. Phillip and Stewart, who had until then shown a conformist orientation, engaged in deviant activities of a minor kind once boys like Pete and Keith had revealed the area as open and safe for such action. Phillip was normally top of the class, but in the appropriate context he would throw raisins, fall over the ironing board, drip water over his paintings and eat the apple he was supposed to be drawing. Mark was also in all the top academic streams, he said he was aiming for university, but in music lessons:

Mark: Our teacher for music, we muck her about something rotten.
Researcher: Why?
Mark: It's just that you don't like the lesson, it is boring . . . you are just sitting there like that.

> *Andy:* The things she says, de dum de dum — rot, you can't keep a
> straight face.

Janet had decided she was 'no good' at history, that was her chosen area: 'I don't
muck about really, just history — chewing. I don't know really.' Diane was
another example. She was normally highly conscientious about her work, but in
art it just didn't matter.

> *Researcher:* Would it worry you if someone said your work wasn't
> very good?
> *Diane:* Yes, except if it was something like Art, then it wouldn't
> worry me, because I don't like art anyway.

There were other places and spaces chosen by these pupils when a supply
teacher took over, or a temporary teacher was in charge, or when a teacher
went out of the room. But the low priority areas of the curriculum were
definitely one of the sites, especially when forays into indiscipline had been
made by other 'ace' deviant pupils. We also suggest that the 'deviants'
employed 'knife edge' strategies too. The danger for them was not 'trouble' as
such, although they would usually avoid a surfeit of it. Rather, their problem
was being mixed up with those who were dubbed 'thick' by their peers. The
deviants, certainly 'the lads' wanted it clearly understood that they were
choosing not to do well, it was not that they couldn't do well if they tried. Again
the uneven values in the curriculum were significant. It did not matter if you
were seen to be 'hopeless' at music or needlework or art, in fact it enhanced
your identity as a 'deviant'. However, it was a different matter if the subject was
maths or English. The 'lads' trod a 'knife edge' in these subject areas; in class
they would work while trying to make it seem that they were not 'straining
meself'. They would not eagerly answer questions, but they would actually get
the work done. They would not profess any interest in tests, but equally they
made certain that they did reasonably well in them. The best example of this
was Roy, who sported full punk regalia together with a skinhead haircut by the
summer term. He was placed in the lowest stream for maths, together with
those he termed 'the dummies'. Within two weeks he had worked sufficiently
hard to get up into the middle stream; he had of course no desire to go into the
top stream.

We now have a picture of the differences that surrounded pupil actions
and reactions to different subjects of the curriculum; and a link is identified
between the pupils' evaluation of a subject's status and their actual behaviour in
lessons. The rationale which pupils employed in making their evaluations of
subjects however remains unclear. It seemed worthwhile to try and understand
why pupils viewed different curriculum areas in the way they did, and
specifically why they placed so much weight on maths and English. The answer
lay in a clear instrumental perspective. Maths and English, we have seen, had
job or career relevance, they alone had an obvious marketability.

> *Christine:* Because to get a job, when you finish, maths and English are what they take you for really.
>
> *Barbara:* I think the same, because you have got to be able to read and spell.
>
> *Christine:* I do think I work harder in maths and English than other things.

On further questioning it seemed as if all subjects were rated on this simple marketability factor. On the issue of science:

> *Diane:* Maths and English are most important.
>
> *Researcher:* What about science?
>
> *Diane:* Yes, well it is important for what I want to do, I suppose I have got to get a science O-level, but I don't really like it — I have got to get one.
>
> *Researcher:* So is science important and useful.
>
> *Michelle:* It depends on what sort of a job you want to do, because if you go to be a housewife, there is no point really in doing too much science. If you are a boy and are going to find a career in engineering or something it is more difficult.
>
> *Researcher:* Yes, but do you think subjects are only important because of what jobs they lead to: do you think there is anything else that makes subjects important?
>
> *Pamela:* I think that English and Maths is important in every job really, they like you to have them. I suppose, well, I want to work with animals, so science is important. For people who want to work in Engineering metal work, things like that are important.
>
> *Sheila:* I think the same.

Again the same rationale is displayed, a positive reaction is given to a school subject, because of its instrumental job value. There were indications that subjects themselves were divided up in the pupils' perspective, and real utility was only given to the parts of subjects that had market relevance.

> *Researcher:* Is science also important?
>
> *Margaret:* Yes, but you should have a choice of what kind of science you do, and if you know what job you want to do, some sciences might be useless to you.
>
> *Researcher:* Which ones?
>
> *Margaret:* If you wanted to be an engineer, and you do biology that would be a bit silly.
>
> *Researcher:* So you think it is only really worthwhile learning subjects that are going to be useful in your work?
>
> *Margaret:* Yes.
>
> *Researcher:* You don't think it is worthwhile learning other subjects?
>
> *Margaret:* Well it makes you more conversationalist. But some people don't like talking, my dad, he doesn't speak up all the time.

For some pupils foreign languages were also seen as important, because of their career aspirations, but this was by no means a common perspective. Foreign languages generally occupied a low status and witnessed more than the average levels of deviance.

> *Barbara:*   I want to be an air hostess, so I'm going to take up German properly.
> *Researcher:*   Do you think it's useful to learn another language?
> *Phillip:*   It could be, if you couldn't get a job, you could go abroad and get one. Or going camping — yes quite useful.
> *Researcher:*   What about French and German, are they important?
> *Margaret:*   It would help you get a job: you could get a more important job overseas or something.
> *Researcher:*   What do you mean by an important job?
> *Margaret:*   Well, if you take a secretary, if you can speak French ... you have got more opportunities — you can get up higher.

While English and maths were 'the basics', other subjects occupied areas of the periphery. Art and music we have suggested were located at the real margins.

> *Researcher:*   Do you think art is important?
> *Rebecca:*   It is for some people, if they want to do it, but it is not for me.
> *Researcher:*   What about you, Julie?
> *Julie:*   Art is not as important as English and Maths, but some people think it is important.
> *Amy:*   Well, because really you can get a job without Art, but most jobs want you to have English and Maths.
> *Julie:*   Yes, if you want to be a typist, you don't really want an art 'A'-level.

This marketability factor may be a partial explanation of why boys viewed cookery more hospitably than needlework, but there was a range of other issues too.

> *Researcher:*   What is the difference between doing cooking and doing needlework? Is cooking girls' stuff?
> *Phillip:*   Er ... no ... not really because the best chefs in the world are men aren't they ... and you don't get men making tapestries and stuff like that. Needlework, it just doesn't appeal to me as doing anything good.

There was for a very few pupils a hint that they were groping towards what might be termed a 'life skills' concept of education. Margaret said she supposed a full education might make you a better conversationalist. Yet even for those pupils who had any such view, maths and English scored high, they were seen to render the individual more competent in the real world.

Researcher: But why are Maths and English so important?

Diane: I suppose it is because you need to know how to write properly.

Julie: And you need to know how to add up for any job.

Researcher: You don't for my job.

Both: That's true — yes.

Diane: But, I think you have got to know how to do it, whether you have the 'O'-level or not, for adding up bills.

Julie: Mortgages on your house and that, you have still got to do it.

Some of the craft subjects too were seen to have a use value, not in the job market but in home-centred skills.

Ian: Technical studies is important.

Researcher: Why?

Ian: Repairing things — if you have got your own home, things like that.

Researcher: But aren't subjects important for any other reason than the job they might lead to?

Stewart: Yes, they are helpful when you are doing odd things round the house — things like woodwork, they are helpful, teach you how to do things.

David: Then you can make your own cupboards or tables like my dad.

Researcher: What about Domestic Science? Is that important?

Both: Oh yes.

Amy: Yes, because I am useless at needlework.

Roz: I don't think they are so important for the boys, but if they're going to live on their own in a flat they've got to learn how to cook, and how to sew their socks.

Diane: But some of the things that we learned to cook, they were stupid — cheese on toast — it's a bit — and how to make a cup of tea — well I would have thought most people know how to do that.

Sport was warmly regarded by many of the pupils; they were pleased by the opportunities the school offered them for a variety of sports. This was the only leisure time interest in which they seemed to feel the school had anything to offer; as we have said, school music was disregarded. Pupils were passionately interested in music, but not the kind that school offered.

The data show the largely instrumental attitudes that almost all of the pupils had toward their secondary school curriculum. Pupils said they wanted decent jobs, they recognized the contribution that school could make towards their future job aspirations, they recognized the need for school-based qualifications to achieve those aspirations. Therefore, school, or certain parts of it, the vocational parts, was useful. This seems to have strongly affected this particular group of pupils, who began their secondary education during a period of economic recession, although they recognized the problems the recession might bring them.

> *Researcher:*   Do you care about doing well at school?
>
> *Jane:*   Yes, because of the job situation at the moment; I wouldn't care so much if there were loads and loads of jobs, but there are hardly any now.
>
> *Gary:*   It's my last school, and I want to get all the exams I can, so I can go and get a nice job. I have got to do well to get a good job. If you don't get a good job you could be on the dole the rest of your life.

The fact that this particular group of pupils lived in a town with especially good employment prospects at that time has probably influenced their reactions to the school curriculum. It is by no means certain that these findings would apply in more depressed economic areas.

The assumption at the base of this paper is that pupils in schools have two sorts of concerns and pressures upon them: the formal demands of the institution, and the informal interests of the adolescent cultures within the school. The assumption is also that the two areas are opposed, and that pupils have to juggle the two against each other. Schutz' notion of 'interests at hand' (1967) may be useful here. In certain arenas the formal concerns predominate; in the highly valued areas, 'the basics', the formal demands gain recognition. In other arenas the informal concerns surface. Where the subject is undervalued, and when it simultaneously confronts values from the informal culture, then a shift in priorities occurs and the informal predominates. In school music, the 'informal' rules — OK? The rationale for deciding which interests come to the fore is that of the perceived instrumental marketability of school subjects. Such perspectives affect teachers in the classroom. Teachers on the periphery (and in Peter Wood's paper we have one such example) face a range of constraints in their practice of realization of their subject.

Notes

1 The school had a twelve form entry; the forms were divided between four 'houses'. The research involved the three forms of one 'house', although one particular form of the three was given greater attention. The three forms were mingled with each other for language teaching and for art and design classes from the beginning of the year. At Christmas they were streamed for maths and science and again mixed around.

References

BALL, S. (1980) 'Initial encounters', in WOODS, P. (Ed.) *Pupil Strategies*, London, Croom Helm.

BALL, S. (1981) *Beachside Comprehensive*, Cambridge, Cambridge University Press.

BERGER, P.L. (1971) *The Social Construction of Reality*, Harmondsworth, Penguin.

DENSCOMBE, M. (1977) *The Social Organisation of Teaching*, unpublished PhD thesis, University of Leicester.

FULLER, M. (1979) *Dimensions of Gender in a School*, unpublished PhD thesis, University of Bristol.

FURLONG, V. (1976) 'Interaction sets in the classroom', in HAMMERSLEY, M. and WOODS, P. (Eds) *The Process of Schooling*, London, Routledge and Kegan Paul.

HAMMERSLEY, M. and TURNER, G. (1980) 'Conformist pupils', in WOODS, P. (Ed.) *Pupil Strategies*, London, Croom Helm.

KELLY, A. (1981) *The Missing Half*, Manchester, Manchester University Press.

LAMBART, A.M. (1976) 'The sisterhood', in HAMMERSLEY, M. and WOODS, P. (Eds) *The Process of Schooling*, London, Routledge and Kegan Paul.

MEASOR, L. (1983) 'Gender and the sciences', in HAMMERSLEY, M. and HARGREAVES, A. *Curriculum Practice: Some Sociological Case Studies*, Lewes, Falmer Press.

MEASOR, L. and WOODS, P. (1984) *Identity and Culture: The Sociology of Pupil Transfer*, Milton Keynes, The Open University Press.

SCHUTZ, A. (1967) *The Phenomenology of the Social World*, trans by WALSH, G., Northwestern University Press.

STEBBINS, R. (1976) *Teachers and Meaning: Definitions of Classroom Situations*, Leiden, E.J. Brill.

VULLIAMY, G. (1977) 'School music as a case study in the new sociology of education', in SHEPHERD, J. *et al.* (Eds) *Whose Music, A Sociology of Musical Languages*, London, Latimer.

WILLIS, P. (1977) *Learning to Labour*, Farnborough, Saxon House.

WOODS, P. (1979) *The Divided School*, London, Routledge and Kegan Paul.

The Amorphous School

John Player

It was in the middle of an investigation into pupils' perceptions of a fourth and fifth year non-examination social education course at Abbey Vale High School,[1] an outer-London comprehensive, that I became increasingly aware of a particular view of school held by many estranged and mainly working-class pupils, whose alienation had led, not to rebellion or active hostility, but to indifference and apathy. For these pupils school had become meaningless and insignificant, its routines and institutions nebulous and amorphous.

The seeds of this notion lay in my conversation with Steven Polakis, a typically unmotivated fifth year boy, as he told me of his feelings towards school:

> S.P.: S'alright ... I like it when I'm here sometimes, but I just don't like coming ... it's getting up in the mornings.
>
> J.P.: Is it on one of the days you've got Maths [the subject he most disliked] you feel 'I don't really want to go to school today'?
>
> S.P.: No, it ain't that 'cos I [pause] 'cos I don't know what lessons I've got; I just find out from me mates. *I don't know what lesson, I just come to school.*

Steven was not the only student to think of school in such vague terms. Mr Percy (English and drama) told me in the staffroom of how he had sent Jimmy Phillips, an estranged working-class 'lad'[2] from his lesson to fetch a tape recorder. Jimmy had had Mr Percy for English for over a term. In the corridor he was stopped by Mrs Sparrowe, head of the English Department, who asked him what he was doing out of lessons. Jimmy replied, 'I gotta get a tape recorder for Mr ... er ... dunno 'is name.' Perhaps Jimmy's ignorance was due more to alienation and to the insignificance of school for him, than to a lapse in memory.

Similarly Mr Boyd (careers) told me of how he had asked another 'lad', Billy Chase, to explain why he had forgotten his books. Had he not checked what lessons he had before he came to school? Billy replied, 'I dunno what lessons, I just got school.' Billy, like Steven, thought of school as an amorphous whole, not an aggregate total of many separate lessons, teachers and rooms.

I asked Steven to think back to his last detention:

J.P.:   What was it about?
S.P.:   [long pause]
J.P.:   Remember?
S.P.:   [pause] I was going to see some teacher and I couldn't go for a couple of days.

He was unsure of the reason for his visit to the teacher in the first place, the teacher's name, the exact cause of his failure to go to see the teacher, or for how long he had procrastinated.

Nigel Smart, however, one of a group of highly motivated fourth year pupils that I interviewed remembered his one detention vividly: 'I had a slight disagreement with Alan Spencer so I kept turning round and poking him and talking and that sort of thing in the lesson.' He remembered the exact context of the detention when I asked him to recall it.

Throughout my interviewing I was struck by the way the motivated children appeared to be so much more aware of their place in school, the 'order of merit' in individual lessons, the rules and procedures they were expected to observe and the subject matter and content of their syllabuses. This was in marked contrast to the way in which the unmotivated pupils tended to speak of school and its structures in hazy, indistinct terms.

I decided to test this notion further, but even before I started, I was aware that whilst I might be able to demonstrate this particular phenomenon, I might also be unable to explain it. Was there a model I could use, a key to unlock this particular door? Several studies appeared to lead in the right direction.

The Correspondence Theory and Beyond

In their 'Correspondence Principle', Bowles and Gintis state that:

> the educational system helps to integrate youth into the economic system through a structural correspondence between its social relations and those of production. The structure of social relations in education not only inures the student to the discipline of the work place, but develops the types of personal demeanour, modes of self preservation, self-image and social class identifications which are the crucial ingredients of job adequacy. (1976, p. 131)

Students are conditioned at school to prepare themselves for the roles they will take in the industrial system of production. This preparation operates at three levels. The highest levels of the hierarchical divisions in education learn to internalize the norms of the economic and industrial enterprise. The middle levels are trained to be dependable, and to show occasional initiative, while the

lowest levels are conditioned into rule orientation. The differentiation processes that take place in schools ensure that the right people enter the economic
system at the appropriate level.

This determinist view of education has received much criticism recently,
not least for its failure to attribute any initiative and free will to the
working-class person, but also because of its exclusive, functionalist concern
with the economic system as the prime causal agent in education. Giroux, in his
critique of the Correspondence Principle, places economic determinism in the
broader context of total ideological hegemony. This

> refers to a form of ideological control in which dominant beliefs, values
> and social practices are produced and distributed throughout a whole
> range of institutions such as schools, the family, mass media and Trade
> Unions. (Giroux, 1981, p. 94)

If a single dominant class chose to exercise such hegemony, it would need
to exert control over every aspect of life, not just by coercion but also by
'positing certain ideas and routines as natural and universal' (Giroux, 1981, p.
94). Thus socio-cultural as well as economic domination would need to be
fostered, yet it is through socio-cultural forms of expression that the oppressed
classes draw up their lines of resistance.

Limited within the confines of economic determinism the Correspondence
Principle portrays the lower levels of society as passive, rule-following func-
tionaries. Yet this is patently not the case; they constantly use their cultural
resources to fill their social relationships both on the shop floor and in the
classroom with acts of resistance and rebellion. Furthermore, Giroux argues,
the Correspondence Principle, by emphasizing the social relationships in
education which parallel those of the work place, tends to disregard the part
played in ideological domination by the selection of 'knowledge', and the
content, methods and evaluations of the curriculum. These and the cultural
values they help to reproduce are also constantly resisted by many working-
class students.

Following this critique, Giroux then moves towards a new theory of
reproduction and transformation. He argues that the dominant culture in
society does reproduce itself in successive generations and that schools act as
agents in this process. Yet, as we have observed, this domination is not just
economic, but a complex weave of the social, cultural and political realms as
well. Hegemony cannot therefore be total since it has to be constantly
reaffirmed, recreated, defended and modified in each of these particular
realms. Correspondingly it is being perpetually resisted, challenged and
limited by the classes it seeks to dominate.

Thus Giroux believes that if the oppressed were to examine their plight,
unite and politicize their opposition and subsequently develop concrete social
relationships that would illuminate and demonstrate liberation, then transformation of society could occur. Giroux, therefore, moves

beyond a theory of correspondence by recognizing that reproduction is a complex phenomenon that not only serves the interest of domination, but also contains the seeds of conflict and transformation. To recognize this is to begin the task of developing an educational theory informed by indictment which is found at the heart of all forms of resistance, an indictment whose central message is that things must change. (1981, p. 109)

In this way Giroux takes into account the element of cultural resistance that seems to be lacking in the subservient and passive image of the working classes portrayed by Bowles and Gintis, thereby providing a useful macrocosmic model for the study of alienated youth. Willis (1976 and 1977), by drawing attention to the links between counter-school culture and shop floor culture, investigates the forms of this resistance and exposes their limitations in failing to convert 'symbolic' power into 'real' power.[3] By distinguishing between the 'them' and 'us' categories[4] in employer/employee relationships, the shop floor 'lads' paradoxically recognize and perpetuate an authority structure. Fatalistically, they volunteer for the lowest levels of the employment market, where they can express their cultural identity with figurative acts of dissidence. Willis adds: 'For all its symbolic resistance, the moving spirit of working class culture till the present has been accommodation to a pre-given reality, rather than an active attempt to change it' (1976, p. 199).

Whereas the 'cultural capital'[5] of the dominant groups in society ensures the success of their offspring and the reproduction of class privilege, the cultural resistance of the working classes plays itself out as a matter of style and symbolic reaction. Steven Polakis' nebulous perception of school and his 'couldn't care less' attitude to his lessons may well represent a stylized form of resistance to alien cultural values which were being imposed upon him. Chewing gum, not having books, lateness to lessons, failure to respond to 'the bell',[6] all epitomize this type of resistance. Willis states: 'In a system where knowledge, and the educational paradigm, are used as a form of social control, "ignorance" can be used in the same way as a barrier to control' (1976, p. 196). However, he goes on to provide an even more productive model.

The Concept of Generalized Labour

In spite of the careers advice they received before leaving school, the 'lads' have their own unique view of the world of work: 'In terms of actual job choice, it is the lad's culture and not the official careers material which provides the most located and deeply influential guides for the future ...' (Willis, 1976, p. 192). This culture 'supplies a set of official criteria by which to judge not *individual jobs* or the intrinsic joys of particular kinds of work ... but *generally* what kind of working situation is going to be most relevant to the individual' (1976, p. 192). Willis argues that particular job choice 'is, in essence, an essentially middle-class construct ... these lads are not choosing careers or particular jobs, they are committing themselves to a future of *generalised labour*' (1976, p. 193).

To the lads, there was little 'differentiation between jobs. It's all labour' (1976, p. 193). In the same indiscriminate manner, Billy Chase observed, 'I dunno what lessons, I just got school' (see above). It would seem, therefore, that a concept of generalized labour is paralleled by an amorphous notion of school. It is more difficult to establish, however, whether such a notion, in the case of an estranged working-class pupil in school, is to be construed as a deliberate form of resistance, or a subconscious anaesthetization of his awareness of an institution with which he cannot identify. An experienced participant observer could perhaps determine whether a particular case of lateness to a lesson was deliberate, or the result of casual unawareness.

Job Satisfactions

One further consideration is that cultural alienation often causes the employee or pupil to seek extrinsic satisfactions from work or school. Hayes and Hopson (1972), drawing from the work of Daws on satisfactions sought from work, list six types: material, status, skill, dominant value, associational, and perceptual.* Perhaps the most significant of these for the shop floor lad are the 'material' (his pay packet) and the 'associational' ('meeting his mates', 'having a laugh'). The latter would particularly apply to pupils of the anti-school sub-culture.

Using these models, I decided that my priority was to seek evidence of the 'generalized' or 'amorphous' school concept at Abbey Vale, while being aware that I would simultaneously be observing and noting more positive forms of resistance and counter-school culture. The study of these forms and of the extrinsic/associational satisfactions which replaced the educational paradigm would, however, remain a secondary consideration.

Methodology and Sample

To test the notion of the amorphous or generalized school I decided once more[7] on the use of a sample of children, or rather, in this case, two larger contrasting samples. In this way it might prove possible to point towards a concept which, with further research, could be more clearly isolated and defined.

The head of the Maths Department, Mr Evans, selected (subjectively) two groups of thirteen and fourteen[8] fifth year students, one which he considered motivated, the other unmotivated. We shall call them the 'M' group and the 'U' group respectively. The 'M' group derived mainly from the 'accelerated' maths set, who had already taken O-level maths and were now studying additional maths in their fifth year. The 'U' group came exclusively from the bottom two maths sets. Quite obviously there was some correlation between the motivation

223

and the academic ability of the students in each group, but I hoped, as far as possible, to test attitudes which were not linked to intellect.

I was able to withdraw each group from three lessons of forty-five minutes duration during which time the students (1) filled in a simple factual questionnaire and an open-ended attitudinal questionnaire; (2) talked to me generally about school; and (3) underwent a photograph recognition test.

I obtained additional information about the twenty-seven students from registers and personal files. Where the data gathered were of a quantitative type, I calculated the 'mean score' for the 'M' group and 'U' group respectively. Pupil absence meant that the statistics are usually based on a group number of between ten and twelve.

Table 1.   *Sources of data on students.*

	Data	Source
1	Father's occupation	(a) student (b) emergency telephone number forms in School Office
2	Number of GCE/CSE examinations students intended to take	student
3	1981 non-verbal reasoning test results	list from Headmaster's Office
4	1981 vocabulary test results	list from Headmaster's Office
5	Fourth year absence figures	last year's registers
6	Fourth year lateness figures	last year's registers
7	Number of occasions per week student is late for a lesson	student estimate
8	Student's knowledge of the times (beginning and ending) of each lesson	student test
9	Whether or not student plans his/her school day in advance	student
10	Student's knowledge of personal timetable	student test
11	Whether or not student carries a bag to school (for books)	student
12	Number of writing implements carried by each student	student (by emptying pockets, bags, etc.)
13	Where student normally keeps school books	student
14	Number of occasions (lessons) per week student chews gum	student estimate
15	Number of detentions since beginning of fourth year	student estimate
16	Ability to recognize members of staff	photograph recognition test
17	General perceptions of school; attitudinal comments which bear relevance to statistical data	open-ended questionnaire

In the following section I propose to:

1 set out the test findings in 'mean' figures, comparing the 'M' and 'U' students as two fairly homogeneous groups in contrast to one another;
2 include among the findings any illuminating or significant comments made by the pupils in relation to the tests;
3 comment where necessary on examples in both groups of atypical pupils who, for one reason or another, significantly deviate from the group norm in any particular test; and
4 explain the significance of each test in throwing light upon the 'amorphous' concept of school.

Table 1 provides a qualitative list of the data gathered on each student and stipulates the source of the data.

Findings and Analysis

1   Father's Occupation

I wanted to establish whether the two groups were characterized by any particular pattern of social class. Parental occupation provided a rough guide. Allowing for my rather clumsy division between manual and professional/ managerial occupations, a preponderance of the former category existed among the parents of the 'U' group and vice versa (see Table 2).

Table 2.   Parental Occupations of Students

	'M'	'U'	
Professional/Managerial	9	0	
Manual	4	9	
Unemployed	0	2	(one a retired pensioner)
No father at home	0	3	
(Total)	(13)	(14)	

2   Number of GCE/CSE Examinations

The students were asked for the number of external examinations they intended to take and the level at which they expected to take them (see Table 3). The figures represent the average number of GCE/CSE examinations being taken per student in each group. With two compulsory subjects (maths and English) and six 'Options', students normally attended courses in eight subjects. Some of these were designated 'non-examination'. It can be seen that the 'M' group, by way of extra classes and early examination dates, was fitting in

Table 3. *Students' Intentions Regarding External Examinations*

	'M'	'U'
C.S.E.	0.9	5.1
G.C.E.	9.3	0.1
(Total CSE + GCE)	(10.2)	(5.2)

more than two examinations above the number allowed for by the exigencies of the timetable. In contrast the 'U' group was spending approximately nine lessons a week (three per subject) following courses which did not lead to external examinations. These particular figures may help to account for the students' perceptions of the 'worthwhileness' of school. Thus the actual number of examination entries might indicate attitudinal as well as academic inclinations in both the 'M' and 'U' groups.

3 and 4   Non-Verbal Reasoning Test/Vocabulary Test

These results can be placed together as the tests were originally conducted in the same week at the end of the students' fourth year at Abbey Vale and also because they are included in this survey for the same reason, that is, they provide a rough guide to the measured intelligence of the students in the two groups (see Tables 4 and 5).

Table 4. *Results of Non-Verbal Reasoning Test*

'M'	'U'
53.5	40.1

Table 5. *Results of Vocabulary Test*

'M'	'U'
46.2	27.9

The scores in both Tables 4 and Table 5 are out of sixty and represent the average mark per person in each group for the two tests. Suffice it to say that the 'M' group appears to perform far better than the 'U' group in measured intelligence tests.

5   Absence from School

Last year's registers provided me with an aggregate figure for each student representing the number of morning or afternoon sessions which had been missed (ten per week). No allowance has been made for the legitimacy of the absence or whether a 'note' had been brought; it is also acknowledged that patterns of absence may have changed in some cases in the first term of the fifth year (see Table 6).

Table 6. Fourth Year Absence Figures (Academic Year 1980/81)

'M'	'U'
13.1 sessions	54.8 sessions
(average number of absences per student in each group)	

If absence from school is a guide to poor motivation, then Mr Evans' subjective group selection receives some justification here. The 'U' group was away from school four times as often as the 'M' group. Although I did not take genuine sickness into account, three students in the 'U' group admitted to occasional truancy:

Questionnaire: I have a day off when ...
'I feel like skipping off' (Robert Walters)
'I am ill or truancy' (Stuart Mancini)
'I fill like it' (Michael Hough)

Yet two students from the 'M' group also admitted to casual absence.

Questionnaire: I have a day off when ...
'I am ill or get bored' (Ivor Brough)
'I'm totally bored with everything' (Trevor Bull)

although it is perhaps noteworthy that both of these boys could be said to come from working-class backgrounds. Furthermore, Trevor Bull's inclusion in the 'M' group was questioned by many members of staff.[9] He certainly transformed the figures for lateness.

6   Lateness to School

Lateness to a morning or afternoon school session is signified by a letter L appearing in an 'absent circle' in a register. These were added up for each student over the whole of the fourth year (see Table 7).

Table 7. Fourth Year Lateness Figures (Academic Year 1980/81)

'M'	'U'
8.1 sessions	20.7 sessions
(3.25 sessions)*	(average number of latenesses per
* discounting Trevor Bull	student in each group)

Trevor Bull actually accounted for sixty-six of the 'M' group's total of 105 latenesses for the year. This exceeded any individual figure for lateness in the 'U' group. Overall, however, the 'U' group's lateness pattern was far worse than that of the 'M' group.[10] This applied also in the case of lateness to lessons.

7   Lateness to Lessons

The figures in Table 8 represent the average number of late arrivals to a lesson per pupil in each group in a thirty-period week.

Table 8.   Lesson Lateness

'M'	'U'
0.73 times	7.6 times

Two members of the 'U' group said that they were always late. Rightly or wrongly I allowed for exaggeration inspired by bravado and counted them late on only twenty out of thirty occasions per week. Nevertheless, the 'U' group was late for one lesson in four (on average) compared with the 'M' group's one lesson in forty.[11] This apparent disregard for official time brings to mind the observations of Willis and Giroux in schools and factories respectively. Both remark that such time-wasting is deliberate: 'an assault on official notions of time' (Willis, 1977, p. 28): 'workers at various levels of production attempt to modify and control the time, pacing and demands made upon them' (Giroux, 1981, p. 96, derived from Aronowitz's (1973) study of General Motor automobile workers). Whilst not for one moment attempting to deny that the pattern of lateness illustrated above by the 'U' group demonstrates an intentional disregard for institutional routines, I believe that the following test results carry the argument a little further.

8   Knowledge of Lesson Times

The students were asked to write down the starting and finishing times of the six lessons of the school day. Precise acquaintance with the lesson times at Abbey Vale is not easy at present, since there have been some recent changes in the school day and because there is also a five-minute change-over period between lessons. The figures in Table 9 represent the average test score (out of twelve) per student in each group.

Table 9.   Lesson Times Test Score

'M'	'U'
9.5	4.7

The 'M' group knew these times of the day twice as well as the 'U' group. Whereas disregard for punctuality can be construed as a deliberate act of anti-school resistance, poor knowledge of the times of the lessons vividly illustrates the shapelessness of the 'U' group's notion of school.

9   Planning the School Day

As a further illustration of the students' perceptions of the importance of their day at school, each of them was asked on a questionnaire: 'Do you usually plan your school day (which books to bring, etc.) either the night or morning before?' Table 10 provides a summary of their responses.

Table 10.   Planning the School Day

	'M'	'U'
Plans day	11	4 (1 girl)
Does not plan day	0	7 (2 girls)
(total)	(11)	(11)

The entire 'M' group thought of school, lessons, books, etc. before they left home. Only four out of the sample of eleven in the 'U' group considered school (and what they learned there?) important enough to be worthy of advanced preparation.

10   Knowledge of Personal Timetable

The shapelessness of school for the 'U' group is again well illustrated by the results of this test. Surely memory alone cannot account for the discrepancy between the two groups highlighted in Table 11. The students were given a blank timetable for a thirty-period week. They were asked to write down the subject, teacher and room for each of the thirty lessons, a total of ninety pieces of information. The average mark out of ninety per student in each group is given in Table 11.

Table 11.   Timetable Test Score

'M'	'U'
82.6	58.3

A few points are worth considering here. As one might expect both groups had little trouble filling in their timetables for the day of the test, but the 'U' group, despite one notable exception,[12] had much more difficulty completing the rest of the week. Their school day was not something they thought much about and they only appeared to contemplate a lesson when they had to go to it. Although the two groups were not tested with regard to their commitment to homework, some of the 'M' group mentioned that they had considered homework nights when they had filled in their timetables. The 'U' group probably did very little homework (especially at home) and did not appear to plan their school week any more than they planned their school day. The subdivision of a school week into separate lesson units was for them a blurred and ill-defined concept.

11 Carrying a Bag to School

It occurred to me that a brief case or executive case was a particularly middle-class appendage and might help to typify the 'style' of the two groups, that is, if any bag were carried to school at all. Furthermore any type of bag carried between home and school might represent a link between the two which the students might or might not wish to forge. Table 12 shows the responses given to the question: 'Do you carry a bag to school (for books, etc.)?'

Table 12.   School Bags

	'M'	'U'
Carry a bag to school	11	4 (3 girls)
Do not carry a bag to school	0	7 (all boys)

Only one boy from the 'U' group carried a bag at all. The boys in the 'U' group did not appear to carry sports bags to school as most of them managed to avoid changing for games. The three girls from the 'U' group who brought bags used them as an all-purpose hold-all for books, make-up, cigarettes, brushes and combs, etc. Their bags were particularly fashionable. Mrs Rawstone (geography) said to me in the staffroom, 'The working-class girls go out of school as if they had never been there. They cover up their school uniforms[13] with large fashionable overcoats and their bags go with the rest of their gear. They could just as well have been to the Hairdressers.' In contrast to the 'U' group boys, everyone in the 'M' group carried a bag. I suspect that they did a lot more homework and books needed to be carried home. The educational paradigm, represented by a brief case, presumably meant much more to them.

12 Possession of Writing Implements

The students were asked to produce every pen and pencil they had with them. Each item was counted separately although packs of felt pens and coloured crayons were counted as one item. Table 13 shows the average number of writing implements per student in each group.

Table 13.   *Number of writing implements*

'M'	'U'
5.0	1.6[14]

This test was included in order to gauge the readiness of the students for their lessons and thereby to gain some further indication of their attitudes to school. Gannaway (1976) places writing in class at the bottom of a 'popularity' list of school activities among a cross section of secondary school pupils. The 'M' group with three times as many pens, etc. as the 'U' group was perhaps demonstrating a greater capacity for 'deferred gratification' by being better prepared to write. It is ironic to note that the type of course being pursued by the 'U' group involves more colouring and drawing, while the 'M' group is required to do much more essay-type written work. Yet it was the 'M' group children who produced a vast array of coloured felt pens and crayons during this particular test.

13   Location of Students' School Books

A more reified, meaningful notion of school would, I suspected, be far more likely to penetrate the home lives of the students. Keeping books at home might be an indication of the importance of school and its related academic activities in their overall life styles. On the other hand, students who left their books at school might be attempting to further separate school from their 'real' lives outside. The students were asked the following multiple-choice question: 'Where do you keep most of your school books? (a) at home (b) in your desk or locker (c) in your bag or (d) somewhere else; state where.' Table 14 shows their responses.

Table 14.   *Where School Books Are Kept*

	'M'	'U'
Home	9	2
Desk/Locker	1	5
Bag	1	1
Elsewhere*	0	3
(total)	(11)	(11)

(* in each case students said that they left their books with subject teachers).

Once again there was considerable evidence of the dichotomy between home and school on the part of the 'U' group. However, it must be added that many staff encouraged this by refusing to release books to members of the 'U' group. Furthermore, location of books also appeared to be linked to normal homework patterns.

14 Chewing Gum in Class

The students were asked to estimate the number of lessons in a thirty-period week in which they chewed gum or ate sweets. As both were offences against school rules, the figures in Table 15 can be interpreted as an illustration of symbolic resistance on the part of the 'U' group in particular. The figures represent the average number of lessons per student in each group in which gum was chewed or sweets eaten.

Table 15. Chewing Gum

'M'	'U'
2.3 lessons per week	7.5 lessons per week

The 'U' group broke this particular school rule three times more frequently than the 'M' group.

15 Number of Detentions

As a further example of the 'U' group's spirit of resistance I asked the students to estimate the number of detentions they thought they had had since the beginning of the fourth year (September 1980). The figures in Table 16 represent the average number of detentions per student in each group.

Table 16. Number of Detentions

'M'	'U'
0.6	19.8

Some members of the 'U' group had considerable difficulty in recalling the exact number in this particular test and a tendency to exaggerate may have occurred. Nevertheless the results are striking.

16   Recognition of Members of Staff

The students were shown thirty-five photographs of members of staff, whose cooperation in this experiment was requested by letter. The thirty-five teachers represented a cross section of ages, departments and different lengths of service from the sixty full-time members of staff at Abbey Vale. The figures in Table 17 represent the average number of correct identifications per student in each group. Students were allowed fifteen seconds to name the teacher.

Table 17.   Results of Staff Photograph Recognition Test (out of 35)

'M'	'U'
31.4	28.6

Several interesting points emerged from this particular experiment.

1   In some cases the students did not know who the teacher was at all, whereas in others they could not remember the name of the teacher. There was no significant difference between the two groups on this particular count.

2   The 'U' group students often expressed their dislike of staff they recognized. One remarked, 'I know 'im; I can't stand 'im.'

3   As expected the students found it easier to name the 'characters' among the staff and those with major responsibilities, for example, both deputy heads and the head of fifth year were known to all twenty-four pupils who took this test.

4   Conversely, 'quieter' members of staff with few responsibilities other than their main subject teaching commitment were less readily recognized by the students.

5   The 'U' group students, if anything, tended to know teachers who had not taught them less well than the 'M' group students. One said, 'I dunno 'im, I've never 'ad 'im.'

Yet overall the difference between the performances of both groups was not marked. What difference there is between the two groups brings to mind, as regards the 'U' group, the comment of Bird (1980, p. 102): 'The teachers appeared to form an insignificant role in these pupils' experience of the school day.'

However, it may well be that the members of the 'U' group are far less vague about members of staff than they are about routines, times and procedures in school, even if they recognize the teachers for negative, antipathic reasons. Curriculum innovations for the 'U' group type of pupil have been numerous in recent years, concerning themselves with such themes as skills and relevance — laudible concepts indeed, but should the emphasis have been rather on people, and the personal qualities, approach and style of the teacher in particular?

The Meaning of School

Whereas the students in the 'U' group tended to hold nebulous notions of school as a whole, and its routines and procedures in particular, they did identify two activities that were a significant part of school life. Bird writes:

> Not only did the school appear to represent a minor part of these pupils' day, but the classroom represented an even smaller part. School was not seen as a learning environment, but one in which to meet friends and to have a good time. (1980, p. 101)

Many of the students in the 'U' group wrote 'Having a laugh', 'Meeting me mates' or the like in answer to the open ended question, 'To me, school means . . .', whereas the educational relevance of school was far more important to the 'M' group students. However, it is not my purpose here to elaborate on these particular features of school life, although they have been well documented by others: Willis (1977), Bird (1980), Corrigan (1979) and Woods (1976), to name but a few.

More central to the argument presented in this paper is the view of Robert Walters ('U' group student) expressed in his questionnaire response: 'To me school means NOTHING.' He even asked his form tutor if it was alright to put 'nothing' down as a reply. The progression from an amorphous to a nihilistic view of school seems a logical one.

The Amorphous School — Posture or Reality?

I began this paper by stating that the concept of the amorphous school needed to be more clearly isolated and defined. Its underlying causes are, perhaps, open to two contrasting interpretations. Either the 'U' group is adopting a deliberate posture of marginality, or their ignorance of the school and its systems is real.

It is likely that the academically less able, whether motivated or unmotivated, would find greater difficulty in learning the routines and procedures of an institution like a school. Yet there were members of the 'U' group who were perfectly capable of acquiring such knowledge, had they had a mind to. It could be further argued that, in an institution which places great value on the acquisition of academic knowledge, those who fail academically lose both self-esteem and dignity. Thus they feel compelled, either consciously or subconsciously, to identify with groups or sub-cultures where other types of knowledge are valued, where it is acceptable, indeed perhaps necessary, to be 'ignorant' of the school and its working practices.

Yet these processes appear to be mutually reinforcing. A posture of deliberate 'ignorance' reinforces a genuine lack of knowledge and vice versa. Knowledge which is the valued currency of the 'M' group, epitomized by such questions as 'What lessons have I got today?', 'What books must I bring?', is both *ignored by* and *unknown to* the members of the 'U' group. In the same way that a sub-culture possesses its own body of knowledge and set of values, it also often fails to possess or give credence to the values and knowledge of other groups or sub-cultures. In other words, it possesses 'non-knowledge', of which an amorphous concept of school is a type. But to assert that calculated marginality is the chicken, and that 'real' ignorance is the egg from which it derives, would be rash indeed.

Conclusion

In this paper I believe it has been possible to identify and demonstrate a particular pupil-held view of school as an amorphous, meaningless institution. This parallels a generalized view of labour held by many of the working-class 'lads' studied by Willis (1977) at Hammerton. It is, however, difficult to explain why these parallels between school and work exist at all.[15] A. Hargreaves (1980) believes that Willis' idea of cross-valorisation between the two cultures is 'not very helpful'.

Yet it would be surprising if a plausible explanation of this particular concept had been discovered, given the limitations of this study. By concentrating exclusively on pupil perceptions, I have obviously neglected the part played in reproducing the amorphous notion of school by the teachers, the school as an institution and society as a whole. Giroux posits the seeds of resistance by pupils within a theory of ideological hegemony (more successfully than Bowles and Gintis). Woods (1977) believes that social, cultural and political control are all manipulated in unofficial ways by teachers at the classroom level. He emphasizes that teachers employ strategies to cope with the situational constraints of the classroom and that children's attitudes are often determined by their perceptions of the teacher at the 'chalk face'. Another view put forward by Reynolds (1976) is that the school may well be the real 'delinquent' and that the ethos and structures of the institution may well accentuate and accelerate deviant patterns of behaviour in pupils.

More recently A. Hargreaves (1980) has argued the need to combine these various paradigms and to approach the sociology of education from all levels, classroom, situation, institution and social structure, both in an interactionist and an interpretative vein. Only by a synthesized plan of research would it be possible to probe more deeply into the complexities of pupil perceptions and strategies.

Why is it important to identify and explain a concept of generalized school? Many teachers, I am sure, are aware of its symptoms and this is reflected in comments on school reports such as 'casual behaviour', 'too easy-going', etc.

Woods discusses how children's characteristics are portrayed on reports as 'personal attributes, well evidenced in different contexts' (1979, p. 206). Do such 'personal attributes' as 'laziness' and 'poor motivation' really represent pupils' perceptions of school as meaningless and unimportant?

Mr Paul, the deputy head at Abbey Vale, said to me:

> We do have our out and out rebels from time to time, but not often. They are quickly dealt with, punished, suspended or transferred to another school. What is more worrying is the number of children who are 'dropping off' in the 4th and 5th Years. It's as if we present them with what they have to do over the last two years, with examinations, career requirements and so forth, and they immediately see the size of the task and give up. They don't necessarily give any trouble, they just 'switch off'.

To make school more meaningful to children like these, then, is our problem as teachers. Perhaps the merest hint of a solution was indicated by the results of the photograph recognition test. Even alienated pupils reacted to members of staff. ('I know 'im. I can't stand 'im' — Alan Oliver.) Teachers are certainly more real and significant to pupils like these than are the institutional routines, rules and ethos. If teachers did but realize that they really do 'make an impression' then their approach to the estranged pupil might be less fatalistic, less defeatist.

Notes

1 Abbey Vale is a pseudonym, as are all the names of teachers and pupils in the school referred to in this dissertation.
2 Using WILLIS' (1977) term.
3 WILLIS (1976, p. 198).
4 *Ibid.*, p. 194.
5 A concept that Willis (*ibid.*) derives from Bourdieu (1971).
6 Except at the end of a lesson!
7 I had used a sample of eight children to examine perceptions of the social education course.
8 I wanted to include at least ten to twelve students in each test sample. The possibility of absence caused me to set out with a higher number.
9 At least five members of staff that I spoke to considered that Trevor Bull was 'casual' and 'sloppy', although very 'gifted'. He was acknowledged to be a 'bit of a mathematician' and this could account for Mr Evans' selection. Mr Evans himself mentioned that Bull was perhaps not typical of the 'M' group as a whole.
10 By a ratio of 2.5:1 or, excluding Trevor Bull, 6.4:1.
11 Even though the school allowed a five-minute change-over period between lessons.
12 Susan Burns scored a maximum of ninety in this test (and had also known all twelve lesson times in the school day), despite having the lowest score for the NVR Test and a relatively low score for the Vocabulary Test. She was, however, in some respects atypical of the 'U' group. She liked PE and had a clear view of her future career in hairdressing. She came from a very large family and her father was unemployed. She

had to do a great deal of work around the house and was obviously very organized. Perhaps her domesticity and family background had encouraged her to be a particularly sharp and efficient time-keeper (incidentally she kept sweets, not cigarettes, in her handbag!).

13 It was particularly interesting how school uniform was stylized by pupils as an expression of sub-cultural resistance. Ties were worn by boys with very large knots at chest level and it would require a Mary Quant to explore and categorize the infinite variety of subtle alterations to basic school colours and clothing that the girls effected.

Hebdige's study of the Mod sub-culture of the 1960s describes the way in which the Mods appropriated consumer commodities and transformed them 'to relocate [their] meanings in a totally different context' (1975, p. 93). As an example he cites the scooter as a 'formerly ultra respectable means of transport' which was 'converted into a weapon and a symbol of solidarity' (1975, p. 93). A similar transformation can happen to a school uniform.

14 I had to lend a pen to Michael Hough to enable him to fill in his questionnaire.

15 However, Willis (1977) argues that the 'lads' notion of a future of generalized labour is, in terms of their own cultural mode, an essentially correct one. 'Working-class kids' see through the rhetoric of most careers advice and make fair assessment of *their* working future: work will be boring, unskilled, manual labour of one type or another; career patterns will be horizontal — the 'lads' will switch from one meaningless job to another; any gratification work provided will be instant — 'diversions' 'laffs' and a weekly pay packet.

This working-class cultural insight appears also to see through the dominant educational paradigm in the same way. Working-class children realize that school knowledge is not a marketable commodity in their culture, that qualifications are rarely worth the sacrifices which need to be made to obtain them, and that conformity, hard work, diligence, etc. still do not permit the unsuccessful to succeed. Some working-class individuals even 'make it' without these qualities, the very qualities that are revered by the dominant ideology of the school.

It is not surprising, therefore, that we should discover how meaningless timetables, qualifications, lessons, books, pens, etc. have become for unmotivated working-class 'lads'. In their own cultural terms their assessment of school is a fairly accurate one. School means nothing, holds nothing for them. Perhaps the 'amorphous school', like the 'generalized concept of labour' is another example of Willis' notion of 'advanced proletarian consciousness'.

16 Derived from Dr Peter P. Daws' research on the occupational satisfactions sought by schoolchildren (1967). This list appears in more detailed form in HOPSON, B. and HOUGH, P. (1973) *Exercises in Personal and Career Development* CRAC/Hobsons Press.

References

ARONOWITZ, S. (1973) *False Promises*, New York, McGraw-Hill.
BIRD, C. (1980) 'Deviant labelling in school: The pupils' perspective', in WOODS, P. (Ed.) *Pupil Strategies*, London, Croom Helm.
BOURDIEU, P. and PASSERON, J.C. (1971) *La Reproduction: Elements pour une Theorie du Systeme d'enseignement*, Editions de Minuit.
BOWLES, S. and GINTIS, H. (1976) 'Education and personal development: The long shadow of work', in BOWLES, S. and GINTIS, H. *Schooling in Capitalist America*, London, Routledge and Kegan Paul.
CORRIGAN, P. (1979) *Schooling the Smash Street Kids*, London, Macmillan.

GANNAWAY, H. (1976) 'Making sense of school', in STUBBS, M. and DELAMONT, S. (Eds) *Explorations in Classroom Observation*, New York, Wiley.

GIROUX, H.A. (1981) 'Beyond the correspondence theory', in GIROUX, H.A. *Ideology, Culture and the Process of Schooling*, Lewes, Falmer Press.

HARGREAVES, A. (1980) 'Synthesis and the study of strategies: A project for the sociological imagination', in WOODS, P. (Ed.) *Pupil Strategies*, London, Croom Helm.

HAYES, J. and HOPSON, B. (1972) *Careers Guidance*, Heinemann.

HEBDIGE, R. (1976) 'The meaning of Mod', in HALL, S. and JEFFERSON, T. (Eds) *Resistance through Rituals*, Hutchinson.

HOPSON, B. and HOUGH, P. (1973) *Exercises in Personal and Career Development*. CRAC/Hobsons Press.

REYNOLDS, D. (1976) 'The delinquent school', in HAMMERSLEY, M. and WOODS, P. (Eds) *The Process of Schooling*, London, Routledge and Kegan Paul.

WILLIS, P. (1976) 'The class significance of school counter-culture', in HAMMERSLEY, M. and WOODS, P. (Eds) *The Process of Schooling*, London, Routledge and Kegan Paul.

WILLIS, P. (1977) *Learning to Labour*, Farnborough, Saxon House.

WOODS, P. (1976) 'Having a laugh: Antidote to schooling', in HAMMERSLEY, M. and WOODS, P. (Eds) *The Process of Schooling*, London, Routledge and Kegan Paul.

WOODS, P. (1977) 'Teaching for survival', in WOODS, P. and HAMMERSLEY, M. *School Experience*, London, Croom Helm.

WOODS, P. (1979) *The Divided School*, London, Routledge and Kegan Paul.

Teacher, Self and Curriculum

Peter Woods

Introduction

To what extent does a teacher find self-expression within the curriculum? How far is a 'subject' as practised in the classroom a realization of an individual teacher's self? These questions are overdue for consideration among sociologists of the curriculum.

As conceived by G.H. Mead (1934), the self is a process, consisting of continual interaction between the 'I' and the 'Me', the former representing the individualized impulsive aspect, the latter the socially regulated aspect, which allows one to regard oneself as object, and stabilizes action (Blumer, 1977). In this way, the self interacts with prevailing social circumstances, now borrowing something from them, now contributing (Berger and Luckmann, 1971). Such a dialectical interplay obtains, I would argue, between teachers and subject specialisms. The proposition is, therefore, that rather in the same way that teachers 'make' rather than 'take' roles (Turner, 1962), they also 'make' the curriculum.

I examined this proposition in a series of interviews with a recently retired teacher. I employed the life history method, the merits of which have been recently argued by Faraday and Plummer (1979), Goodson (1980) and Bertaux (1981). It seemed important to consider the teacher's total life and career, and to try to identify some of the major strands of development of self, and the important influences upon it. The teacher (whom I call 'Tom') and I talked in consequence on a number of occasions for a total of some twelve hours, yielding over 500 pages of transcript. I had, too, my fieldnotes and interview transcripts from previous projects in which Tom had figured prominently (Woods, 1979 and 1981). In the course of these discussions, a second proposition suggested itself, namely, that if the curriculum and self are in dialectical interplay, large elements of that self have been formulated in early life.

What follows is a framework for the consideration of these two propositions. First, I abstract from the many hours of interaction with this man what I perceive to be major components of his self. I go on to consider the implications of these elements for his strategical action as a teacher, and for his attitude to the curriculum. I next trace the origins of the elements in his earlier life, including a consideration of macro-influences and mediating factors. Finally, I suggest that the actual degree and quality of self-subject interaction depends on ranges of coordinates that we can specify for any particular teacher.

I must stress again the speculative nature of this framework. It is based on only one teacher, and covers a vast field, some parts of which are inevitably sketched over lightly. My purpose is not to present a comprehensive model or an exhaustive biographical account, but more simply to raise some of the issues in this hitherto unexplored area.

A Brief Overview of Tom's Career

1922	Born in the Borders, Scotland. Father, Scottish, civil engineer; Mother, Irish, Catholic. Tom eldest child in family of six. Goes to Catholic primary school.
1934	Tom wins scholarship and goes to local grammar school. Matriculates 1939.
1939	Joins army on eight-year contract. Trains in Signals.
1939–47	Serves in Europe with BEF and invasion force, and training troops in England; after 1945, in India and Japan; 1947, demobbed; married 1943.
1947–50	First experience of teaching in two primary schools in Lincolnshire as emergency-trained teacher.
1950–52	Teacher training college.
1952	Returns to primary school.
1953–55	Takes up post at all-age school (Catholic) in home town.
1955	Moves to all-age school in Midlands; this becomes a secondary modern in 1957, and a comprehensive in 1978. Tom progresses from teacher of general subjects in all-age school to Head of Design in Secondary Modern. He retired through ill-health in 1979.

Aspects of the Self (Summary)

Prominent among the esteemed values of the preferred self were humanitarianism (love of, and trust and faith in people), pacifism (after the war), tolerance, honesty and independence. Tom also has two major dispositions: (1) a questioning, curious, critical outlook on life and the world, and (2) an artistic temperament, involving love of beauty, creativity and self-expression.

Yet, at times, certain bi-modal features are apparent, Tom at one time espousing one value or cause, or a certain trait or disposition, at another, its opposite. The main features here were:

Tolerance	Intolerance
'Straightness'	'Deviousness'
Idealism	Pragmatism
Romanticism	Realism
Collectivism	Individualism
Involvement	Detachment
Outgoingness	Reserve
Confidence	Uncertainty

In the tension between these features lies the key to Tom's survival. It represents the means by which he engages with society, but continues to stay 'at one' with himself (though in some respects there are *two* selves). Thus, he is an 'incurable romantic', yet even in the identification of that fact shows himself to be basically a realist. Much of his teaching ideal is contained within the community philosophy of A.S. Neill, professing togetherness, friendship, equality, democracy, and found expression, as well as in school, in local pub, entertaining at home and running the Adult Education Centre. But Tom also feels strongly individualistic, independent, detached, aloof. In some respects, he feels this may be a result of an inherent shyness, but in other respects he cultivates it. It is what he wants — to be a 'loner', even among his own family. One of the great lessons he has learned through life is tolerance, yet here and there he shows an intolerance, at times understandable in the light of other things he holds dear (such as his disdain of certain incompetent teachers), at other times more difficult to comprehend (such as his total condemnation of the French as a nation). Then, too, he is a great admirer of 'straight' behaviour, involving fairness, honesty and directness, without fuss or favour, but considers himself a most 'devious' character in finding ways to achieve his own ends if his more direct approaches are rejected.

Such apparent inconsistencies well illustrate the Meadian notion of self, not as a fixed entity, but as a process, constantly in flux as it encounters different situations and interacts with different others. It does not discount the possibility of a 'core' self (Berger *et al.*, 1973; Turner, 1976). Tom says his 'real me' is the detached, aloof, individualistic 'loner'. Here he can indulge his idealism and romanticism. But in the outside world, in interaction with others, he has acquired the hard edge of realism. Though a romantic at heart, he is nobody's fool. He can see through humbug, other people's strategies, his own failings. Though he has never lost or tempered his ideals, he has never entertained illusions about their chances of realization.

Implications of the Self for Strategical Action and for Curriculum

Tom's tolerance, humanitarianism and 'straightness' are evident mostly in his day-to-day interactions with pupils and parents. There are no threats, subterfuges, coaxings to get pupils to do what he wants, beyond the provision of a friendly atmosphere and the cultivation of a sense of togetherness. His view of the teacher is as a 'facilitator', and of the subject, 'it is what it does to people, not what it is'.

The 'artistic' line comes through his subject, but also his general approach to teaching and child development. For Tom, art is not a body of knowledge, or a collection of skills and techniques. Nor does a product like examination results matter.

> Technique is totally unimportant, in art, you know. When all is said and done, it's what you achieve, not how you achieve it, and even if I read any simple little manual on 'How to paint in oils' — you can imagine all these things, you can learn all these techniques in one night. You may make mistakes at first, but if you are intelligent this sort of thing is only really a matter of commonsense.... You don't need instruction.... A boy serves an apprenticeship, he just hangs around a bench where people are doing it and just picks it up....

Art thus is not a subject, but a medium for the expression of the self. And the important outcome is not the painting, but what it does to people. Above all, it should increase their sensitivity.

> I'm concerned with bringing art to the populace, making life a little bit richer for them, making a girl understand that laying a table is a work of art, it can either be pleasant and seductive and complementary to the food, or it can just be a lot of crockery chucked down. That's all. That's the basis of all art in my terms ... just open their eyes a little, and making them feel more.

It follows that you cannot *teach* art. Tom saw his job as 'to create an environment in which these creative things could flourish ... and children can only create this environment within themselves. You certainly don't "teach".'

Further, art is only part of, and subservient to, the grander design, which is the whole person. Tom is a convinced child-centred integrationist.

> My kind of teaching depends on integration.... I didn't waste time on history sessions drawing little Norman Castles, you could do that in Art. Everything worked together, when you were doing one subject you were talking about another.... These teachers [in his last school] were taught in a discipline — their educational training is nil. They don't know what inter-relationships and coordination is about.

Thus he bemoaned his failure to get links with the woodwork and metalwork teachers, who resisted all his overtures. His best memories of teaching were of a time when, as head of art, he could cover his responsibilities for the subject to the whole school in two days, and had one form only for the other three days of the week. Here he could perpetrate an integrated curriculum and cultivate relationships in the holistic, full-blooded way he liked best.

242

Tom insists he had to do things 'his way', and his solution to the problem caused by the one school where he was not allowed sufficient rein, was to move on. He said he told his prospective new headmaster, at interview:

> I'm very impressed with the school, but I'd like to point out I don't fit very easily into tramlines. I can guarantee that if I come to this job, I'll try very hard to put the school first and keep everything going, but I can only do it my way. I don't know any other way of teaching except my way. It might at times conflict, but we should be roughly going in the same direction.

What is 'his way'?

> It isn't a way, it's not a religion, I've worked out. It's just that I tend to play things off the cuff you know, I work by and from the children. I think about the responses I get and I build on those, and I sense what's happening around me, and if I feel there is a more productive line, I'll drop the other with pleasure, because I don't see any point in flogging dead horses if you've got live ones in the stables.... I tend to tack furiously if I'm losing wind on that side, I veer over here.... I never worked to a time-table.[1] That's another reason no Head liked me very much. I swallowed the timetable, and regurgitated it to suit myself.

In the Borders' Catholic school where he taught, he tried to humanize what he saw as the dogmatic teaching of the church. He aimed to give his 'senior lads a more interesting life, and some freedom'. He got woodwork and cookery going 'with a bit of pushing, twisting and cajoling'. He took on 'the school gardens' and 'the kids loved that — there was a certain sort of freedom. We would talk together outdoors freely and easily ... and we learned a lot together.' Football, youth club — you name it, Tom did it in those days, and he 'loved it'. His method was built on *trust*. He had trusted people, and children in particular, all his life, and had not often been let down. So he developed close relationships with them, and much of his important 'teaching' he feels took place around the edges of the official timetable. For example, 'walking to the swimming pool, on the way I would talk to the kids ... about the town, and they knew nothing really about it ... and then we'd spend some time on the seashore inspecting shells and weed and so forth ... it's so easy to lead children, I've found. I could get topics going in a million things.' While he had the freedom and opportunities to 'teach' in this particular way, he was happy, but opposition built up among his superiors and he felt forced to leave.

However, if much of this smacks of 'redefinition' (Lacey, 1977), Tom had his periods of 'compliance', notably at the beginning and at the end of his teaching career. The latter had something to do with the 'side-bets' (Becker, 1960) he had made by that time (see below), the former with the animal instinct to survive. In his first (junior) school, he really did have a very hard training. I had 60 odd children in one room, and he [the headmaster] 60 odd in the other, with a glass partition between us. For the first six months the partition stayed back all the time, and I taught with his listening to me with his left ear while he listened to his own lot with the other, and every move I made was checked and double-checked. I had to cycle six miles to work, and he insisted on my being there at 8.30 a.m., and by 8.45 I had to show him not only my teaching notes for the day, but my blackboards for the day.

At 8.55, these blackboards were inspected, as was Tom's person and clothing. If all was acceptable, he was given pen, inks and register, and supervised while he completed it. He had a hard training, but never held it against that man, and was able to 'put it into proper perspective later'.

Tom learnt the 'nuts and bolts' of the business from these people (his first two junior school headmasters) — preparation, organization and discipline. He had high ideals, but 'was very tied down by them'. He accepted everything the way they presented it and 'did what he was told'. He had a little bit of fun with the children on the side, but only when the head was not around. He was little more than a monitor in his first school, a 'minireplica' of the head. But

I thought it wasn't hurting me. His way worked, so let's understand that first. I had big ideas ... but I didn't know how to implement them. Controlling sixty odd children when you have had no experience is a hairy business, so I found the best thing was if his routine worked, use it, if you've nothing better, and when the time comes, chuck it out of the window ... but in the first instance, you must have some control. Without that there is no hope in life.

When he remembers the vast numbers of young teachers he has met in his career who just could not cope, he counts himself 'very lucky to have had this monster Welshman to put me right when I started'.

By the time he went to training college, he 'really did know the ropes, and was well trained. I didn't get away with anything like a young teacher might today.' He had served his apprenticeship in practical skills and in 'coping', had a better idea of what was and what was not possible, and in some respects had had his horizons broadened, first by his second headmaster, a man after his own heart, imaginative, caring, progressive, and who gave Tom rather more scope and allowed him to spread his wings a little; secondly, by the educational literature he was always saturating himself in, and the 'emergency' courses for trainee teachers he went on. This early period, therefore, found Tom 'situationally adjusting', acquiring the necessary kit of a teacher practising in the state system, momentarily subordinating his preferred self to the indispensable framework of the role, but finding more scope in his second school for his own personal style of teaching — child-centred, de-institutionalized, relevant, free, exciting, fun. This freedom, however, was gained at some cost to other interests — his own creative painting, for example. But it enabled him to 'rise above' his two-year training course, which, for him, was an in-service one. It gave him justification for some of his ideas.

Eventually, at his second primary school, he felt that he began to exercise a reciprocal influence on the head, as he did with a later one 'rejuvenating them. . . . They had probably been such as I was in their youth, but had got in the doldrums, hadn't kept up with the literature, and had lost the desire to keep it up. So I was like a little refresher course to them. . . .' This is the kind of strategic redefinition identified by Lacey (1977, p. 73) — influencing 'those with formal power to change their interpretation of what is happening in the situation'. But it also indicates a readiness to 'trade' on Tom's behalf, accepting some of their ideas and practices, though they might have a totally different concept of education from his, while they accepted some of his. 'I believe one must compromise on the way to winning — and winning is what it is all about. Sell the chap a record — there is a chance he will buy a record player. In the meantime, tolerate his phonogram.' His criterion for judgement here was results, not examination results, but the effect on the person that he held so dear.

In his last school, a secondary modern, eventually to become a compre-hensive, Tom felt caught between a number of intractable forces — an unyielding headmaster, a subject-centred staff, the need to remain where he was for his son's sake, and later, periodic illness. He 'wasn't given enough' freedom to develop, and having to justify yourself to idiots — that was very upsetting.' The whole concept of education was different — 'I wanted a lot more freedom, a lot more integration. I wanted everything we did to be meaningful.'

There were satisfactions, however, notably on the social side of his teaching, in the administration of the developing design area, and in rela-tionships in the community at large. While at this school, he deployed the following strategies:

1 to fight for the things he believed in. He and a colleague spearheaded a major 'complaints' exercise against the head. It achieved little, except, Tom suspects, their non-promotion. He feels he may have had more success with younger teachers, struggling to cope.

2 to compromise, but only to seem to give way in 'smaller battles in order to win larger wars'. Similarly, to bargain, for example, to offer his services for work above the call of duty in exchange for greater freedom. Thus at one stage he opted to take over the terrors of the school, 3D.

> I became known as Mr 3D. Three dimensional Tom. But it had one good effect. I could lay down my rules about this — 'if you don't like what I'm proposing for these children, well find somebody else. . . . I got my own way, you see. I could do what I liked. . . .

3 to seek a more conducive situation — perhaps even out of education altogether. For a time, he flirted with the notion of personnel work or the social services. He felt they 'worked in smaller units, and that you could be responsible for your own thing ... your case load would be your own, rather than this restrictive practice I was going through day by day.' Family commitments (see later) prevented him, and his efforts, in any case, were double-edged. Asking the head weekly for a testimonial was, he thought, one form of pressure.

4 to cultivate marginality. 'I just lived in a little island within the school, you know. I really did.' Within the art room, he could put into practice his educational ideas, as far as the situation allowed, secure liaisons with the occasional like-minded member of staff, succour the young, inexperienced teachers, and seek to influence those with power in the school whom he felt he could relate to.

5 to compartmentalize his self. It was another contradiction within Tom that, although a convinced integrationist with regard to the curriculum and a believer in the whole person of the pupil, he divided his own self between private and public arenas (Berger et al., 1973). He increasingly reserved his 'real' self for home, and felt that his public self as teacher was comparatively unreal. After marriage, and particularly as his son grew up, Tom fell into line to stabilize his career for utilitarian purposes. The ideal Tom thus became even more displaced to the interstices of life. Most of the elements of this ideal self were intensely privatized, but this did facilitate the management of the public self.

Derivations of the Self: Micro

So far, I have considered aspects of Tom's self, and their relationship to his views of teaching and of the curriculum. From whence did this self derive?

1   Home and Parents

For Tom, his home life, particularly during his adolescent years, was by far the greatest influence. The major aspects were:

(a) *The general ambience* — critical, enquiring, down-to-earth factual, religious (Catholic) but undogmatic. His home was a meeting place for young people in the town, and he spent many evenings during his teens witnessing and joining in discussions and arguments about matters of current concern. Tom says, 'They had a big influence over me. . . . I got the impression that I was just a piece of putty floating through this world.' His home became a kind of club for the young people who came to the town — mainly young teachers from the high school, grammar school and convent. (Religion was a unifying feature here, for the area was predominantly Calvinist, and Catholics 'stuck together'.) You didn't stay in a place like that long, so there was a considerable turnover, always young people with their specialities in literature, Greek, Latin, politics and so forth. But they weren't all teachers. He could remember a doctor, a dentist, a lawyer, and a manager of the local gas works coming round. So between the ages of 11 and 14, he 'sat on the fringes of life', when they discussed politics, religion, philosophy, psychology and so on. Occasionally, when he asked a question, he would get drawn in, and they would give him books to read.

In general, Tom liked everybody he met during his childhood. 'They were lovely people because they were straight.... Nobody told you lies ... they were dead straight.' In this, too, lay the kernel of a later belief that the medium was more important than the message. He had witnessed so many debates and arguments, he could see all points of view, and agree with all. More important to him was 'the quality of the delivery [which] almost overcomes the message underneath. I love a good argument [like his father], presentation of an argument, I get so enthralled by the way it's presented, I wonder sometimes if I've missed the essence.'

(b) *Father* — possible Tom's strongest influence. '. . . the more I thought about my father, the more I got to understand him since he died, believe it or not, because I am so similar.... Everything I do I see my father in me, you know ... I *am* my father, and I do mean that.'

Tom was the eldest child in a family of six, he had his father's name, he was the one 'carrying on his family'. This was why, he thinks, his father wanted him to know everything he knew. So he taught him many practical skills, but also socialized him into a mode of thinking while he was doing it. The one thing he does remember, very positively, was '. . . never, never accept anything — question, question, question! Always ask why . . .'

> He loved an argument, not just for opposition's sake, but for the quality of argument. He would say, for example, 'We've got to get this damn priest of yours over here one night. I can't get any sense out of you people. There's got to be a better argument than this, you know.'

'And he loved it when these priests came, especially the old one, because he would argue and argue and argue. He just loved arguing, and we grew up in this atmosphere. Dad's at it again, just listen to him!'.

Like Tom, his father was a survivor. A civil engineer, he can never remember his father doing any engineering. Tom's teenage years were during the depression of the 1930s, and his father put his hand to all manner of jobs to keep the family supplied, and to use what talent he'd got for his own personal ends ... making things for the house, etc. Even so, if he set his mind on something he would achieve it, even as a boy. Tom had a massive confidence in his father's ability to manipulate what were basically unfavourable situations.

247

The classic example of this, perhaps, was his conversion to Catholicism (from atheism) shortly before his death.

There are many minor examples of this optimistic approach to life. All things were possible to his father. As a boy, Tom was 'the most nervous, shy, introverted thing' who perpetually thought himself 'not good enough'. But his father gave him confidence and a defence. He said 'you are better than most around you. There are plenty better than you, but on average, you are above most of them. What you've got to develop is a "brass neck" attitude to this world. Walk into a room and say of course I can do it. That's the attitude in life.' 'Now I remember that, and very distinctly I can remember the room, the occasion, all about it, and that stuck with me.' He was a 'dour, taciturn Scot . . . but always there, as a rock. He had become essentially a "private" man, for he did a hundred jobs, and none of them really possibly matched up to what he was capable of doing. So to overcome his frustration, he worked at home using what talent he'd got for his own personal ends . . . making things for the house, etc.'

Tom already appreciated the distinction between private and public. The 'critical' outlook engendered at home was not suited to school, where they preferred unquestioning obedience. His nonconformity was already well in evidence, and in the latter days he played truant for about two and a half days a week. 'Being a devious little kid I got away with it for a year. I was awfully clever! . . . it's escapism.'

Arguments with teachers led to his giving up at an early stage two of his favourite subjects — maths and art. But his home was his own 'personal university'. They coached him, for example, through the School Certificate after years of non-achievement at school. Also, his father encouraged him, by, for example, taking his drawings to show his friends. One of these friends advised Tom to go in for teaching — that or architecture. In fact, Tom got a place at Art College in Edinburgh, but it was too far and too costly to take up. His father got him offers of jobs, one with a petrol company, one in an architect's office, but he chose to go into the army, basically to get away from home. He loved his childhood, but now he wanted independence. But going into the army he regards as a romantic act. He didn't want to be a 'soldier' — that was not the intention.

(c) *Mother.* Tom's mother was the focal point of the family, a clever woman who had wanted to be a teacher, but her family could not afford to sustain her, and she was headed off by marriage. She provided the intellectual drive and climate for the family, and sought to compensate for her frustrations through her children. She was thus always drawing Tom's attention to the benefits and virtues of teaching as a profession. 'I think it's a great profession. I think teaching is a wonderful thing. To be able to pass things on to children . . . to learn and understand, themselves, you know.' But more important than this direct lesson, perhaps, was the climate that she created in the home, the people she invited there, the intellectual soirées that she hosted.

She was a 'garrulous, lovely' woman, Irish by birth, whose ancestors were 'all pure Irish, and extreme romantics. . . . Nothing practical in their world at all.' In this, she contrasted with his father's side, one of dour, almost obstinate practicality. It was her religion that held in the home, but it was a 'very liberal sort of religious house. They were total believers . . . but they were free. Most of the people coming into our house, a lot of these youngsters, were agnostics, well, you name it, they were it.'

Tom's parents had faith in their children. They were never shocked by anything he did. And they never took anything for granted. 'Mother would never hear people knocked. She always felt that there could be a reason that we just couldn't know about, and might never know about. . . . Nothing was odd to her really.'

(d) *Grandparents.* Tom feels his mother's Irish parents were a significant influence upon him. He remembers in particular the wild romanticism of his grandfather's stories and his grandmother's generosity, not only to him, but to all comers; also, his grandfather's strong sense of independence, and rejection of any normal career.

> . . . He had it made. He retired when he was thirty odd. He didn't like the idea of this bloody work and he just thought it pure farce being used by other people, and he retired. I don't know how he lived, because he didn't draw anything from the government. . . . But he had talents, and he used them. He used to mend clocks. He didn't get worried about it, it didn't seem important to him.

Tom was also impressed by the degree to which he had his life organized in a series of routines governed by the pub's opening hours.

Running through these accounts are all those aspects of Tom's later self that were to find expression in his teaching — a strong sense of individuality, of critical awareness, of coping almost triumphantly in the face of adversity, of marginality, almost brinkmanship, of freedom, and of love of, and respect for, people.

2   Books, literature, art

Tom has been an avid reader all his life. He remembers in particular, in his early days, a book on the miners' strike of the 1920s, which converted him to socialism (the 'official' politics of the family, represented by his mother, was liberalism). When he read *And Quiet Flows the Don*, he wrote to the Russian Embassy to find out more about Russia and was inundated with communist propaganda.

Later in life, of particular note was his encounter with the writings of A. S. Neill — during the war, in fact, before his teaching career had begun. Neill's ideas became the cornerstone of Tom's philosophy about teaching, unsurprisingly, for all the features of his earlier socialization are there — the emphasis on democracy, equality, independence, freedom, open discussion and debate, 'straightness', mutual caring, growth and learning from within. Neill convincingly tied all these ideals to education at a time when Tom was becoming interested in instructing in the Signals Corps.

3   Teachers, Coaches

In general, teachers at school, he recalls, were more of negative than positive influence, cooling him out of maths and art, and being hidebound by rules and routines, which to him were anathema. One example of this he recalls from his infant days concerned a woman teacher who enthused over a sketch of a cat he had made, and fetched the head to see it. While they were away, Tom noticed he had omitted an important detail — the 'belly button' — so he put it in. On her return, with the head, she flew into a temper and boxed his ears:

> 'You naughty boy, you wicked boy, and I've just brought the Headmaster here to see this.' And I can still see his face when he looked at it, as much as to say, Oh God, you know, what's the boy done wrong, but he couldn't say it to her or to us, you know, and honestly that was about the first time I'd got the sort of understanding of dealing with awkward people. You could never be right. And also, that adults didn't necessarily back each other up, except on the surface.

He has often drawn on the moral of this memory in his own teaching of art to children. He would never disparage anything. Anything that somebody produced must have value in it. He remembered once when he was sorting through some pupil folders to decide which to keep and which discard, he recalled that incident when 'that good work had been missed by one mark, which wasn't interpreted artistically but biologically', and wondered who was he to judge. 'Half the stuff in the bin may be more valuable to those children than this other work.'

The immediate result of that kind of teacher attitude was the privatization of those areas of the curriculum most dear to him. His art teacher 'made a snide comment to him about religion. . . . It was an effort to put me down without the right of reply. . . . "Shut up, get out" sort of thing. So I just stopped doing Art in school. I attended all lessons, but I never painted any more. I did it all at home, . . .' where, needless to say, he was duly encouraged by his father, and his father's friends, among whom there was one in particular with strong artistic leanings and connections.

It is no curiosity, then, that Tom should come to believe that art cannot be taught. Later, 'when I went to college, I deliberately didn't take Art. I thought I could deal with that on my own. This is personal development as far as I am concerned. I can read, I can look and . . . do it myself, and I went into fields which I thought would be more difficult.'

But he admired the headmaster of the grammar school. He had to cane

Tom every Friday because of his habitual transgression of the rules, and it went on so long they developed a strange relationship over the business, the head executing his duty with an understanding and bonhomie that Tom much admired. As with his father, it seems this man practised role distance to good effect. Tom was always impressed with that ability in people, and was to use it himself to good effect in his own teaching.

4   Side-Bets (Becker, 1960)

Tom married during the war. This immediately influenced where he went after the war and to some degree what he did — to England (Lincolnshire), instead of India where he really wanted to go (his wife did not wish to go India). On demob, he took up teaching. He says that the first thing he wanted was to get back into the swing of painting again, and

> had I not been married I most certainly wouldn't have taught, because I realized that if you are going to be a full-time teacher, dedicated to his job, you couldn't possibly be an artist as well ... it's time consuming, body consuming, mind consuming. So I think I knew then that in a sense I was giving up art for teaching.... If you are in education, you have to use your art for other people, and help them along the road, and while you are doing that, you are not developing yourself.... And I don't think you can even be a good artist and be married and lead a normal happy married life. That's ridiculous. You've got to be a bit more selfish.

Later in his career, his options within teaching were profoundly affected by family considerations. For example, he certainly would have left his final school because of frustration through the policy of a new headmaster, but for his wife and son, whose education and subsequent career he now put first.

> When A was about 13 he used to get petrified when he saw me looking through the back pages of the Times Ed. He knew by then this was a danger signal, a man looking for a job somewhere, and he was a very nervous boy, and it had taken him a long time to settle in his school. He was worried sick he'd have to leave his friends and start all over again. It was about that time I thought, well what's the point, I'm not ambitious really.... I was as happy here as I would be anywhere....

Here we see Tom surrendering some of his interests as artist and as teacher in return for satisfactions as husband and father.

Derivations of the Self: Macro

Throughout his career, certain structural and macro-considerations appear influential in the formation of the self, notably the following.

Social Class

Tom himself disputes his 'middleclassness'. It is never a term he has used in connection with himself, because he considers he 'came from working-class antecedents . . . We all had to work. Of course we had to do jobs that were very menial.' His father may have been a 'cut above, if you like, the average man in the street, in theory, but in practice he was having to do what they did.' His ancestry was rural — farming figures prominently as far as Tom could remember, his father being the first one to break out of the rural mould and go into a more industrial type of work.

What distinguished Tom's parents from most others in the town was their education, and their aspirations. They could be considered members of the 'service' class. As used by Halsey *et al.* (1980), this consists of those 'exercising power and expertise on behalf of corporate "authorities", plus such elements of the classic bourgeoisie,. independent businessmen, and "free" professionals, as are not yet assimilated into this new formation' (Goldthorpe and Llewellyn, 1977, p. 259). His father had been educated and trained to the position of the professional, working on behalf of civil authorities. His mother had been a brilliant pupil at school in Perthshire, had won a County Scholarship, studied as a pupil-teacher, but then the family had moved to the Borders, where there was no transfer of scholarships, and so her aspirations to be a teacher were thwarted. However, she never lost the interest. Tom recalls doing some research for her on the history of the Labour Party shortly before she died, because she wanted to talk to someone's group about it. 'She wanted to tell other people . . . she was trying to keep her intelligence on the boil all the time.'

So, although the actual positions were lacking, the reality of a 'service class' home was there. This applied to material things as well as to status and prestige:

> We were, in a sense, better than others, though I don't like saying these things. We had our own house for one thing, and we lived well, you know, what I mean by everybody else's standards we lived well. By their standards we were bloody well off. We had fruit when nobody else ate fruit. They had bread and dripping, you know, when we had fish, steak, and all the rest. We were well off.

Tom thus had the material advantages of such a home, and the motivational example and desire to become more firmly established in a professional occupation. But none of his family was class conscious. Tom prefers to think of himself as 'classless', and feels more affinity for the working class than any other. Objectively, of course, by virtue of his occupation, he would be classified as middle or 'service' class, firmly settling in to a niche offered but then not opened to either of his parents. He has consolidated the position aspired to by his parents. And the intellectual progression from his parents led him from a very early age into socialism. But it is one tempered with the cult of the individual. There are shades, here, of his mother's brand of liberalism, but more potently, I would suggest the influence of significant others who, in a sense, seemed to stand outside and defy society, living on their own wits and their own terms. His father and grandfather are the two outstanding examples of this. This 'marginality' has become Tom's own style.

Religion

As a member of a Catholic family in a predominantly non-Catholic area, Tom was conscious of the fact that he was different. 'Very conscious of that, and I remember asking about it, questioning it, why *should* ... and maybe to some degree that's the trigger to my questioning so much, you know.'

Religion was more clearly an integrator and differentiator than social class. They were in different primary schools for a start, and there was great antagonism between the RC school and the rest, 'to a degree that one chose one's time to go along a certain road, or one was prepared for attack.' At the grammar school he was fairly well accepted by the children, though he was conscious of being different from the vast majority of them. But he remembers lots of problems with staff. 'It was always the subtlety ... in history in particular, and I insisted on going to the lessons which I didn't have to [as a Catholic] because it seemed to me to be important to know what the others were talking about, and I didn't want to be outside it.... I found most of the teachers couldn't resist the snide comments at my expense.' There was, he says, a partisan business going on in the area at the time, 'rather like the Northern Ireland thing today, in a minor key.' Even then, he says, he could identify it as that, he knew it wasn't him personally they were getting at. Again, he felt he could rise above it as an individual, being '... bloody devious and twisted and odd, and I think even then I could use what little knowledge and intelligence I had to escape from most of these situations. And humour, I realized early, was the best "let-off".'

There were many doctrines of the church he could not accept. He remembers being worried about the church's teaching on matters like birth control, transubstantiation, purgatory. He was always questioning. Nonetheless, he came to believe that every person should have a belief, 'no matter whether it's Catholicism, Communism, or whatever. I don't think we're big enough on our own to stand on our own feet, mentally or emotionally. We feel the need for something to support us.' This is the basis of his respect for other people's beliefs. Tom was captivated by the romance, beauty and communality of Catholicism.

What other Church went in for such colourful displays, you know, everything was beautiful ... and the Latin, and the Vestments. The fact that there was historical significance to it all ... and equally important, the word Catholic, universal ... it was the universality of it

I think that intrigued me ... that, and the sheer romance.... The church itself was the best little museum in town.

In short, Tom's association with Catholicism sharpened his appreciation of beauty, taught him the values of belief and tolerance, and the virtues of sociation, and provided substance for the exercise of his critical judgement. Where, on occasions, religion acted as a constraint, he sought a new situation where he would be free from it. For example, at one stage in his career he returned to his home town to take up a post in the Catholic school. While many aspects of this were delightful, renewing friendships, dealing with parents who were actually contemporaries of his when he was a schoolchild in the town, and generally enjoying the community relations he values so greatly, he found the religion there oppressive. It dominated the school day. His efforts to liven up the teaching of it were frowned upon. Who was he to set himself up as a radical innovator against centuries of development in the church?

Needless to say I did it my way, I didn't do it the formal way which would be chattering out the questions and the answers.... I did it my way which I thought was more interesting and more humorous, with cartoon strips and the like.... I was severely castigated for this ... people don't make inroads into my life like that, not my teaching life you know. I organized my teaching and if they didn't like it, they could say so.

Also, to carry on teaching there, he would have to have the 'Bishop's certificate', but had the bishop any qualifications in teaching? That again illustrates how religion predominated over teaching within the school. It choked his personal style, and was one of the main reasons for his leaving the school after a stay of only two to three years. The other major reason was the headmaster who had been appointed on the strength of his religious rather than teaching qualifications. 'I got more and more frustrated. I had done about all I could do. I needed more freedom....'

Social, Political and Economic Climate

Tom's career runs parallel with four distinct phases:

pre-war: marked by the economic crisis of the thirties, and mounting international tension
the war of 1939–45
post-war: optimism, but economic scarcity; 'secondary education for all'
1960s affluence, and later, comprehensive education.

I select just one of these here — the war — to illustrate the impact on self. The army 'was an important part of my life. If that little bit in my adolescence was an introductory course, this was a postgraduate degree I took in the army.

It was a very maturing process.' He has had 'a very enclosed life, like a monastery in a way' and the army got him away from home and stood him on his own feet, where he was able to put into practice his father's precepts. He learnt a trade in the Signals, and quickly learnt that you could get money by educational advancement. This induced him to 'improve', and soon he was training new recruits, most much older than himself. He went with them, with the BEF to France, and was driven out with them at Dunkirk. After the BEF it was 'a piece of cake', lots more training and courses.

Again Tom adapts, and not only survives, but enjoys — the horrors of the war apart (such as the relief of two concentration camps in 1945). It gave him what he wanted — 'a place of his own' as head of a small workshop unit. Here he had his first real experience of teaching, savoured the satisfaction of getting across difficult concepts, saw the point himself of much discussion, such as that on the gestalt theory, that had taken place at his mother's soirées. There was experiment and research on things like radios for tanks, in an atmosphere at that time of continual urgency and excitement. As for the horrors of the war, they are burned into his mind, not only the excesses of the enemy but also of troops on his own side, and by the end of the war he was a total pacifist. The best of his army experiences were in India and Japan, countries and people that he learned to love, though initial expectations from propaganda had led him to expect otherwise. He was fascinated by the religions, which were not inhibiting but encouraged a certain way of life; and found them both 'totally amenable people', who accepted you for what you were. These experiences helped him to understand other people, not to pre-judge. His teaching activities also expanded, becoming in charge of the army bureau of current affairs. His 'deviousness' ('it was my middle name') developed apace, advancing the interests of his unit. 'I must have been an awful little bastard but I was out to get what I wanted.' In India, too, he came across many marvellous books, including some by A.S. Neill. For the first time he realized how important it was 'to belong to and be living with, and be totally part of the community which one was trying to have an impact on.' Above all, the army injected a strong note of realism and practicality. Old soldiers, later, were not going to be 'pushed around' or take kindly to 'airy fairy' ideas. The army also made him supremely adaptable. 'Thanks to the army, moving around, I've never had any problems settling in. I could settle into a pig-sty tomorrow and be happier than the pigs.'

Thus the army made Tom independent, reinforced in practical terms the values he had learnt theoretically at home, expanded his horizons, giving him a rich experience of the world on which his future career could be based, gave him experience of teaching, and sharpened certain aspects of his personality, such as his critical stance and his 'deviousness'. It also meant that he went into teaching as a mature student 'who wasn't going to be pushed around any more'. When he went to training college three years after demob, he and others like him reacted strongly to expectations of conformity. At one of their first meetings with the Principal, they told him 'please understand we've had our ration of this [being pushed around]. We are reasonable human beings, we want to create a life for ourselves, we want to be trained, but we are not boys who have just come from school ... we had been forced to conform too long. . . .'

Mediating Factors

Between the broad, general developments and structures and the everyday detail of the classroom lie a number of mediatory factors, which may hold keys to personal fulfilment. For Tom, three were of special significance:

1 the position, role and person of the headteacher,
2 the reference group, and
3 the subject.

1   The Headteacher

The negative repercussions for staff of the decisions and actions of the headteacher as 'critical reality definer' have been vividly portrayed by Riseborough (1981). But there is still considerable room for individual manoeuvre.

During Tom's career as teacher, he served under five headmasters. Two were 'admirable', showing an openness of mind and spirit, a good intelligence, and a dedication to teaching which matched Tom's own aspirations. He was still not allowed free rein. Under the first (at his second primary school), he was still learning the *craft* of teaching. Under the second (at the all-age school in the Midlands), he began well, but after a while became sickened with the 'iron discipline', where 'the kids were flogged for nothing'. He could take the daily inspections of staff, but not the military discipline the pupils were subjected to — he 'had been through all this nonsense in the army'. He was on quite good terms with the head, and one night, after a number of drinks, voiced his objections. There followed an uncomfortable period, during which the head checked the books in Tom's room and raised objections about 'every other one', and an eventual amicable agreement which resulted in compromise on both sides.

> So he made his amends and then well, what he really came up with then was all the worries he had from the beginning when he gave me permission to start this thing [for Tom to do it 'his way']. That's what worried him. He maybe thought he'd given me too much freedom. How could he justify someof the things I was doing when an inspector came around?

But Tom admired this man. 'I take my hat off to that old boy. He worked the kids hard, he was an absolute tyrant, but they had everything when they left, because they'd been stretched. He did a good job within his own lights.'

But if he showed Tom the value of discipline and system, Tom also felt that *he* had an effect on the head, making him 'a little more free, letting him see that he didn't have to go along these narrow routes, that you could have a lot of fun and freedom and get just as far if not further.' In fact, this head did not get the top post at the new secondary modern when it was built, because he 'had become very stroppy and fell out with the authority ... mostly because he demanded so many things for that school.' He took up a post with another authority, where he began with a 'six-month terror campaign clearing out the dead-wood teachers left over from the previous all-age school', a policy Tom thought 'pretty rotten, but in a way, I think, right'.

This headmaster illustrates for Tom the best form of adaptation to the mediatory role. Though a person of very strong views and commitment, who would not brook failure, weakness or idleness, he showed a degree of flexibility which allowed Tom's basically diametrically opposing libertarian style some scope — within reason. If Tom exceeded his bounds, the head would complain, but reasonably, and as a colleague, not as a superior authority. In this way, they gained a sense of 'common cause' though their methods vastly differed.

Not so with Tom's final headmaster. Under him, according to Tom, the school, though a 'new concept in education' at the time, became organized on very rigid and traditional lines, with a heavy emphasis on external appearance, and a sacrifice of more power than was necessary to external agencies. The chances for partial autonomy and individual expression, especially of the kind Tom favoured, were therefore lost, with the result that Tom in his final years as a teacher became more marginalized.

2 Reference Group

Modelling himself on his parents, grandparents and the coterie of intellectuals who frequented his home when he was a child, Tom became a kind of 'conditioned free-thinker'. In later life the sort of people he related to were firstly those like his early headmasters who taught him the discipline of coping, but chiefly people most like himself — liberal free-thinkers in constraining positions of authority, skilled in the practice of role-distancing. They included, in his later years, a canon, chairman of the school governors, who showed the same breadth of view as the canon of Tom's younger days, an educational adviser, previously a close, like-minded colleague in the last beleaguered situation, and the deputy head in the school, who shared many of Tom's educational ideals.

Throughout his life, Tom, a marginal man, picked out other marginals to relate to in society. At the end of his career, destitute of such companionship on an equal basis, he appeared to occupy the role of mentor or counsellor to other marginals in the school, either those young teachers not yet firmly established, or older teachers, who, for one reason or another, were having difficulties. At slightly more distance, Tom related to the local community of art teachers. He helped form an art teacher's group in the county, and 'this was a great help when we came to set up the secondary moderns you know, because we knew each other, we could share experiences, and could discuss courses and things like that.'

Above all, perhaps, as genuine child-centredness would demand, Tom took his main cue from the pupils and their parents. In all the vagaries and uncertainties, they were the one constant. To Tom, 'they are the only known factor'. When he went back to his home town 'every parent I met was my peer, and my relationships with people were great. We'd been to school together. . . . And I loved the kids, because I've got a great feeling for these under-privileged country kids, you know. They're tough, hellishly tough, but by God they're good, they're great and I loved them!' In his final years of teaching, the pupils past (as, now, parents) and present, were his major referent.

3 Subject

Tom had to systematize his teaching and discipline pupils for O-level and CSE, and, at times, serve another function in 'public display'. He felt cramped by the non-integrated curriculum, but there were opportunities for creativity and freedom along the lines he desired. The external reference group of art teachers helped in strengthening this particular bridge. There were also links with galleries and artists, with other schools, and with the Art College, and the activities that involved him in attending or giving talks and lectures to local bodies, to primary schools, and in holding exhibitions.

However, Tom's prime evaluation of himself as a teacher relates not to art as such, nor to pupils formally assigned to him, but to 'spontaneous interaction', where pupils (many of whom he may not have taught) sought him out 'just to talk'. The 'Art Club' was highly informal, and markedly outside the official curriculum. Pupils came in the evenings, in very casual clothes, they made coffee, talked, had background music; they were self-motivated, governed by their own rules; they could just 'talk' if they wished, or, when they chose to apply themselves to tasks, pursue an 'integrated' curriculum.

> So instead of using our art club just for painting, we used to do a bit of research into the county's history — the Mechanics' Institute, and things like that. We put on an exhibition in working-class history in the county.

Tom's whole approach is epitomized by his first ever O-level candidate, who had to be fitted into other classes, because he was the only one. He got a grade 1, but for Tom that was not important.

> What was important was that in the odd moments in between dealing with all the other children in there, one could talk to him. I remember introducing him to T.S. Eliot. The boy got fascinated by poetry

through Eliot, and his pictures improved, because he started to see visions, if you like, in poetry and literature. He's a policeman now, but he hasn't lost his love of poetry and art. Now that to me is success — it's got nothing to do with the 'O' level he got. . . . I made a total friend of that boy.

These activities, as Tom noted himself, are remarkably similar to the family soirées of his youth, which he recalls as his most educational experiences as learner, and which he now as teacher sought to perpetuate in as many ways as he could in and around the formal curriculum.

Conclusion

The case of Tom shows that a teacher's self, in part at least, both finds expression in and gives expression to a curriculum area. The dialectic involves persistent and complex strategies, trade-offs, gains and losses. Tom, for example, finds a disjuncture between his professional and personal development, with his real self ensconced in the latter, but with great satisfactions as well as disappointments in each. His successes as a teacher, though very gratifying to him, were made at a considerable sacrifice, he feels, to his own creativity. Nor is it retrievable. Tom has given his best years to teaching and feels his own creative edge has been blunted. 'Tom the artist' remains an unknown, untried character of another life. But he takes comfort in the facts of his involvement in teaching.

We have seen that the quality and extent of that involvement depended on the conjunction of a number of coordinates. 'Self' coordinates are rooted in Tom's personal history. These are the values, beliefs and dispositions to do with such things as creativity, expressivity, romanticism, love of beauty, freedom, individuality, sociability, independence, questioning, a critical attitude, holism. Then, there are 'subject' coordinates, which permit the integration of those of the self. In the case of art, obviously the subject matter and activity speak to the self coordinates at the beginning of the list. Otherwise, its comparatively low status within the curriculum as a whole, as well as its professed need for creative 'space', means that there is less restraint and less pressure than there is on some mainstream subjects, and hence more room for the individual. As far as Tom is concerned, it is integrational and holistic in its approach to people; yet separatist and interstitial within the overall curriculum of the school. It has distinct social and community aspects which emphasize relationships; and it allows scope for creating the kind of environment and atmosphere the teacher wishes. Of all subjects, art arguably offers more opportunity for achieving the ideals of A.S. Neill, Rousseau and Dewey than other subjects within the modern curriculum.

There are institutional coordinates, such as nature and power of the headteacher, teacher culture and sub-cultures and school ethos. There are also macro-considerations to do with socio-economic and political events and trends, and structural factors, such as social class. There are 'private life' coordinates, deriving from family and leisure interests and commitments. At different times and in different places all these coordinates come together in different ways, presenting the individual with a mixture of opportunities and difficulties in varying proportions. I have attempted to show how one teacher steered a personal course through various conjunctions of these factors, trying to ensure the predominance of the 'self' coordinates, and how the strategies employed in this task themselves have roots deep in his past.

Viewed in this way, a curriculum area is a vibrant, human process lived out in the rough and tumble, give and take, joys and despairs, plots and counter-plots of a teacher's life. It is not simply a body of knowledge or set of skills; nor simply a result of group activity (Goodson, 1983). Tom's case shows that, to some extent at least, individuals can and do chart their own courses, and can engage with the curriculum at a deep personal level. For a full appreciation of this I have argued that we need to take a whole life perspective. Our data have suggested how the formulation of self in the early years may relate to later teaching and handling of a subject area, and the part played in the formulation of that self by such factors as home environment, parents, teachers, marriage and socio-economic and political factors. We need to give more consideration to this whole life perspective, within which individuals personally engage with the process of a subject area if we are to do the study of the curriculum — and the people involved in it — full justice.

Notes

1 For the most part, Tom worked in schools where teachers retained the same form for a whole year for most subjects, and often more than a year.

References

BECKER, H. (1960) 'Notes on the concept of commitment', *American Journal of Sociology*, 66, July.

BERGER, P.L. and LUCKMANN, T. (1971) *The Social Construction of Reality*, Harmondsworth, Penguin.

BERGER, P.L. *et al.*, (1973) *The Homeless Mind*, Harmondsworth, Penguin.

BERTAUX, D. (1981) *Biography and Society: The Life History Approach in the Social Sciences*, Beverly Hills, Calif., Sage.

BLUMER, H. (1966) 'Sociological implications of the thought of G.H. Mead', *American Journal of Sociology*, 71, March, pp. 535–44.

FARADAY, A. and PLUMMER, K. (1979) 'Doing life histories', *Sociological Review*, 27, 4, pp. 773–98.

GOLDTHORPE, J.H. and LLEWELLYN, C. (1977) 'Class mobility in modern Britain: Three theses examined', *Sociology*, 11, 2.

GOODSON, I.F. (1980) 'Life histories and the study of schooling', *Interchange*, 11, 4.

GOODSON, I.F. (1983) *School Subjects and Curriculum Change*, London, Croom Helm.

HALSEY, A.H. *et al.*, (1980) *Origins and Destinations: Family, Class, and Education in Modern Britain*, Oxford, Oxford University Press.

LACEY, C. (1977) *The Socialization of Teachers*, London, Methuen.

MEAD, G.H. (1934) *Mind, Self and Society*, Chicago, Ill., University of Chicago.

RISEBOROUGH, G.F. (1981) 'Teacher careers and comprehensive schooling', *Sociology*, 15, 3, pp. 352–81.

TURNER, R.H. (1962) 'Role-taking: Process versus conformity', in ROSE, A.M. (Ed.) *Human Behaviour and Social Processes*, London, Routledge and Kegan Paul.

TURNER, R.H. (1976) 'The real self: From institution to impulse', *American Journal of Sociology*, 81, 5.

WOODS, P. (1979) *The Divided School*, London, Routledge and Kegan Paul.

WOODS, P. (1981) 'Strategies, commitment and identity: Making and breaking the teacher role', in BARTON, L. and WALKER, S. (Eds) *Schools, Teachers and Teaching*, Lewes, Falmer Press.

Seals of Approval: An Analysis of English Examinations

Douglas Barnes and John Seed

The relationship between the process of learning in the classroom and public examinations at 16+ is both close and complex. Examinations reflect certain major priorities of state education yet appear to be in conflict with other values commonly espoused by teachers. At the same time, however, the examination system determines in very precise ways what goes on within the school and within each classroom — constraining the teacher and narrowing his options, looming as a dark threat to the pupil.[1] As the pamphlet by members of the London Association for the Teaching of English, *English Exams at 16*, has stressed: 'Any examination in English embodies a view of language, however ill-defined, and conveys a view, however inarticulate, of how competence in language can be developed.'[2] In preparing this article we have analyzed examination papers in English Language and English Literature in GCE O-level and CSE in order to get access to whatever 'views of language' these embody, including views about what constitutes an appropriate study of literature.[3] The point of looking into examination papers in search of a view or model of language is that a public examination is never merely a way of testing candidates, but is also a message about curriculum priorities. Examination papers, rather than syllabuses or examiners' reports, were chosen for analysis because they offer to teacher and taught the most persuasive arguments about what model of the subject is appropriate, what should go on in lessons, what knowledge, skills and activities should be emphasized and what can safely be ignored.

The LATE pamphlet, *English Exams at 16*, set out to discuss the principles which should inform the examining of English. We owe considerable debt to their excellent discussions; however, we begin at the other end with a close analysis of a large sample of the English examinations available in the summer of 1979, and attempt to clarify and elucidate the demands and expectations operating at that time.

Our original intention was to provide a detailed account of what was going on in English examinations so that judgements could be made about how they could be improved. To this end we tried to develop ways of elucidating and comparing certain characteristics across a bewilderingly complex range of papers. The apparatus of categories and tables that we have used in the analysis represents no more than one way of presenting for public scrutiny the data and criteria of our discussions: no doubt other methods would have been possible.

We have called this paper 'Seals of Approval' because of the power wielded by examinations in classifying and attributing status to young people. It is perhaps as a result of this power that examination boards are so sensitive to the public scrutiny of their papers. Some boards have responded to this analysis not by confronting the major issues that we have raised but by seeking possible errors in the tables, as if one error would delegitimize the whole project. We are confident, however, that whatever disagreements might emerge about the specific weighting of this or that element in a paper, the broad characteristics of English examinations are accurately represented in the following pages.

Table I indicates the range of examinations scrutinized. (See Appendix I for full details.) We acknowledge that as well as the forty-three papers analyzed there were others which we did not look at. Most of these were intended for special groups of candidates and did not attract large numbers; we have no reason to believe that their inclusion would have radically changed our conclusions.

Table 1.   Papers Chosen for Analysis

	O-Level	CSE	16+
English Language	11	7	3
English Literature	10	3	1
Joint Language and Literature	0	9	0

It is necessary to acknowledge an important omission which might considerably change the overall picture. All the papers considered here are Mode I, set by an examining board on the basis of a published syllabus. The CSE system allows also for Mode 2, papers set centrally on syllabuses provided locally, and Mode 3, examinations carried out by schools or groups of schools on the basis of their own syllabuses, Mode 3 being much the more significant in scale.[4] In some cases these CSE Mode 3 syllabuses extend still further those characteristics that tend to differentiate CSE from GCE, so that if it had been possible to include them it would have further dichotomized the two. Others are very like O-level papers; to analyze them would be very informative but beyond the range of this study.

Part 1 of this report deals with English Language papers, considering first composition tasks and then tests of comprehension, in each case taking O-level first and then CSE; part 2 deals with English Literature papers, again GCE first and then CSE, and also the literary element in some combined language and literature papers; part 3 offers some interpretations and comments.

I   English Language

The remarkable and sometimes bewildering diversity of English examining is the first point to make. Some generalizations can be made however. The O-level language papers tend to display a common balance of elements and the same shape: an essay/composition, a comprehension, a shorter exercise of some kind in functional/practical prose. Greater emphasis (in terms of total marks though not necessarily in the range of marks awarded) falls upon the former two types of writing, usually about 80 per cent. Summary as a separate exercise occurs in only three of the eleven papers analyzed.[5] A majority of boards have an additional exercise or two, generally consisting of a letter or report, in which the candidate is to carry out a precisely defined task of information, persuasion, etc., in which accuracy and succinctness are at a premium. AEB (I/025) is unique in preserving the old-fashioned tests of vocabulary, usage and grammatical competence. Table 2 provides a detailed breakdown of the balance of elements in different O-levels, using the proportion of marks awarded as an approximate indication of relative emphasis. (What in fact determines emphasis is the *range* of marks awarded to each question, and not the total, but this information is not available.)

The situation in CSE English Language exams is much more difficult to summarize succinctly. Because of the complex and variable balance of examination paper, folder of assessed coursework, and oral and other assessments the nature of the question paper will play a smaller part — in comparison with GCE — in the overall assessment. As Table 3 indicates, a formal examination paper can constitute as little as 35 per cent of the total assessment or as much as 80 per cent. Examinations that test what is called 'Unitary English' complicate the issue further by combining language and literature testing: the latter, for instance, frequently has a comprehension format though the questions require more interpretative comment than do the usual comprehension questions. Though CSE boards by stressing oral and course work have moved away from the traditional mode of examining still predominant in O-level within the actual examination itself the essay or composition, the comprehension and, less often, a letter, are as in GCE O-level the central forms of writing required from candidates and thus deserve detailed study. These tables of the elements in O-level and CSE Language papers are a fairly superficial index of what is actually involved for the candidate. This requires a more detailed analysis of the character of compositions and comprehension tests.

Compositions

We will begin with the kinds of writing called variously 'essays and compositions'. Analyzing these required a complex set of categories, since the starting point, the content and the mode of writing all needed to be taken into account.

Table 2. Proportions of Marks Allocated to Each Element in GCE English Language Papers

O-level examining board	Essay/composition	Comprehension	Summary/précis	Exercise in functional writing	
London	50	35	15	0	
Cambridge	50	50	0	0	
Southern Universities	45	35	20	0	
Welsh	40	50	0	10	
Oxford	35	50	0	15	
Oxford and Cambridge	25	75	0	0	+14% grammar and vocabulary
AEB (I/025)	35	20	16	15	
AEB (II/069)	50	50	0	0	
JMB (B)	50	26	0	24	
JMB (C)	33	35	0	32	
JMB (A)	35	50	0	15	
AEB/SEREB (16+)	40	20	0	0	+40% oral
ALSEB/JMB/YREB (16+)	40	40	0	0	+20% oral

Table 3. CSE English Language Examinations: Elements

	Exam as percentage of total assessment	CSE Board	Essay/ composition	Comprehen- sion	Other exercises	
CSE Language	50	TWYLREB	1 or 2	1	none	+25% oral assessment and 25% course work
	80 or 40	NWREB	2 (40%)	1 (40%)	none	+20% oral (folder optional in place of essays)
	35	EAST ANGLIA(S)	1	1	none	+25% oral + course work
	60	NRB	1	3	1 (letter)	not available
	70	EAST MIDLANDS	1	2	1 (letter)	oral 30%
	50	SWEB	1	1 (multiple choice)	2 (short essay and letter)	+25% oral +25% course work
	50	SREB (R)	1 (incl. letter)	1	1	+20% oral + 30% course work
	50	EAST ANGLIA (N)	1 or 2	1	1	+ literature paper
	70	ALSEB	3 (1 imaginative, 1 descriptive, 1 persuasive)	1	1	+ literature paper
Unitary English	50	YREB	2	1	none	+ literature paper
	80 or 40	WEST MIDLANDS	1	2	1	+ literature paper (or option of folder)
	65	MIDDLESEX	1	2	none	+35% oral and literature paper
	30	SEREB	2	1	none	+ optional literature paper + oral
	70	METROPOLITAN	1	1	none	+ literature paper
	40	WELSH	1	1	none	+ oral and aural + literature paper

Was the candidate provided merely with a title or a longer and more detailed set of instructions or was there a different kind of initiating device, such as a picture? What kind of experience was called upon? What mode of writing was involved — was it open to choice or was it predetermined? The following were the categories used:

(a) *Starting points:* This set of four categories deals with the nature and extent of the guidance given.

1 Title: Often a simple title is provided, such as 'Bargains' or 'Making Up'; sometimes a longer title but still without instructions or a model of any kind, such as 'Is competition in schools beneficial or harmful?'.

2 Instruction: This is where some explicit guidance is provided about content, style, form, etc. of the writing. For instance: 'We can learn a lot about people from the way they dress. Write about the suitability of various types of clothing for work and leisure, and explain why, in your opinion, so much importance is often attached to people's outward appearance.'

3 Verbal stimulus: Where a passage of prose, poetry or a newspaper extract, etc. is provided to hint at content and/or a mode for a piece of writing: for instance, eleven lines from an R.S. Thomas poem on a thunderstorm followed by an invitation to write a description of a summer storm.

4 Picture: A photograph or painting is provided and used to initiate a piece of writing.

(b) *Content:* These categories give a rough indication of the *theme* of the writing, what kind of experience it calls upon:

1 Public: An issue of public, usually social, significance — essays on pollution, stories on a public theme, descriptions of places, objects, etc.

2 Private: Where the writing calls upon private/personal experience: family life, subjective feelings, personal relationships.

3 Open: Where the writing can be manipulated to include various contents.

(c) *Mode of writing:* Here the concern is with genre, how the question has determined the form of the writing:

1 Open: Where a variety of modes are possible: for example, the simple title 'Making up' could be interpreted as justifying a story, a description, an autobiographical passage, or a piece of reflective writing.

2 Story: Where a fictional narrative is quite clearly indicated.

3 Autobiographical: Where personal reminiscence, memories, are called upon; a narrative of personal life.

4 Descriptive: Calls for detailed representation of an object, a place, an event.

5 Analytic: By which is meant a piece of reflective/discursive prose calling for evaluation and abstraction: for instance, 'What development, now in its infancy, seems to you to hold the greatest hope for mankind in the future? The development you choose may be in any field you like — for example, science, medicine, travel or social organization.'

In some cases, of course, no single category applied — though this was fairly infrequent. In such cases a question was split into two (half) categories. To give a couple of examples: A YREB question where the starting point is a cartoon, a drawing and a couple of extracts from newspapers: this is categorized as $\frac{1}{2}$ picture, $\frac{1}{2}$ verbal stimulus; another example involves the mode of writing: 'Write an account of any sponsored walk or swim, or similar event designed to raise money, in which you have been involved. Did you enjoy the activity and what problems, if any, did you encounter in seeking sponsorship and in collecting money after the event?' This involves both descriptive and some analytic writing.

Table 4 provides an example of the information gleaned from a CSE paper (East Anglia South, paper 1) in which the candidate had to do one essay or composition — from a range of eight possibilities — in one and a quarter hours. In this way a general profile of aspects of essays/compositions across a whole range of examinations was built up, so that certain regularities begin to show themselves. Sometimes candidates are presented with a range of possibilities with minimal indication of precisely what is wanted, and sometimes, conversely, with highly explicit instructions and precise guidance. This polarity of implicit/explicit or closed/open is important because it characterizes typical differences between O-level and CSE essay and composition questions. Provisionally we can make the following distinction between 'ideal types' of essay/composition questions:

O-level   Few explicit instructions; topics tending to be public or open, that is, concerned with topics distant from everyday life; open-ended as to mode, though often couched in a style that seems to imply impersonal discussion;

CSE   Detailed instructions and guidance; tending to private topics close to everyday life; mode of writing fairly precisely defined and delimited: instructions often addressed directly to the candidate as if spoken face to face.

When 'Mode of Writing' is considered in isolation, there is a considerable overlap between GCE and CSE papers in the proportion of writing tasks which leave the candidate free to choose. We examined thirteen GCE and 16+ and sixteen CSE papers: of these more than half — nine GCE and ten CSE — fall into a central band in which between 14 and 40 per cent of the titles leave the mode of writing 'open'. Sharp differences appear, however, when some of the remaining papers are compared: *all* of the Oxford and Cambridge GCE board's

Table 4. *Content Analysis of CSE Paper*

	Starting points:				Content:			Mode of writing:				
	Title	Instruction	Stimulus	Picture	Public	Private	Open	Open	Story	Autobiographical	Descriptive	Analytic
Eight Questions	0	6	1	1	6	0	2	2	0	1	2½	2½

titles are open, while *none* of the titles set by three CSE boards (YREB, ALSEB, NWREB) is open.

The analysis of 'Starting Points' showed more widespread differences of emphasis. The proportion of writing tasks in the form of a title alone without any instructions is higher in O-level: it averages 35.3 per cent of all O-level questions compared to 28.05 in CSE papers. The 'Oxford and Cambridge' O-level, for example, has 50 per cent of its questions as titles only and all its questions are *open* in respect to mode of writing. There are no general instructions and titles include such open possibilities as 'Bargains', 'You are never alone', 'Useless knowledge' and 'The synthetic creations of man's inventive mind'. Contrast this with, for instance, the ALSEB paper where the candidate has to do three pieces of writing, one from each of three sections: section A requires a 'vivid piece of writing'; section B demands 'you should write as clearly and methodically as possible'; section C states that the aim is 'to write persuasively . . . to persuade someone to your point of view'. In each case the required style is made explicit, and with it, of course, the criteria by which the writing will be assessed: in section B, for instance, key phrases include 'very carefully' (about a description), 'clear, factual report', 'Plan in some detail. . . .' There is nothing open-ended in this paper at all: the candidate is directed to do three different kinds of writing — a story or imaginative description, a clear factual report, a persuasive piece of public writing — and is provided with precise instructions and guidance. East Anglia (North) CSE, while it provides some choice from a broad range of modes of writing and subjects, similarly provides very detailed instructions and in no case is a title only provided. This is one of the more open-ended options: 'We can learn a lot about people from the way they dress. Write about the suitability of various types of clothing for work and leisure, and explain why, in your opinion, so much importance is often attached to people's outward appearance.' One question has nearly ninety words of detailed instruction, another nearly seventy and a third fifty.

We are not offering here a hard and fast categorization of the differences between O-level and CSE. The situation is more complex than that. (See Appendix 2 for a detailed breakdown of the different elements in the testing of writing in various English Language papers.) The SREB CSE, for instance, conforms to the O-level ideal type. There is a wide choice: one topic is to be chosen from twenty-one possibilities; seventeen are merely titles and thirteen are open as far as the mode of writing is involved. One of the questions says: 'Write, in any way you wish, about ONE of the following titles' and there follow eight words: Peace, Exhaustion, Hatred, Laughter, Hero-worship, Desolation, Memories, Meditation. Conversely, the London University O-level paper — though in one sense conforming to the O-level pattern in that four of the questions are titles only and nearly half of the ten questions are *open* in mode of writing — provides at the head of the paper a detailed set of instructions (over fifty words) which call for 'interest' and 'relevance', an appropriate form and style, technical accuracy and a minimum length of 450 words. In spite of such irregularities it is possible to represent O-level and CSE questions as tending towards two contrasting ideal types. If one considers discursive essays only it is possible to say that O-level questions present in brief outline a public situation, call for evaluation which is abstract, impersonal and intellectual; while CSE questions present in some detail a private situation, with instruction and guidance, demand personal opinion, 'viewpoints' and subjective experience, and are closed, determining content, occasion and even style of the essay. The CSE question is made 'relevant' to a picture of the teenager's world — in style of language (a personal tone, as if addressed to an acquaintance) and in content (concrete situations, with heavier presence of family, friendship, sport, and a contrasting lack of issues requiring theoretical discussion).

Consider the following pairs of questions where the same content has been moulded into contrasting examination forms:

> O-level Cambridge local: 'Do the British run themselves down too much? What things can we be proud of?'
> CSE East Anglia (N): 'An American pen-friend who has never visited England and who knows nothing about the country apart from what she has read in the press or seen on television, asks you what it is like to be a young man or young woman growing up here in 1979. Write the reply you would send.'
> O-level Cambridge local: 'What attracts people to clubs and societies? What is your own attitude to group activities?'
> CSE ALSEB: 'You have started a new club at your school. Write an article for the school magazine giving details of the activities of your club and trying to persuade other pupils to join.'

In such cases the contrast is palpable between: a brief, open-ended question versus more detailed instructions and a delimited form; intellectual, abstract debate versus a personal, persuasive, concrete account; a self-sufficient and autonomous discourse versus a social 'occasion'. It can probably be assumed that there will be a similar divergence between the criteria used in assessing such different tasks.

Ironically, the highly explicit tasks typical of CSE are probably set because the teachers who set them believe that less able pupils need writing that offers them the support of a ready-made structure, content that is near to their own first-hand experience, and an indication of the style expected. Whether or not the supporting structure helps or hinders, it is clear that attempting to specify first-hand experience risks setting up a stereotype of 'ordinary boys' and girls' lives and interests' which may in many cases be inappropriate. The close specification of an expected style may rest upon the belief that pupils who do not meet a wide range of reading matter outside school will need to be protected in the examination room from an inapposite choice of style, and indeed there is much to be said for making such criteria available to candidates. We have perhaps said enough to indicate that what results are two contrasting kinds of test, assessing different abilities, and containing implicit within them different models of young people and the writing abilities they will need. It must be admitted, however, that we have no access to the two sets of criteria used in assessment, so that we cannot be certain that they follow the differences we have described.

In many composition questions there are quite specific assumptions about the nature of normal social and cultural life: often questions call for candidates to project themselves into a social situation which may be alien to their experience. In some cases this is simply a matter of regional particularity, such as a question on 'country characters' (Cambridge local) or several questions on rural life (SWEB CSE). More often it is a matter of class culture. How far do exam questions in English project a stereotyped and inappropriate social ethos — a stable nuclear family (the 'Janet and John' syndrome) or the traditional grammar school culture — or subtly suggest a particular moralized version of social behaviour? Many questions — both O-level and CSE — assume the existence of a particular school culture of speech days and head boys, pupil clubs and societies, pen pals, school magazines. Candidates are asked to write articles for the school magazine, to write a speech introducing to the assembled school a famous former pupil, to debate the virtues of school societies, and so on. Consider, for instance, the hint in the words 'usefully spent' of an unstated set of preferences for ways of spending money: 'If a former pupil left your school a large sum of money, describe the various ways in which you think it could be usefully spent' (Welsh CSE). Essay questions about pupils' uses of leisure time — a common subject — frequently invoke the 'Protestant ethic' of useful and constructive hobbies which may be inappropriate to more casual and sociable ways in which many pupils pass their free time. Other questions call for the assumption of a public role outside the repertoire of many capable 16-year-olds — public speeches, letters to the press. The point here is to suggest that part of the essay content in current English exams may be failing to engage with the range of experience of a substantial section of the school population. When pupils are forced to project themselves into an alien situation the weakness of the resulting writing may not stem from a lack of communication ability but from a socially induced incomprehension of the appropriate codes. It is important that exam questions should avoid reduplicating either outdated or socially restrictive writing situations.

Of course, there are many essay questions which do not embrace only a narrow section of social and cultural life. One thinks of familiar essay themes such as pollution and the environment, war, sport and other important public matters. How far, though, are some of these same values and assumptions still operative? To be more specific, how far are particular social issues articulated in questions in such a way that their content is neutralized and depoliticized so that only a particular kind of response is legitimate? This is a difficult point; examination questions may simply confirm a boundary between legitimate and illegitimate response which is constructed over time in the classroom. At the same time a particular tone of balanced 'objectivity', a sense of rational choice between given alternatives — the procedure of BBC current affairs offers the liberal paradigm here — does seem to be present in the exam style. For instance, a question on the social position of women provides about seventy words of debate between two extreme positions on the relative superiority of male and female: the candidate is asked then to give his own views. Here he is 'placed' between two caricatured positions neither of which he could rationally hold and is thus forced to play the honest broker, the tolerant and balancing liberal. This tends to be the ascribed position for the candidate in many questions on contentious issues such as nuclear energy, pollution, feminism. One suspects that rationally defensible 'extreme' positions may be subtly delegitimized in the course of evaluation, though this would be difficult to prove. This is often underwritten by the cool tone of the questions, couched in grey discursive vocabulary, which is not the only valid 'colour' for serious discourse. While it is true that in the end it is the markers' values and preconceptions which determine what grade a particular essay will receive, it is the examination paper that will be referred to in future years, and will indicate to teacher and taught alike what kinds of writing are preferred. (Oblique evidence on these preconceptions is available in examiners' reports. Roger Knight's penetrating analysis of these in his article 'Examiners' English[6] shows that the criteria used in assessing O-level compositions are 'poorly articulated and sometimes very dubious'.)

This points us towards the other side of the coin — what is excluded. Certain contentious themes recur, as indicated, but others — which include important historical and social experiences and genuine cultural resources — are absent. There are no examples of questions on race and racial conflict, the realities of unemployment, poverty and wealth, areas of contested authority and other potent moments of everyday life. Similarly, there are no examples of the use of English in ways other than the dominant mode — standard English. Here the examination is doing little more than responding to the concerted erosion of regional dialects in the classroom and in the whole established culture: their demotion to the level of slang, their labelling as the argot of a low status social class. This has a particular urgency in the context of assessing Caribbean English.

Tests of Comprehension

In the case of comprehension tests — which continue to play an important part in determining what English competencies are tested in O-level and CSE — we consider two issues: the character of the passage which the candidate has to read and comprehend; and the nature of the questions that test that reading. These two, taken together, offer us a means of characterizing what constitutes 'comprehension' in each of the examination papers.

In considering comprehension questions, we introduce a different mode of analysis from those used with essays. How far are the examiners calling for the candidate to exemplify what has been called 'an active interrogation of the text'?[7] How far, on the other hand, is the current mode of assessing understanding based not so much on the active involvement of the reader in constructing meaning out of a test for himself as on a view of understanding as a decontextualized functional competence? These questions involve consideration not just of internal questions of format and style but also of broader matters of context.

In O-level Language papers there are usually two comprehension passages (in seven out of eleven cases) often divided into literary (fiction, less often *belles lettres*) and discursive. The literary type of passage tends towards 'high culture' — extracts from the fiction of E.M. Forster, Wilkie Collins, D.H. Lawrence, John Steinbeck, Ted Hughes, L.P. Hartley are examples, as well as two cases of poetry (Robert Frost, JMB(A); John Betjeman and Stephen Spender, Oxford and Cambridge). Non-fiction passages vary from a highly-wrought vestige of Victorian culture about the spirit of human endeavour in exploring miscellaneous Arabian deserts (AEB) to carefully reasoned arguments on ecology (Oxford local, Oxford and Cambridge). Other themes of non-fiction comprehension passages include: life in contemporary Moscow (JMB C), the character of industrial towns in the West Riding (JMB/West Midlands), biographical remarks on Marie Curie (AEB/SERB), the vicissitudes of life on a Burmese plantation (AEB 069), the world of Victorian railway navvies (AEB 025). The criteria for selection of many of these passages would seem to have little to do with the 'life-world' of the 16-year-old but rather to do with their intrinsic literary value or conceptual content.[8] CSE passages, on the other hand, tend to aim for some kind of familiarity or relevance. Prose extracts include Jack Common on youthful work experience in the earlier part of the century (NRB), passages on poverty and childhood in South Africa by Alan Paton (TWYLREB), on countryside by Ted Hughes, a cautionary moral tale (anonymous) on fire risks in the countryside (East Midlands), on television's effect on social life by Brian Aldiss. Of course, the distinction between O-level-type fiction and CSE-type fiction in Comprehension extracts is not clear-cut. The Metropolitan CSE board, for instance, has a passage from Ernest Hemingway and a poem by Andrew Young. Amongst the non-fiction passages in CSE the following themes occur: the habitat of badgers, polishing seaside pebbles, autobiographical account of mountaineering in the Himalayas, meeting the Queen, hurricanes in the US, skateboarding, television, elm trees, fishing, the representation of violence in the press, housing estates and spoliation of natural beauty. Again there is some overlap with O-level passages but in the range of CSE material there are indications that selection has been made with an eye on the world of the candidate, aiming for relevance through some image of adolescent interests (hobbies, television, the outdoor life). There is certainly little of the stylistic affectation of some of the O-level passages. Simplicity, clarity and pertinence seem to have been among the criteria for selection.

The social situation of the examination candidate is of crucial importance, since making sense of a passage requires some kind of orientation, some sense of purpose and situation. In some CSE papers there are welcome signs of an intention to construct a context for the passages, and for the questions which are to be answered. Thus the Welsh CSE presents a photograph, a government leaflet and some prose; the YREB paper presents newspaper extracts and an advertisement. East Anglia (N) not only gives newspaper extracts but also situates the whole comprehension: 'Imagine that you live in the village of Nordwich. You and some friends, having read the newspaper extracts, are exchanging ideas. Answer the following queries which your companions have raised. . . .' The tasks in such comprehension tests as these are contextualized in three ways: the material is drawn from recognizable sources and situations, in contrast with writings drawn from the *belles lettres* tradition; several pieces are often associated in the same task; and there is an attempt at setting the questions in a situation in which explanation and paraphrase would be reasonable.

It is when we turn from the content of the passages to the questions set that the artificiality of the typical comprehension test is most striking. In order to understand what skills of understanding are typically emphasized we placed all comprehension questions in one of seven categories, as follows:

1   *Select quotations:* the candidate is directed to the passage to select from it a quotation — a word, a phrase, a longer extract; for example: 'Find a word in the second paragraph which means the same as footprint.'
2   *Short paraphrase:* asks for simple rephrasing of a word or phrase (or any unit shorter than a sentence).
3   *Longer paraphrase:* this asks for the rephrasing of a sentence or longer extract.
4   *Short interpretation:* to expound the meaning and implications of a word or phrase in the light of the context it appears in.
5   *Longer interpretation:* to expound the meaning and implications of a sentence or longer passage in the light of the context it appears in.
6   *Imaginative reconstruction:* to rewrite in fictional form some part of the passage.
7   *Further development:* using the passage as a jumping-off point, to develop either a piece of discursive writing or imaginative/descriptive prose in another direction. The difference here between 6 and 7 is in the relationship to the passage: 6 is a transposition or reconstruction from within data already given in the passage, while 7 is a development into autonomous territory.

The boundary between paraphrasing (as in 1, 2, 3) and interpretation (as in 4 and 5) is perhaps worth clarifying. Paraphrase is a matter of simple rephrasing, of rewriting information already provided. Interpretation involves going beyond the literal meaning, and using the rest of the passage and possibly background knowledge to extrapolate implications and interrelationships. The following examples from the same CSE paper should make this difference clearer:

'Explain what Bill meant by: "his should have been the glory of a refusal".'

This is categorized as 'short interpret' because it concerns *part* of a sentence and requires an understanding of the whole passage and context and because it calls for interpretation of meaning which is implicit in a complex situation.

'Give two reasons why Bill was worried as soon as he saw the typewriter he had to use.'

This is an example of paraphrase (long). The meaning here is not implicit but is explicitly contained in two sentences and requires simple identification and rewriting: little or no contextualizing is involved.

Every question asked in the comprehension sections of the papers analyzed was assigned to one of these categories. We wished, however, to show for each comprehension test the relative emphasis on one kind of question or another, but faced the problem that there was no standard total of questions, nor were questions equivalent in scale. Nor did we have in all cases the number of marks assigned to each question. In order to make the results comparable we resorted to an admittedly subjective method: one of us distributed ten points amongst the question categories in such a way as to represent approximately the relative emphasis placed on each of them by that particular examination paper. Thus the Comprehension questions on one O-level paper were estimated as follows: select quotations 1/10; short paraphrase 1/10; long paraphrase 2/10; short interpret 1/10; long interpret 3/10; imaginative reconstruction 0/10; further development 2/10. In this way it became possible to compare one paper with another.

Table 5 distils the results of analysis of the nature of questioning in O-level

Table 5. Comprehension Questions in O-level

O-level board (including 16+)	Percentage of questions asking for paraphrase	Percentage of questions asking for interpretation of word or phrase	Percentage of questions calling for longer interpretation	Percentage of questions asking for imaginative/ development
AEB (025)	95	5	0	0
JMB (C)	90	10	0	0
OXFORD local	80	20	0	0
London (multiple choice)	65	30	5	0
AEB (069)	62	33	5	0
SUJB	60	25	15	0
AEB/SEREB (16+)	58	42	0	0
ALSEB/JMB/YREB (16+)	27	12	55	5
JMB/West Midlands (multiple choice)	48	32	20	0
Welsh	48	37	16	0
JMB (B)	40	10	50	0
Oxford and Cambridge	30	11	36	23
JMB (A)	20	20	30	30
Cambridge local	11	28	11	50

and reveals the stress on close attention to the passage, especially via paraphrase. In ten out of thirteen papers there were no questions at all which asked for 'imaginative reconstruction' or 'development'. In only two O-level papers did more than a third of the questions call for making sense of a sentence or longer part of the passage; four papers had no question of this kind at all. Here, it is clear, paraphrase and the understanding of single words or short phrases are predominant in all but four O-level comprehensions. A particular kind of competence is being tested which is very different from the broader capacity to construct meaning which the Bullock Report called for.

With CSE the situation is a good deal more complex. CSE exams use the comprehension format to initiate different kinds of writing such as short essays and imaginative reconstructions. More than half of CSE papers (eight out of fourteen) have a substantial element of this kind of writing. Perhaps equally important is that in many of them much greater weight is given to questions which demand interpretation of sentences or longer sections: in four papers this is the most substantial element in the whole range of questions. (It can be seen from Table 5 that the 16+ paper set by the ALSEB/JMB/YREB consortium conforms rather to the CSE than to the GCE pattern by placing the major emphasis upon questions requiring 'longer interpretation'.) However, as Table 6 shows, there are several CSE boards for whom comprehension is seen, in the same way as in O-level papers, as a test of competence to paraphrase sentences and passages and to understand particular words or phrases. In general,

Table 6. Comprehension Questions in CSE

CSE board	Percentage of questions asking for paraphrase	Percentage asking for interpretation of word or phrase	Percentage calling for longer interpretation	Percentage asking for imaginative/ development
Middlesex	100	0	0	0
West Midlands (English Studies)	80	0	0	20
NRB	75	25	0	0
West Midlands	70	15	15	0
SWEB	60	20	20	0
SREB	55	20	0	25
NWREB	50	15	15	20
East Midlands	45	55	0	0
SEREB	30	50	20	0
Metropolitan	25	20	40	15
Welsh	25	0	0	75
TWYLREB	20	40	40	0
East Anglia (N)	20	20	10	50
East Anglia (S)	20	20	35	25
ALSEB*	12	8	72	8
YREB*	0	0	65	35

* In these papers the comprehension format is being used as part of the Literature component of Unitary English. East Anglia (N) has both a Language and a Literature Comprehension: the former only is under scrutiny in this table.

however, CSE comprehension is a more flexible, multi-purpose activity — with a broader range of questions, some attempts to give passages which relate to recognizable contexts in the world inhabited by most young people, and questions which place more emphasis upon inference, and the ability to use larger verbal contexts as aids to understanding, and to cope with larger-scale and more implicit aspects of meaning.

II   English Literature

We now turn to English Literature examinations in order to determine whether they display patterns similar to those in English Language papers. The character of the books to be read is obviously of central importance in the experience of studying literature. Here the individual English department and teacher have some limited autonomy in selecting from an examining board's syllabus, just as the individual pupil has some choice in what he selects from his course of study for revision and from the actual questions on the examination paper. We begin with English Literature in O-level.

Choice is usually restricted in precise ways. For instance, the University of London examination (Syllabus A) requires four questions to be attempted: one compulsory essay on Shakespeare; one compulsory essay on poetry (either Keats, a general anthology or a selection of modern English poets) one compulsory essay on fiction (Harper Lee's *To Kill a Mockingbird*, or Hardy's *Far from the Madding Crowd*, or an anthology of modern short stories); plus an additional question chosen from any of the three sections, so that the candidate attempts questions on various genres. In some cases, however, candidates have some leeway and are able to avoid answering a question on, for example, Shakespeare or poetry.

Shakespeare still figures prominently: five of the papers include a compulsory Shakespeare question, and in Cambridge local and SUJB candidates are required to attempt both a context and an essay on Shakespeare, two questions out of five. Oxford local (02) includes two compulsory Shakespeare questions out of six required of the candidate. In Oxford local (Gen) and London (A) one Shakespeare question out of four is required. In other papers Shakespeare figures as an option. (AEB is unique in having no Shakespeare question whatsoever; the 1980 syllabus states: 'The emphasis of the paper is on twentieth century literature but the syllabus is not limited to this period.') Other former rivals in the English literary pantheon — Milton, Wordsworth, Tennyson — have faded almost without trace; Shakespeare remains towering over the landscape of 'real' Literature presented to the 16-year-old initiate.

Most papers contain a substantial section of poetry questions, and in four cases this includes more questions than any other section. In three papers the candidate is required to answer a poetry question. The older tendency to insist on the study of a classical text such as *Paradise Lost* or *The Prelude* has gone. Many of the papers do have a remaining classical author but anthologies now bulk very large (thirteen titles out of nineteen). All this obviously permits a good deal of selection on the part of both teacher and pupil. However, further detailed analysis of what is included and excluded from these anthologies — the principles of their selection — would provide more exact data on the range of poetry which examinations recognize. The poetry prescribed in 1979 is listed in Table 7. We can ask, for example, whether there is concentration on particular periods, or upon groups or poets who share a style or a view of the world. Certainly there has been a shift during the last thirty years away from an insistence on the poetry of earlier periods, including at times considerable emphasis on the Victorians. If they so wish, teachers can choose to confine their attention entirely to poetry written in the latter half of our own century and in the papers we have analyzed this means the poets of the fifties, especially Hughes, Larkin, Betjeman, Causley and R.S. Thomas.

Table 7. Poetry Set Books in O-Level Literature

Board	
Oxford local (02)	Chaucer/Tennyson/Hardy/Modern Anthology
Oxford local (GEN)	Poetry and Ballad Anthologies: including 'Palgrave' and 'Oxford'
London (A)	Selected Keats/Anthology/Selected modern poets including Hughes, Causley, R.S. Thomas
SUJB	Anthology
AEB (027)	Three Anthologies
AEB (028)	No prescribed poetry texts
JMB (A)	Selected Keats/General Anthology/Selected modern poets including Hughes, R.S. Thomas, Larkin
Cambridge local (200/1)	Chaucer/Anthology
Cambridge (Plain Texts)	Unspecified
Oxford and Cambridge	Chaucer; Anthology of narrative poems
Welsh	Choice from three anthologies

Do these poets have enough in common to constitute a cultural prescription or limitation on the range of literary experience offered to pupils? With the possible exception of Hughes, they all seem to participate in a slightly prosaic acceptance of the cultural and social *status quo*, though in other respects they differ widely. Certainly there is no disturbing or radical questioning to be found amongst them. Nor is English verse from the United States, or from Australia, or from African countries chosen. And the poetry of the earlier part of the century now appears but seldom. Clearly this *is* a restricted range of verse though the work of earlier poets is available as alternatives. The restriction we refer to is perhaps analogous to the stereotypes we have described as shaping the choice of essay topics in the English Language papers. How the restriction should be interpreted we shall consider later.

In prose fiction there is a relative pancity of nineteenth century fiction in O-level Literature syllabuses. In only three papers does it have a substantial presence and in three other papers it is the smallest category (see Table 8). Dickens and Hardy share first place in appearances — five each — and have no challengers. There are notable absences from the early twentieth century, George Orwell, for example. In the case of modern prose there is a surprisingly limited range of options. Two examinations — Oxford local (Gen) and Cambridge local — both of which stress nineteenth and early twentieth century fiction, have no modern fiction at all. The two AEB papers place a good deal of emphasis on non-fiction with autobiographies by Siegfried Sassoon and Richard Church, Priestley's *English Journey* and Durrell's reminiscences. But in the other seven exams the same texts recur: Harper Lee's *To Kill a Mockingbird* (three papers), Golding's *Lord of the Flies* (five papers), L.P. Hartley's *The Go-Between* (four papers) and Laurie Lee's *Cider with Rosie* (three papers). This is a remarkable concentration of texts. Whether they are so well represented because they are regarded by examiners and teachers as the best recent fiction in the English language or because they are eminently 'examinable', or for some other reason, cannot be settled on the evidence we have available.

Table 8.   Prose Set Books in O-Level Literature

Board	Nineteenth century	Early twentieth century	Mid twentieth century
London (A)	Hardy	Twentieth Century Short Stories	Harper Lee
JMB	Jane Austen	—	Harper Lee, William Golding
SUJB	—	—	William Golding, L.P. Hartley, Laurie Lee
Oxford local (02)	Dickens, Eliot George	—	Laurie Lee
Oxford local (GEN)	Dickens, Brontë, Hardy	—	—
Cambridge local (200/1)	Thompson, Eliot George	E.M. Forster, Joseph Conrad	—
Cambridge local (Plain Texts)	Dickens, Hardy	—	Harper Lee, William Golding, L.P. Hartley
AEB (027)	Dickens, Twain Mark	Bennett, J.B. Priestley, Sassoon (memoirs)	Gerald Durrell, J.G. Farrell, Short Stories
AEB (028)	Hardy	E.M. Forster	G. Greene, G. Durrell, Richard Church
Oxford and Cambridge	Dickens	Lawrence	Sillitoe
Welsh (0a)	Austen Hardy	Aspects of the Short Story	William Golding, L.P. Hartley, Laurie Lee

Finally, modern drama is in all but two O-level papers (AEB 028 and Welsh)[9] among the two weakest categories. There is none at all on London University's examination paper. Here again there is a good deal of unanimity about which are the central texts and authors: Shaw appears on five papers; Bolt's *A Man for All Seasons* on three papers; Miller's *The Crucible* on three papers, and Dylan Thomas' *Under Milk Wood* on two. Other modern plays such as Shaffer's *Royal Hunt of the Sun*, O'Casey's *Juno and the Paycock* and Miller's *All My Sons*, appear once each. There is almost nothing written within the last twenty years and nothing which breaks with the conventions of theatrical realism, except *Under Milk Wood*. We now turn to the questions asked about these books.

The categories which we used to analyze the different types of questions in O-level literature exams were as follows:

1 *Selective narration:* this asks for unreflective paraphrase, simply retelling some part of the story. A question on E.M. Forster's *Where Angels Fear to Tread* provides an example: 'Describe Caroline's visit to Gino and the baby, explaining what happens to make her change her mind about the idea of bringing the baby back to England.'

2 *Imaginative reconstruction:* this involves rewriting a scene from a play from the point of view of one of the characters.

3 *Close textual:* directs towards close scrutiny of the text and asks for analysis of specific words, phrases, lines in stylistic terms. (This kind of question matches the concern for the texture of language, the 'words on the page', characteristic of F.R. Leavis and the Cambridge school of criticism.)

4 *Thematic reading:* involves extracting from within the text and eluci-dating a particular theme or idea. Here is a succinct example: 'How important is the idea of magic in *The Go-Between?*'

5 *Character:* the description or interpretation of a character in a play or story.

6 *Moral evaluation:* this involves evaluation — not, as in 3 and 4 above, from within a particular repertoire of specialized skills (literary critic-ism) — but from a moral or more broadly ideological standpoint: it directs the candidate to relate literary work to a particular cultural model of the world or to a particular implicit rationality. An example is: '"Schooldays should be happy days." Discuss Lee's village school, in the light of this comment.'

7 *Stagecraft/Transposition:* this involves considering the technical form of a particular literary work and being able to transpose it into a different one. A rare example: 'What advantages might a film version of *A Midsummer Night's Dream* have over a stage production?'

This is not a typology of the full range of different kinds of examination questions: rather these categories attempt to isolate specific kinds of intellec-tual practices which the answering of questions involve. Any particular question (as in the examples given for 1, 4, 6 and 7 above) may fall squarely into a single category. But sometimes different kinds of practices are involved in a single question. Consider, for instance, the following question: 'Give an account of the scene in which Antony addresses the crowd in the market place, from the beginning of his speech up to the point where the crowd leave. What methods does Antony use to gain the support of the crowd and what do we learn of his character in this science?' This calls for both 'selective narration' and 'character analysis'. In such cases — and they are frequent — the question is categorized under two separate headings ($\frac{1}{2}/\frac{1}{2}$), though this is unlikely to represent the emphasis placed on the two elements by markers, who usually expect more narrative than comment.

For example, one O-level literature paper contained twenty-seven questions distributed thus: Selective narration 9, Imaginative reconstruction 0, Close textual 1, Thematic reading 6, Character 11, Moral evaluation 0, and Stagecraft 0. Forty per cent of the questions on the paper involve character analysis, a third of them involve selective narration, and so on. A general picture emerges of what practices are predominant in literature papers and what are peripheral.

In the majority of examinations the essay is the only form of answer expected in response to questions about literature, but there are a few other formats. Two papers (SUJB and Cambridge local) contain a compulsory context question on Shakespeare in which the candidate answers a number of shorter questions about a passage chosen from the set play and printed on the examination paper. In another paper (Oxford local O2) this format is used for three out of the six questions. In these cases we have used the seven categories to analyze them, as if they were essay questions. Table 9 shows how all of the questions were distributed across the categories.

The first point which emerges from Table 9 is the marked predominance of two categories: 'Thematic reading' and 'Character analysis'. Across the ten papers these two categories involve just under 70 per cent of the emphasis: indeed, on one paper (Oxford local (Gen)) these constitute the only types of writing about literature made available to the candidate. Despite fluctuation there is unanimity here across all the boards. If we add a third category, 'Selective narration', which though absent on two papers is strongly represented on others, then we find 85 per cent of all questions on examination papers are covered.

The central stress in the O-level testing of reading, then, falls on a relatively restricted range of skills — the ability to remember, select appropriately and paraphrase parts of a text, the ability to select appropriate incidents from a story or play and to utilize them to attribute stylized motives or personality characteristics to a fictional person, and the ability to relate a simple theme given in the question to statements and incidents in the texts. How far is the aim of this kind of questioning simply to reassure the sceptical examiner that the candidate has actually read the set texts — and with enough attention to be able to retrieve the basic plot and characters? This possibility is

Table 9. Nature of Writing in O-Level Literature (estimated in percentages)

O-level board	Selective narration	Imaginative reconstruction	Close textual	Thematic reading	Character	Moral evluation	Stagecraft/Transposition	Total
SUJB	10	0	6	32	36	4	12	100
JMB	0	0	12½	38	38	12½	0	101
Oxford local (02)	25	0	16	35	25	0	0	101
Oxford local (GEN)	0	0	0	50	50	0	0	100
Cambridge local (200/1)	33	0	4	22	40	0	0	99
Cambridge local (Texts)	6	6	6	30	36	16	0	100
London B	21	0	2½	58	13	0	5	99.5
London A	29	0	9	36	23	2	0	99
AEB (028)	21	0	5	40	31	3	0	100
AEB (027)	18	0	7	25	39	10	0	99
Oxford and Cambridge	11	8	7½	38	27	4½	4	100
Welsh (0a)	22	4	11	23	21	13	5	99
Average	16.3	1.5	7.2	35.6	31.6	5.4	2.2	

underlined by key instructional terms in many papers: 'Show . . .', 'Describe . . .', 'Give an account of. . . .' For instance, in the JMB (Syllabus A) paper, which is dominated by thematic and character questions, the instruction 'Give an account of' occurs ten times in sixteen questions and a subsidiary phrase — 'pointing out' — also occurs ten times: so that the typical question format consists of 'Give an account of, . . . pointing out. . . .' Again and again evidence for acquaintance with the text is demanded rather than serious discussion about what the work actually means to the candidate. Moreover, the candidates have to learn to operate a convention that places limits upon what is to be considered to be a facet of 'character' or an exemplification of a 'theme', though it would not be easy to define those limits.

This last point is reinforced if we look at those categories which are markedly underrepresented. 'Imaginative reconstruction' and 'Stagecraft' are absent from nine out of twelve and eight out of twelve papers respectively, and where they do appear they are amongst the smallest categories, that is, those given least emphasis in that paper. The intelligent candidate who is actively involved in literature — as a keen reader of fiction, as an actor in school or local drama group, even as someone who wants to be a writer — has no means of deploying his concern. More importantly, one type of knowledge about literature is being disqualified here. The development in fictional form of a given character, the transposition of a play into a story, the rewriting of a novel's ending — these can be a medium for valuable and legitimate forms of knowledge about literature. Similarly the 'practical' knowledge of theatre is a valid means of approaching a dramatic text. However, only four papers (SUJB, London B, Oxford and Cambridge, Welsh) offer any opportunity for this kind of writing about drama.

The situation in CSE literature is more complex and open-ended. The different combinations of course-work and examination, the development of 'Unitary English' in which language and literature are examined together, the much greater autonomy of the individual English department and teacher — all these make any kind of overall picture difficult to clarify. We cannot specify which texts are actually being read because of the long lists of options offered to teachers: the best we can do is to show the overall pattern. The NWREB, for instance, specify as set texts a list of twenty-seven prose works, ranging across nineteenth century novels (five, including Austen, Dickens, Brontë), five early twentieth century novels (by Lawrence, Huxley, Orwell twice, Wells) and a large range of post-war English fiction — as well as twenty-two dramatic works including plays by Sophocles, Shakespeare, Goldsmith, G.B. Shaw (four titles) and familiar modern plays by Arthur Miller, Rattigan, Wesker and Dylan Thomas. ALSEB offer a choice of three specific options: the first (1895–1939) includes H.G. Wells, Arnold Bennett and John Steinbeck fiction, poetry by D.H. Lawrence, Hardy, Frost and De La Mare and drama by O'Casey, Shaw and Wilder; the second (1945–present) includes a similar range of fiction, poetry and drama including Harper Lee's *To Kill a Mockingbird*, Stan Barstow stories, poetry anthologies, drama by Delaney, Bolt's *A Man for All Seasons* and Arthur Miller; a third general option is more wide-ranging, stretching from science fiction stories to a Dickens novel, and from Shakespeare to Terson's *Zigger Zagger*.

In CSE literature questions, modern fiction and drama play a far larger part than in GCE. Shakespeare's plays and nineteenth century fiction do appear on CSE lists but this does not imply that they are frequently chosen: the contents of the lists do not necessarily reflect the distribution across the 16+ population of either literature studied in the classroom or the individual's choices within the examination itself. There is some possibility that this wide range of options disguises the predominance of a few texts, perhaps *A Taste of Honey*, *A Kestrel for a Knave (Kes)* and *Billy Liar*, in the choices actually made by teachers.

This wide range of texts poses a particular problem to the examiner who sets the questions. Each task must be framed so that it can be carried out in terms of numbers of different texts, yet not to be so vague and unspecific as to favour prepared answers. This dilemma undoubtedly plays a major part in determining the kinds of questions set in CSE papers, yet it is also possible to detect within the questions a model of literary study which is appreciably different from that implicit in O-level literature papers. It is necessary in discussing the examining of literature in CSE to make a distinction between (1) boards setting an independent paper in English Literature, and (2) boards setting a 'Unitary English' paper of which literature is only part. (In the latter cases the literary element often appears in a 'comprehension' format, with the questions based upon passages printed on the paper.)

Only three of the eight papers we have inspected fall into the former category; the nature of the questions set is displayed in Table 10, using the same categories that were used in analyzing the O-level questions.

Table 10.   Nature of Writing in CSE Literature Questions

Board	Selective narration	Imaginative reconstruction	Close textual	Thematic reading	Character	Moral evaluation	Stagecraft
NWRB	21	27	0	12½	33	6	0
NRB	50	0	2	6	25	16	0
ALSEB	7	0	8	45	30	8	0

We comment on each of these three papers in turn:

NWRB: Half the questions involve some 'Imaginative reconstruction' fused usually with a non-reflective category, for example: 'Imagine yourself to be a character from one of the books you have read who is involved in an incident in the future. Describe the incident and your feelings and reactions to it.' Other questions use personal response/private opinion as the mechanism for writing, for instance: 'Write about ONE character, from a book you have studied, whose experiences you would like to have shared, making clear why you would have enjoyed this.' This paper combines a stress on backing up any statement with reference to the text and a strong presence of selective narration and character analysis with, on the other hand, the use of either fictional format or personal response/private opinion.

ALSEB: The model of literary activity in this CSE paper is close to the predominant pattern in GCE papers (see Table 9): there is no use of 'Imaginative reconstruction' and minimal 'Selective narration' (indeed less than in a number of O-level examinations). But another characteristic sharply differentiates it from them: nearly half of all the questions are broken down into different elements. Hence the difficulty of a structured interpretative essay is eased by demanding instead shorter answers. For instance, the following question on Bolt's *A Man for All Seasons:*

12 a) What important matter is discussed in More's meeting with Wolsey?
    b) What are the essential differences between Cromwell and More?
    c) How relevant to modern life do you think to be More's sense of right and wrong?

This guidance seems analogous to the support given to candidates in essays set in CSE English Language papers: the candidate's sense of relevance is less searchingly tested, since he or she is given general guidance about what should be included.

NRB: In this paper there is no 'Imaginative reconstruction' and no breaking down the question into shorter answers. Instead there is a massive investment in 'Selective narration'. Only six out of twenty-five questions do *not* involve some element of retelling events. In addition, as with other CSE papers, personal opinion carries the weight of interpretation and reflection, for instance: 'Basing your answer on two different stories, write about the character of one person you admire and of one person you do not admire'. In some of the questions literary criticism is transmuted into moralizing — note the relatively high incidence of 'moral evaluation' (16 per cent) — but reinforced, of course, with evidence that the candidate 'knows' the books.

English Literature as a separate examination subject, though more common than it was in the sixties, is still less frequent in CSE than Unitary English where both language and literature are tested together. In some examinations the English Literature component takes the form of interpretative essays on set-books but in others it has a comprehension format. The Metropolitan CSE, for instance, has its examination divided into a Language paper (Comprehension and Composition/Essay) and a Literature paper. The latter requires the candidate to do four different questions (as well as an 'unseen') — but while there are a couple of Shakespeare questions (6 per cent of total), two poetry questions and four questions on nineteenth century fiction, the vast bulk of questions are on post-war fiction and drama and the candidate can complete the paper solely on the basis of modern fiction and drama. The nature of the questions is in line with what was found in CSE literature examinations and in the whole CSE examination paradigm: questions were very detailed; there was a high incidence of questions broken down into several shorter parts; selective narration (33 per cent) and character analysis (30 per cent) predominated: questions were couched in personal idiom, and opinion and moralizing replaced the impersonal/interpretative dimension of O-level. (It should be noted that 'moral evaluation' constitutes nearly one-quarter of the whole paper.) This is representative of other Unitary English examinations which have a literature paper of essays: it is possible to complete the paper largely on the basis of modern fiction and drama; selective narration predominates (Middlesex 40 per cent, West Midlands 50 per cent, West Midlands English Studies 33 per cent); the tone of the questions is personal, and moralizing is invited.

Other Unitary English examinations have the literature component in a form similar to that of a comprehension test in a language paper: a series of questions is to be answered on the basis of a passage usually drawn from one of the listed set books, either from a novel or a play, or a poem drawn from a book of verse. The ALSEB paper, for instance, has three passages with questions — one prose (Bill Naughton), one poem and one drama (Shaw). Though the format is a 'comprehension', with four or five questions on each passage, the questions mostly involve interpretation and the final question in each case (with largest allocation of marks) demands fairly sophisticated interpretative skills; for instance: 'From the poem, choose two images (word pictures) which you find particularly interesting. Explain what the poet is trying to show in these images, and show how well she does so.'

East Anglia (North) similarly uses the comprehension format and has separate parts on prose, poetry and drama (again all modern). In each case the series of short questions on the passage (mostly interpretative) is followed by a longer question which is in fact a short literary essay, for instance, following up a passage of social realist fiction from the 1930s on the brutalizing effects of poverty: 'People's lives and actions (especially the ways in which they treat others) are often dictated by the times and/or circumstances in which they live. By referring to two other books/plays/poems show you have found this to be true in your own reading.'

YREB conforms to precisely the same pattern of passages and questions. Here, however, the final and most substantial question on each passage is not an interpretative literary essay but is wholly concerned with developing in either imaginative or autobiographical form an aspect of the original passage; for instance, this on *Walkabout*: 'Imagine yourself to be the Aboriginal. Describe the white children as they appear to you, and your feelings about them.'

Thus Unitary English uses some of the strategies of CSE literature to make the questions more appropriate to candidates of a wider ability range: breaking away from the impersonal critical essay, dissolving it into shorter parts, giving instructions that reduce the emphasis on the candidate's ability to apply literary critical criteria of relevance, or calling for imaginative/personal writing that enables candidates to relate what they have read to their own experience and view of the world, thus shifting the criteria of relevance into their hands. This summary account perhaps attributes rather too much consistency to the eight papers we have examined. There is undoubtedly a sharp dichotomy between those papers which place great emphasis on selective narration and those which use the comprehension test format. The former can be said to soften the cognitive demands of the test by aiming for the simplest level of response, mere reproduction; the latter eschew such a test of memory, and place their emphasis upon various kinds of interpretation. It is difficult to account for such a divergency.

III Commentary

In commenting on what has been described in the previous two sections we will discuss the limitations of the traditional examination as a context for the testing of English, consider what implicit models can be abstracted from the papers we have analyzed, and commit ourselves to some value judgements.

Since communication in its very nature concerns interplay between people, to test English — whether language or literature — by isolating the candidate in an examination room is paradoxical. Denied reference to texts or to other sources, denied the opportunity to think, plan, draft and redraft, or to try out ideas in discussion with others, the candidate is in a position unlike most of the occasions when adults — even academics — write in the course of their lives, and indeed unlike the conditions set up by many English teachers in their lessons. As we have shown, most of the tasks candidates are given are equally unlike those of real life: when adults write they do so for a purpose and in a context that defines what is important, what should be included and excluded, what form and tone is appropriate, what account should be taken of possible readers, and so on. Similarly with reading: apart from reading for pleasure, we read because what we read relates to some context in our lives which defines what matters, what should be remembered, how new ideas and information are likely to be used in the future, a context, that is, which orients our sense of relevance. It is very difficult for the examiner to supply such purposes and relevancies; examination tasks, since they must be seen to be unbiased, are thought to be of necessity decontextualized. If a context is provided it can be no more than a ghostly simulation: to tell a writer that he is writing a letter to a friend is unpersuasive when he knows that he is writing an answer for an examiner. Nevertheless, we welcome those attempts to simulate a context that we have already referred to.

The assessment of coursework provides one way of dealing with the problem of context. We indicated in Table 3 what proportion of the marks awarded in the CSE examinations is drawn from performances in a traditional test, as against school assessments of coursework and oral abilities. The availability of coursework goes some way towards alleviating the artificiality of traditional examinations, though it does not tell us what use teachers make of these opportunities for more naturalistic settings for work in English.[10] With the notable exception of NUJMB's O-level Syllabus D, which is based entirely on school assessments, these opportunities have been more readily available in CSE examinations, where they have drawn the fire of those who equate decontextualized testing with objectivity.

It will be clear to readers who have persevered thus far that our analysis has hinted at two 'ideal types' of English embodied to a greater or lesser degree in the papers we have analyzed. We cannot report a neat GCE/CSE division, for the pattern is far more complex. Nevertheless, by a summary act of abstraction we can describe two models of English which can claim to represent tendencies. We call the two models Public and Private, in order to make it quite clear that many O-level papers do not conform to the former model, and that many CSE papers diverge from the latter. If what follows appears to oversimplify, the reader can turn back to the appropriate part of our analysis to correct any misrepresentation.

Though we call the models Public and Private, both are public in the sense that a candidate must display competence publicly in ways and according to criteria not chosen by him or her. The Public model, however, detaches English from everyday life. Topics for writing often require the ability to stand back from social issues and coolly put arguments from various viewpoints. The test looks for the ability to sustain a public mode of writing, in which the writer holds a topic at arm's length and examines it without personal commitment. Though the *belles lettres* tradition still survives in some of the passages chosen for comprehension, the expected style of composition seems to correspond more to certain kinds of middlebrow journalism. In both general and literary essays, the choice of content, format and style is largely left to the candidate, though this is not to imply that he is free since one senses in the impersonal style of the rubric a whole world of assumptions and values. In this Public model, what is being tested includes whether the candidate has internalized these assumptions and values enough to be able to judge what topics and perspectives will be preferred, and what kinds of writing count as at once well-balanced, rational and inventive. In strange contrast to this apparent openness, comprehension questions tend to stay close to the surface meaning of texts, even when they are not very literal ones; it is as if credit will be given only for publicly produceable meanings, and not for those more oblique implications which are open to debate and uncertainty. The passages set for comprehension tests are predominantly literary; when they are not fictional they tend to be contemplative writing at a remove from the everyday. Similarly the essays required in literature examinations of the Public model stress stylized literary critical tasks concerned with 'characters' and 'themes'. What is required is a special kind of public performance within traditional modes: the candidate's own world, whether of everyday life or fantasy, is implicitly held at a distance. Even the non-fiction works prescribed for literature examinations are distant from most people's lives. The Public model tests a version of English that extracts the learner from the purposes and particularities of daily experiences, and isolates him in a special context where he needs to show that he has available to him the styles, preferences and rationalities appropriate to a small number of stylized modes of language use. Such examinations are decontextualized not only in the sense discussed at the beginning of this section — the isolation of the candidate from stated purposes and relevances — but also in the sense that they separate the abilities and preferences tested from any context likely to be familiar to 16-year-olds. (It should perhaps be added that this is not necessarily a criticism, since it could be argued that education *should* lift students out of the commonplace.)

The examiners whose papers exemplify the Private model, on the other hand, might almost have had the above description of the Public model available to react against. It is as if they had said: 'Not all pupils have equal access to these public modes, or to the implicit values that underlie acceptable choices of content or style, so we will choose writing and reading tasks which since they are close to everyone's daily concerns will give an equal opportunity to all to show their language abilities.' But in order to avoid the implicit values concealed in open tasks, the Private model examiners committed themselves to the task of specifying areas of experience and modes of representing them which would be relevant to every pupil. Thus the books and extracts that they choose and the writing and reading tasks they set exemplify a stereotype, a lowest common denominator of urban life that in its way is as stylized as the Public stereotypes. This is a world of domestic experience, the world of the family, the peer group, the club, at worst a kind of parody of urban working-class life. This world dominates the choice of reading with the ubiquitous 'kitchen sink' novels and plays, and equally dominates the topics and tasks set in composition tests. The expectations are predominantly private and personal: tasks in language and literature papers alike are designed to tap first-hand experience. If public issues, local or national, appear, they are personalized so that they are reflected primarily in their impact on the individual. In literature, the Private model, by asking for interpretation rather than paraphrase, and sometimes through tasks of imaginative reconstruction, rewards the candidate who is able to commit himself at some depth to the works read in a way quite different from literary criticism. Tasks are spelt out in a friendly face-to-face tone which reinforces the emphasis on the first-hand, the anecdotal, the domestic: experience, including literary experience, is represented as individual and private. Alongside this privatization is a second characteristic. The examiners in the Private model try to make fully explicit what kinds of writing are expected, and what criteria will be used in evaluating them, with the probable intention of giving all candidates equal access to them. Essay tasks define content, sequence, purpose, audience and style: the task is contextualized, but at the expense of denying the candidate any room for manoeuvre. It is as if the examiners could not trust candidates to order their thoughts in an acceptable way, and the result is that the stereotype cannot be escaped. The Private model, by making expectations and criteria explicit, treats the candidate as the prisoner of a set of social conventions, and indeed prescribes what those conventions shall be, the stylized picture of urban life that has already been referred to.

Although the Public model appears to throw responsibility on the candidates, in effect it tests whether they have internalized certain practices and values. The subject matter and tasks tend to be decontextualized, testing stylized abilities distant from naturalistic contexts and concerns. The Private model seeks to escape this by providing context and making criteria explicit, though this too imprisons candidates in a set of cultural conventions which purport to be realistic but may be quite unlike any individual's experience. The Private model is from one point of view no more than an alternative Public model, excluding whole areas of a learner's concerns as effectively by its explicit requirements as the Public model does by implicit means.

In describing these two idealized models we have endeavoured to step temporarily outside our own values in suggesting the concerns that inform each of them, and in hinting at their implications for candidates and for the teaching of English. We do not intend to make a crude choice between the Public and the Private models: in any case these are abstractions which do no more than suggest tendencies present in the examinations we have considered. These two tendencies imply different views of the world. The candidates must master the expectations implicit in the examination they are to sit: the topics to choose, the roles and tones to be adopted in writing about them, the books to read and how to write about them. All this amounts not merely to skills to be mastered but social values and ways of understanding the world. Yet pupils participate outside school in a bewildering variety of cultural experiences. Education, we believe, should respond to the social, cultural and ethnic diversity of the school population. English is in a particularly sensitive position. Its stress on personal, affective, experiential kinds of knowledge as opposed to formalized 'school knowledge' places it at the boundaries of school and out-of-school life, public and private experience. Quite divergent languages are thus brought into play, some of which may seem marginal, eccentric, illegitimate to the bearers of the dominant culture. This is crucial when it comes to evaluation of any writing which embodies contents which to the marker/examiner may seem alien or hostile. The pertinent question as far as examination papers are concerned is how far their questions veto certain kinds of experience and language and thus make certain cultural traits a disqualification. The restrictive and artificial situation in which writing occurs in an English examination already fits with certain individualistic, competitive dispositions and opposes other more cooperative traits. The two stereotypes we have described are far from sensitive to this diversity: we can only hope that in constructing them we have underestimated the cultural possibilities present in existing examinations. Are there topics and emphases that never appear in the written tasks? Is the range of literature unnecessarily restricted? Are there skills, purposes and contexts in real life communication which are not represented in these examinations? Do they embody a restricted view of how one can participate in literature? Our impression is that these restrictions do exist, though we find promising possibilities in some papers, and these must be acknowledged.

Finally, we commit ourselves to some judgments about ways in which we believe English examinations at this level should develop.

1   We welcome attempts to provide a context for the language skills being tested, whether by specifying purposes, audiences and relevances for reading and writing tasks, or by the use of coursework. Comprehension testing in a number of CSE papers has made progress in this direction and goes some way towards providing recognizable contexts and questions which establish a possible or imaginable situation. It must be recognized, however, that such specification can lead to cultural stereotyping of the kind we have described.

2   In spite of the difficulties of moderating coursework it is essential that this should form a substantial part of all English examinations, since by no other means can the problems of decontextualized tests be fully solved.

3   The low status of spoken language in English examinations at GCE O-level is patently absurd, if examinations are to test skills valued outside the classroom. (As Table 3 shows, oral assessment appears in many CSE examinations; a separate study would be needed to find out to what extent and in what ways these assessments influence the teaching of English.)

4   It seems unreasonable that in English Language examinations the candidates are often confronted with unseen passages which in style and content are alien to both the first-hand experience and the reading background of most 16-year-olds. In such cases the initial leap of faith that the reader has to make is for many candidates a leap away from their own developing field of meanings, so that it can be no just test of their reading abilities. This is not, however, to be interpreted as a plea for lowering standards, or as a capitulation to what we have described as a stereotype of urban culture.

5   Testing understanding mainly by means of short questions requiring paraphrase and localized interpretation misrepresents the nature of comprehension which requires active use of clues from the text as a whole and the mobilizing of the reader's existing knowledge and understanding.

6   We regret the tendency to examine literature by setting questions that primarily test the ability to recall and reproduce details of texts. This is a poor way of representing literary response, and encourages teaching methods that teachers themselves regard as undesirable, and which do harm to pupils' enjoyment of literature. Poetry is a special problem here. Considerable numbers of younger children can write verse which is genuinely interesting and can respond to verse forms, ballads and songs, riddles, language games and so on. Yet poetry is notoriously

difficult for 16-year-olds to handle in examination classes. This discrepancy suggests the need for a radical reappraisal of how poetry is both taught and examined in the fifth year.

7   At a more subtle level, we note that in some boards literature is tested in a way which enshrines a detached and contemplative attitude to texts, and presented as something complete in itself, distant from the reader, and untouched by the secular world. The activities which we have called 'Imaginative reconstruction' have the virtue of transgressing this traditional aesthetic by disrupting the finality of the given text. Similarly, it would be valuable if poetry could more often be shown as the provisional result of a human being's labour and thus demystified; too often, it is enshrined in print, not represented in changing draft. Such challenges to the traditional assumptions of literary criticism seem to us to be healthy ones.

8   We have recognized the presence of stereotypes of 'suitable reading for 16-year-olds'. Such stereotypes are undesirable, even those which are motivated by a desire to catch pupils' interest. One of the purposes of schooling is to widen the range of pupils' cultural understanding and sympathy.

9   We welcome such innovations as those of Cambridge local (Plain Texts) and SUJB in allowing candidates to consult texts in examinations.

Acknowledgements

We wish to record indebtedness to the University of Leeds School of Education for financing John Seed's contribution to the research, and for giving permission to reprint this paper which originally appeared as a pamphlet issued by the School of Education. We are glad too to acknowledge critical advice from Dorothy Barnes, Mike Raleigh and Gordon Whalley, who read an early draft of this paper.

Notes

1   For an excellent account of the nature of examining and its effects on the educational process see Pearce, J. (1972) *School Examinations*, London, Collier-Macmillan.

2   London Association for the Teaching of English (1980) *English Exams at Sixteen: An Analysis and Some Proposals for the Future*, LATE, 3 Bucharest Road, London, SW18.

3   At the same time we analyzed three randomly selected 16+ examinations, and included the figures relating to them in the tables that refer principally to O-level. (It may be necessary to explain for some of our readers that 16+ examinations are designed to incorporate within a single examination system the full range of pupils that GCE O-level and CSE together have come to serve.)

4   There are also some Mode 3 Syllabuses at O-level: AEB, for instance, have some

eighty syllabuses with a combined entry of around 25,000 candidates. Oxford and Cambridge offer an internal assessment option in both Language and Literature: entries 4761 and 4941 respectively.

5 In Table 2 we have taken summary or précis to be a separate exercise requiring shortened paraphrase of the whole of a given passage. Two GCE Boards (Oxford local, and Oxford and Cambridge) include what amounts to a summary as a sub-section of their tests of comprehension.

6 Knight, R. 'Examiners' English', in *English in Education*, 11, 2, pp. 24–34.

7 Though the source of this phrase is not known to us it well summarizes the view of reading expressed in Lunzer, E. and Gardner, K. (Eds) (1979) *The Effective Use of Reading*, London, Heinemann.

8 It is sometimes difficult to construe what these criteria are. Consider the following paragraph from a passage set for comprehension in an O-level paper.

> For me, exploration was a personal venture. I did not go to the Arabian desert to collect plants nor to make a map; such things were incidental. At heart I knew that to write or even to talk of my travels was to tarnish the achievement. I went there to find peace in the hardship of desert travel and the company of desert peoples. I set myself a goal on these journeys, and although the goal itself was unimportant, its attainment had to be worth every effort and sacrifice. Scott had gone to the South Pole in order to stand for a few minutes on one particular and almost inaccessible spot on the Earth's surface. He and his companions died on their way back, but even as they were dying he never doubted that the journey had been worth while. Everyone knew that there was nothing to be found on the top of Everest, but even in this materialistic age few people asked, 'What point is there in climbing Everest? What good will it do everyone when they get there?' They recognised that even today there are experiences that do not need to be justified in terms of material profit.

9 The Welsh Board's paper offered the widest choice in drama: the candidate had to choose a question to answer from three on *Under Milk Wood*, three on *Conflicting Generations: Five Television Plays*, three general questions, and three appropriate to *She Stoops to Conquer, Pygmalion, The Royal Hunt of the Sun* or *The Importance of Being Ernest*.

10 The relationship between examination mode (coursework or examination paper) and alternative emphases in the teaching of writing has been investigated empirically during the research project from which the present discussion of examinations originally derived. See Chapter 3 of Barnes, D. and D. (1984) *Versions of English*, London, Heinemann.

Appendix 1. Full List of English Exam Papers (Summer 1979) under Analysis Here

Type	Abbreviated title	Full title	Total numbers entered in summer 1979
O-level English Language	Welsh	Welsh Joint Education Committee	23,163
"	London	University of London	70,000
"	AEB (II/069)	The Associated Examining Board	34,608
"	AEB (I/025)	The Associated Examining Board	80,944
"	SUJB	Southern Universities Joint Board	Numbers not supplied
"	Oxford local (01)	Oxford Local Examinations	c.50,000
"	Cambridge local (116)	University of Cambridge Local Examinations Syndicate	40,256
"	Oxford and Cambridge	Oxford and Cambridge Schools Examination Board	11,921
"	JMB (A)	Joint Matriculation Board	38,766
"	JMB (B)	Joint Matriculation Board	40,334
"	JMB (C)	Joint Matriculation Board	3,711
16+ English Language	JMB/West Midlands	Joint Matriculation Board/West Midlands Examinations Board	6,864
"	AEB/SEREB	The Associated Examinations Board/South East Regional Examinations Board	5,547
"	ALSEB/JMB/YREB	Associated Lancashire School Examining Board/Joint Matriculation Board/Yorkshire Regional Examining Board.	17,500
CSE English Language	TWYLREB	The West Yorkshire and Lindsey Regional Examining Board	2,033
"	NWREB	The North West Regional Examining Board	49,482
"	East Anglia (S)	East Anglian Examinations Board (South)	11,913
"	NRB	The North Regional Examining Board	26,861
"	East Midlands	East Midland Regional Examinations Board	24,837
"	SWEB	South Western Examinations Board	28,030
"	SREB (R)	South Regional Examinations Board (Syllabus)	c.23,000

Category	Code	Board	Numbers
CSE Unitary English	East Anglia (N)	East Anglian Examinations Board (North)	11,285
"	Welsh	Welsh Joint Education Committee	17,123
"	ALSEB (A)	Associated Lancashire School Examining Board	6,285
"	YREB	Yorkshire Regional Examining Board	5,720
"	West Midlands (ES)	West Midlands Examining Board: English Studies	18,372
"	West Midlands (E)	West Midlands Examining Board: English	12,835
"	Metropolitan	Metropolitan Regional Exam Board: English	Numbers not supplied
"	Middlesex	Middlesex Examinations Board	9,141
"	SEREB	South East Regional Examinations Board	11,249
O-level English Literature	London (A)	University of London	40,000
"	London(B)	University of London	58,725
"	JMB (A)	Joint Matriculation Board	Not supplied
"	SUJB	Southern Universities Joint Board	c.35,000
"	Oxford local (02)	Oxford Local Examinations	c. 5,000
"	Oxford local (GEN)	Oxford Local Examinations	23,062
"	Cambridge local (200/1)	University of Cambridge Local Examinations Syndicate	8,847
"	Cambridge local (Plain Texts)	University of Cambridge Local Examinations Syndicate	32,529
"	AEB (027)	The Associated Examining Board	3,113
"	AEB (028)	The Associated Examining Board	
16+ English Literature	JMB/West Midlands	Joint Matriculation Board/West Midlands Exam Board	5,390
CSE English Literature	NRB	North Regional Examinations Board	15,987
"	ALSEB (A)	Associated Lancashire Schools Examining Board	560
"	NWRB	North West Regional Examinations Boards	25,186

Appendix 2. Breakdown of Elements of Essay/Composition Writing

Choice from total	Examination	Starting points: Title	Instruction	Stimulus	Picture	Content: Public	Private	Open	Mode of writing: Story	Open	Autobio-graphical	Descriptive	Analytic
1/10	Welsh	3	5	2	0	3	1	6	2	2	½	2	2½
1/10	London	4	1	3	2	1	1	8	2	4½	1	½	2
2/10	AEB (II/069)	4	5	1	0	6	1	3	1	3	0	1½	4½
1/8	AEB (I/025)	6	1	1	0	4	1	3	0	3	0	1	3
1/6	SUJB	3	3	0	0	5	0	1	0	2	0	1	3
1/5	Oxford local	3	2	2	0	2	1	2	1	2	½	½	1
2/16	Cambridge local (116)	5	7	2	2	11	1	4	3	4	2	1½	5½
1/8	Oxford and Cambridge	4	1	3	2	4	0	4	0	8	0	0	0
1/10	JMB (A)	0	6	3	0	5	1	4	2	3	1	1	3
1/7	JMB (B)	2	2	2	1	4	1	2	1	1	½	2½	2
3/12	JMB (C)	2	6	2	2	8	1	3	1	1	1	4	5
1/14	JMB/West Midlands	6	3	4	1	10	0	4	1	7	0	3	3
2/10	AEB/SEREB	7	3	0	0	8	2	0	1	4	0	1	4
2/13	ALSEB/JMB/YREB	6	3	2	2	4	7	2	1	3	0	5	4
1/9	East Midlands	2	7	0	0	3	4	2	1	1	2	2	3
1/8	NRB	4	1	1	2	4	0	4	1	2	0	2½	2½
1 or 2/7	TWYLREB	1	1	5	0	4	2	1	1	1	0	1½	3½
2/10	NWREB	0	6	2	2	4	3	3	3	0	3	1	3
1/21	SREB	17	2	1	1	6	1	14	5	13	0	2	1
1/8	SWEB	2	4	1	1	7	0	1	1	3	0	1	3
1/8	East Anglia (S)	0	6	1	1	6	0	2	0	2	1	2½	2½
1 or 2/12	East Anglia (N)	0	10	0	2	7	2	3	3	2	1	3½	2½
1/10	Welsh	5	3	2	0	4	0	6	3	2	1	1½	1½
3/11	ALSEB	0	7	1	3	10	1	0	3	3	1	6	3
2/3	YREB	0	0	2	1	3	0	0	1	0	1	1	1
1/10	West Midlands (Eng. St.)	3	6	0	1	5	2	3	2	4	0	2	2
1 or 2/8	Metropolitan	2	3½	1½	1	1	4	3	2	3	2	½	½
1/10	West Midlands	4	3½	1½	1	4	1	5	3	2	1	1½	2½
1/10	Middlesex	3	5	0	2	5	1	4	1	6	0	1	2
2/9	SEREB	1	5	2	1	5	1	3	0	3	1	2½	2½

Contributors

Clem Adelman, Senior Lecturer in Education, Bulmershe College of Higher Education.

Stephen J. Ball, Lecturer in Education, University of Sussex.

Douglas Barnes, Reader in Education, University of Leeds.

Robert G. Burgess, Lecturer in Sociology, University of Warwick.

Barry Cooper, Lecturer in Education, University of Sussex.

Ivor F. Goodson, Director of The Schools Unit, University of Sussex.

Martyn Hammersley, Lecturer in the Sociology of Education, The Open University.

Lynda Measor, Research Assistant, School of Education, The Open University.

John Player, Second Master, Stowmarket High School, Suffolk.

June Purvis, Lecturer in Educational Studies, The Open University.

William A. Reid, Senior Lecturer in Education, University of Birmingham.

John Seed, Lecturer in History, Roehampton Institute.

Louis M. Smith, Professor of Education, Graduate Institute of Education, Washington University, St Louis, Missouri.

Peter Woods, Reader in Sociology of Education, The Open University.

Author Index

Adams, C., 107, 108, 109, 113
Adelman, C., 1, 2, 8–9, 77–88
Adelman, C. and Walker, R., 78, 87
Akinsanya, S.K.
  see Roberts and Akinsanya
Alakija, O.A., 143, 146
Anderson, H.H. and Brewer, M., 165, 175
Anderson, J., 117–18, 119,126, 128, 132, 134, 137, 138, 146
Archer, H.
  see Parry and Archer
Archer, M.S., 4, 12, 25, 54–5, 62
Arensberg, C.M.
  see Chapple and Arensberg
Arensberg, C.M. and Kimball, C.T., 170, 175
Arensberg, C.M. and MacGregor, D., 170, 175
Aronowitz, S., 228, 237
Ashby, J., 100, 104
Ashby, M.K., 91, 100, 113
Azikiwe, N., 143

Bacus, K., 118–19, 140, 146
Ball, S.J., 3, 4, 9, 15, 16, 17, 22, 52, 61, 62, 117–47, 202, 216
Ball, S.J. and Goodson, I.F., 1–12
Ball, S.J. and Lacey, C., 52, 61, 62, 182, 198, 199
Barnes, A., 105–6, 113
Barnes, D. and Barnes, D., 295
Barnes, D. and Seed, J., 11, 263–98
Barnes, S.B., 47, 62
Barton, L. and Meighan, R., 199
Barton, L. and Walker, S., 114, 261
Batten, 127–8

Becker, H.S., 53, 62, 243, 251, 260
Beechey, V., 112, 113
Beidelman, T.O., 118, 119, 120, 146
Beittel, K.R., 153, 175
Ben-David, J., 29, 46, 60, 62
Ben-David, J. and Collins, R., 29, 34, 41, 44, 46, 56, 62
Bennett, M., 106
Berger, P.L., 201, 217
Berger, P.L. and Luckmann, T., 17, 23, 239, 260
Berger, P.L. et al., 241, 260
Bernstein, B., 25, 37, 44, 46, 49, 61, 62, 86, 87, 138–9, 146
Bertaux, D., 15, 23, 239, 260
Bhaskar, R., 54–5, 62
Bidwell, C.E. and Windham, D.M., 75
Bird, C., 233, 234, 237
Birksted, I.K., 181, 199
Blackstone, T.
  see Mortimore and Blackstone
Block, M., 20
Blumer, H., 239, 260
Board of Education, 113
Boorstin, D.J., 159, 175
Bourdieu, P. and Passeron, J.C., 236, 237
Bowles, S. and Gintis, H., 220, 222, 235, 237
Bradburn, E., 85, 87
Brewer, M.
  see Anderson and Brewer
Brock, J.A.M. and Smith, L.M., 165, 167, 175
Bryan, Prof., 30
Bucher, R., 8
Bucher, R. and Strauss, A., 29, 40, 44, 53–4, 57, 60, 62

Subject Index